the NILE

A TRAVELLER'S ANTHOLOGY

the NILE

A TRAVELLER'S ANTHOLOGY

DEBORAH MANLEY

CASSELL

Cassell
Wellington House
125 Strand
London
WC2R 0BB

First published 1991
First paperback edition 1996

The editor and publisher acknowledge with thanks the use of material in this book to the following:
Jonathan Cape Ltd for excerpts from *The Travels of Ibn Jubayr* translated by R. J. C. Broadhurst; and Constance Sitwell's *Lotus and Pyramid*; Academy Chicago Publishers Inc for excerpts from *Flaubert in Egypt* translated by Francis Steegmuller; Michael Haag for material from his *Discovery Guide to Egypt*; Peter Owen Ltd for excerpts from Jean Cocteau's *Maalesh*; Faber and Faber Ltd for excerpts from Lawrence Durrell's *Spirit of Place* and William Golding's *Egyptian Journal*; Peter Frasers & Dunlop Group Ltd for excerpts from Jan Morris's *Places* and *Cities*; Hamish Hamilton Ltd for the excerpt from Alan Moorehead's *The Blue Nile*; B. T. Batsford Ltd for the excerpts from Cecil Beaton's *Near East*; Methuen London for excerpts from *A Wayfarer in Egypt* by Annie Quibbell and *Through the Lands of the Bible* by H. V. Morton; Harcourt Brace Jovanovich Inc for excerpts from Princess Marta Bibescû's *Egyptian Day*; Penguin Books Ltd for excerpts from Charlie Pye-Smith's *The Other Nile*; Curtis Brown Ltd for excerpts from Sir Winston Churchill's *The River War*; Michael Simmons of *The Guardian* for his article about a visit to Egypt and Alan Pryce-Jones for an excerpt from *The Spring Journey*.

Distributed in the United States
by Sterling Publishing Co., Inc.
387 Park Avenue South, New York, NY 10016–8810

Distributed in Australia
by Capricorn Link (Australia) Pty Ltd
2/13 Carrington Road, Castle Hill, NSW 2154

British Library Cataloguing in Publication Data
The Nile: a traveller's anthology.
1. Africa. Nile River region. Description & travel
I. Manley, Deborah
916.204

ISBN 0 304 34843 0

Typeset by Input London Ltd

Printed and bound in Great Britain by Mackays of Chatham Ltd

Cover: *Beside the Nile, 1859* by Leon Belly (reproduced by courtesy of the Mathaf Gallery, London)

Contents

Contents

Contents

Introduction

Egypt is the Nile. That is no epigram or figure of speech: the street I tread on in Cairo, the beef and potatoes I take for lunch – they are just solidified, organified, vitalised Nile. Every rod of tilled land in Egypt was washed hither from the Abyssinian mountains, and laid down to fertilise the desert, by the Nile. The great river not only gives water to a rainless land, it makes the very soil. If the land is hardened by the brown, mud-bearing water each flood-time, it will bear well; if not, it will soon go back to desert again. If the water is not drained off after flood-time the flat land will become waterlogged. And if the full Nile should burst its banks the land will become a lake. The Nile is Egypt's all in all – to be trained and cockered, filled up now, emptied out then, coaxed into giving the greatest possible life and leaving behind the least possible death. Egypt is, of all others, the land of the engineer: he makes or unmakes it, enlarges or diminishes it, according as he succeeds or fails in managing the Nile.　　　　　　　　　　　　　　　　　　　　　　　　G. W. Steevens, 1898

Literary archaeology was what I came to call the activity of sifting through layer after layer of travellers on the Nile. I could have worked through the layers from the present backward in time; or from the distant past to the present. But I used no particular point in time as a start. The start was the Nile.

It has flowed through all our imaginations since we were children. For that reason our knowledge tends to be simple, uncomplicated by too much detail, and dramatic. We know that the Nile is the life blood of Egypt in an almost miraculous way, and that along its banks once dwelt a civilization which raised monuments so spectacular that they still make pygmies of us all today.

This is the knowledge that most of us bring to Egypt and the Nile. And we tend to come with guidebook in hand. Beside every hotel pool there will always be people swotting up on the next day's visit, or trying to work out what it was they saw that morning. People cling to every word of the modern dragomans, the tour guides, clustering around to miss no detail. As the holiday week or fortnight goes on, everyone becomes noticeably more knowledgeable, and more determined to increase their comprehension. This includes a desire to under-stand the manners and customs of the modern Egyptians as well as of their ancient ancestors. On the plane home the talk is not only of sights seen and bargains struck but also of people met and even homes visited. Everyone is certain they must come to Egypt again.

Egypt has always fascinated foreigners in this way, and the experience of being there has urged people to record what they have seen. Steevens, the young *Daily Mail* correspondent who followed Kitchener to Khartoum, commented that the writing room of Shepheard's Hotel in Cairo was filled each evening with people scribbling away in their journals, and it is obvious that the writing up of one's journal was an important part of each day for many Nile travellers.

Although the records and comments in this book are arranged to follow the Nile up from Alexandria to Wadi Halfa, just below the second cataract, and therefore cover today's man-made Lake Nasser, there is a historical layering too. As you read you will find Herodotus rubbing shoulders with Robert Curzon because, although 2,000 years separated them, they were interested in the same aspect of the Nile. Harriet Martineau and Gustave Flaubert were not high up on the Pyramids together, but we listen to their reports together. That is an important purpose of this book: to bring together like-minded or contrasting travellers from different times in the same place.

From earliest times there were travellers, like Herodotus and Strabo, who tried to put the Nile and its people 'on the map', describing what was going on and what had been happening in the not so distant past. Then, much later, came the medieval Arab travellers, like Ibn Battuta and Ibn Jubayr, coming from other parts of Africa or from Moorish Spain; and there were a few Christians, spilling over from pilgrimages to the Holy Land or seeking the edges of the known world.

Late came the entertaining Dane, Frederick Norden, the rambling Scot, James Bruce, and, with Napoleon, the middle-aged, scholarly, brave and enthusiastic Frenchman Vivant Denon. It was their writing that began to excite people in Europe about the idea of what lay south of Cairo. Then, thick and fast, came a fascinating collection of adventurers, treasure seekers and scholars to the places of which they had read. Most memorable among these were undoubtedly the Swiss Muslim John Lewis Burkhardt, trudging up to Abu Simbel, the vast Italian 'strong-man Egyptologist' Giovanni Belzoni, with his courageous wife, and the scholars Edward Lane and Gardner Wilkinson, with their careful sifting and describing of the manners and customs of Egyptians ancient and modern. Intermingled with these famous figures were an extraordinarily likeable group of people who travelled and wrote with charm and an appreciation of the country which those who followed sometimes lacked. There were the ex-naval officers Irby and Mangles, who, meeting up by chance with Belzoni, stripped off to labour with him to open up the great temple at Abu Simbel in 1817. There were young men like Henry Light and Frederick Henniker and the Frenchman Comte de Forbin, who came just to look, and, of course, to write about what they saw. And in the background at this time was always the shadowy, hospitable figure of Mr Henry Salt, the British Consul General in Cairo, who had the money to make the search after ancient Egypt more possible, and his rival, Drovetti, the French Consul.

Irby and Mangles described this Anglo–French rivalry in 1817:

Demand for papyrus and other antiquities is so great in consequence of opposition between the French party, employed by Mr Drovetti, and the English employed by Mr Salt that [the local people] are now getting five times what they once received for their finds. In consequence about half a dozen of the leading characters of Gournu [the village near the Valley of the Kings], or rather the greatest rogues, have headed their comrades, and formed themselves into two distinct digging parties, or resurrection men, designating themselves the French and English party; these people are constantly occupied in searching for new tombs, stripping the mummies, and discovering antiquities.

But even then it was not only men who travelled and recorded what they saw. Edward Lane's sister, Sophia Poole, and her two sons spent several years with Lane and his Greek wife in Cairo and contributed much about life beyond the harem wall which he could never have learned on his own. Mrs Colonel Elwood happily followed her man to India and back with all the uncomplaining enjoyment and zest that any man exhibited. And Sarah Belzoni lived with her husband in a Theban tomb and accompanied him on his first visit to Abu Simbel dressed as a man. Equally surprising, though more low key, were Lady Belmore and her companion, Miss Brookes, in 1816. Lord Belmore, seeking relics in the company of his wife, two sons, brother and others travelled up beyond the cataract, and made the Frenchman Comte de Forbin so disheartened by constantly meeting a lady with a pink parasol in Aswan that he decided to turn back from what appeared to be too well worn a path.

It was a combination of Napoleon's troops under General Desaix, with Vivant Denon closely accompanying them, and the long, firm and often harsh rule of Mehemet Ali (1805–47) that opened up the Nile to somewhat less intrepid travellers – who might even have described themselves as tourists. These were that large group who had read the 'big square' books published by earlier travellers and been fired with the urge to follow them.

The German Henry Rhind commented in 1856:

Although the fame of the monumental remains, the novelty of Eastern life, the characteristic scenery of the Nile, and many historical associations both sacred and profane, have long combined to impart to Egypt a varied attractiveness, such as perhaps no other country could hope to claim ... still, so great were the difficulties, possible dangers ... that few were so adventurous as to make the attempt ... to overcome ... the palpable discomforts of travelling in a country where the way was little more than pioneered ... However, the establishment of the overland route to India through Egypt [partly by Samuel Bevan] made it 'more familiarly known, and more easy of access – and a voyage up the Nile became gradually less difficult of accomplishment ...'

Indeed, each autumn from the 1840s onwards, tourists began to pour into Egypt, mainly through Alexandria, although some came through Sinai on their way from the Holy Land. They would spend some days in Cairo, visiting the 'lions' (sights) and choosing and arranging for the hire of a *dahabeeyah*, the most popular type of river boat for the traveller. They would also take on a dragoman or general factotum and guide, and a *reis* or pilot-cum-skipper for the boat. The dragoman would then look after their interests with more or less enthusiasm, provisioning the boat for the journey and along the way. The travellers, nailing their personal pennant to the masthead and their national flag to the stern, would then set off up the Nile from Boulak, some in haste and others at leisure.

The trick was to go up against the stream as fast as possible, sailing when the wind from the north was favourable, and when the wind dropped, as it often does, to be hauled along by the sailors tracking along the bank, sometimes for days. The traveller could then go ashore and walk in the countryside, observe human and animal life and visit the towns and villages along the way. For many, this was a time too for shooting much of the wildlife they saw – one Victorian sporting lord was said to have killed 10,000 birds in one season. The one thing the travellers could not do was look at the monuments of ancient Egypt – the movement ever upward and southward was too important. The sights were viewed as the river's flow carried the boat downstream and northward on the return journey, when using the wind was not so vital to progress. On the journey downstream the *reis* would allow you to stop where you wanted; on the upstream journey you stopped only where *he* wanted.

However, Amelia Edwards, one of the most redoubtable and entertaining of all the travellers, cautioned against this arrangement in 1873:

It is the rule of the Nile to hurry up the river as fast as possible, leaving the ruins to be seen as the boat comes back with the current; but this, like many another canon, is by no means of universal application. The traveller who starts late in the season has, indeed, no other course open to him. He must press on with speed to the end of his journey, if he would get back again at low Nile without being irretrievably stuck on a sand-bank till the next inundation floats him off again. But for those who desire not only to see the monuments, but to follow, however superficially, the course of Egyptian history as it is handed down through Egyptian art, it is above all things necessary to start early and to see many things by the way.

By the time Amelia was making the journey it would have been perfectly possible to go by steamer and to stop as and when one chose. Harriet Martineau in any case disagreed with her in 1848:

Moreover, there was great advantage in going up quickly while the river was yet high enough to afford some view of the country. In returning, we found such a change produced by the sinking of the waters only a few feet, that we felt that travellers going up late in the season can hardly be said to have seen the country from the river. At all times, the view of the interior from the Nile must be very imperfect, and quite insufficient to justify any decision against the beauty of the great valley. This arises from the singular structure of the country. Everywhere else, where a river flows through the centre of a valley, the land either slopes from the base of the hills down to the river, or it is level. In Egypt, on the contrary, the land rises from the mountains up to the banks of the Nile: and where, as usually happens, the banks are higher than the eye of the spectator on the deck of his boat, all views of the interior, as far as the hills, are precluded. He sees nothing but the towns, villages, and palm-groves on the banks, and the mountains on the horizon. My attention had been directed upon this point before I went by the complaints of some readers of Eastern travels that, after all their reading, they knew no more what the Egyptian valley looked like than if it had never been visited. As this failure of description appeared to regard Egypt alone, there must be some peculiar cause for it: and thus we found it. The remedy was, of course, to go ashore as often as possible, and to mount every practicable eminence. I found this so delightful, and every wide view that I obtained included so much that was wonderful and beautiful, that mounting eminences became an earnest pursuit with me. I carried compass and note-book, and noted down what I saw, from eminence to eminence, along the whole valley, from Cairo to the Second Cataract. Sometimes I looked abroad from the top of a pylon; sometimes from a rock on the banks; sometimes from a sandy ridge of the desert; sometimes from a green declivity of the interior; once from a mountain above Thebes, and once from the summit of the Great Pyramid. My conclusion is that I differ entirely from those who complain of the sameness of the aspect of the country. The constituent features of the landscape may be more limited in number than in other tracts of country of a thousand miles: but they are so grand and so beautiful, so strange, and brought together in such endless diversity, that I cannot conceive that any one who has really seen the country can complain of its monotony.

Besides Harriet Martineau with her ear trumpet, among the people who were making the journey at this period – from the 1840s to the 1870s, were Florence Nightingale getting her first taste of Oriental life; Mark Twain laughing at everybody, including himself; the outrageous Frenchman Gustave Flaubert; and Amelia Edwards herself, in Egypt almost on a whim yet preparing to become to Egyptology what Henry Salt had been a generation before – the provider and the spur.

There were many, many more and increasingly among their number were Americans. I especially warmed to William C. Prime, a lawyer turned journalist from New York who managed to combine a liking for the country and a sense of inquiry about the past with a great deal of energetic pleasure in the present – his description of his visit to the crocodile pits is a classic.

Not a traveller in the same sense but a resident, Lady Duff Gordon was in Egypt hoping to recover from consumption. After she had published her *Letters from Egypt* in 1865, she herself became one of the 'lions'.

Overlapping with this group of independent travellers, from the end of the 1860s onwards right up to the present day, were the 'Cook's excursionists' and their heirs, the package holidaymakers. Gradually the number of people who travelled the Nile under sail diminished as the group travellers, insulated from life along the Nile's banks on the steamers took over. In 1868 the Prince of Wales managed to combine both methods of travel, having sailing boats drawn upriver by steamer – hasting along, according to William Howard Russell of Crimean fame, to escape from Cook's first tour of Egypt. Miss Riggs, one of those initial tourists, however, seemed less interested in the royals than they appeared to be in her.

From the 1870s to the end of the century and beyond, travel on the Nile was dominated by the all-pervasive figure of John Mason Cook, Thomas Cook's son. He wrote very detailed instructions on exactly how a Nile steamer was to be managed, and even today, a century later, Nile steamers are still run in much the same way.

The British, apparently more by coincidence than by design or with forethought, took charge of Egypt after the extravagances of Ishmael Khedive and the nationalist uprisings of 1882. But at the same time events in the south were beginning to produce a new sort of traveller, still serviced entirely by Cook's – the soldiers on their way to Khartoum. Here it is G. W. Steevens again and the young Winston Churchill describes Nile life with the passage of the troops, including American Indians and others brought in from Canada to traverse the cataracts. The British soldiers themselves seem to have written little apart from signing their names, dates and regiments all over the temple at Abu Simbel and elsewhere.

Towards the end of the nineteenth century all the great and the good passed along the Nile under the guidance of Cook's and other tourist agencies. In the Nile season of 1895–6 Cook's published a brochure of some of the 'Royal and Distinguished Persons' who had travelled with them. It included queens and emperors, the Shah of Persia (by order of the British government), two empresses, an archduke, a sultan and a maharajah, along with no less than twenty-three bishops and three archbishops. With them went two dozen members of parliament and such well-known figures as Mr Holman Hunt, RA, Mr Rider Haggard, Herr Krupp, Count Metternich, General Pitt Rivers, Dr Schliemann, the Very Reverend Dean Spooner, Sir Arthur Sullivan and Mr Vanderbilt. (One could make up a great story about who travelled with whom and what the consequence was . . .)

As Rudyard Kipling observed, every nationality was also represented among the residents in 1913:

Here is a country which is not a country but a longish strip of market-garden, nominally in charge of a government which is not a government but the disconnected satrapy of a half-dead empire, controlled pecksniffingly by a Power which is not a Power but an Agency, which Agency has been tied up by years, custom, and blackmail into all sorts of intimate relations with six or seven European Powers, all with rights and perquisites, none of whose subjects seem directly amenable to any Power which at first, second, or third hand is supposed to be responsible. That is the barest outline. To fill in the details (if any living man knows them) would be as easy to explain baseball to an Englishman or the Eton Wall game to a citizen of the United States. But it is fascinating play. There are Frenchmen in it, whose logical mind it offends, and they revenge themselves by printing the finance-reports and the catalogue of the Bulak Museum in pure French. There are Germans in it, whose demands must be carefully weighed – not that they can by any means be satisfied, but they serve to block other people's. There are Russians in it, who do not very much matter at present but will be heard from later. There are Italians and Greeks in it (both rather pleased with themselves just now), full of the higher finance and the finer emotions. There are Egyptian pashas in it, who come back from Paris at intervals and ask plaintively to whom they are supposed to belong. There is His Highness, the Khedive, in it, and *he* must be considered not a little, and there are women in it, up to their eyes. And there are great English cotton and sugar interests, and angry English importers clamouring to know why they cannot do business on rational lines or get into the Sudan, which they hold is ripe for development if the administration there would only see reason. Among these conflicting interests and amusements sits and perspires the English official, whose job is irrigating or draining or reclaiming land on behalf of a trifle ten million people, and he finds himself tripped up by skeins of intrigue and bafflement which may ramify through half a dozen harems and four consulates. All this makes for suavity, toleration, and the blessed habit of not being surprised at anything whatever.

16

War in our century brought others to Egypt who were not there of their own choosing, including Noël Coward, Cecil Beaton and Lawrence Durrell. Already there was a very fashionable foreign population, not unlike the memsahibs and sahibs of India. Between the wars came Major Jarvis, pointing fun at all the others, and Constance Sitwell, one of the most delightful of travellers.

Today most of us fly in, spend a couple of weeks there and fly out, promising but possibly failing to return. A few, like Charlie Pye-Smith, are more leisurely, and in 1984 William Golding even hired a *dahabeeyah* and did the journey in the 'proper' way. As I delved through the literary mound, I became increasingly convinced that it was time to open the Nile again to the *dahabeeyah*-classes. There are hardy people who travel along the river by felucca, living in the open and using the river bank as a 'bathroom'. Maybe I too would once have enjoyed that. But at Luxor someone is restoring a *dahabeeyah* – perhaps that is the start of bringing them back to the river.

The alternative 'going on the boats', the Nile steamers, is still a very special experience. As one of our party said excitedly on the first morning, 'I looked out of the window. I couldn't believe it – it was as if a movie was going past me!'

However you go, it is worth reading up on Egypt. Murray's *Egypt Handbook* in 1880 and many similar books encouraged the traveller to read a great deal in preparation and along the way. Of course, any self-respecting eighteenth- or nineteenth-century visitor would have read their Bible and their Latin histories. They were familiar with Herodotus and Strabo and knew all about the seven lean and the seven fat kine. To include all the vast literature of Nile travel was no more possible then than it is now. But this collection will at least provide an overview of travellers from earlier times. It is *not* a guidebook, but to enter Karnak temple sharing Denon's astonishment or Amelia Edwards's awe adds to the dimension of the experience. To know what William C. Prime or Giovanni Belzoni thought as they entered the tombs 'on the other side' brings an extra resonance to one's own experience. The adventure of the cataract is long since gone, but you can still in imagination go up it with Harriet Martineau or down it with Florence Nightingale. Even the Aswan Dam has been overshadowed by the High Dam, but Douglas Sladen's description makes one appreciate it for what it is. Philae is more wonderful because one shares it with Edward Lear and Dean Stanley; Nubia possibly more memorable seen through the eyes of Arthur Conan Doyle and Rudyard Kipling.

As you travel, you will be told that the holes carved in the temple columns at various heights are where people tethered their animals in the shade of the buildings when the ground level was high above where it is today. The guides will tell you this, but it is not so often that they will point out to you, high above your head, the places where previous travellers stood on the rubble to carve their names. Frederick Henniker describes Esneh in 1822:

> ... nothing remains visible except a portico; and this, though in the middle of one of the principal towns, is filled for the greater part with dirt, and the remainder of bales of merchandise – the first is collected to such a height that the road-way is on a level of the roof of the body of the temple, and on this are built the pygmy houses of the Arabs.

Among these carved names are those of the poet Rimbaud and of Belzoni himself. And there are others too. As early as 1817 the Frenchman Viscount Forbin commented crossly:

The names of several *domini terrarum*, lords of the earth, are discernible on the feet of the colossus [at Thebes], but our eyes rest with a rational, a fondly cherished esteem, on the name of Germanicus, inasmuch as the progress of his journeyings into Upper Egypt was universally marked by the most pleasing and authentic traits of his benificence. I know not whether it will excite a smile of contempt, but the scene produced in me a singular stage effect, when I found an obscure baronet commemorating his route to Thebes, with his name on the granite in close connexion with Caesar's. It had been recently done and not without some trouble. I will not say that this gentleman showed the superiority of his intellect when he records the particular part of London where he dwells.

In putting together a book like this one starts with bibliographies. The first sight of the 'site' in literary archaeology is another book. In my case Michael Haag's admirable *Guide to Egypt* was the first sight of the treasures which lay hidden. One book leads to another, one author to another: Thomas Legh met John Burkhardt in Cairo and again on the banks of the Nile; Belzoni worked with Irby and Mangles at Abu Simbel and they then met up with Legh in Asia Minor; Amelia Edwards was told with love, years after her death, of Lucie Duff Gordon.

Once I had found the starting points in the bibliographies (and I much regret that Jane Robinson had not published her *Wayward Women* until it was almost too late for me to use), I was lucky enough to live near the Bodleian and Rhodes House libraries in Oxford, and my daily pleasure in just being in those lovely buildings is all part of the book. I would like to thank their staffs for their efficiency and kindnesses. I was lucky enough to be able to use the library of the Royal Commonwealth Society in London before Mammon and 'progress' threatened to destroy one of the last open libraries of British academic heritage, and I would like to thank Terry Barringer and her staff for that pleasure. I had great delight in using the Thomas Cook Ltd archive, with those enthusiastic historians of travel, Edmund Swinglehurst and Joy Hooper. Their collection of ephemera brought the past to life even more than any book. But it was not only libraries in Britain that were searched. Helen Small delved for me in Ottawa, and Madga Hall searched for me at Berkeley, and I am very indebted to them. In Egypt, Michel Chawki, then Assistant Manager on Eastman's ms *Atlas* told me how a modern Nile boat is organized.

I dug for myself in London's Portobello Road and in bookshops up and down the country. I unearthed my 1929 Baedeker reprint in Luxor, in the shop of the descendants of the very Aboudi who is recommended in it as a dragoman. I am very grateful to the literary archaeologists who have gone before and have reprinted books and written about people and places, and particularly to Alan Moorehead for his *The Blue Nile*, which, along with Amelia Edwards's *One Thousand Miles up the Nile*, would be my 'desert island' reading for a Nile voyage.

Finally, I am deeply grateful to my husband and to my sister, Peta Rée, who travelled to Egypt with me and who listened and helped as I unearthed more and more of the story of the Nile and its travellers.

A Brief Historical Background

A very rapid historical resumé will help the reader to understand the background of the travellers in Egypt.

Only Herodotus, of our travellers, visited Egypt in the days of the pharaohs (in about 460 BC). In 276 BC Eratosthenes, the Greek geographer, sketched the course of the Nile and hinted at its source. In 332 BC Alexander the Great conquered Egypt, founding a new capital at Alexandria. He died within a year, distributing his vast empire among his generals: the start of the Ptolemy line of pharaohs.

Roman influence began in 168 BC, and by 30 BC Egypt had become a province of Rome. It was during this period that Strabo, Pliny and Diodorus Siculus were on the Nile. It is important to remember that although today they may be no more than names to most of us, they were read and absorbed by Victorian travellers, who also knew their Bible well, as Dean Stanley's remarks in 1852 show:

> Egypt, among its many aspects of interest, has this special claim – that it is the background of the whole history of the Israelites; the land to which, after Palestine, their thoughts either by way of contrast or association immediately turned ... The first migration of Abraham from Chaldea is one continued advance southward, till he reaches the valley of the Nile; and when he reaches it he finds there a kingdom, which must have been to the wandering tribes of Asia what the Roman Empire was to the Celtic and gothic races when they first crossed the Alps. Egypt is to them the land of plenty, whilst the neighbouring nations starve ... Egypt became 'The Holy Land'; ... it is therefore a fitting, it may almost be called a necessary, prelude to Sinai and Palestine.

The Romans used Egypt as a granary for over six centuries, but their rule declined and in AD 641 the Islamic Arabs were welcomed into Egypt. In 1171 Saladin established himself and his Aiyubid line as sultans of Egypt. It was at this time that Ibn Jubayr was in Egypt. In 1250 the last Aiyubid was murdered by his mercenary Mameluke bodyguard, starting three centuries of the strange rule of the Mamelukes. They were a slave aristocracy, a military caste, first of Turks and Mongols, later of Circassians. None reigned for long, each ousted by endless intrigue and bloodletting.

In 1517 the Ottoman Sultan Selim absorbed Egypt into his empire. The Mamelukes continued to dominate the country under the pasha, the viceroy of the Ottoman sultan. Egypt was heavily taxed, sadly neglected and sank into dire poverty, with the additional threats of plague or the failure of the inundation always looming.

By the end of the eighteenth century the Mamelukes were at full strength again, raping the land they ruled. But even so such travellers as the Dane Frederick Norden managed to travel along the Nile in 1737 and bring back amazing tales of what they saw to whet appetites in Europe.

In 1798 Napoleon landed near Alexandria with 40,000 men. His ostensible purpose was to sever Britain's links with the East and to restore control of the Mamelukes to their Ottoman sultan. But, surprisingly, the people rose up against the invaders, rallying to their leaders. Nelson destroyed the French fleet in

Aboukir Bay, and Napoleon was virtually trapped in a hostile Egypt. Although he did defeat the Mamelukes in 1799, their leader, Murad Bey, escaped. General Desaix sought him up and down the Nile, and along with him went Vivant Denon, attempting and often succeeding to record ancient Egypt.

In 1801 the British landed at Alexandria and compelled the French to withdraw. They attempted to take some relics with them, but the Rosetta Stone was wrested from them by William Hamilton. The British too withdrew finally in 1807.

In 1805 Mehemet Ali, a young Albanian officer in the Turkish army, became governor of Cairo. Ruthless and skilful, he dragged Egypt into the modern world. In 1807 he took complete control after massacring over 400 of his Mameluke allies. He sent young Egyptians to France to study and brought in specialists from abroad to help with Egypt's resurrection. His army, under his son Ibrahim, brought the Sudan under control.

The European powers were increasingly interested in Egyptian affairs. Egypt was becoming the fast overland route to the East. After Mehemet Ali's death in 1847, power descended to his line, but the peasantry did not share in the new prosperity, and at times there were insurrections along the Nile. The Reverend A. C. Smith, for example, was caught up in one as he returned from his lengthy holiday in 1868. Ishmael, the grandson of Mehemet Ali, achieved self-government for Egypt, the title of Khedive for himself, the completion, in the world's spotlight, of the Suez Canal in 1869 and bankruptcy for his country. In 1879 he was forced into exile.

Financial advisers were appointed by Britain and France (the main creditors of Egypt) and, in reality, became the government of the country. The nationalist leader Colonel Ahmed Arabi demanded freedom from foreign domination and in 1882 there were riots in Alexandria in which Europeans and Christians were killed. Britain stepped in. She stayed in Egypt for seventy years, ruling theoretically through a consul-general under the sultan of Turkey. The first of these was Lord Cromer, who was in charge until 1907. The First World War disrupted plans to return Egypt to self-government, but after more troubles Britain proclaimed the end of her protectorate in 1922 and recognized Egypt as an independent state with a hereditary constitutional monarchy.

However, British influence and garrisons remained, and after the Second World War King Farouk's interference in government and his intrigues led to his overthrow by military coup. Egypt became a republic. The Suez crisis of 1956 brought the whole world to the brink of war and resulted in Russian involvement in the building of the High Dam. It was nations from all over the world which, through UNESCO, contributed to the lifting of the great temple at Abu Simbel (and other temples) from the inundation of the High Dam. Thus did the world acknowledge, in the most practical of ways, its debt to the civilization of ancient Egypt.

The Travellers: Biographies

Inquire about your neighbours before you build, and your companion before you travel.
Arabic proverb

There are two extremes in travellers. One who is just arrived, has never before been in the country, and of course has no knowledge of customs and things, cannot see one-fourth of what he should see; the other is so thoroughly initiated into their customs and manners, that those which shock at first sight, lose their effect on him; he almost forgets his own ways, and does not reckon any thing he beholds extraordinary or worth attention, though perhaps even of the greatest consequence.   Giovanni Belzoni, 1817

There is comfort, when travelling eastward, in meeting Englishmen. You are very certain, in coming in contact with the English pleasure-traveller, to meet a gentleman. Exceptions are very rare. It is also worthy of remark, that the English gentleman, so soon as he learns that you are American, regards you as a fit companion, which is a degree of confidence that he is very far from reposing in one of his own nationality. Englishmen meeting Englishmen, look on one another as so many pick-pockets might, each of whom was certain that each of his neighbours meant to rob him on the first available opportunity.

This perhaps arises from the danger that foreign acquaintances may entail unpleasant and impractical recognitions at home. There is no apprehension of this in meeting Americans, and this may serve to explain a willingness to find society for the time which will not prove troublesome in the future.
William C. Prime, 1855

It is a question whether those who go to Egypt for only two or three weeks and live in hotels ever see the real Orient life or character. They meet too many of their own race and language, and not enough of the natives. In the hotels they live as they do in Europe or America, and the Egyptian ways must be to them no more than an Oriental drop scene in a theatre of modern manners. It is impossible to acquire a good knowledge of the Cairo people unless one has a house among them, with native servants and away from the caravansaries.

The charm of Eastern life is only found among the people and in living like the people, and that cannot be done in a hasty, flying visit. Their docility and gentleness, their ignorance and dirt, their good humour and childishness combined, are delightful to recall in other lands, among other people and under different skies.

A few months' residence there is as fascinating as a hashish dream. The country grows on one.   Jeremiah Lynch, 1889

The travellers in this book stayed in Egypt for periods from only a couple of weeks to several years. Their communality is that they travelled on the Nile – and that they wrote about what they saw and did there.

Bartlett, William Henry (1809–54)

A topographical draughtsman, Bartlett was employed to make sketches for architectural publications in England. He branched out on his own, travelling in Europe, the Middle and Far East and America. The results of his journeys were a number of highly illustrated books. His journey to Egypt in 1845 led to his book *The Nile Boat*, from which illustrations in this book and some commentary are taken.

Beaton, Cecil (1904–80)

The famed stage designer and photographer worked for the Ministry of Information during the Second World War, and from his travels came a book, *Near East* (1943). He designed stage sets and costumes for numerous theatrical productions and films, including *Gigi* and *My Fair Lady*. He published many books of his own photographs and provided photographs and drawings for many others.

Belzoni, Giovanni Baptista (1778–1823)

Born at Padua, Belzoni was a man of many parts: actor, engineer, traveller, archaeologist and showman. 6 foot 7 inches tall and broad to match, he was a remarkable physical figure and (comments the *Dictionary of National Biography*), 'When his origin and first steps in life are considered, it must be allowed that he is one of the most striking and interesting figures in the history of eastern travel.'

He went to England in 1803 to seek his fortune, married and with his wife exhibited feats of strength in street fairs and on stage. However, he had studied hydraulics in Rome and he also began to exhibit his own water-engineering inventions. The Belzonis moved on together to Spain and Portugal, 'where he personated Samson', and in 1815 they found themselves in Egypt, where the Pasha Mehemet Ali employed him to create one of his hydraulic machines. The experiment was a disaster.

However, John Lewis Burkhardt recommended him to Mr Henry Salt, the British Consul-General in Egypt, and in 1816 Salt employed him to remove the colossal granite figure, known as the Young Memnon, from Thebes and ship it to the British Museum.

Belzoni's amazing appearance and Mr Salt's money gave him great influence over the local people and he travelled freely in Egypt. He excavated the great temple of Ramses II at Abu Simbel, discovered by Burkhardt, and opened the grotto-sepulchre of Seti I. There he discovered the pharaoh's sarcophagus, which is exhibited today in the Sir John Soane Museum in London. 'With the same happy instinct for discovery', he lighted upon the entrance to the second pyramid at Gizeh and found the sarcophagus of King Khafra (Chephren). Back in London he made a facsimile of Seti's tomb and exhibited it with great success.

In 1823, thirsty for new possibilities, Belzoni set out for Timbuktu in the hope of tracing the source of the Niger. He contracted dysentery and died on 3 December 1823 at Gato in Benin, where 'a simple inscription marks his grave beneath a spreading tree'.

Bevan, Samuel (*fl.* 1859)

In the spring of 1848 Bevan went to Egypt to assist Thomas Waghorn in establishing a practical overland route to India and 'divesting the Egyptian portion of that route of its varied discomforts; facilitating by the aid of steam the passage of the Mahmoudieh Canals of the Niles; and rendering safe, and even agreeable, the once dreaded desert'.

Bevan completed his mission to the satisfaction of Waghorn and stayed on in Egypt before wandering back to London by way of Italy and more adventures.

Bibescû, Princess Marta Lucia (1888–1973)

A descendant of a distinguished Romanian family and married (at the age of sixteen) to a Romanian nobleman, Princess Bibescû was renowned as one of the outstanding women writers in the French language. She wrote her first book – about her travels in Persia – when she was only eighteen, and went on to write novels and studies of Proust and Winston Churchill. She had a rare beauty which led all men to fall in love with her, and, according to her *Times* obituary, 'she made any man she liked feel that he was the only man in the world for the moment' – a talent she exercised on Howard Carter while she was recovering from an illness in Egypt in 1930.

Browne, William George (1768–1813)

In 1792 Browne set off for Egypt, journeying to Abyssinia in 1793–6. He returned to England by way of Syria and Constantinople and published the narrative of his travels in 1800. He travelled again in Turkey and the Levant from 1800 to 1802, and set out once more in 1812, intending to reach Tartary. His journey ended with his murder near Tabriz in Persia.

Bruce, James (1730–94)

Bruce's early life was one of multifarious ambitions, but on the death of his wife, he began to study Arabic and the language of Abyssinia, and the idea of reaching the true source of the Nile became his main purpose in life. In 1768 he sailed up the Nile, crossed to the Red Sea and thence to Abyssinia. He faced many problems but was eventually led to what he thought was the source of the Nile; of course, he was mistaken, having located only the source of a tributary, not of the Nile itself. On his return to Europe he was lionized in France, but rather laughed at in England. He retired to Scotland and published his travels in 'five massive, ill-arranged, ill-digested but most fascinating volumes' in 1790.

Sir E. A. Wallis Budge (1857–1934)

Budge became an assistant at the British Museum in 1883, rising to be Keeper of the Department of Egyptian and Syrian Antiquities from 1894 to 1924. He edited the standard text of the *Book of the Dead* (1898) and other learned tomes, and he also wrote *The Nile*, which was given to all Thomas Cook Nile travellers.

Burkhardt, John Lewis (1784–1817)

Born in Lausanne, Burkhardt studied in Germany and in 1806 moved to England. He offered his services to Joseph Bankes of the African Association. He spent some time in Syria, was the first European to see Petra, and arrived in Cairo in 1812. He made two journeys up the Nile to Nubia, the first in 1813, and was the earliest European to encounter the temple at Abu Simbel.

Burkhardt always travelled in disguise and lived as an Arab at all times. In 1817 he was struck down by dysentery in Cairo and, aware of his approaching death, asked that he be buried as a Muslim, 'with all the proper regard to the respectable rank which he was held in the eyes of the Natives'.

Carne, John (1789–1844)

Educated at Queen's College, Cambridge, Carne travelled in the East in 1821. In 1826 he was ordained as a deacon and resided from then on in Penzance, where he recorded his travels, as well as penning several biographies of eminent missionaries. It must have all seemed dull after Cairo.

Christie, Agatha (1890–1976)

The most famous of all crime novelists drew on her own experience of a winter in Egypt for *Death on the Nile*. She said in an introduction to the Penguin edition in 1953, 'when I read it now I feel myself back in again on the steamer from Asswan to Wadi Halfa'.

Churchill, Sir Winston (1874–1965)

After a not very satisfactory school career, Churchill was commissioned in the 4th Queen's Own Hussars in 1895. He saw action in Cuba with Spanish forces and then joined his regiment in India, serving on the North West frontier. On his return to Britain he asked to be sent to Egypt and the Sudan. He took part in the Battle of Omdurman in 1898, and a year later published the two volumes of *The River War*. He resigned his commission and went to South Africa, where he was captured by the Boers. He escaped in 1899 and resumed his writing. In the following year he became a Unionist MP for Oldham, and from there on he embarked upon his now-famous and distinguished political career.

Clarke, Edward Daniel (1769–1822)

Clarke, well known for his interest in mineralogy, was also a noted antiquary and traveller. He accompanied various lords, keeping a journal and collecting coins, antiques and minerals. In 1801 he was in the Holy Land and Egypt. He collected along the way, acquiring among other things, a huge marble statue now in the Fitzwilliam Museum, Cambridge, and seventy-six cases of antiquities. Returning to England in 1802, he became professor of mineralogy at Cambridge.

Clemens, Samuel Langhorne (1835–1908)

Better known by his pen name, Mark Twain, Clemens had a career suited to a book jacket: apprentice to a printer at the age of twelve, a river pilot on the Mississippi for a short time, private secretary to his brother, and city editor of a Virginia newspaper. He alternated between mining and newspaper work until becoming 'noted as a humorist', writer and lecturer. *The Innocents Abroad* (1869) tells of his tour through Europe and around the Mediterranean.

Cocteau, Jean (1889–1963)

Known more perhaps as a film producer than a poet, much of Cocteau's poetry has, however, been translated into English. His films include such eternal works as *La Belle et la Bête* (1945) and *Les Enfants Terribles* (1948). His book *Maalesh* (1949) is the story of a theatrical tour through the Middle East.

Cook, John Mason (1834–99)

Son of Thomas Cook (1808–92) and in partnership with his father in the travel business from 1864, Cook became agent for passenger traffic on the Nile in 1870. In 1880 he announced that he had signed a contract for the entire control of the steamboat service on the Nile for ten years, and was granted the exclusive right of carrying mails, specie, and civil and military officials between Asyut and Aswan in 1889. He made a similar contract with the British government and performed valuable services in the Nile Campaigns.

G. W. Steevens, the young journalist, described the 'Real Governor' in 1898:

The nominal suzerain of Egypt is the Sultan; its real suzerain is Lord Cromer. Its nominal Governor is the Khedive; its real Governor, for a final touch of comic opera, is Thomas Cook & Son. Cook's representative is the first person you meet in Egypt, and you go on meeting him. He sees you in; he sees you through; he sees you out. You see the back of a native – turban, long blue gown, red girdle, bare brown legs; 'How truly oriental!' you say. Then he turns round, and you see 'Cook's Porter' emblazoned across his breast. 'You travel Cook, sir,' he grins; 'alright.' And it is alright: Cook carries you, like a nursing father, from one end of Egypt to the other. Cook has personally conducted more than one expedition into the Sudan, and done it as no Transport Department could do. The population of the Nile banks raises produce for Cook, and for him alone. In other countries the lower middle-classes aspire to a Government position; in Egypt they aspire to a Cook position. 'Good Cook job all the time,' is the native's giddiest ambition – a permanent engagement with Cook.

Curzon, George Nathaniel, 1st Viscount (1859–1925)

Curzon was Secretary of State for India from 1891 to 1892 and was then at the Foreign Office. From 1898 to 1905 he was Viceroy of India, where G. W. Steevens watched his inauguration. He travelled extensively, and wrote several books both about travel and about politics. He served in the War Cabinet and was Secretary of State for Foreign Affairs from 1919 to 1924.

Curzon, Robert (1810–73)

Curzon left Oxford without a degree in 1831, when he became a member of parliament. In the following year his seat, Clitheroe, was disenfranchised under the Reform Bill. Curzon set out almost immediately on his Grand Tour in Egypt, Syria, Greece and Turkey. His main purpose was to seek ancient manuscripts in monastic libraries.

He returned to the Middle East in 1836–8 on a private tour. In 1841 he was Private Secretary to the British Ambassador in Constantinople, and later was a commissioner defining the Russo–Turkish frontier.

Denon, Baron Dominique Vivant (1747–1825)

Denon, the son of a lesser nobleman, studied law in Paris. His winning way with the ladies won him advancement and in 1772 he was attached to the embassy in St Petersburg. Thereafter he was sent on various diplomatic missions. The French Revolution found him in Venice, and, although he was proscribed, he bravely returned to Paris. He was spared and invited to join Napoleon's commission in Egypt. With General Desaix he went up and down the Nile in pursuit of Murad Bey, recording the antiquities as he went.

He writes in his reminiscences of his excitement at this mission:

I was about to tread the soil of a land covered since immemorial time with a veil of mystery and closed for the past two thousand years to all Europeans. From Herodotus to our own times, all the travellers here are content to sail up the Nile rapidly, not daring to lose sight of their boats, leaving them for a few hours only in order to inspect, hastily and uneasily, the objects closest to the shore . . .

On his return to France, Denon was appointed Director of the Central Museum of Arts, and in 1804 Director General of Museums. He played an important part in establishing the Louvre collections.

Diodorus Siculus (*fl.* 1st century BC)

Born in Sicily in the time of Julius Caesar and Augustus, Diodorus travelled in Egypt during 60–57 BC. His universal history consisted of forty books, of which only the first five, dealing with the mythic history of the Egyptians, Assyrians, Ethiopians and Greeks, and the last nine still survive.

Doyle, Sir Arthur Conan (1859–1930)

Conan Doyle, the creator of Sherlock Holmes, trained as a doctor, but was not a very successful one. In his early thirties gave up medicine for a full-time career as a writer. After his visit to Egypt he wrote a novel, *The Tragedy on the Korosko*, in which a party of English tourists are attacked by dervishes (1897).

Duff Gordon, Lucie (1821–69)

At the age of nineteen Lucie married a Scottish baronet, Sir Alexander Duff Gordon. Their home welcomed a wide circle including Dickens, Thackeray, Eliot Warburton, Tennyson and Kinglake. In 1862, unable to live in the English climate, Lady Duff Gordon settled in Egypt, mainly at Luxor. Her vivid letters to her family were published and brought her fame. Other travellers on the Nile visited her with as much reverence as they visited temples. But it was the Egyptians who truly loved her, seeing her as 'the great lady who was just and had a heart that loved the Arabs'.

Durrell, Lawrence (1912–90)

We know of Lawrence Durrell's youth from his brother Gerald's books. During the war he became a Foreign Service press officer in Athens and Cairo. He later went on to various press attaché posts. He is the author of, among other books, the great *Alexandria Quartet*, published between 1957 and 1960. The extracts here come from *Spirit of Place: Letters and Essays of Travel*, published in 1969.

Eden, Frederic (*fl.* 1870)

In the spring of 1869 Frederic Eden and his wife resolved to avoid the next European winter and go up the Nile. They had to economize, so did not employ a dragoman. Eden's book *Up the Nile Without a Dragoman* was written to show how 'such luxuries' may be dispensed with.

Edwards, Amelia B. (1831–92)

Amelia Edwards's book *A Thousand Miles up the Nile* came with me to Egypt and we read her visit to each sight before we went ourselves.

She was a contributor to those splendid journals *Household Words* and *All the Year Round*, and also wrote criticisms for other journals. She was the author of eight not very memorable novels and two books of travel about Belgium and the Dolomites. She was in Europe for the third time when, because the weather proved miserable, she and her companion decided, almost on the toss of a coin, to go to Egypt. She never looked back. Her journey lasted six months and she became so absorbed that even today her book retains its authority as an introduction to the spirit of the ancient civilization.

Shocked by the wanton destruction going on in Egypt, with rapacious locals and collectors removing everything they could, she determined to fund scientific excavations. Her Egypt Exploration Fund (founded in 1882) still finances archaeology in Egypt today. Her second book about Egypt, *Pharaohs, Fellahs and Explorers*, was published in 1891.

Elwood, Anne Katherine (*fl.* 1825)

In October 1825 Anne Katherine and her husband set off on a journey which was to take them from Sussex to Bombay by way of Egypt and the Red Sea and back again via Ceylon and the Cape. Writing under the title of 'Mrs Colonel Elwood', Anne Katherine described her journey with great enjoyment, relishing the scary bits and laughing a great deal all the way. She deserves to be better known.

Fabri, Friar Felix (1441–1502)

A Dominican brother from Ulm in Germany, Friar Felix left his quiet priory on two occasions (in 1480 and 1483) to visit the Holy Land. H. F. M. Prescott, the scholar, teacher and author, chronicled his two journeys in *Jerusalem Journey* (1940) – called *Friar Felix at Large* in America – and *Once in Sinai* (1958).

Flaubert, Gustave (1821–80)

Born in Rouen, the son of a distinguished medical man, Flaubert early on developed a strong dislike of 'received ideas'. He studied law in Paris, but apparent epilepsy and the death of his father led to his retirement, with his mother, to the family estate near Rouen. From that time on he devoted his life to literature. He travelled in the Near and Middle East from 1849 to 1851, with his friend, the writer and photographer Maxime Du Camp.

Forster, E. M. (1879–1970)

The novelist E. M. Forster worked for the Red Cross in Alexandria during the First World War. His two books, *Alexandria: A History and a Guide* (1922), quoted here, and *Pharos and Pharillon* come from this experience.

Golding, Sir William (1911–93)

Winner of the 1983 Booker Prize, William Golding was always fascinated by Egypt, and in 1984 he set off with his wife, Ann, up the Nile as travellers did a century earlier, except that his boat had an engine. The result of this journey is his book *An Egyptian Journal*, which shows that although much had changed over the decades, a great deal also remained the same.

Grey, Catherine (1838–1901)

Catherine Grey was the only daughter of the Inspector General of Swedish cavalry. She married William Grey, the eighth son of the 2nd Earl Grey in 1858, but he died seven years later. She was Bedchamber Woman to the Princess of Wales. In 1873 she married the Duke d'Otrante.

Haag, Michael (b. 1943)

Michael Haag is a writer, photographer and publisher with a special interest in Middle Eastern history and travel. He has written *Discovery Guide to Egypt* (4th edition, 1990), and is working on a history of Christianity in Egypt.

Haggard, Sir Henry Rider (1856–1925)

As a young man Rider Haggard worked in South Africa and on the Queen's birthday in 1877, 'formally hoisted the British flag over the South African Republic at Pretoria'. In 1884 he was called to the Bar. He became involved in various official committees and travelled around the world between 1912 and 1917 as a member of the Dominions Royal Commission. He wrote a vast number of books of which the most famous must be *King Solomon's Mines* (1885). *Ayesha, the return of She*, which contains a reflection of the near disaster at the Pyramids, was published in 1905.

Henniker, Sir Frederick (1793–1825)

Succeeding his father to the baronetcy shortly after he graduated from Cambridge, Sir Frederick set off on the Grand Tour through Europe to Egypt and the Holy Land and back through Greece in 1816. He considered going into parliament in 1825, but withdrew his candidacy and died soon after.

Herodotus (*c.* 484–424 BC)

Probably born into a wealthy family in a Greek colony in Asia Minor, Herodotus began his travels as a young man. He visited a swathe of lands around the Mediterranean, including Babylon, Egypt, Scythia and Greece. Judging by his observations, these journeys must have been leisurely affairs, giving him the opportunity not only to see the physical make-up of the place but also to learn about the manners, customs and tales of the people.

His time in Egypt is thought to have been between 460 and 455 BC, when the Athenian armies controlled the country. He probably moved from Asia Minor to Athens in about 447 BC. In 443 BC he joined colonists sent out by Pericles to Italy and was given land and citizenship there. He settled down, travelling little even within Italy, in order to perfect his writings.

Hopley, Howard (*fl.* 1880)

Howard Hopley wrote the Nile version of three men in a boat, *Under Egyptian Palms* (1869), and then, although he was the author of a certain amount of popular literature for magazines, sank into obscurity, being ordained in 1871 and recorded as 'vicar of Westham since 1885'.

Hoskins, George Alexander (1802–63)

Hoskins first visited Egypt and Nubia in 1832–3 and wrote his *Travels in Ethiopia* (1835). He returned for his health and wrote *A Winter in Upper and Lower Egypt* in 1863, the year of his death in Rome. He is especially interesting for his observations about the changes over this period – particularly how much of the ancient monuments had been carried off or destroyed.

Huxley, Sir Julian (1887–1975)

By training a biologist, by belief a humanist, Huxley, a university lecturer, was involved in Lord Hailey's African Survey (1933–8) and became the first Director General of UNESCO from 1946 to 1948. He wrote widely on scientific matters, especially as they touched humanity. *From an Antique Land* (1954) was written after visits around the Middle East on behalf of UNESCO.

Ibn Battuta (1304–*c.*1365)

Born into an important family in Tangier, Ibn Battuta set out on a pilgrimage to Mecca in 1325. His purpose was not only religious; he wanted to broaden his knowledge through contact with famous scholars. But, as time went on, his ruling passion became 'to travel through the Earth'. This ambition led him to further journeys: by a different route to Mecca and then onward to East Africa and the Persian Gulf, and then on yet another pilgrimage to Mecca in 1332, when he also travelled through Asia Minor, across to the Crimea, overland to the Khan's camp in the Caucasus and back to Constantinople. From there he set out through Central Asia for India, reaching the River Indus on 12 September 1333. In Delhi he was employed for some time by the Sultan and was sent in 1342 as the Sultan's envoy to China. He returned by way of Sumatra in 1347, was back in Mecca in 1348 and then went westward again to Morocco. Ibn Battuta went to Spain and then travelled south to the various kingdoms of West Africa. After this he seems at last to have settled down in obscurity.

Ibn Jubayr (1145–?)

The son of a good family from Valencia that had come to Spain in 740 with the army of the Caliph of Damascus, Ibn Jubayr worked as secretary to the Moorish governor of Granada. In 1183 he set out on a pilgrimage to Mecca, and for the next two years he kept a daily chronicle. After visiting Alexandria and Cairo, he went up the Nile to Qus before joining a caravan to cross over to the Red Sea. From there he went on to Mecca and Medina, then to Baghdad and Damascus, where he witnessed the triumphant return of Saladin's army, and then on to Acre and eventually homeward.

Irby, Charles Leonard (1789–1845)

Resigning his commission in 1816, Irby set off with his old friend and messmate James Mangles to tour Europe. The journey extended far beyond their original design, and they ended up helping Giovanni Belzoni to clear out the temple at Abu Simbel.

Their letters formed the basis of *Travels in Egypt and Nubia, Syria and Asia Minor during the years 1817–1818*. After marrying Mangle's sister in 1825, Irby served for a further period in the navy from 1826 to 1828.

Jarvie, William (1841–1921)

Born in Manchester, Jarvie went to America with his family as a boy. He was in dental practice in Brooklyn, New York, from 1872 to 1916. In 1903 he accompanied his younger brother James, a self-described 'capitalist', and sister, Maggie, on a long holiday in the Middle East, for James's health. The letters he wrote home to his wife and daughter were later printed for family members, and a copy was eventually given to Thomas Cook Ltd.

Jarvis, Major Claude Scudamore (1879–1953)

After service in the Army, Jarvis joined the Egyptian Government Service in 1918. He became Governor of the Sinai Peninsula (1923–36) and this out-of-the-way posting may have encouraged him to write his range of entertaining books, which included *Oriental Spotlight* (1937), and *Through Crusader Lands* (1938).

Kinglake, Alexander William (1809–91)

Kinglake made the eastern tour described in his much-loved and much-read book *Eothen* (meaning 'the East' in Greek), which was published in 1844 though written in 1835. Jan Morris says in the modern edition that it 'cast a spell over the genre from that day to this'. It is a book which combines the 'frankness and wonderment' in a young man who was interested in life rather than the monuments. On his return to England he was called to the bar in 1837, but did not settle to the law. In 1845 he accompanied the flying column of St Arnaud to Algiers. He followed the English expedition to the Crimea and was present at the Battle of Alma in 1854. Lady Raglan invited him to write the history of the campaign. From 1857 to 1868 he was MP for Bridgwater in Somerset, remaining until his death a popular bachelor at London dinner parties.

Kingsford, W. E. (*fl.* 1900)

Mr Kingsford's book *Assouan as a Health Resort* was published in 1900 to coincide with the opening of the Cataract Hotel, and was undoubtedly a public relations exercise.

Kipling, Rudyard (1865–1936)

Born in Bombay, Kipling was sent home to school at the United Services College, which provided the background for *Stalky and Co.* (1899). He returned to India as a journalist and writer. His tales and poems brought him fame, and he settled in England in 1889, continuing to write and travel. Among his many books *The Jungle Book* (1894–5), *Just So Stories* (1902) and *Kim* (1901) are probably the best known today. He refused the Poet Laureateship in 1905, but was awarded the Nobel Prize for Literature in 1907.

Lear, Edward (1812–88)

Lear became a draughtsman in the gardens of the Zoological Society, and then, from 1832 to 1836, was employed to draw the menagerie of the Earl of Denby (it was for his patron's children that he produced his *Book of Nonsense*). He left England for his health in 1837 and never settled there again, though his letters show that he longed to return. He taught art in Rome, then wandered and sketched around the Mediterranean. He visited India in his sixties as a guest of the viceroy. Everywhere he went he painted delightfully and wrote very individual letters to friends and relatives.

Legh, Thomas, MP (1795–1857)

Legh was a Cheshire gentleman with an interest in science. He travelled widely as a young man and planned to visit the Levant in 1812. However, discouraged by 'the unhealthy state of the countries there' on his first journey, he redirected his steps to Egypt. His intention was to be a tourist: 'to admire the remains of antiquity scattered over the face of that wonderful country'. However, when he and his companion Charles Smelt were unexpectedly permitted to penetrate the interior of Nubia, they did so. On their way back they met 'Shekh Ibrahim', in fact John Lewis Burkhardt, who was journeying towards his discovery of Abu Simbel.

Leland, Charles Godfrey (1824–1903)

The son of a Philadelphia merchant, Leland was educated at Princeton, Heidelberg and Paris. He practised law in Philadelphia in 1849–53, and then became 'engaged in writing books and took part in the Civil War'. In 1869 he went to Europe, living mainly in London and Florence as a writer. His publications range through books on the Celtic tongue, gypsies, ballads, legends and travel books, including *Egyptian Sketches* (1873).

Light, Henry (1782–1870)

A captain in the Royal Artillery garrisoned at Malta, Light obtained leave to travel for 'curiosity and amusement' in 1814, the year after Burkhardt and Legh had gone into Nubia. He hired a small boat in Cairo, took his writing and sketching materials and sailed up to Deir, well south of the Second Cataract. He always wore European dress, sometimes his uniform. After returning to Cairo and publishing his charming book in 1818, he went on to the Holy Land and Cyprus. When he retired from the army, he was appointed to a governorship in the West Indies.

Loti, Pierre (1850–1923)

A long-serving French naval officer who wrote novels and other books about the countries he had visited, Loti was made a member of the French Academy in 1891.

Macaulay, Dame Rose (1881–1958)

Author of such well-loved novels as *Potterism* (1920) and *The Towers of Trebizond* (1956), Rose Macaulay travelled widely, terrorizing those who accompanied her with her driving. Her travels led to such books as *Going Abroad* (1934), *Fabled Shore* (1948) and *Pleasure of Ruins* (1953), from which the excerpt on Luxor is taken.

Madden, Dr Richard Robert (1798–1886)

Madden's sojourn in Egypt was brief, but his work elsewhere was such that it is surprising he is not better known in our day. Born in Ireland, he qualified as a surgeon. He travelled in the Levant and Egypt between 1824 and 1827, and wrote the letters that became his book *Travels in Turkey, Egypt, Nubia and Palestine*. In 1833 he went to Jamaica as a special magistrate to administer the statute abolishing slavery. He soon came into conflict with the landowners and moved on to America. In 1836 he returned to the Caribbean as Superintendent of Liberated Africans. In 1840 he was again in Egypt, this time with Sir Moses Montefiore on his philanthropic mission to the Middle East. In 1841 Madden was on the west coast of Africa, inquiring into the administration of British settlements. In that year he published a study of Mehemet Ali, the Pasha of Egypt. For some time he lived in Lisbon as the correspondent of the *Morning Chronicle*, and then in 1847 was appointed Colonial Secretary of Western Australia, where he exerted himself on behalf of the Aboriginals. In 1850 Madden returned to his native Ireland, deciding to work to improve the conditions of the peasantry in his own country.

Mangles, James (1786–1867)

Joining the navy a year before Charles Irby, Mangles served in some of the same areas and also in South America. He set off on his travels with Charles Irby in 1816 (this part of his life is covered in Irby's biography). He was elected a Fellow of the Royal Society in 1825, and in 1830 was a founding member of the Royal Geographical Society. He wrote books on various subjects, ranging from windowbox gardening to Thames estuary navigation and a geographical dictionary of the British Isles.

Manley, Deborah (b. 1932)

Deborah Manley was an army daughter born in Aldershot, and spent her early childhood at British Army stations in India. During and after the war she lived for several years in Canada and Vienna. After university she spent eight years in Nigeria and the Cameroons, where her husband was an education officer. Since then she has lived in London and Oxford, working in publishing. She has continued to travel whenever possible, mainly in Europe, North Africa and America. Her journey across the Soviet Union by train to China led to her book *The Trans-Siberian Railway: A Traveller's Anthology* (1988). On her first journey to Egypt she fell in love with the place and its people. On her latest visit she travelled up the Nile with nineteenth-century authors in her luggage, sharing their experiences alongside her own.

Manning, Samuel (1822–81)

Mr Manning's bright, breezy prose is perhaps surprising as he was renowned mainly as a Baptist minister, although he was for some years editor of the *Baptist Magazine* and became the general book editor of the Religious Tract Society in 1876. There he promoted a series of illustrated books of travel.

Martineau, Harriet (1802–76)

Miss Martineau was the daughter of a Norwich manufacturer of Huguenot origins. She suffered from 'feeble health and deafness' (we see one but not the other in her ascent of the Pyramids). She began to publish writings of a philosophical, political and feminist nature in 1821. By 1834, with books on the Poor Law and Taxation behind her, 'she was consulted by cabinet ministers'. She visited America in 1834–6 and later recorded this journey in *Society in America* (1837), and *A Retrospect of Western Travel* (1838). Her first novel, *Deerbrook*, appeared in 1839. In 1848 she set off to explore Egypt and Palestine, a journey she recorded in the three volumes of *Eastern Life* (1848). She continued writing all her life, and wrote an autobiography which was published posthumously (reprinted by Virago in 1983).

Maspero, Sir Gaston (1846–1916)

Maspero was born in Paris, and after studying and teaching he was by 1869 a professor of Egyptology. He succeeded Mariette Bey as Director of the Boulak Museum in Cairo, from 1881 to 1886. He was Director of Excavations in Egypt from 1899 to 1914. He wrote a number of books on archaeology and in 1910 a book of reminiscences, *Egypt: Ancient Sites and Modern Scenes*. He was often accompanied through Egypt by Charles Edwin Wilbour.

Melly, George (*fl.* 1850)

In 1850 Melly, who came from a Liverpool business family, visited Egypt in the company of his mother and father, sister and brother. They went right up into Nubia and as far as Khartoum, where, according to Melly, 'few travellers had preceded us and to which town no ladies had ever penetrated before'. They returned across the desert via Korosko, following in the footsteps of Bruce. Sadly Mr Melly senior died at Gagee. With the agreement of the chiefs of the village he was, with a Christian service, buried in the village cemetery. Melly coined the pleasing name 'the Alps of Art' for the Pyramids.

Merrick, E. W. (*fl.* 1900)

Of herself E. W. Merrick said, 'I am an artist.' She was a portrait painter who went to Egypt with friends. While there she met the great explorer H. M. Stanley and was commissioned to paint his portrait. Having painted the Khedivah, she realized there must be a large field for a lady artist in India and took herself off there with success.

Moorehead, Alan, CBE (1910–83)

Born and educated in Melbourne, Moorehead worked as a foreign correspondent for the *Daily Express* from 1936 to 1939, one of his first assignments being to cover the Spanish Civil War. He was a war correspondent in the Middle and Far East and in Europe. His masterly books *The White Nile* and *The Blue Nile* (1960 and 1962) brought together the whole fabric of the search for the source of the Nile, and, along with Amelia Edwards's *A Thousand Miles up the Nile*, these are the books I would take with me on a Nile journey.

Morris, Jan (b. 1926)

As a journalist Jan (*née* James) Morris worked on *The Times* and *The Guardian* from 1951 to 1962. As James Morris he wrote a great number of wonderful travel commentaries, including *Coronation Everest* (1958), *Venice* (1960), *Cities* (1963), *Oxford* (1965), *Places* (1972); then as Jan Morris (since 1973), *Travels* (1976), *Stones of Empire* (1983), *Journeys* (1984), *Last Letters from Hav* (1985) and *Pleasures of a Tangled Life* (1989), an autobiography.

Morton, H. V. (*c.* 1890–1975)

H. V. Morton entered journalism in 1910, and worked on several major newspapers. His *In Search of* books began to appear in 1927, after a series on London. His books continued to pour out to within three years of his death, and have never been out of print. His *In the Steps of the Master* appeared first in 1939, and his *Middle East* in 1941.

Nightingale, Florence (1820–1910)

It is amazing to think that Florence (named after her birthplace) lived well into this century. Her interest in nursing began early and, before her visit to Egypt in 1849–50 she had already engaged herself in cottage nursing and had visited hospitals in London and abroad. On her way back from Egypt she went to the Kaiserwerth Institute (for deaconesses and nurses) in Germany and returned there to train the following year. In 1854 she reached Scutari in the Crimea, having been invited to take nurses there by Sidney Herbert, Secretary for War. We all know about the 'lady with the lamp', but less well known is her work over the next half-century in promoting nursing and hospital design in Britain, in improving the health of the British Army and in powerfully supporting education in India. Even when she was nearly bedridden, she ruled the world of medicine from her bedchamber, demanding the presence of ministers there and allowing her cats to leave their footprints on great state papers.

Norden, Frederick (1708–42)

The son of a colonel of Danish Artillery, Norden was educated in the Danish Corps of Cadets. Showing great promise in mathematics, the art of building vessels and drawing, he was sent off travelling by King Christian VI in order to study the galleys and rowing-vessels of the Mediterranean. In 1737 the King also ordered him to Egypt, from whence he returned with 'many memoirs upon everything that had appeared to him interesting ... together with an ample collection of designs and sketches made on the spot'. He died in Paris four years later, apparently of consumption.

Olin, Stephen (1797–1851)

A cleric and academic, Olin became president of Wesleyan University, Connecticut. His two volumes of travels in Egypt and the Holy Land were published in 1843.

Pliny the Elder (AD 23/24–79)

A Roman savant, Pliny practised as an advocate and was later in military service, in Spain, Africa and elsewhere. Of his many literary works, only the *Natural History*, in thirty-seven books, survives. He died during the eruption of Vesuvius, having gone to the Bay of Naples to help his friends.

Pococke, Richard (1704–65)

Described as a man of 'solemn air, mild manners and primitive simplicity' Pococke came from a family of the cloth and appears to have been given preferment in the church by his relatives. From 1733 to 1736 he travelled widely in Europe with his cousin, the Dean of Exeter. By now imbued with a passion for travel, he planned a journey to the East. He reached Alexandria in September 1737, and set off up the Nile, reaching Philae. He and the Danish traveller Norden passed each other in the night unknowingly, Norden going upriver and Pococke going down. He went on to Jerusalem, Asia Minor and Greece, and later won a reputation as a pioneer of Alpine travel.

On his return to England in 1743 he began to publish a record of his journeys. Preferment in the church continued and he became Bishop of Meath, where he planted the seeds of a cedar from Lebanon.

Poole, Sophia (1804–91)

Sophia, the sister of Edward William Lane, was an important link in a chain of men who made Egypt their study. In 1829 she married a barrister in holy orders who was a notable book collector, and had two sons. By 1842 we find her (with the two boys) on her way to Egypt to join her brother. She was to live there for seven years. While her brother was making his studies for *Manners and Customs of Modern Egypt*, Sophia was learning about the life of the women of Egypt. This she wrote up in her book *An Englishwoman in Egypt*. On her return to England, she collaborated with her younger son, Reginald Stuart Poole, on a series of photographic books on the Middle East. He became keeper of the Department of Coins and Medals at the British Museum, and her later years were spent at his house at the Museum.

Pryce-Jones, Alan (b. 1908)

The book critic, author and journalist was assistant editor of the *London Mercury* when he went to Egypt and wrote about it in *The Spring Journey*. He became editor of the *Times Literary Supplement* and book critic of the *New York Herald Tribune*. He has published poems, a musical play, an opera and his autobiography *The Bonus of Laughter* (1987).

Prime, William Cooper (1824–1905)

Son of a headmaster, Prime graduated in 1853 as a lawyer, but ten years later rather strange circumstances made him go into journalism. The *New York Journal of Commerce* was suppressed in 1861 (for 'disloyalty'); on its rebirth Prime became editor, for eight years. He combined this position with the presidency of Associated Press. He also accumulated a notable collection of early illustrated books and a major coin collection, and wrote authoritative books about coins (1861) and porcelain (1878). His travel in pursuit of his hobbies led to various 'vacation' books, and in 1855 his visit to the Middle East was followed up with *Boat Life in Egypt and Nubia* (1857) and *Tent Life in the Holy Land* (1857). He was one of the principal promoters of the Metropolitan Museum of Modern Art in New York.

Pye-Smith, Charlie (b. 1951)

Born in Huddersfield, Charlie Pye-Smith studied ecology in Newcastle and London. He wrote two books on related subjects and various articles on environmental matters and travel, and did research for the BBC series *Only One Earth*. He went first to Egypt, the Sudan and Ethiopia in 1975, and returned nine years later to find that not only had Africa changed but so had he. The result of this journey, *The Other Nile*, was published in 1986.

Quibell, Annie (1862–1927)

Herself an excavator and draughtswoman (she was an assistant to Flinders Petrie, helping on a number of his excavations and contributing to several of his volumes), Annie married the archaeologist James Edward Quibell (1867–1935) in 1900. She published two popular books, *Egyptian History and Art* (1923) and *A Wayfarer in Egypt* (1926). Her husband was keeper of the Cairo Museum from 1913 to 1925 and then for two years Secretary-General of the Antiquities Department.

Richardson, Dr Robert (1779–1847)

Having graduated as a doctor at Edinburgh in 1807, Richardson practised for a time in Dumfrieshire and then became travelling physician to Viscount Mountjoy, later Earl of Blessington. In 1816 he joined the Earl of Belmore and his party for a two-year tour through Europe, Egypt and Palestine. His *Travels* were published in 1822. Having read them, Byron remarked, 'The author is just the sort of man I should like to have with me for Greece – clever, both as a man and as a physician.' Richardson later set up an extensive medical practice in London.

Roberts, David, RA (1796–1864)

The son of an Edinburgh shoemaker, Roberts became a scene painter, eventually at Covent Garden. Were he alive today and receiving royalties, he would be a rich man, for postcards of his work are on sale all over Egypt. He began to travel after he moved to London in 1823, 'in search of picturesque subjects'. His work was rightly popular. He spent five months in Egypt from 1838 to 1839, producing a prodigious amount of work. In 1851 he was one of the commissioners of the Great Exhibition.

Sandys, George (1578–1644)

The seventh son of Edwin Sandys, Archbishop of York, Sandys went on an extended tour abroad in 1610, publishing an account of his travels in four volumes in 1615. In 1621 he went to America as treasurer of the Virginia Company, remaining there for about ten years. On his return to England, he became a Gentleman of the Privy Chamber to Charles I.

Simmons, Michael (b. 1935)

Michael Simmons, a journalist who would like to be a writer, has written on political and industrial matters for various newspapers, specializing in Eastern Europe since 1968. He has written books on that area, his latest being *Vaclav*

Havel, the Reluctant President. He found his visit to Egypt in 1989 a mind-blowing experience.

Sitwell, Constance (1888–1974)

The younger daughter of a tea planter who became an MP, Constance was born in Ceylon and lived there until she was nine. She lived the life of a daughter of the Edwardian gentry: having London seasons, spending summers in Scotland and travelling with her parents. She went to Egypt first with her parents (described in her autobiography *Bright Morning*, 1942) and then again in 1927, evoked so wonderfully in *Lotus and Pyramid*. She also wrote about other travels, as well as one novel. She is the writer I really felt I had 'discovered' – no one seems to know her, though she writes with a very special quality.

Sladen, Douglas (1856–1947)

Sladen made very good use of all his travels, writing numerous books on the various angles of each place he visited. Born in London, he travelled the world and held many interesting posts, including being the first Professor of History at Sydney University and the editor of *Who's Who* from 1897 to 1899. His historical writing included books on the Spanish Armada and the Black Prince. He published *On the Cars and Off* about his journey across North America by rail, and various books about Japan and Egypt, including *Egypt and the English*, *The Tragedy of the Pyramids* (1909), *Queer Things about Egypt* (1910), *Oriental Cairo* (1910), *The Curse of the Nile* (1913). He wrote various novels and two plays.

Smith, Reverend Alfred Charles (*c*. 1822–?)

The only son of another clergyman, he was educated at Eton and Christ Church, Oxford, and became the Rector of Yatesbury. In the 1860s he travelled to Egypt with his father and a third clergyman, publishing in 1868 his *Attractions of the Nile and Its Banks*.

Stanley, Dean (1815–81)

At school at Rugby, in the time of the headship of Dr Arnold, Arthur Penrhyn Stanley was respected by his contemporaries as 'a being of higher order', despite being no good at games. The character of Arthur in Hughes's *Tom Brown's Schooldays* is supposed to be modelled on him. He became a fellow and a tutor at University College, Oxford, and was canon of Christ Church and Regius Professor of Ecclesiastical History in 1856, when he visited Egypt. He was Dean of Westminster from 1864 until his death.

Steevens, George Warrington (1869–1900)

At Oxford Steevens was a brilliant but very shy classics scholar. It was only later that his talent for 'vivid journalism of a literacy quality' was recognized and in 1893 he took up a serious career in journalism. In 1896 he joined the staff of the newly founded *Daily Mail*. He visited America and wrote *The Land of the Dollar* (1897). He then covered the Graeco-Turkish war and went on to Egypt, a visit which resulted in his *Egypt in 1898*. He returned a year later as a war correspondent to report on Kitchener's campaign to destroy the power of the Khalifa in the Sudan. This led to his most popular book, *With Kitchener in Khartum* (1899). He followed Lord Curzon to India and then, back in Europe, reported on the Dreyfus trial. He was ordered to South Africa and was involved in the siege of Ladysmith. Sadly, at the age of thirty-one, he died of enteric fever, depriving readers of a writer who might have given pleasure for many more years.

Strabo (*c.* 63 BC–*c.* AD 23)

Of a distinguished Greek family, Strabo was sent abroad at an early age to study under famous teachers in Rome and elsewhere. Geographer and historian, he boasted of having travelled more widely than any of his predecessors: 'East to West from Armenia to the Tuscany region and North to South from the Black Sea to the borders of Ethiopia'. But with the major exception of his journey up the Nile, *c.* 25 BC, there are practically no details of these journeys.

Stuart, Henry Windsor Villiers (1827–95)

Villiers Stuart was ordained in 1850, but in 1873 surrendered holy orders and successfully contested County Waterford as a Liberal. He travelled extensively in South America and Egypt. After the English occupation of Egypt, he was attached to Lord Dufferin's mission of reconstruction, and in 1883 was commissioned to investigate the condition of the country.

Taylor, Bayard (1825–78)

Brought up in a Quaker household in Pennsylvania with direct links to William Penn, Taylor first published before he was twenty. As a result of his early work he was given commissions from the *Saturday Evening Post* and *New York Tribune* and he set off on his travels. He soon became 'his own age's young hero among travellers', moving around Europe (*Views Afoot*, 1846). The California gold rush took him west and then, after a short, sad marriage, to the Middle and Far East. Then he remarried and settled to a rather dull life in America, but was eventually sent as US ambassador to Berlin, where he died.

Warburton, Eliot (1810–52)

A lifelong friend of Kinglake (of *Eothen* fame), Warburton was called to the Irish bar in 1837 but gave up his profession to travel and write. In 1843 he made an extensive tour through Syria, Palestine and Egypt, and wrote about this in *The Crescent and the Cross* (1844). It went into seventeen editions and was admired for its 'terse, simple but most telling touches'. Warburton led a wandering life, beloved wherever he roved. He also published various historical works and considered writing 'an impartial history of Ireland . . .' In January 1852 he was deputed by the Atlantic and Pacific Junction Company to arrange a friendly understanding with the Indian tribes on the Isthmus of Darien. He embarked on the West Indian mail steamer *Amazon*. Two days later the ship caught fire and Warburton was among those who perished.

Wilbour, Charles Edwin (1833–96)

Wilbour combined business with travel. Although very knowledgeable, having studied Egyptology under Gaston Maspero in Paris and Berlin, he was a helpful spectator rather than a scholarly Egyptologist. For several seasons he was Maspero's guest on the Egyptian Antiquities Service steamer, where he performed useful services to other archaeologists. He also formed a valuable collection of antiquities, which is now in the Brooklyn Museum, New York.

Wilkinson, Sir John Gardner (1797–1875)

Wilkinson's father was a member of the African Exploration Society and the Society of Antiquaries, and his mother was a classical scholar. The researches of Thomas Young and Champollion had revealed the meaning of hieroglyphics and, as a result, shown the way to understanding ancient Egypt. Wilkinson was just the man to take up the challenge. He went to Egypt first in 1821 and from then, making Cairo his base, he spent twelve years pursuing his studies.

In 1813 he visited Nubia, although no account of this journey appeared until 1832. He spent much of the years 1824, 1827 and 1828 at Thebes, where he carried out elaborate explorations and where Mrs Elwood and her party enjoyed his company. Ill health forced him back to England in 1833, and he began to publish seriously. His three-volume *Manners and Customs of Ancient Egypt* (1837), with splendid colour drawings and many illustrations, was very well received. Amelia Edwards had read it diligently as a child and when she came to Egypt recognized many old friends on the walls of the temples and tombs. His books, including Murray's *Traveller's Handbook* in 1847, positively encouraged travellers to follow him. He returned to Egypt often between 1842 and 1855.

1

Entering upon Egypt and Alexandria

Introduction

Nothing can be more secure and peaceable than a journey on the Nile, as every one knows nowadays. Floating along in a boat like a house, which stops and goes on whenever you like, you have no cares or troubles but those which you bring with you. I can conceive nothing more delightful than a voyage up the Nile with agreeable companions in the winter, when the climate is perfection. There are the most wonderful antiquities for those who interest themselves in the remains of bygone days; famous shooting on the banks of the river; capital dinners, if you know how to make the proper arrangements; comfortable quarters, and a constant change of scene.

Robert Curzon, 1837

Today would-be travellers on the Nile fly into Cairo or Luxor, seeing the Nile first from the air, and travel around the country by train or taxi or coach and along the river on a cruise. Until this century most travellers arrived either at Alexandria after a long and sometimes arduous journey by land and sea from Europe, or overland from Suez as a continuation of a journey through the Holy Land and Sinai or even from India. A few arrived across the desert from the Red Sea to Luxor.

For those who arrived across the desert it was like coming to the promised land, as Friar Felix Fabri in 1483 and Alexander Kinglake in 1835 record.

Without warning the hoped-for moment arrived. From the edge of a plateau we looked down to where, over against us, far below, lay a country of a different kind ... from ... our barren and enormous waste. For we looked down upon a part of Egypt, a kindly land ... And seeing it we were seized with both joy and amazement: with joy because we saw the end of the dreadful wilderness, men's dwellings, plentiful water, and many other things we had lacked in the desert. Yet amazement too, because we looked at a strange land. For we saw a great gathering of waters, as if it had been the sea, and high above those waters grew groves of tall palms, and other fruitful trees, and towers and other lofty buildings rose from the waters, towns and villages stood wonderfully in the midst of the waters ... For it was the time of the rising of the Nile, which river, leaving his bed, enriches and irrigates the whole of Egypt.   *Felix Fabri*

When evening came I was still within the confines of the Desert, and my tent was pitched as usual; but one of my Arabs stalked away rapidly towards

43

the West without telling me of the errand on which he was bent. After a while he returned. He had toiled on a graceful service: he had travelled all the way on to the border of the living world, and brought me back for a token an ear of rice, full, fresh, and green.

The next day I entered upon Egypt, and floated along (for the delight was as the delight of bathing) through green wavy fields of rice and pastures fresh and plentiful, and dived into the cold verdure of groves and gardens, and quenched my hot eyes in shade, as though in a bed of deep waters.

Alexander Kinglake

For the main flow of travellers arriving through Alexandria the approach and arrival was often a mix of pain and pleasure. The Reverend Smith in 1868, the year before the gala opening of the Suez Canal, defied any European mind to be prepared for their first view of Eastern life. Even to people accustomed to Eastern life, the going over given to travellers, either by the twelfth-century officials who confronted Ibn Jubayr or their successors who awaited nineteenth- and twentieth-century travellers – unless, like Catherine Grey in 1869, they were accompanying royalty – was pretty gruelling.

Once on shore Ibn Jubayr found the city of Alexandria itself fine and spacious. In the 1840s the writer Harriet Martineau, Dr Samuel Bevan (there to help with the development of the overland route to India) and Dr Madden were less enthusiastic. Robert Curzon in 1833 was amused by the passing scene.

Nowadays a visit to Alexandria is likely to be no more than a day trip from Cairo. But then it was the place where travellers began to learn about Egypt. Baedeker's *Guide* was often present to teach them, although in words we now deplore. Major Jarvis in 1937 viewed the city with the fond cynicism of his age and Lawrence Durrell disliked and used it in the 1940s. Jean Cocteau was disappointed and James Morris in 1972 discovered a memory which survived. But then it was also where travellers like E. M. Forster began to learn about Egypt.

Alexandria is only a prelude to the Nile and Egypt and once past it the real journey begins. Many, many people who passed along the river had read their Herodotus, so it is useful here to know what they knew.

The Gift of the River
Herodotus, *c.* 460 BC

What they said of their country seemed to me very reasonable. For anyone who sees Egypt, without having heard a word about it before, must perceive, if he has only common powers of observation, that the Egypt to which the Greeks go in their ships is an acquired country, the gift of the river . . .

The following is the general character of the region. In the first place, on approaching it by sea, when you are still a day's sail from the land, if you let down a sounding-line you will bring up mud, and find yourself in eleven fathoms' of water, which shows that the soil washed down by the stream extends to that distance.

From the coast inland as far as Heliopolis the breadth of Egypt is considerable, the country is flat, without springs, and full of swamps. As one proceeds beyond Heliopolis up the country, Egypt becomes narrow, the Arabian range of hills, which has a direction from north to south, shutting it in upon the one side, and the Libyan range upon the other. The former ridge runs on without a break, and stretches away to the sea called the Erythræan; it contains the quarries whence the stone was cut for the pyramids of Memphis; and this is the point where it ceases its first direction, and bends away in the manner above indicated. In its greatest length from east to west it is, as I have been informed, a distance of two months' journey... On the Libyan side, the other ridge where on the pyramids stand, is rocky and covered with sand; its direction is the same as that of the Arabian ridge in the first part of its course. Above Heliopolis, then, there is no great breadth of territory for such a country as Egypt, but during four days' sail Egypt is narrow; the valley between the two ranges is a level plain, and seemed to me to be, at the narrowest point, not more than two hundred furlongs across from the Arabian to the Libyan hills. Above this point Egypt again widens.

From Heliopolis to Thebes is nine days' sail up the river; the distance is eighty-one schoenes, or 4860 furlongs. If we now put together the several measurements of the country we shall find that the distance along shore is, as I stated above, 3600 furlongs, and the distance from the sea inland to Thebes 6120 furlongs. Further, it is a distance of eighteen hundred furlongs from Thebes to the place called Elephantiné [present-day Aswan].

A Multitude of Ships
Reverend A. C. Smith, 1868

The novelty of the scene rivetted our attention, and kept most of us in open-mouthed astonishment and admiration. Vessels of all sizes and shapes thronged the harbour, but we had no eyes for ships – their crews occupied all our attention. Arabs, Egyptians, Nubians, Syrians, Turks, Greeks, with swarthy skins and flowing robes – and all apparently screaming, at the top of their voices, the most unintelligible jargon – formed such a scene of indescribable novelty, confusion, and noise, as positively paralysed all our attempts to prepare for disembarking, and held us fixed in a long stare of amazement and wonder. I defy any European mind, however well regulated, to be prepared for this first view of Eastern life. Let a man be never so well read in Oriental travels; have drank never so deeply of the stores of information as to its habits and customs; have realised as far as possible all the imagery of the Arabian Nights, and other glowing pictures of Eastern scenes – still the reality will so far surpass all his previous conceptions, as literally to take away his breath, when he comes into personal contact with Eastern life for the first time. Now, the harbour of Alexandria is perhaps better calculated than any other spot in the world for this introduction to Oriental scenes; and as the European traveller steams into it, and threads the long lanes of vessels which always congregate therein, a new world seems to open to his astonished eyes and ears, and he stands amazed at the sight. At least that was our experience: there were such multitudes of ships, of every build and of every rig, the elegant lateen-sail of the Levant of course prevailing; sailors in every imaginable costume, the universal fez (or *tarboosh*) and the full trousers of the East of course predominating; and such a hubbub and very Babel of tongues, screeched at the highest pitch of which the human voice is capable, Arabic of course in the ascendant: these sounds and sights absorbed our whole attention, and kept us thoroughly occupied till we were fairly landed on the quay.

The Day of Our Landing
Ibn Jubayr, 1183

The first day of the month was a Sunday and the day after our arrival in Alexandria. The day of our landing, one of the first things we saw was the coming on board of the agents of the Sultan to record all that had been brought in the ship. All the Muslims in it were brought forward one by one, and their names and descriptions, together with the names of their countries, recorded. Each was questioned as to what merchandise or money he had, that he might say *zakat,** without any enquiry as to what portion of it had been in their possession for a complete year and what had not. Most of them were on their way to discharge a religious duty and had nothing but the [bare] provisions for the journey. But they were compelled to pay the *zakat* without being questioned as to what had been possessed by them for the complete year and what had not . . .

The Muslims were then ordered to take their belongings, and what remained of their provisions, to the shore, where there were attendants responsible for them and for carrying to the Customs all that they had brought ashore. There they were called one by one, and the possessions of each were produced. The Customs was packed to choking. All their goods, great and small, were searched and confusedly thrown together, while hands were thrust into their waistbands in search of what might be within. The owners were then put to oath whether they had aught else not discovered. During all this, because of the confusion of hands and the excessive throng, many possessions disappeared. After this scene of abasement and shame, for which we pray God to recompense us amply, they [the pilgrims] were allowed to go.

There is no doubt that this is one of the matters concealed from the great Sultan known as Salah al-Din [Saladin]. If he heard of it, from what is related of his justice and leanings to pity, he would end it. But God is sufficient to the Faithful in this unhappy case, and [in the life to come] they will pay the *zakat* with the happiest heart. In the lands of this man [Saladin], we found nothing bad that merits mention save this affair, which was provoked by the officials of the Customs.

Landing at Alexandria
Samuel Bevan, 1849

I shall never forget the scene that awaited us on landing at the hard. Camels, donkeys, merchandise of every description, shrieking women, boys, and greasy Arabs, were jumbled together in indescribable confusion; the men fighting and cuffing one another, with the most violent gesticulations, in their anxiety to

* *Zakat* in its primitive sense denotes 'purification', whence it is used to describe that portion of property bestowed in alms as a sanctification of the remainder to its owner.

appropriate the luggage of the newly arrived passengers, in order to convey it to the city. Furner, armed with a huge whip, which I learnt to call by the name of '*Korbash*', dealt his blows right and left on the heads and shoulders of the natives, and speedily cleared a way for us to where a group of donkeys were standing, all saddled and bridled. My friend, selecting the two which he considered the best, told me to mount; an injunction which I mechanically obeyed, for I scarcely knew what I was doing, and was querying with myself whether my Ramsgate and Blackheath experience in donkey-exercise would avail be aught on the present occasion. The saddles were of stuffed carpet, and very high, and my stirrup-leather broke with me on getting up, an accident no sooner remarked by Furner, than my donkey-boy was rewarded with a little of the '*korbash*'. To tie it up again, was the work of a moment, and then off we went at a gallop, with a boy at each tail, through some narrow streets, between high walls, where, in addition to the exertion required in keeping my seat, I had continually to bob my head to avoid being knocked off my perch by some passing camel, which, with its ponderous and enormous load, would fill up the whole of the street. Ever and anon, my donkey-boy, by a fearful thwack '*a posteriori*', would give my animal a right or left-handed bias, sufficient almost to make me lose my equilibrium, while Furner, who rode behind, could scarce keep his seat for laughter. Five minutes hard riding brought us into the middle of a crowded bazaar, and we were forced to relapse into a trot, our boys clearing a space before us by repeated cries of '*shimalek! aminak! ariglak!*'* &c.

Arrival by Sea
Karl Baedeker, 1929

Most of the steamers berth at the wharf of the Inner Harbour. As soon as the passport examination and health inspection is over the traveller should have his luggage conveyed to the hotel or station by the hotel-servants, or by one of the representatives of Cook's or the Cairo hotels, who swarm out in small boats to meet the incoming steamer (about 5 piastres a trunk). These are recognizable by their official caps. Those who employed unauthorized persons will certainly be cheated.

Royal Arrival
Catherine Grey, 1868

The first sight of Alexandria was really very striking. The weather, though cold, was very bright, and nothing could be more gay and interesting than the whole scene as we came into the harbour. The vessels in the port had all 'dressed ship,' as I had learnt to call it on board the *Ariadne*, that is, they were covered with flags from the top of each mast to the water's edge, and all saluted and manned yards; while hundreds of boats of the most picturesque shapes, and very gaily painted, filled with black and bronze faced half savage-looking people, dressed in the brightest Egyptian costumes, came out to see us, and pulled

* 'To the left; to the right; mind your legs!'

round the ship. I was immensely amused and interested by the sight. The band of the *Ariadne*, meanwhile, played on board; and music, such as it was, in many of the boats, added to the effect.

At eleven o'clock we disembarked under salutes from the *Ariadne* and other ships, and from the shore, and were met on landing by the Viceroy's eldest son, Mehemet Taafik Pasha, as well as by numbers of officers and official persons of all sorts, in full uniform. The officers appointed to attend upon the Prince during his stay in Egypt – Mourad Pasha and Abdel Kader Bey – came on board the *Ariadne* before we landed. State carriages were provided for us in the railway, to which we walked up; a regiment of Zouaves of the Guard lining the way up to the station, where there was a guard of honour. The number of people out to see us was enormous, forming, indeed, a regular wall of natives on both sides all the way up! The effect of their beautifully bright dresses was very striking; even those who were scantily clothed, or not clothed at all, having always some bright cap or handkerchief on their head, which gave them a bright appearance; and I must say I was immensely struck by it all.

Discovering Alexandria
Michael Haag, 1987

'If a man makes a pilgrimage around Alexandria in the morning, God will make for him a golden crown, set with pearls, perfumed with musk and camphor, and shining from the East to the West' (Ibn Duqmaq). Today even the most determined seer of sights will be able to catch the evening train back to Cairo. A Roman odeon, Pompey's Pillar, the tombs at Kom Shogafa; these and a medieval fortress squatting on the foundations of the Pharos lighthouse are the principal but paltry remains of Alexandria's resplendent past. Some will see nothing in her. Others will voyage through the phantom city and listen to her voices and music.

Some Features and Antiquities of Alexandria
Ibn Jubayr, 1183

First there is the fine situation of the city, and the spaciousness of its buildings. We have never seen a town with broader streets, or higher structures, or one more ancient and beautiful. Its markets also are magnificent. A remarkable thing about the construction of the city is that the buildings below the ground are like those above it and are even finer and stronger, because the waters of the Nile wind underground beneath the houses and alleyways. The wells are connected, and flow into each other. We observed many marble columns and slabs of height, amplitude, and splendour such as cannot be imagined. You will find in some of its avenues columns that climb up to and choke the skies, and whose purpose and the reason for whose erection none can tell. It was related to us that in ancient times they supported a building reserved for philosophers and the chief men of the day. God knows best, but they seem to be for the purpose of astronomical observations.

One of the greatest wonders that we saw in this city was the lighthouse which

Great and Glorious God had erected by the hands of those who were forced to such labour as 'a sign to those who take warning from examining the fate of others' [Koran XV, 75] and as a guide to voyagers, for without it they could not find the true course to Alexandria. It can be seen for more than seventy miles, and is of great antiquity. It is most strongly built in all directions and competes with the skies in height. Description of it falls short, the eyes fail to comprehend it, and words are inadequate, so vast is the spectacle.

We measured one of its four sides and found it to be more than fifty arms' lengths. It is said that in height it is more than one hundred and fifty *qamah*.* Its interior is an awe-inspiring sight in its amplitude, with stairways and entrances and numerous apartments, so that he who penetrates and wanders through its passages may be lost. In short, words fail to give a conception of it. May God not let it cease to be an affirmation of Islam and (for that creed) preserve it. At its summit is a mosque having the qualities of blessedness, for men are blessed by praying therein ... We went up to this blessed mosque and prayed in it. We saw such marvels of construction as cannot faithfully be described.

Amongst the glories of this city, and owing in truth to the Sultan, are the colleges and hostels erected there for students and pious men from other lands. There each may find lodging where he might retreat, and a tutor to teach him the branch of learning he desires, and an allowance to cover all his needs. The care of the Sultan for these strangers from afar extends to the assigning of baths in which they may cleanse themselves when they need, to the setting up of a hospital for the treatment of those of them who are sick, and to the appointment of doctors to attend to them. At their disposal are servants charged with ministering to them in the manner prescribed both as regards treatment and sustenance. Persons have also been appointed to it who may visit those of the strangers who are too modest to come to the hospital, and who can thus describe their condition to the doctors, who would then be answerable for their cure.

First Sights
Harriet Martineau, 1848

In this garden, as in every field and garden in Egypt, the ground was divided off into compartments, which are surrounded by little ridges, in order to retain whatever water they receive. Where there is artificial irrigation, the water is led along and through these ridges, and distributed thus to every part. I found here the first training of the eye to that angularity which is the main characteristic of form in Egypt. It seems to have been a decree of the old gods of Egypt that angularity should be a prime law of beauty; and the decree appears to have been undisputed to this day: and one of the most surprising things to a stranger is to feel himself immediately falling into sympathy with this taste, so that he finds in his new sense and ideas of beauty a fitting avenue to the glories of the temples of the Nile.

The gardens of Alexandria looked rude to our European eyes; but we saw

* One *qamah* is a man's height.

few so good afterwards. In the damp plots grew herbs, and especially a kind of mallow, much in use for soups: and cabbages, put in among African fruits. Among great flowering oleanders, Marvel of Peru, figs and oranges, were some familiar plants, cherished, I thought, with peculiar care under the windows of the consular houses; – monthly roses, chrysanthemums, Love-lies-bleeding, geraniums, rosemary, and, of course, the African marigold. Many of these plots are overshadowed by palms – and they form, in fact, the ground of the palm-orchards, as we used to call them. Large clusters of dates were hanging from under the fronds of the palms; and these were usually the most valuable product of the garden. The consular gardens are not, of course, the most oriental in aspect. We do not see in them, as in those belonging to Arab, the reservoir for Mohammedan ablution, nor the householder on the margin winding on his turban after his bath, or prostrating himself at his prayers.

Alexandrian Sightseeing
Samuel Bevan, 1849

In the evening, Furner insisted on my taking another lesson in donkey-riding, so selecting two of the best looking from the *stand* close to our office door, we cantered through the square towards Cleopatra's Needle, which forms a prominent object on the sea-shore, just outside the town. On our way, we passed through a dirty Arab village, where we were besieged by a crowd of urchins who begged of and then threw stones at us. We were compelled to gallop away as fast as our donkeys would go, to get out of the reach of the heavy missiles with which they occasionally obliged us, though had their numbers been less formidable, it is probable we should have stood our ground and shewed fight. For this sort of reception we were indebted to our Frank costume; for I found a few weeks afterwards, when I had adopted the dress of the country, that I could pass the same spot, and others equally notorious, unmolested.

From the Needle, we made a long round to Pompey's Pillar and the Baths of Cleopatra. There is a good view from the base of the former over the Mahmoudieh Canal, which fertilizes in its course a narrow strip of country, and studded as it mostly is with numerous sails, forms a curious feature in the landscape. The pillar stands out in solitary grandeur from a vast plain of ruins and tombs, the site of ancient Alexandria. Hard by is a little building bearing some resemblance to a temple; this is a refuge for hard-pressed debtors, a strong-hold against all pursuit, and so long as they remain under its friendly shelter, neither law nor remorseless creditor has power to lay hands upon them. Our road to what are said to be the Baths of Cleopatra, lay through a bustling and most dirty street of low Arab dwellings, to a kind of quay or shipping place for corn, near to which is a group of quaint looking wind-mills with six or eight sails each, the whole in full motion, spinning round with a rushing noise that sorely alarmed our poor donkeys, although it served to prove to us that there was at least no lack of corn in Egypt. A dusty gallop of another mile then brought us to the shore, where we tethered our beasts, and proceeded to examine the spot where it is alleged that the 'Queen of Beauty' used to perform her ablutions. The Baths consist of three or four rocky caves open to the sea, where sheltered from the scorching rays of the sun, the water acquires an enticing temperature, and ripples in and out at a depth of several feet. Close by the Baths, in a sandy cliff, are some excavations of prodigious size, which an old Arab informed us were Catacombs, but as they contain no bones or relics of mortality, and do not even boast of a stray skull or two, he found us somewhat sceptical; the old man conducted us through the outermost apartments, but having no candles, and the evening closing in, we could see but little of their distinction, so pitching him a few paras we hastened homewards.

Pompey's Pillar
Dr R. R. Madden, 1825

Another of the few existing monuments of Alexandrian magnificence is Pompey's Pillar ... This column may be divided into four separate parts: the shaft, the capital, the base and the pedestal. The shaft is one solid block of granite, sixty-four feet in height and eight and a quarter feet in diameter; the column together is eighty-eight and a half feet high. It is calculated to weigh one million one hundred and ten thousand pounds, and would require a vessel of five hundred tons to transport it ... I have seen ladders rigged to the top by English sailors, who contrived to pass a rope over it by a common kite.* I made two fruitless attempts to ascend, but I found it impossible; an Irish lady, however, a Miss Talbot, had the courage to mount, and breakfasted on the summit.

Alexandrian Street
Robert Curzon, 1833

We took possession of all the rooms upstairs, of which the principal one was long and narrow, with two windows at the end, opening on to a covered balcony or verandah: this overlooked the principal street and the bazaar. Here my companion and I soon stationed ourselves, and watched the novel and curious scene below; and strange indeed to the eye of an European, when for the first time he enters an Oriental city, is all he sees around him. The picturesque dresses, the buildings, the palm-trees, the camels, the people of various nations, with their long beards, their arms, and turbans, all unite to form a picture which is indelibly fixed in the memory. Things which have since become perfectly familiar to us were then utterly incomprehensible, and we had no one to explain them to us, for the one waiter of the poor inn, who was darting about in his shirt-sleeves after the manner of all waiters, never extended his answers to our questions beyond 'Si, Signore', so we got but little information from him; however, we did not make use of our eyes the less for that.

Among the first things we noticed was the number of half-naked men who

---

* This method of passing a rope up was used also for measuring the height of tall structures. Reverend Michael Russell reports that the officers of a Glasgow man-of-war in 1827 'passed a string over the top of the column – to this they fastened a cord, and, eventually, a rope-ladder. Their example has been followed by the crew of almost every king's ship since stationed in that port ... But the national flag having on one occasion having been left by a party, the governor took so much offence as to prohibit all such frolics for the time to come.' Russell also notes that a similar feat was accomplished in 1777 by an English captain.

went running about, each with something like a dead pig under his arm, shouting out 'Mother! mother!'* with a doleful voice. These were the *sakis* or water-carriers, with their goat-skins of the precious element, a bright brass cupful of which they sell for a small coin to the thirsty passengers. An old man with a fan in his hand made of a palm branch, who was crumpled up in the corner of a sort of booth among a heap of dried figs, raisins, and dates, just opposite our window, was an object of much speculation to us how he got in, and how he would ever manage to get out of the niche into which he was so closely wedged. He was the merchant, as the Arabian Nights would call him, or the shop-keeper as we should say, who sat there cross-legged among his wares waiting patiently for a customer, and keeping off the flies in the meanwhile, as in due time we discovered that all merchants did in all countries of the East. Soon there came slowly by a long procession of men on horseback with golden bridles and velvet trappings, and women muffled up in black silk wrappers: how they could bear them, hot as it was, astonished us. These ladies sat upon a pile of cushions placed so high above the backs of the donkeys on which they rode that their feet rested on the animals shoulders. Each donkey was led by one man, while another walked by its side with his hand upon the crupper. With the ladies were two little boys covered with diamonds, mounted on huge fat horses, and ensconced in high-backed Mameluke saddles made of silver gilt. These boys we afterwards found out were being conducted in state to a house of their relations, where the rite of circumcision was to be performed. Our attention was next called to something like a fourpost bed, with pink gauze curtains, which advanced with dignified slowness preceded by a band of musicians, who raised a dire and fearful discord by the aid of various windy engines. This was a canopy, the four poles of which were supported by men, who held it over the heads of a bride and her two bridesmaids or friends, who walked on each side of her. The bride was not veiled in the usual way, as her friends were, but was muffled up in Cachmere shawls from head to foot. Something there was on the top of her head which gleamed like gold or jewels, but the rest of her person was so effectually wrapped up and concealed that no one could tell whether she was pretty or ugly, fat or thin, old or young; and although we gave her credit for all the charms which should adorn a bride, we rejoiced when the villanous band of music which accompanied her turned round a corner and went out of hearing.

Some miserable-looking black slaves caught our attention, clothed each in a piece of Isabel-coloured canvas and led by a well-dressed man, who had probably just bought them. Then a great personage came by on horseback, with a number of mounted attendants and some men on foot, who cleared the way before him, and struck everybody on the head with their sticks who did not get out of the way fast enough. These blows were dealt all round in the most unceremonious manner; but what appeared to us extraordinary was, that all the beaten people did not seem to care for being beat. They looked neither angry nor affronted, but only grinned and rubbed their shoulders, and moved on one side to let the train of the great man pass by. Now, if this were done in London, what a ferment would it create!

The prodigious multitude of donkeys formed another strange feature in the

* *Moyah* means 'water'.

scene. There were hundreds of them, carrying all sorts of things in panniers; and some of the smallest were ridden by men so tall that they were obliged to hold up their legs that their feet might not touch the ground. Donkeys, in short, are the carts of Egypt and the hackney-coaches of Alexandria.

In addition to the donkeys, long strings of ungainly-looking camels were continually passing, generally preceded by a donkey, and accompanied by swarthy men clad in a short shirt, with a red and yellow handkerchief tied in a peculiar way over their heads, and wearing sandals; these savage-looking people were Bedouins, or Arabs of the desert. A very truculent set they seemed to be, and all of them were armed with a long crooked knife and a pistol or two, stuck in a red leathern girdle. They were thin, gaunt, and dirty, and strode along looking fierce and independent. There was something very striking in the appearance of these untamed Arabs: I had never pictured to myself that anything so like a wild beast could exist in human form. The motions of their half-naked bodies were singularly free and light, and they looked as if they could climb, and run, and leap over anything. The appearance of many of the older Arabs, with their long white beards and their ample cloak of camel's hair, called an abba, is majestic and venerable. It was the first time that I had seen these 'Children of the Desert', and the quickness of their eyes, their apparent freedom from all restraint, and their disregard of any conventional manners, struck me forcibly.

Intercourse with Orientals
Karl Baedeker, 1929

The average Oriental regards the European traveller as a Croesus, therefore as fair game, and feels justified in pressing upon him with a perpetual demand for bakshish, which simply means 'a gift'. The number of beggars is enormous, but bakshish should never be given either to adults or children, except for services rendered or to the aged and crippled; and the government appeals to the tourist by public placards not to encourage the habit of begging. A beggar may be generally silenced with the words, 'Al Allah' or 'Allah yihannin, aleik': (God have mercy on thee) or 'Allah yatik' (May God give thee). The best reply for more importunate cases is 'Mafish' (I have nothing for you) or 'Mafish bakshish' (there is no gift), which will generally have the effect of dispersing the assailants for a time.

It is, of course, inevitable that cabmen, guides, donkey-boys, and the like should expect a gratuity in addition to the stipulated fee for their services, and the traveller should therefore take care to be amply supplied with small change at all times, and especially with pieces of half a piastre. Payment should never be made until the service stipulated for has been rendered, after which an absolutely deaf ear should be turned to the protestations and entreaties which almost invariably follow ... if the attacks which ensue are not silenced by an air of calm indifference the traveller may use the word 'ruh' or 'imshi' (be off) or 'uskt' (be quiet) in a quiet but decided and imperative tone. At the same time it must be admitted that the increasing number of visitors to Egypt tends to raise prices during the height of the season, so that a larger bakshish than is mentioned in the handbook may be sometimes necessary.

While much caution and firmness are desirable in dealing with the people, it need hardly be added that the traveller should avoid being too exacting or suspicious.

Spotlight on Alexandria
Major C. S. Jarvis, 1937

Alexandria is a city on the Mediterranean coast of Egypt that all Government officials find necessary to visit on inspection during the summer heat when Cairo is becoming unpleasantly close and stuffy. Every self-respecting Department in the service maintains some sort of an excuse for inspection – a workshop, stores, or even a resthouse, and these are assiduously inspected by everybody during the summer months and left entirely on their own devices for the rest of the year.

The bathing at Alexandria is supposed to be excellent, but of late years the sea has become heavily impregnated with Jockey Club-scented brilliantine, and there is a definite film of hair oil, sunburn lotion and face powder on the surface of the waves that extends to the three-mile limit and slightly beyond.

Looking Down
Lawrence Durrell, 1944

... Meanwhile the ubiquitous dust and blackness; the faces of the Arabs with their weakness and cupidity.

The thin exhausted lusts of the Alexandrians running out like sawdust out of dummies; the shrill ululations of the black women, the rending of hair and clothes in mourning – a skilled occupation – outside the whitewashed hospital. The tarbush, the dark suit, the rings, the French accent; the scrofula, the pox, the riches, the food. Even in your Italian brothel I cannot think how to write or speak to you from this flesh-pot, sink-pot, melting-pot of dullness.

Looking Back
Jean Cocteau, 1949

As I love permanent things and hate to see beauty disappear – I even feel the loss of certain restaurants and shops belonging to the days of my childhood – I was immensurably charmed by this road, for here the scene has not changed since Bible days. It even gives an antique air to a bicycle. Here there are villages made of baked mud and here also are men who are coloured mauve, pink or beige; there are noblemen with profiles which look as if they were carved in terra-cotta, and here and there is a fine group consisting of a man mounted on his donkey with which he forms a single whole, sculptured out of the pallor of stone. An earthly mimetism mingles sky, ground, trees, animals and aborigines, rendering them barely visible. (In the theatre, mechanics, who sleep on the floor, become so invisible that people walk on them). On the banks of the Nile slaves with their hands behind their backs, bent forward as beneath a storm, with ropes around their necks, drag along the barges, with their tall billowing sails, full of sacks and earth. Barges, slaves, sacks and earth, white with the same pale dust, go up the Nile whose water, fluted by the wind, takes on the evil shade of absinthe.

As we approach Alexandria the air becomes lighter. Lungs can breathe in more oxygen. We go alongside the jetty with its yellow buildings facing the sea, frothing and dancing and shading into a greenish tinge as it reaches the turquoise horizon, making us forever think of Cleopatra. Cairo is a city of streets; everything happens in the streets. Alexandria is a city of houses; everything happens in the houses.

Alexandria
James Morris, 1972

Grandfather's view of Alexandria still has a pathetic majesty. Legend says that Alexander the Great, who personally decreed the shape of the city, is buried somewhere beneath its streets, intact in a crystal coffin, and a few years ago a dedicated Greek waiter arrived from the Piraeus to unearth him. Night and day his fanatic figure was to be seen at work, digging away behind advertising hoardings, peering into manholes, and sometimes so disrupting the traffic by pursuing his researches in the middle of main streets that in the end the tolerant city authorities had to expel him.

For even now there is a magnetism to the old grandeur of Alexandria. Only a few hidden stones are left of the Pharos, seventh wonder of the world, and over them the Arabs long ago built the fort of Qait Bey: but the very knowledge of their existence is enough, and from the imaginary shadow of that metaphysical lighthouse – once 400 feet high, with a gigantic figure of Poseidon on top – the eye sweeps respectfully around one of the grandest of all waterfronts. The corniche at Alexandria is ten miles long, and never seems to peter out: it is lined with block after block of massive four-square buildings, white or sandy-coloured, and is so fuzzed about with balconies that from a distance it seems to be permanently in scaffolding. There is an ex-royal palace at each end: Ras el Tin serene in the west, from whose quay King Farouk sailed away into exile in his own yacht, Montazah flamboyantly in the east, a turreted ogre's lair in a park, set about with lascivious legend.

From one to the other runs that magnificent promenade, with no particular structure to strike the eye, only a fine sweep and a sense of consequence. Alexandria is not a city of notable monuments – 'a day', says Hachette's guidebook hopefully, 'is hardly enough for a visit of the city'. But as you stand there in the salty sunshine, with a gusty wind from Asia Minor blowing out of the sea, you can scarcely forget that over there the Canopic Way ran straight as a die between a thousand pillars from the Moon Gate to the Sun Gate, and that in the harbour at your feet Mark Antony's triremes came to anchor. A sentry of the Egyptian Army stands sentinel at Pompey's Pillar, an indeterminate monument of antiquity on a hillock near the station, as if to show that even the severe republicans of modern Egypt retain a respect for the imperial splendours: and when, not long ago, they discovered an enchanting little Greek theatre beneath a building site in the centre of the city, the roughest urchins of the back streets, momentarily tamed by its unearthly grace, were to be seen loitering in silent wonder on the edge of the excavation, gazing down upon that white prodigy beneath.

The scale and some of the pride survive. Alexandria is haunted by superb ghosts – queens, admirals, sages, poets. During the Muslim fast of Ramadan the sunset gun is fired each evening from the mole of Qait Bey: and across the silence of the Eastern Harbour, in that brief pearled hush of the Egyptian twilight, its white puff of smoke drifts mystically and disperses, long after the bang, as though virgins are sacrificing to their gods out there, or they are stoking up the Pharos.

To Sum It Up
E. M. Forster, 1922

Such are the main features of Alexandria as it has evolved under Mohammed Ali and his successors. It does not compare favourably with the city of Alexander the Great. On the other hand it is no worse than most nineteenth century cities. And it has one immense advantage over them – the perfect climate!

2

Alexandria to Cairo

Introduction

From this river, there ascendeth no vapors, the humour being rarified by so long a progress, so that although exhaled it assumeth no visible body, but undistinguishably mixeth with the purer air, agreeing with the same in tenuity. Than the waters thereof there is none more sweet: being not unpleasantly cold, and of all other the most wholesome. Confirmed by that answer of Pescenius Niger unto his murmuring soldiers: What? crave you wine, and have Nilus to drink of?　　George Sandys, 1610

Until the railway went through in the 1850s the journey by boat through the delta to Cairo could be a delight or a disaster. The Mahmediah Canal, completed with great cost in lives in 1835, made the journey somewhat easier. James Webster in 1826 found the journey boring, whereas Robert Curzon found everything delightfully fresh and green, Gustave Flaubert dreamed of Cleopatra, and Florence Nightingale enjoyed herself despite little sleep. W. H. Bartlett in 1845 described and illustrated the delights and torments along the way. Reverend Smith went by railway and found the journey enthralling. For Harriet Martineau the journey was crowned by her first view of the Pyramids and by the excitement of reaching Cairo.

The Father of Rivers
Robert Curzon, 1833

The banks of the canal being high, we had no view of the country as we passed along; but on various occasions when I ascended to the top of the bank while the men who towed the boat rested from their labours, I saw nothing but great sandy flats interspersed with large pools of stagnant muddy water. This prospect not being very charming, we were glad to arrive the next day on the shores of the Father of Rivers, whose swollen stream, although at Atfeh not more than half a mile in width, rolled by towards the north in eddies and whirlpools of smooth muddy water, in colour closely resembling a sea of mutton-broth.

In my enthusiasm on arriving on the margin of this venerable river I knelt down to drink some of it, and was disappointed in finding it by no means so good as I had always been told it was. On complaining of its muddy taste I found that no one drank the water of the Nile till it had stood a day or two in a large earthen jar, the inside of which is rubbed with a paste of bitter almonds.

This causes all impurities to be precipitated, and the water thus treated becomes the lightest, clearest, and most excellent in the world. At Atfeh, after a prodigious uproar between the men of our two boats, each set claiming to be paid for transporting the luggage, we set sail upon the Nile, and after proceeding a short distance, we stopped at a village or small town to buy some fruit. Here the surrounding country, a flat alluvial plain, was richly cultivated. Water-melons, corn, and all manner of green herbs, flourished luxuriantly; everything looked delightfully fresh and green; flocks of pigeons were flying about; and multitudes of white spoon-bills and other strange birds were stalking among the herbage, and rising around us in every direction. The fertility of the land appeared to be extraordinary, and exceeded anything I had seen before. Numberless boats were passing on the river, and the general aspect of the scene betokened the wealth and plenty which would reward the toils of the agriculturist under any settled form of government. We returned to our boat loaded with fruit, among which were the Egyptian fig, the prickly pear, dates, limes, and melons, of kinds that were new to us.

Whilst we were discussing the merits of these refreshing productions, a board, which had been fastened on the outside of the vessel for four or five men to stand on as they pushed the boat with poles through the shallow water, suddenly gave way, and the men fell into the river: they could, however, all swim like water-rats, and were soon on board again; when, putting out into the middle of the stream, we set two huge triangular lateen sails on our low masts, which raked forwards instead of backwards, and by the help of the wind made our way slowly towards the south. We slept in a small cabin in the stern of our vessel; this had a flat top, and formed the resting-place of the steersman, the captain of the ship, and our servants, who all lay down together on some carpets: the sailors slept upon the deck. We sailed on steadily all night; the stars were wonderfully bright; and I looked out upon the broad river and the flat silent shores, diversified here and there by a black-looking village of mud huts, surrounded by a grove of palms, whence the distant baying of the dogs was brought down upon the wind. Sometimes there was the cry of a wild bird, but soon again the only sound was the gentle ripple of the water against the sides of our boat. If the steersman was not asleep, everyone else was; but still we glided on, and nothing occurred to disturb our repose, till the blazing light of the morning sun recalled us to activity, and all the bustling preparations for breakfast.

From Alexandria to Cairo
Gustave Flaubert, 1849

Sunday morning, 25 November

Leave on a boat towed by a small steamer carrying only its engine. Flat, dead banks of the Mahmudiyeh [Canal]; on the shore a few naked Arabs running, from time to time, a traveller trots by on horseback, swathed in white in his Turkish saddle. Passengers: ... an English family, hideous; the mother looks like a sick old parrot (because of the green eyeshade attached to her bonnet) ... At 'Atfeh you enter the Nile and take a larger boat.

First night on the Nile. State of contentment and of lyricism: I gesticulate, recite lines from Bouilhet, cannot bring myself to go to bed; I think of Cleopatra. The water is yellow and very smooth; a few stars. Well wrapped in my pelisse, I fall asleep on my camp-bed, on deck. Such rapture! I awoke before Maxime; in waking, he stretched out his left hand instinctively, to see if I was there.

On one side, the desert; on the other, a green meadow. With its sycamores it resembles from a distance a Norman plain with its apple-trees. The desert is a reddish-gray. Two of the Pyramids come into view, then a smaller one. To our left, Cairo appears, huddled on a hill; the dome of the mosque of Mohammed Ali; behind it, the bare Mokattam hills.

Arrival in Bulak (Cairo's harbour or port), confusion of landing, a little less cudgeling than at Alexandria, however.

From Bulak to Cairo, rode along a kind of embankment planted with acacias. We come into the Ezbekiyeh [Square], all landscaped. Trees, greenery. Take rooms at the Hôtel d'Orient.

To Cairo
Florence Nightingale, 1848

17 November

My Dearest People,

Here we are, our second step in the East. We left Alexandria on the 25th, at 7 o'clock a.m. Were towed up the Mahmoudieh Canal by a little steam-tug to Atfeh, which we reached at 5 p.m. The canal perfectly uninteresting; the day gloomy. I was not very well, so I stayed below from Alexandria to Cairo. At Atfeh, as we were seventy people on board a boat built for twenty-five, Mrs. B. and I plunged out, without a plank, upon the bank, and ran across the neck of land which still separated us from the river, to secure places in the *Marchioness of Breadalbane*, which was waiting to take us to Cairo. Then first I saw the solemn Nile, flowing gloomily; a ray just shining out of the cloudy horizon from the setting sun upon him. He was still very high; the current rapid. The solemnity is not produced by sluggishness, but by the dark colour of the water, the enormous unvarying character of the flat plain, a fringe of date trees here and there, nothing else. By 6 o'clock p.m. we were off, the moon shining, and the stars all out. Atfeh, heavens! what a place! If you can imagine a parcel of mud cones, about five feet high, thatched with straw, instead of tapering to a point, a few round holes in them for windows, one cone a little larger than the rest, most of them grovelling up the bank, and built in holes – that is Atfeh, and the large anthill is the Governor's house.

On board our steamer, where there is no sleeping place, but a ladies' cabin, where you sit round all night, nine to the square yard, we have hardly any English, no Indians, for luckily it is not the transit week. Out condition is not improved physically, for the boat is equally full of children, screaming all night, and the children are much fuller of vermin; but mentally it is, for the screams are Egyptian, Greek, Italian, and Turkish screams; and the fleas, &c are Circassian, Chinese, and Coptic fleas.

Mr. B. comes down into the cabin, and immediately from off the floor a

Turkish woman rose in her wrath, adjusted her black silk veil, and with her three slaves, who all put on theirs which were white, sailed out of the cabin like a Juno in her majestic indignation, and actually went for the night on board the baggage steamer which followed us. She was the prettiest woman I ever saw, more like a sylph than a Juno, except on that occasion, and sat in her close jacket and trousers, with a sash around her waist, when with us. The women who *stood* the onset, were a bride from the island of Lemnos, a fat ugly woman, who had been married at eleven, and was being brought up by two duennas, rather nice old hags in turbans, to Cairo to her husband. The bride was magnificently dressed, and would have been handsome if she had not looked such an animal and so old. Her duennas always sat on either side of her, like tame elephants, and let her speak to none. She was covered with diamonds and pearls, had one jacket on of blue velvet trimmed with fur over another of yellow silk, &c. Most of the women crouched on the floor all night, and talked the whole time. They were amazingly puzzled by us, and I was asked some fifty times if I were married. This redoubled the difficulty; I could not conceive why one said to me so often, 'But you *did* go to the opera at Alexandria,' and would believe no denial. What we could be going to do in Upper Egypt was another difficulty; and that we should not travel by a caravan. At last we heard them settling in Greek that we were the singing people of the opera at Alexandria; but what could we be going to sing at Dongola for? Another woman was explaining her views on marriage. English, she said, married late, and fifteen *was* late. She never would marry her daughter later than ten or twelve, and when you *began* to think of it, the man ought not to be more than seven. (By the by, we saw a marriage at Alexandria; one horse bore the wedded couple, of six and seven, the lady riding behind her bridegroom, and preceded by men playing single stick.)

At 2 o'clock the moon set, and the stars shone out. At six the bright and morning star Venus rose; presently the pyramids appeared, three, against the sky, but I could not muster a single sensation. Before ten we were anchored at Boulak; and before eleven, with our baggage on camels, ourselves with the Efreet running before us, the kourbash cracking in his hand (it is impossible to conceive anything so graceful as an Arab's run), we had driven up the great alley of acacias from Boulak to Cairo to the Ezbekeeyeh and the Hôtel de l'Europe.

I would not have missed that night for the world; it was the most amusing time I ever passed, and the most picturesque.

Miseries and Pleasures
W. H. Bartlett, 1845

Notwithstanding the very great conveniences enjoyed in travelling by a steamer, I shall always rejoice that my first impressions on the Nile were received in another kind of craft. I arrived at Atfeh, where the canal joins the river, in the evening, and found a small boat belonging to the then existing Transit Company, newly painted and fitted. A servant was on board to provide for and attend the hirer. Though it could not be deemed an economical conveyance, it was, for the size, exceedingly comfortable, and fitted with every requisite save bedding, which I had with me. It had, moreover, the honourable distinction of being the fastest sailer on the river, as I soon perceived, to my great satisfaction, by leaving everything behind. Happily, I had not yet learned the trifling drawback to this advantage which afterwards came to light, that from its sharp build and the heavy press of sail that it carried, it had been more than once capsized.

I hastened on board; the sun had sunk and given place to a rosy twilight, and the moon peeped up above the rich level of the Delta. And here I must notice, that what reconciles the traveller to this land of plagues – of flies and beggars, of dogs and dust and vermin, is not alone the monumental wonders on the banks of the Nile, but the beauty of the climate, the lightness of the air, inspiring a genial luxury of sensation, the glorious unfailing sun-set and serene twilight, reflected in the noble river, and casting over the hoary remains of antiquity a glow and gorgeousness of hue which heightens their melancholy grandeur, and gilding over a mud village until even its filth and misery are forgotten. I mounted the roof of the little cabin as the broad latine sail swelled smoothly under the pressure of the Etesian wind, which, at this season of the inundation, by a wonderful provision of nature, blows steadily from the north, thus alone enabling vessels to stem the powerful current of the rising Nile.

The boat, with her broad sails and her long wake whitening in the moon, and her Arab crew, lying upon deck, chanting their peculiar and plaintive songs, flew rapidly along through those historic waters. I sat up to a late hour, so delightful was my first impression of the patriarch of rivers.

But on the following morning the scene was wholly changed. On awaking, we were close to the alluvial chocolate-coloured bank, the rich deposit of countless inundations, and the crew on shore were engaged in the toilsome task of tracking or hauling the boat, (a process represented on the ancient sculptures,) to the music of a monotonous chant, which they seemed scarce able to utter. There was not a breath of air, and the warm, soft, cloudless sky was reflected back from the glassy surface of the broad yellow river. The heat was close and overpowering. Hours like these, of which the traveller on the Nile must make up his mind to not a few, are indeed awfully wearisome. It is too hot to go on shore and walk through the deep dust of the unsheltered bank, and cooped up and panting for breath in the narrow cabin of your boat, you seem doomed, ere the ardours of noon abate, to be roasted alive, like a crab in its own shell. Every thing inspires listless, restless, irritable ennui, only to be alleviated, if haply at all, by the fumes of the consoling pipe. It is well if, when thus becalmed and panting in a Nile boat, you are exempt (as from the recent painting and cleansing of mine was happily my case) from the company of bug, fleas, cock-roaches and other creatures more minute and 'familiar to man'. But to the incursions of flies and mosquitoes you lie helplessly exposed. The former, stingless though they be, may fairly take the lead as the principal of Egypt's plagues, and at the bare recollection of past sufferings one cannot help being animated with a feeling of vengeance. Their name is legion. You can neither eat nor drink without the risk of swallowing them, nor doze, or read, or draw, without a constant trial of temper from their incessant trailing over your eyes and ears and nostrils. The natives, being used to it, contrive to drop off into an uneasy slumber, but for a new comer this is a hopeless attempt. You sit all day with a fly-switch in your hand, and though a dozen times you rise in murderous mood, and clear the walls of the cabin with wholesale slaughter, a few moments afterwards they blacken its panels as before, and you piteously invoke the breeze which would perhaps disperse the buzzing swarm of your mud-born tormentors, or, peradventure, waft you beyond their reach. In the fat slime of the Delta they are particularly numerous and active. I was told by a friend, who one evening pitched his tent on this rich level, that in addition to these plagues, he was visited by a numerous company of toads, which he kicked out of his tent without much ceremony. One, however, was accidentally left behind; upon which, recumbent on his carpet in the midst of a tormenting swarm of flies and mosquitos, the traveller's eye mechanically rested. The creature, 'perdu' in his nook, was deeply intent on snapping up fly after fly as they darted past his open maw; upon which sight my friend immediately arose, and drove in again the whole company of the toads, in the hope of some trifling diminution, through their exertions, of the number of his petty tormentors.

Abundance
Reverend A. C. Smith, 1868

I shall always regard that railway journey [to Cairo] as the greatest ornithological treat I ever had in my life. I was not altogether a perfect novice in observing the birds of other countries, yet I was quite amazed at the profusion of birds which presented themselves before my astonished eyes on that memorable occasion. I had been told by more than one friend of Egyptian experience, when in England I was making preparations for a collecting campaign, that with the exception of hoopoes, pigeons, and clouds of water fowl to be seen on the sandbanks, but never to be approached, I should find no variety to reward my exertions; and though I knew from the lists in the pages of the 'Ibis', hereafter to be specified, that such was by no means the case, but only the opinion of careless travellers, who generally have one eye closed to the objects of nature around them, yet I certainly was not prepared for the abundance as well as the great variety which this first day's journey brought before my eyes. Immediately after leaving Alexandria, as we skirted the shores of the Lake Mareotis, water fowl of many species literally swarmed: *grallatores*, as well as *natatores*, in incredible numbers, well waited on by *raptores*. I shall allude to all these birds again in an after page of this volume; suffice it to say here that vultures of three species, kites of three species, hawks, kestrels, buzzards and harriers were to be seen far and near during our entire passage through the Delta. Here there were dogs on one side, vultures on another, tearing at the carcase of a dead camel, while hooded crows were always at hand to take their share. There were herons and spoonbills in abundance, and flocks of the russet-backed heron fearlessly attending the ploughman, just as rooks are wont to do here; though the Egyptian teams were certainly as strange to our eyes as were the birds which followed them, to wit, a pair of camels, or a pair of cows, or a camel yoked with a cow, or even a tall gaunt camel with a diminutive donkey, an oddly matched pair indeed. There there were sandpipers and little ringed plovers running on the shallows, flocks of geese and ducks roused from the adjoining marshes by the noise of the advancing train, and, for the first twenty miles or so, gulls and terns of various sorts.

First Sight of the Pyramids
Harriet Martineau, 1848

Till 3 p.m. there was little variety in the scenery. I was most struck with the singular colouring – the diversity of browns. There was the turbid river, of vast width, rolling between earthy banks; and on these banks were mud villages, with their conical pigeon-houses. The minarets and Sheikhs' tombs were fawn-coloured and white; and the only variety from these shades of the same colour was in the scanty herbage, which was so coarse as to be almost of no colour at all. But the distinctness of outline, the glow of the brown, and the vividness of light and shade, were truly a feast to the eye.

At 3 o'clock, when approaching Werdán, we saw large spreading acacias growing out of the dusty soil; and palms were clustered thickly about the town; and at last we had something beyond the banks to look at; – a sandy ridge which extends from Tunis to the Nile. – When we had passed Werdán, about 4 p.m., Mr. E. came to me with a mysterious countenance, and asked me if I should like to be the first to see the Pyramids. We stole past the groups of careless talkers, and went to the bows of the boat, where I was mounted on boxes and coops, and shown where to look. In a minute I saw them, emerging from behind a sandhill. They were very small; for we were still twenty-five miles from Cairo; but there could be no doubt about them for a moment; so sharp and clear were the light and shadow on the two sides we saw. I had been assured that I should be disappointed in the first sight of the Pyramids; and I had maintained that I could not be disappointed, as of all the wonders of the world, this is the most literal, and, to a dweller among mountains, like myself, the least imposing. I now found both my informant and myself mistaken. So far from being disappointed, I was filled with surprise and awe: and so far was I from having anticipated what I saw, that I felt as if I had never before looked upon any thing so new as those clear and vivid masses, with their sharp blue shadows, standing firm and alone on their expanse of sand. In a few minutes, they appeared to grow wonderfully larger; and they looked lustrous and most imposing in the evening light. – This impression of the Pyramids was never fully renewed. I admired them every evening from my window at Cairo; and I took the surest means of convincing myself of their vastness by going to the top of the largest; but this first view of them was the most moving: and I cannot think of it now without emotion.

Between this time and sunset, the most remarkable thing was the infinity of birds. I saw a few pelicans and many cormorants; but the flocks, – I might say the shoals – of wild ducks and geese which peopled the air, gave me a stronger impression of the wildness of the country, and the foreign character of the scenery, than anything I had yet seen. – We passed by moonlight the spot where the great experiment of the Barrage is to be tried; and here we could distinguish the point of the Delta, and the junction of the other branch, and knew when we had issued upon the single Nile. – Soon after, the groves of Shoobra, – the Pasha's country palace, – rose against the sky, on the eastern shore. Then there were glimmerings of white houses; and then rows of buildings and lights which told of our approach to Boolák, the port of Cairo. The palace of Ismael Pasha, who was burnt at Sennaar twenty-nine years ago, rose above the bank; and then there was a blaze of cressets, which showed where we were to land. A carriage from the Hotel d'Orient awaited our party; and we were driven, under an avenue of acacias, a mile or two to Cairo. By the way, we saw some truly Arabian dwellings by torchlight, which made us long for the morrow.

In the morning I found that my windows looked out upon the Ezbekeeyeh, – the great Square, – all trees and shade, this sunny morning; and over the tree tops rose the Pyramids, apparently only a stone's throw off, though in fact more than ten miles distant. A low canal runs round the Square, just under my windows; and on its bank was a striking group, – a patriarchal picture; – an Arab leading down his flock of goats to water. The sides of this canal were grass-grown; and the interior of the Square, the area of 400,000 feet within the belt of trees, was green with shrubs, fieldcrops, and gardens. While I was gazing upon this new scene, and amusing myself with the appearance and gestures of the people who went by on foot, on asses, or on camels, Mr. Y. and Mr. E. were gone to Boolák, to see about a boat which we had heard of as likely to suit us for our voyage up to the First Cataract. At breakfast they brought us the news that they had engaged the boat, with its crew. We afterwards mounted donkeys, and rode off to Boolák to examine this boat, which has the reputation of being the best on the Nile.

The Nile: from Alexandria to Aswan, 1850

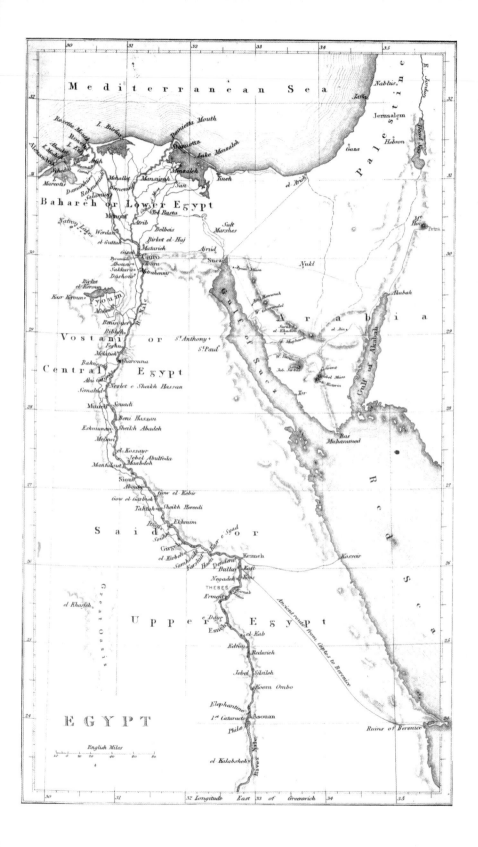

Bayard Taylor in local dress.

The Princess of Wales riding a donkey through the bazaar.

'The indefatigable donkey boys rush on you before you have well set foot on this historic land.' W. H. Bartlett, 1845.

Pompey's Pillar, Alexandria.

Village in the Nile Delta.

Donkey boys and foreigners, about 1880.

Shepheard's Hotel, about 1880.

*Shops in a Cairo street from
Edward Lane's* Manners and
Customs of the Modern
Egyptians, *1836.*

The ferry to the Pyramids in Old Cairo, 1845.

*Panoramic view
of Cairo, 1880.*

Market boat at Minieh, 1873.

Sphinx and Pyramid, showing 'the Sphinx cleared from the sand'.

3

Cairo

Introduction

Rolling grandly northward out of the African interior, at last the noble River Nile splits into the several streams of its Egyptian delta, and creates a region so rich, so old, so deep-rooted in constancy, so sunk in the cycles of fertility and decay, that there is something almost obscene to its fecundity. At the head of this country, at the point where the river divides, there stands the city of Cairo. She is the capital of Egypt, the largest city in Africa, the metropolis of the Arab world, the intellectual centre of Islam, and for more than a millennium she has been one of the great places of the earth. Cairo straddles the Nile, and the river is at once her raison d'être, *her life-blood, her pleasure-ground, her highway, and the thread of permanence that has bound together many centuries of fluctuating and often sanguinary history. The Nile, the sacred river of the ancients, is still the oracle of Cairo. If you look downstream from the city, there shimmers a mirage of the Mediterranean. If you look upstream, there lies Africa, brown and enigmatical. If you look away from the water, east and west, there stretch the wide deserts that have fostered the peculiar arid genius of the Arabs. The horizons of Cairo are wide, and visionary, and heavy with symbolism. She is a city half African, half Arab, Muslim with pagan undertones, softened over the generations by a sporadic soft breath of humanism playing upon her from the north. You can call her a hybrid city, or a mongrel; but she can perhaps serve as an archetype of the half-caste society of the future, a* mélange *of colours and tastes and prejudices and heritages, fused into a fitful unity, like an ingot white-hot but flickering in the furnace.*

James Morris, 1958

It took time to make arrangements in Cairo to travel on up the Nile, but in that magnificent, throbbing city, there was always more than enough to do.

To Ibn Battuta in 1326 Cairo was the 'mother of cities' and three centuries later George Sandys found much magnificence. Many others beside Reverend Smith felt as if they had wandered into an Arabian Nights entertainment, and the leisurely American Charles Edwin Wilbour must have felt this more than any when he beheld the Holy Carpet from Mecca in 1883. In 1868 the Viceroy himself received Catherine Grey with the Prince and Princess of Wales.

The appearance of Cairo and the appearance of Egypt changed with the inundation of the Nile. Robert Curzon discussed it in 1833, as had Charles Thompson in 1767. John Carne was there in 1827 when the waters flowed in.

There was always so much to see and do. Jean Cocteau enjoyed the Museum;

during the war the great photographer Cecil Beaton found the city thronging with soldiers.

To nineteenth-century travellers and to others until its destruction in 1952, Cairo meant Shepheard's Hotel. John Ripley, who accompanied an early Cook's tour in 1871, bring it to life for us again. George Melly paints in the voices and the faces of 1851, but G. W. Steevens, the brilliant young journalist, there on his way to join Kitchener in Khartoum, suffered Cairo out of season.

The City of Misr
Ibn Battuta, 1326

I arrived at length at the city of Misr [Cairo], mother of cities and seat of Pharaoh the tyrant, mistress of broad provinces and fruitful lands, boundless in multitude of buildings, peerless in beauty and splendour, the meeting-place of comer and goer, the stopping-place of feeble and strong. Therein is what you will of learned and simple, grave and gay, prudent and foolish, base and noble, of high estate and low estate, unknown and famous, she surges as the waves of the sea with her throngs of folk and can scarce contain them for all the capacity of her situation and sustaining power. Her youth is ever new in spite of length of days, and the star of her horoscope does not move from the mansion of fortune; her conquering capital (*al-Qâhira*) has subdued the nations, and her kings have grasped the forelocks of both Arab and non-Arab. She has as her peculiar possession the majestic Nile, which dispenses her district from the need of entreating the distillation [of the rain]; her territory is a month's journey for a hastening traveller, of generous soil, and extending a friendly welcome to strangers.

It is said that in Cairo there are twelve thousand water-carriers who transport water on camels, and thirty thousand hirers of mules and donkeys, and that on its Nile there are thirty-six thousand vessels belonging to the Sultan and his subjects, which sail upstream to Upper Egypt and downstream to Alexandria and Damietta, laden with goods and commodities of all kinds. On the bank of the Nile opposite Cairo is the place known as al-Rawda ['the Garden'], which is a pleasure park and promenade, containing many beautiful gardens. The people of Cairo are fond of pleasure and amusement. I once witnessed a fête there which was held for al-Malik al-Nâsir's recovery from a fracture which he had suffered in his hand. All the merchants decorated their bazaars and had rich stuffs, ornaments, and silken fabrics hung up in their shops for several days.

Cairo
George Sandys, 1610

Cairo represents ... the shape of a crescent stretching south and north with the adjoyning suburbs five Italian miles, in breadth scarce one and a half where it is the broadest. The streets are narrow, and the houses high built; but the private buildings are not worth the mentioning, if compared to the publick, of which the mosques exceede in magnificency, the stones of many being curiously carved without, supported with pillars of marble, adorned with what art can devise and their religion tollerate.

The streets are unpaved, and exceedingly dirty after a shower, over which many beames are laid athwart on the tops of the houses, and covered with mats to shelter them from the sunne. Than Cairo no citie can be more populous, nor better served with all sorts of provision.

Water and Minarets
Reverend A. C. Smith, 1868

Then the strange architecture, the really handsome fountains, which abound at the corners of the bazaars for the continual refreshment of this water-loving people: the mosques, many of which have no slight pretensions to beauty – above all the minarets, the most graceful and elegant of buildings, and which catch the eye at the distant ends of the streets; the light and airy lattice-work of the windows, which admits the air, but keeps out prying eyes from the rigidly secluded interior; these and many a charming bit of detail, on which one continually stumbles in the more retired parts of this extensive city, made our daily rides through the streets of Cairo fascinating and amusing during the whole time of our stay. At intervals, and more especially at the quieter hours of evening and night, came the musical chant of the Muezzins from the galleries of the tall minarets, calling the faithful to prayer; and as the solemn sound of these aërial invitations to devotion float over the city, it seems like the melodious voices of angels calling out of heaven: 'God is great; God is merciful. There is no Deity but God: Mohammed is the Apostle of God. Come to prayer; come to prayer. Prayer is better than sleep. There is no Deity but God'.

But what continually came uppermost in the minds of us all, and I suppose of most of our fellow-countrymen in Cairo, was the strong feeling we had that we were living in the midst of the scenes so familiar to us in childhood from that favourite book, the 'Arabian Nights Entertainments', but never realised till now.

As we rode among the bazaars of Cairo, and watched the habits and manners of the people, it is wonderful how that old highly-prized volume, the delight of our childhood, was always recurring to our thoughts; and we almost felt inclined to wonder whether we were not in a dream, so familiar to our astonished eyes was many a scene which we had never beheld before, but which was indelibly impressed upon our memories in our childish days, when engrossed, as doubtless we all have been in turn, in the 'Thousand and One Nights'.

The Holy Carpet from Mecca
Charles Edwin Wilbour, 1883

This morning at nine I was awakened by cannon and supposed Fred, Charles and Brugsch had come. But no, it was the Holy Carpet from Mecca.* So I coffeed, mounted a donkey for the first time since I have been here and galloped

* Celebration on the return of the pilgrims from Mecca.

to the citadel. With a white donkey and a white beard you may go anywhere in a Moslem crowd so I was soon within ten yards of where the Khédive alighted and the Mahmal* was reviewed. The crowd was wonderfully picturesque and of all the colors that have yet been invented, in fact as well as in costume. In places of vantage were close carriages from which veiled faces looked, some with beautiful eyes. The tall bearded blacks who guard such veils tried to keep a clear space between them and the show with remittent success. The Khédive, who looks like Mr. Dennis whom we used to see at Bien Faisance, though he is not so tall, came after the troops, English and Egyptian, had been placed, and then amid more booming of cannon came the peaked-top, camel-borne tabernacle which holds the carpet, gorgeous with embroidered trappings. The next camel bore a fat sheikh, a descendent of Mohammed; the next a fatter one naked to the waist who wagged his head with a persistance which only true religion could maintain; the third carried the white-bearded Father of the Cats, who held a little boy who held the black and white cat. The cat did not seem very anxious to get away. I suppose Lane tells all about this; what I admired was the color, which was a feast to the eyes.

Cairo and the Prince of Wales
Catherine Grey, 1868

At five we arrived at Cairo, where we were received by the Viceroy; the special train running through the public station to the Viceroy's private one, opposite the garden of Kazr-el-Nil.

The Viceroy and his eldest son took the Prince and Princess to an immense hall in the Palace, where I and all the suite followed, and were all presented to the Viceroy. We then went straight to carriages, which were waiting for us in the large courtyard, – English carriages and horses, with postilions and liveries in the English fashion – and then, with regiments of Zouaves drawn up all round, and an escort of Lancers following each of the first carriages, we drove to the Palace Esbekieh, which has been appropriated to the Prince of Wales during our stay in Egypt. The Prince and Princess and the Viceroy were in the first carriage; the young Prince and I, with Mourad Pasha, in the next, and so on.

The Palace of Esbekieh is beautiful; full of French luxury, but without the real comfort of an English house. The Prince and Princess have an immense bedroom, full of rich French furniture. The beds are very beautiful, made of massive silver, and cost, I believe, £3,000 each! My room is so large that even when the candles are lit, there might be somebody sitting at the other end of it without your knowing it. You could not even hear people speaking from one end to the other. It is as high as it is long, with nine large windows. There is a beautiful silver bed; a large divan (rather high and hard for comfort) round half of the room; a common writing-table and washhand-stand (put in all the rooms at the request of Sir S. Baker); a large sofa, and quantities of very smart chairs round the walls. The curtains and covers of the furniture are all made of the richest silk. Add to all this, one immense looking-glass, and you have

---

* An ornamented frame carried by a camel, with two scrolls from the Koran attached.

the whole furniture of my room, which is more like a state drawing-room at Windsor, than a bedroom. All the other rooms are furnished in the same way.

The Rise of the Nile
Robert Curzon, 1833

In England every one talks about the weather, and all conversation is opened by exclamations against the heat or the cold, the rain or the drought; but in Egypt, during one part of the year at least, the rise of the Nile forms the general topic of conversation. Sometimes the ascent of the water is unusually rapid, and then nothing is talked of but inundations; for if the river overflows too much, whole villages are washed away; and as they are for the most part built of sunburned bricks and mud, they are completely annihilated; and when the waters subside, all the boundary marks are obliterated, the course of canals is altered, and mounds and embankments are washed away. On these occasions the smaller landholders have great difficulty in recovering their property; for few of them know how far their fields extend in one direction or the other, unless a tree, a stone, or something else remains to mark the separation of one man's flat piece of mud from that of his neighbour.

But the more frequent and the far more dreaded calamity is the deficiency of water. This was the case in 1833, and we heard nothing else talked of. 'Has it risen much today?' inquires one, – 'Yes, it has risen half a pic since the morning'. 'What! no more? In the name of the Prophet! what will become of the cotton?' – 'Yes; and the doura will be burnt up to a certainty if we do not get four pics more'. In short, the Nile has it all its own way; everything depends on the manner in which it chooses to behave, and El Bahar (the river) is in everybody's mouth from morning till night. Criers go about the city several times a day during the period of the rising, who proclaim the exact height to which the water has arrived, and the precise number of pics which are submerged on the Nilometer.

This Nilometer is an ancient octagon pillar of red stone in the island of Rhoda, on the sides of which graduated scales are engraved. It stands in the centre of a cistern, about twenty-five feet square, and more than that in depth. A stone staircase leads down to the bottom, and the side walls are ornamented with Cufic inscriptions beautifully cut. Of this antique column I have seen more than most people; for on the 28th of August 1833, the water was so low that there was the greatest apprehension of a total failure of the crops, and of the consequence famine. At that time nine feet more water was wanted to ensure an average crop; much of the Indian corn had already failed; and from the Pasha in his palace to the poorest fellah in his mud hovel, all were in consternation; for in this country, where it never rains, everything depends on irrigation – the revenues of the state, the food of the country, and the life or death of the bulk of the population.

Two Seasons
Charles Thompson, 1767

It has been justly observed indeed, by the Ancients as well as the Moderns, that nothing can be a finer sight than Egypt at two Seasons of the Year; for if a Man ascend some Mountain in the Month of *August* or *September*, he beholds a wide Sea, in which appear almost innumerable Towns and Villages, intermixed with Groves and Fruit-trees, whose Tops are only visible, and here and there a Causeway for Communication between one Place and another; which all together form a Prospect as agreeable as it is uncommon. On the other hand, in the Spring Months ... the whole Country is like one continued Meadow, whose Verdure, enamell'd with Flowers, charms the Spectator, who likewise sees Flocks and Herds dispersed over all the Plains, and the Peasants busied in their rural Employments. In a word, Nature, which is then dead as it were in other Climates, seems here to be in its Bloom and Gaiety.

Celebration
John Carne, 1826

The 16th of August was the day fixed on for the celebrated cutting of the bank of the Nile; a time of great rejoicing with the Egyptians, the inundation being now at its height.

It is the custom for a vast number of people of different nations to assemble and pass the night at the appointed spot. We resolved to go and mingle among them, not doubting that something highly interesting would occur. We arrived at the place about eight at night, it being a few miles distant from the city: there was firing of canon, illuminations in their way and exhibitions of fireworks. The shores of the Nile for a long way down from Boulac were covered with groups of people, some seated beneath the large-spreading sycamores, smoking; others gathered around parties of Arabs, who were dancing with infinite gaiety and pleasure, and uttering loud exclamations of joy, affording an amusing contrast to the passionless demeanour and tranquil features of their Muslim oppressors.

[Carne then crossed to the opposite shore.]

Perpetually moving over this scene which (both shores and river, and groups of palms), was illumined by the most brilliant moonlight, were seen Albanian soldiers in their national costume, Nubians from the burning clime of farther Egypt, Mamelukes, Arabs and Turks. At a number of small sheds, each of which had its light or small fire, you might have meat, fish etc ready dressed.

[Carne dozed off, but was roused by a desperate quarrel between some Arabs and Albanians, and again joined in the activity.]

The other side of the beautiful river which shone like glass in the splendid light, still presented a gay appearance; lights moving to and fro amid the trees, boats pushing off with new comers, and sounds of gaiety, with the firing of musquetry being still heard.

At last day broke, and soon after the report of a cannon announced that the event so ardently wished for was at hand. We proceeded to the spot, around which immense crowds were rapidly gathering. The high and shelving banks of the canal, into which the Nile was to be admitted, were crowded with spectators. We obtained an excellent situation for observing the ceremony, by fortunately meeting with Osmin, a Scotch renegade, but a highly respectable man, and the confidential servant of Mr Salt [the British Consul].

The Kiaya Bey, the chief man of the Pacha, soon arrived with his guards, and took his seat on the summit of the opposite bank. A number of Arabs now began to dig down the dyke which confined the Nile, the bosom of which was covered with a number of pleasure-boats, full of people, waiting to sail down the canal into the city. Already the mound was only partly demolished, when the increasing dampness and shaking of the earth induced the workmen to leave off. Several Arabs then plunged into the stream, and, exerting all their strength to push down the remaining part, some openings were soon made, and the river broke through with irresistable violence. For some time it was like the rushing of a cataract.

According to custom, the Kiaya Bey distributed a good sum of money, throwing it into the bed of the canal below, where a great many men and boys scrambled for it. Several of them had a sort of net, fastened on the top of a pole, to catch the money as it fell. It was an amusing scene, as the water gathered fast round them, to see them struggling and groping amidst the waves for the coin; but the violence of the torrent soon bore them away; and there were some who had lingered to the last, and now sought to save themselves by swimming, still buffeting the waves, and grasping at the money showered down, and diving after it as it disappeared. Unfortunately this sport every year costs a few lives, and one young man was drowned this morning.

The different vessels, long ere the fall had subsided, rushed into the canal and entered the city, their decks crowded with all ranks, uttering loud exclamations of joy. The overflowing of the Nile is the richest blessing of Heaven to Egypt: as it finds its way gradually into the various parts of the city and neighbourhood, the inhabitants crowd to drink of, and wash in it, and rejoice in its progress.

The Museum
Jean Cocteau, 1949

Visited the Museum with Dr. Drioton, a jovial person who seems to infuse cheerful life into the necropolis. He slips from one century to another, spares us from looking at minor works and only stops before the masterpieces. The more I walk along, the more I listen, the more I move around the columns, the more do I experience the feeling of a dark world which fastens on to ours and which will not loosen the suckers through which it takes its life. Whatever it may cost, they find it necessary to confirm their existence, to perpetuate themselves, to incarnate, to re-incarnate, to hypnotise nothingness and to vanquish it. Fists closed, eyes wide open and fixed, the Pharaohs march against the void, put it to sleep, braving its powers. For this reason it does not seem a sacrilege to move them to a museum. They have exacted this nominal glory, a glory as of a tragedian in the limelight. They did not hide themselves in order to disappear, but in order to await the cue for their entry on the stage. They have not been dragged from the tomb. They have been brought from the limbo of the wings with masks and gloves made of gold.

Besides, I had proof of this in the room where the mummies lie. It is now closed to the public, but the Doctor opened it with his key. Here they lie side by side in their death, under the windows, in a kind of hospital, where the wounded are sorted out, a morgue where one bends down over the corpses in order to identify the victims. These prodigious men have to the end won the toss from Fate and have continued from effigy to effigy, sloughing and changing their skins. The mania for survival has sculptured the outlines of the leather and bronze faces which seem to threaten us with closed fists. In the waiting room where the great haughty family lives together, everyone escapes and finds again an honoured place in the museum where some gigantic form gives it permission to be at home, to put on a soul and to cry out, 'It is I'.

Seti the First! How beautiful he is, with his little nose, his pointed teeth showing, his little face, like that of a human beast of prey, his little face which belongs to death, reduced to one requirement alone – not to die. 'I! I! I!' This is the word which the rafters throw back. And the rich dignitary who, from his stela, repeats the attitude of the king, shouts it at the top of his voice. His double, facing him, echoes back the repeated image in which he contemplates himself, with or without a wig, with or without a loin-cloth. On the top of the coffer containing his entrails, the four little faces of Tut-Ankh-Amun look at each other as though the central one were reflected in a triptych mirror, and say, 'I! I! I!'

Thanks to the Doctor we pass over the crude, uncouth period when women had men's faces, and over the subsequent long period of academic art, to the period influenced by the grace of Thebes when men had the faces of women. Thereafter King Amenophis IV changed the play and its setting. The sun became the only god (that which the sun foreshadows). By his order art became realist, then sur-realist. Portrayal was carried to its limits, till a grandiose folly was reached, when they decided that heads should be lengthened, until at last they hung down like pilgrim's gourds. But from one age to another distortion of effigies is always overshadowed by the necessity of adopting the intra-uterine position and even the Queen's chaise carried by her flunkeys made her publicly contract herself like the foetus within the womb or within the egg.

Everywhere death protects itself against evil forces which might detract from its purpose of not being truly dead, of not being engulfed in slumber.

The Egypt which shows its flat road by means of living milestones, is only the culmination of a Neolithic Egypt lost to us because she had no writing, and because she carved her flintstones into weapons but into nothing else. We can only guess her outlines through those lay figures of ivory which blaze the trail for the future to follow. We have seen the costumes and stage setting, here now is the theatre and the stalls full of the accessories from which nothing is lacking: – the Halls of Tut-Ankh-Amun.

We shall be able to imagine the luxury surrounding this young invalid, born of what would now be deemed incest. Everything is there, almost untouched by time: – seats, coffers, rings, ear-rings, false beards, gloves, beds, waggons, walking sticks, clasps and little switches. Everything is new, shining, ready for use. The quality of this shining is held for us still, lambent in the alabaster lotus from which he drank. His chariot still holds for us the black horse comparisoned for his use, the make-up box seems ready to open, full of the kohl for his eyes, and his golden sandals await to shod his royal feet, to take him where he would go.

Cairo in Wartime
Cecil Beaton, 1942

It was arranged I should wear RAF uniform with 'official photographer' on the shoulders instead of a rank. I should stay one week in Cairo before my first job in the desert.

So now I would explore Cairo, 'the magnificent slum', 'the fly-blown mecca of artifice and noise', 'the melting pot of a pre-war decadence' – that much-abused city in such strange contrast to the desert from which the troops come for their days of leave.

At first sight the city seemed French in spirit – somewhat like Nice, or the suburbs of many large French towns. The indeterminate architecture reminded me of the pretentious villas in stage scenery of the 'eighties.

A dust storm was blowing in from the desert on to the Louis Philippe buildings, which already looked as if they were originally built of compressed dust; the dust blew in gusts into the Opera House, put together in a fortnight by Ismail for the visit of the Empress Eugenie at the opening of the Suez Canal. It blew in swirling eddies on the pavements, on to the slices of water melon, into the cafés, laundries and post-card shops. It blew through the jalousies into the 'Art Moderne 1900' interiors, and the French 'Louis style' salons, over-crowded with bric-à-brac. The young Arab, barefooted in his cotton galabyiah, carrying a mountain of faded red roses, looked worried as he stepped off the curb while a taxi dashed by, for he feared a khamsin would blow for four days. The camels were unperturbed, as they walked with the slow dignity of Pont Street dowagers, whom they so closely resemble.

The general noise was made up of hurdy-gurdies, bicycle bells, news-vendors, trams, bag-pipes, loud-speakers, and the braying of donkeys.

The troops on leave thronged the streets in their thousands. The hawkers pestered them, and plucked at their arms in an attempt to sell coloured spec-tacles, fly-whisks, and hopelessly out-of-date American magazines. The bars, cafés, cabarets, and cinemas were crowded. A few canteens and rest centres were advertised, and shops purveyed scarabs and watches which were 'sand, water and shock proof'.

The famous Shepheard's Hotel was a seething mass of young officers – gay and debonair in tropical uniforms – a sight one would see nowhere else. They were mostly sun-burned, their fair hair bleached – the new arrivals distinguish-able by their rosy knees that look like white heart cherries.

So this was Shepheard's – a crowded but infinitely respectable hotel, with dark oriental halls, ebony women with richly carved rotundities, holding aloft frosted lights, pearl inlaid furniture, palms, drab hangings, marble corridors, brass bedsteads and Arab servants.

So these were the men who have received such criticism for idling away the hours drinking on the terrace. In contrast to the Long Range Desert Group who, unpublicized in the desert, are building up a legend with their romantic daring and bravery, these so-called 'Gabardine Swine' have also been named the 'Short range Shepheard's Group'. What incites such ire and criticism? For were not these men, too, recently wearing battledress, and will they not wear it again to-morrow? They were spending only one day of leave here for each month passed in the desert. Those civilians on the terrace, there, were the representatives of the Maritime Commission, and at the large round table were the war correspondents waiting for the next story to break. Those officers were the American observers with the army, here for a night before catching an airplane to London or India, and the women in white and scarlet were the nurses in tropical uniform.

A young man of the Scots Guards, powdered with desert dust, with bright eyes and a patch of sores in place of a moustache, but with an otherwise particularly clear sunburnt skin, loped into the bar. 'An iced brandy and ginger ale with a lump of lime in it.' He took a gulp, 'Gosh, that's good.' He has been thinking about that drink for much of the time he spent in the desert, certainly for most of the journey here.

'Now for a bath! Do you know', he confided to the barman, 'I haven't had a bath for five months!' The barman, ever ready with the right phrase, said 'the French believe only dirty people need to wash.'

Another day in one of the local carriages, gharries, we toured the Arab town, the largest Moslem city in the world. The gharry, with a mound of clover for the horse's next meal dumped on the board by the driver's foot, is looked down upon as being inelegant by the dragoman, doormen, and the miscellaneous group of snobs always clustered around the entrance steps of the large hotels. But, in spite of this, the gharry makes the most delightful means of leisurely locomotion and of surveying the changing scenes. From such a vantage point, even the humblest among us feels like royalty. We drove in the Moski through the narrow overhung lanes, with the pretty wiry balconies of the harems, almost meeting above the jostling crowds. The tarbush and coloured turbans of the various sects, dynasties and families formed a bobbing sea below us, as we sat aloft, processing along lanes lined with brilliantly coloured sweetmeats, or butchers' shops, or alleyways with gold necklaces arrayed in glittering splendour against a black background. The whole thoroughfare given over to engraven brasswork rolled past us, followed by another of pearl inlay work. The most romantic is the spice quarter, with its fragrance of the Arabian Nights. In bulging, buff-coloured sacks, the cedar wood, rose, mint, sandalwood and innumerable varieties of curry powder are equally seductive in scent and beauty. It was alarming to see the young men swinging a large heavy shell-shaped weapon, with which they pounded the nutmeg in stone jars. They save themselves from madness by singing in unison a loud and monotonous dirge, the rhythm of which carries them along through the physical agony of effort. Heaving to and fro, they looked like Blake engravings of tormented souls writhing in Purgatory. Once they give up this work their muscles contract, and they are unfit for further effort.

Evening at Shepheard's
John Ripley, 1871

[The writer accompanied Cook's third tour of the Nile, and in the *Excursionist*, having enjoyed the peace and quiet which descended on the hotel in the middle of the day, now watches the tourists returning after their day's activities.]

Towards evening the tide of life, of noise, and excitement, that ebbed from the Hotel, begins to flow with tenfold vigour: fresh arrivals, burned and bronzed, return from their tour up the Nile; dusty travellers come from crossing the Desert; and the Tourists out for the day are back again; and now till the hour for dinner the scene is lively indeed. Costumes of every kind, complexions of every shade, and tongues of every nation, greet the eye and salute the ear: dragomans settling accounts with victimised Tourists, vendors of photographs, shawls and jewellery, offering their wares; now one's attention is distracted by a juggler, who with carpet spread, is 'thimble rigging', and drawing long strings of medals out of his throat, before he finishes his conjuring tricks; another arrives with trained monkeys, dog and goat, and solicits our attention to his exhibition; scarcely have we time to look at him when an Egyptian serpent charmer comes, and shows with what familiarity he can handle reptiles and turn them into neckties; but his familiarity with them is soon eclipsed by a close-shaven, dirty, black boy, who arrives and commences to eat a live snake . . . And thus the time speeds on to 6:30 pm, when the sound of the dinner gong disperses the artistes, and calls the visitors to the table d'hôte, and darkness and silence fall upon the city.

Shepheard's
Amelia B. Edwards, 1873

It is the traveller's lot to dine at many *table-d'hôtes* in the course of many wanderings; but it seldom befalls him to make one of a more miscellaneous gathering than that which overfills the great dining-room at Shepheard's Hotel in Cairo during the beginning and height of the regular Egyptian season. Here assemble daily some two to three hundred persons of all ranks, nationalities, and pursuits; half of whom are Anglo-Indians homeward or outward bound, European residents, or visitors established in Cairo for the winter. The other half, it may be taken for granted, are going up the Nile. So composite and incongruous is this body of Nile-goers, young and old, well-dressed and ill-dressed, learned and unlearned, that the new-comer's first impulse is to inquire from what motives so many persons of dissimilar tastes and training can be led to embark upon an expedition which is, to say the least of it, very tedious, very costly, and of an altogether exceptional interest.

His curiosity, however, is soon gratified. Before two days are over, he knows everybody's name and everybody's business; distinguishes at first sight between a Cook's tourist and an independent traveller; and has discovered that nine-tenths of those whom he is likely to meet up the river are English or American. The rest will be mostly German, with a sprinkling of Belgian and French. So far *en bloc*; but the details are more heterogeneous still. Here are invalids in search of health; artists in search of subjects; sportsmen keen upon crocodiles; statesmen out for a holiday; special correspondents alert for gossip; collectors on the scent of papyri and mummies; men of science with only scientific ends in view; and the usual surplus of idlers who travel for the mere love of travel, or the satisfaction of a purposeless curiosity.

The Tourists
George Melly, 1851

Here an ingenious youth, clad in a suit of grey, is thrashing an impertinent donkey-boy for making an overcharge of five piastres for going to the pyramids; whilst at the next hotel there is a spectacle of a totally different character, in a young girl, of extraordinary beauty, setting forth on a ride, whose cough and hectic colour declare that she has only been brought here to die.

The lovely sky, the splendid sunset, and the numerous picturesque scenes of Cairo, are certainly well worth a visit; but in her position 'the old familiar faces' of home, I should have thought, would have been preferable for the light of the fading eye to rest upon. Possibly she does not know her danger, or her friends are sanguine as to the effect of a change of climate; but it is melancholy to think that a creature so brilliant should be brought to a place so foreign in all its features, to wander a few days among its scenes of rainbow-tinted life, and then be buried into an obscure nook among its gloomy dead.

We met several intelligent travellers at the *table-d'hôte* – among others a Russian Prince, an American gentleman, and an Englishman – all of whom had visited different parts of the world; and their conversation was equally interesting and instructive. The latter had come from England by Stockholm, St. Petersburg, Constantinople, Syria, had been up to Assouan and back, and was about to return to England by the Lower Pyrenees and Spain. He considers the voyage down the Volga as extremely interesting.

Colonel W—, an American, who sat at the bottom of the table, a fine old man, with a magnificent white beard, was singularly characteristic in his conversation.

'Here now,' said he exultingly, drawing a frame about the size of a farthing from his pocket, 'here is a greater wonder than anything you ever saw – beats the Pyramids hollow. It is the Lord's Prayer written in the smallest hand that ever anything was written in – and I wrote it: with the finest crow-quill that ever was made – and I made it: from a crow, the smallest that ever was killed – and I killed it: with the best gun that ever was shot with – and I shot with it: the pen made with the sharpest knife that ever was bought – and I bought it.'

Everything he had, or had anything to do with, was the best and the fastest that could be found throughout the world. His boat passed everything on the Nile – and he had the fastest horse that ever was created. We could not test the qualities of his steed – because it remained in the States: but the boat, though it had had four days start, was subsequently passed by a friend of ours at Keneh.

Egypt out of Season
G. W. Steevens, 1898

All that was no more than you expected: you knew that no tourists came to Egypt in July. But native Egypt was out of season too. The streets that clacked with touts and beggars, that jingled with every kind of hawker's rubbish – you passed along them down a vista of closed jalousies and saw not a soul, heard not a sound. The natives must be somewhere, only where? A few you saw at road-making, painting, and the like jobs of an off-season. But every native was dull, listless, hanging from his stalk, half dead. Eyes were languid and lustreless; the painter's head drooped and swayed from side to side, and the brush almost fell from his lax fingers. In the narrow bevel of shadow left under a wall by the high sun, flat on back or face, open-mouthed, half asleep, half fainting, gasped Arab Cairo – the parasite of the tourist in his holiday, the workman leaving his work, donkey-boy and donkey flat and panting together.

Well might they gasp and faint; for the air of Cairo was half dead too. You might drive in it at night and feel it whistle round you, but it did not refresh you. You might draw it into your lungs, but it did not fill them. The air had no quality in it, no body: it was thin, used up, motionless, too limp to live in. The air of August London is stale and close, poor; exaggerate it fifty-fold and you have the air of July Cairo. You wake up at night dull and flaccid and clammy with sweat, less refreshed than when you lay down. You live on what sleep you can pilfer during the hour of dawn. As you drive home at night you envy the dark figure in a galabeah stretched on the pavement of Kasr-en-Nil bridge; there only in Cairo can you feel a faint stirring in the air.

To put all in one word, Egypt lacks its Nile. The all-fathering river is at his lowest and weakest. In places he is nearly dry, and what water he can give the cracked fields is pale, green, unfertile. He was beginning to rise now, slowly; presently would come the flood and the brown manuring water. The night wind would blow strongly over his broadened bosom, the green would spring out of the mud, and Egypt would be alive again.

Only in one place was she alive yet – and that was the Continental Hotel. Here all day sat and came and went clean-limbed young men in flannels, and at dinner-time the terrace was cool with white mess-jackets. Outside was the only crowd of natives in Cairo – a thick line of Arabs squatting by the opposite wall, nursing testimonials earned or bought, cooks and valets and grooms – waiting to be hired to go up the Nile. Up at the citadel they would show you the great black up-standing 40-pounder guns with which they meant to breach Khartum. Out at Abbassieh the 21st Lancers were changing their troop-horses for lighter Syrians and country-breds. The barrack-yard of Kasr-en-Nil was yellow with tents, and under a breathless afternoon sun the black-belted Rifle Brigade marched in from the station to fill them. The wilted Arabs hardly turned their heads at the band; the Rifles held their shoulders square and stepped out with a rattle.

The Egyptian may feel the sun; the Englishman must stand up and march in it. You see it is his country, and he must set the example. And seeing Egypt thus Nileless, bloodless, you felt more than ever that he must lose no time in taking into firm fingers the keys of the Nile above Khartum.

4

Pyramids and Sphinx

Introduction

I confess, however, that at the first sight of the Pyramids, the only sentiment I felt was admiration. Philosophers, I know, can sigh or smile at the reflection that the most stupendous monument ever erected by the hand of man is a tomb: but why should we behold in the pyramid of Cheops nothing but a heap of stones and a skeleton? It was not from a sense of his nothingness that man reared such a sepulchre, but from the instinct of his immortality: this sepulchre is not the boundary which marks the termination of the career of a day, but the entrance of a life without end, 'tis an everlasting gate erected on the confines of eternity.   F. R. Chateaubriand, 1806

Today's visitors may find the Sphinx overshadowed by scaffolding as Egypt tries to shore up the great creature, and today's visitors can no longer climb the Pyramids, but that makes them no less staggering.

In 460 BC Herodotus queried the cost of their building and Pliny dismissed them as a foolish exhibition of royal wealth, but for all others, the reaction to them is astonishment and admiration.

The journey from Cairo to the Pyramids took most of a day before the motor car and coach, but John Carne and Dr Madden refreshed themselves with the water of the Nile on the way. Nowadays the thought of drinking Nile water may make one shudder, but perhaps if we followed Dr Madden's advice we too would find it health-giving...

Venturing inside the Pyramids, as Frederick Norden did in 1737, sounds like caving in a morgue, despite the merriment of his description. Sir Gardner Wilkinson had advice to give to such adventurers in his *Handbook to Egypt* of 1847. Alexander Kinglake describes well the sense of admiration and awe that these mighty edifices produce. But, turning aside here to the Sphinx, Dean Stanley provides a brief introduction, and Flaubert laughs at it.

The Pyramids are indeed astonishing: Sir Julian Huxley's description in 1948 simply reinforces our astonishment. In Harriet Martineau's day the great ambition was to climb to the top – pulled and pushed there by eager assistants. Miss Martineau achieved this ambition and was so overwhelmed by the experience that she forgot her most 'precious articles of property'. Mark Twain's descriptions of his adventures were, as always, of great charm. Many found the helpers on the Pyramids a necessary nuisance, but Rider Haggard saw them act as saviours and Constance Sitwell enjoyed their company.

The Cost of the Pyramids
Herodotus, *c.* 460 BC

... Thus the upper part of the Pyramid was first finished off, then the next part, and last of all the lower ground part. Now, the sum that was spent on radishes, onions, and garlic for the workmen, is marked in Egyptian characters on the Pyramid ... If these things be so, how much besides may we calculate was spent on the iron with which they worked, and on bread and clothes for the workmen ... as they were constructing these works.

Extravagance
Pliny the Elder, *c.* AD 50

We will mention also cursorily the Pyramids, which are in the same country of Egypt, – that idle and foolish exhibition of royal wealth. For the cause by most assigned for their construction is an intention on the part of those kings to exhaust their treasures, rather than leave them to successors or plotting rivals, or to keep the people from idleness. Great was the vanity of those individuals on this point.

The Delights of Nile Water
John Carne, 1826

Fatigued with heat and thirst [on his journey to the Pyramids] we came to a few cottages in a palm-wood, and stopped to drink of a fountain of delicious water. In this northern climate no idea can be formed of the exquisite luxury of drinking in Egypt: little appetite for food is felt, but when, after crossing the burning sands, you reach the rich line of woods on the brink of the Nile, and pluck the fresh limes, and, mixing their juice with Egyptian sugar and the soft river-water, drink repeated bowls of lemonade, you feel that every other pleasure of the senses must yield to this. One then perceives the beauty and force of those similes in the Scriptures, where the sweetest emotions of the heart are compared to the assuaging of thirst in a sultry land.

Nile Water
Dr. R. R. Madden, 1825

In its wholesome properties, I believe the water of the Nile exceeds that of any other river in the world. Even when turbid, as at its rise, and depositing a sediment in a tumbler, in thickness an eighth of an inch at least, and alive with animal-culae, visible to the naked eye, even then it loses none of its salubrious qualities; but, on the contrary, by its gentle action as an aperient, it benefits health.

Into a Pyramid
Frederick Norden, 1737

The most agreeable way of seeing the Pyramids is with a party; they mutually excite each other's curiosity. All the prodigies related by those who have seen them there before are not to be too credulously swallowed. From Cairo the tour to them may be made in a day or two. Those who have a mind to spend two days, ride off on asses ... through the city, cross the canal, and afterwards traverse the isle of Rhodda; on the left of which ... they and their asses embark, and land at Gize, a village opposite to Cairo. There no stop is to be made for the curious, not until a league farther, where is the inn with some chambers to let. There a very disagreeable night is passed by the curious, without beds or other convenience, they are tormented by bugs, but one night is soon over, and when curiosity eggs, such difficulties are most easily born. Next morning ... the road to the Pyramids is entered on ... two Arabians are taken as guides ...

At the opening of the first Pyramid fire some pistols in order to dislodge the bats, then order the two Arabs to clear away the sand, that almost chokes up the farther entrance to it.

This done, the next precaution is to strip to your shirt, on account of the excessive heat within the Pyramid; in this trim you get through, each person a bougie* in his hand, for in this narrow avenue, it would be dangerous to use flambeaux† on account of the suffocating smoke ... At the end of it there is a passage made of force, whose opening is scarce one foot and a half high and two broad. And through this hole must curiosity pass, on Belly Couchant, while the two Arabs who have wriggled themselves through before, seize each leg, and drag their gentleman through this probation cleft, all covered with filth. Happily this narrow passage is not above two yards long, other wise such tugging would be unsupportable to all ... then a large space opens, where the traveller takes breath, and some refreshments ...

The progress continues with great difficulty until at last the traveller reaches a salon 'and their past difficulties are swallowed up in admiration.'

Here, by way of amusement, pistols are fired, which excite a noise equal to that of thunder. No further objects to be seen, they return the same way with the same difficulty.

The first care of the tourists when they come out of the Pyramid must be to dress instantly, cover themselves warmly, and drink a glass of generous wine, in order to prevent a pleurisy, which they are very liable to, on account of the sudden transition from a very hot to a more temperate air. This precaution observed ... they ascend the Pyramid to contemplate the landscape all around, which is delightful. Thereon without, as well as in the chambers within, are inscribed the names of many persons who have visited this Pyramid, and by so doing meant that their having travelled thither should be transmitted to posterity.

This first Pyramid well examined, go to the second which being shut is soon dispatched.

* Candle.
† Flaming torch.

Advice
Sir Gardner Wilkinson, 1847

In going into the pyramid, I need scarcely suggest the necessity of being provided with candles and a lantern, lucifers, and a supply of water; and a long stick to raise a light upon, in examining the upper part of the rooms, may be useful. I should also recommend a cloak, to put on in coming out, particularly in the evening, which is by no means a bad time for visiting the interior. It may be as well not to intrust it to the care of the Arabs, when not wanted within the Pyramid, as they are not particularly clean.

The Pyramids and the Sphinx
A. W. Kinglake, 1835

Familiar to one from the days of early childhood are the forms of the Egyptian Pyramids, and now, as I approached them from the banks of the Nile, I had no print, no picture before me, and yet the old shapes were there; there was no change; they were just as I had always known them. I straightened myself in my stirrups, and strived to persuade my understanding that this was real Egypt, and that those angles which stood up between me and the West were of harder stuff and more ancient than the paper pyramids of the green portfolio. Yet it was not till I came to the base of the great Pyramid that reality began to weigh upon my mind. Strange to say, the bigness of the distinct blocks of stones was the first sign by which I attained to feel the immensity of the whole pile. When I came, and trod, and touched with my hands, and climbed, in order that by climbing I might come to the top of one single stone, then, and almost suddenly, a cold sense and understanding of the Pyramid's enormity came down overcasting my brain.

Now try to endure this homely, sick-nursish illustration of the effect produced upon one's mind by the mere vastness of the great Pyramid. When I was very young (between the ages, I believe, of three and five years old), being then of delicate health, I was often in time of night the victim of a strange kind of mental oppression. I lay in bed perfectly conscious, and with open eyes, but without power to speak or to move, and all the while my brain was oppressed to distraction by the presence of a single and abstract idea – the idea of solid Immensity. It seemed to me in my agonies that the horror of this visitation arose from its coming upon me without form or shape – that the close presence of the direst monster ever bred in Hell would have been a thousand times more tolerable than that simple idea of solid size; my aching mind was fixed and riveted down upon the mere quality of vastness, vastness, vastness, and was not permitted to invest with it any particular object. If I could have done so, the torment would have ceased. When at last I was roused from this state of suffering, I could not of course in those days (knowing no verbal metaphysics, and no metaphysics at all, except by the dreadful experience of an abstract idea) – I could not of course find words to describe the nature of my sensations, and even now I cannot explain why it is that the forced contemplation of a mere quality, distinct from matter, should be so terrible. Well, now my eyes saw and knew, and my hands and my feet informed my understanding that there was nothing at all abstract about the great Pyramid – it was a big triangle, sufficiently concrete, easy to see, and rough to the touch. It could not, of course, affect me with the peculiar sensation I have been talking of, but yet there was something akin to that old nightmare agony in the terrible completeness with which a mere mass of masonry could fill and load my mind.

And Time too – the remoteness of its origin, no less than the enormity of its proportions – screens an Egyptian Pyramid from the easy and familiar contact of our modern minds; at its base the common Earth ends, and all above is a world – one not created of God, not seeming to be made by men's hands, but rather the sheer giant-work of some old dismal age weighing down this younger planet.

Fine sayings! but the truth seems to be, after all, that the Pyramids are quite of this world; that they were piled up into the air for the realization of some kingly crotchets about immortality – some priestly longing for burial fees; and that as for the building, they were built like coral rocks by swarms of insects – by swarms of poor Egyptians, who were not only the abject tools and slaves of power, but who also ate onions for the reward of their immortal labours! The Pyramids are quite of this world.

And near the Pyramids, more wondrous and more awful than all else in the land of Egypt, there sits the lonely Sphinx. Comely the creature is, but the comeliness is not of this world; the once worshipped beast is a deformity and a monster to this generation, and yet you can see that those lips, so thick and heavy, were fashioned according to some ancient mould of beauty, some mould of beauty now forgotten – forgotten because that Greece drew forth Cytherea from the flashing foam of the Ægean, and in her image created new forms of beauty, and made it a law among men that the short and proudly wreathed lip should stand for the sign and the main condition of loveliness through all generations to come. Yet still there lives on the race of those who were beautiful in the fashion of the elder world, and Christian girls of Coptic blood will look on you with the sad, serious gaze, and kiss your charitable hand with the big pouting lips of the very Sphinx.

The Sphinx
Dean Stanley, 1852

... if ... the Sphinx was the giant representative of Royalty, then it fittingly guards the greatest of Royal sepulchers; and, with its half human, half animal form, is the best welcome and the best farewell to the history and religion of Egypt.

Sphinx and Pyramids
Gustave Flaubert, 1849

We sit on the sand smoking our pipes and staring at it. Its eyes still seem full of life; the left side is stained white by bird-droppings (the tip of the Pyramid of Khephren has the same long white stains); it exactly faces the rising sun, its head is gray, ears very large and protruding like a negro's, its neck is eroded;

from the front it is seen in its entirety thanks to a great hollow dug in the sand; the fact that the nose is missing increases the flat, negroid effect. Besides, it was certainly Ethiopian; the lips are thick.

From the top of the Pyramid one of our guides pointed out the site of the battle, and said: '*Napouleoun, Sultan Kebir? Aicouat, mameluks,*' and using both hands he mimed the act of beheading.

At night, strong wind; struck by great gusts, the tent shudders and flaps like the sail of a ship.

*

A cold morning, spent photographing; I pose on tip of a pyramid – the one at the S.E. corner of the Great Pyramid.

In the afternoon we ride in the desert ... We pass between the first and second Pyramids and soon come to a valley of sand, seemingly scooped out by a single great gust of wind. Great expanses of stone that look like lava. We gallop for a while, blowing our horns to try them; silence. We have the impression that we are on a beach and are about to see the sea; our moustaches taste of salt, the wind is sharp and bracing, footprints of jackals and camels half obliterated by the wind. One keeps expecting to see something new from the top of each hill, and each time it's only the desert.

We ride back; the sun is setting. Beyond, the green Egypt; to the left, a slope that is entirely white, one would swear it was snow; the foreground is all purple – the small stones covering the ground glitter, literally bathed in purple light; it is as though one were looking at them through water so transparent as to be invisible; coated with this light as though with enamel, the gravel gleams with a metallic sheen. A jackal runs up and disappears to the right: at this hour of nightfall one hears them barking. Back to the tent, skirting the base of the Pyramid of Khephren, which seems to me inordinately huge and completely sheer; it's like a cliff, like a thing of nature, a mountain – as though it had been created just as it is, and with something terrible about it, as if it were going to crush you. It is at sunset that the Pyramids must be seen.

The Actuality of the Pyramids
Sir Julian Huxley, 1948

At first almost everybody equates the Pyramids with the mighty three of Giza: only later does he realize the existence of the other sixty-odd pyramidal constructions spread out along the seventy-mile stretch of the Nile's left bank across from Memphis, memorials of the Pyramid Age.

Familiarity (though at second-hand) had led me, not to despise the Pyramids, but to discount them. They had become international commonplaces, degraded to the level of the tourist souvenir. They had passed through so many million minds as one of the 'Wonders of the World' that their sharp edge of real wonder had been blunted. Like Niagara, and Rio de Janeiro, they had been thrust down my throat so often that I was sure I was not going to be impressed by them.

But in actuality, they make an overpowering impression. It is not one of beauty, but on the other hand not one of mere bigness, though size enters into it, and there is an element of aesthetic satisfaction in the elemental simplicity of their triangular silhouette. But this combined with an element of vicarious pride in the magnitude of the human achievement involved, and with a sense of their bold novelty and their historical uniqueness, to produce an effect different from that of any other work of man.

Jomard, who was among the men of learning on Napoleon's expedition to Egypt, has well described this effect. 'The general aspect of those monuments,' he writes, 'gives rise to a striking observation: seen from a distance they produce the same kind of effect as do high mountain peaks of pyramidal form, outlined against the sky. The nearer one approaches, the more this effect decreases. But when at last you are within a short distance of these regular masses, a wholly different impression is produced: you are struck by surprise, and as soon as you have reached the top of the slope, your ideas change in a flash. Finally, when you have reached the foot of the Great Pyramid, you are seized with a vivid and powerful emotion, tempered by a sort of stupefaction, almost overwhelming in its effects ... What you experience is in no wise the admiration provoked by a great work of art, but it is profound and impressive.'

Napoleon's mind reacted characteristically to the sight. He first demanded to know the measurement of the Great Pyramid: and then astonished his staff, on their return from climbing to the top, by pointing out that its cubic content would suffice to build a wall ten feet high and a foot thick entirely surrounding France. This is one way of bringing home its staggering bulk. Originally this solid mass of stone was over 480 feet high – 115 feet higher than the top of the cross on St Paul's; its base covered over 13 acres – an area, we are assured by the guide-books, sufficient to accommodate St Paul's, Westminster Abbey, St Peter's, and the Cathedrals of Florence and Milan all at once; and it contained over 2 million blocks of stone, averaging 2½ tons in weight. It is an artificial mountain, which would reach from the seashore almost to the summit of Beachy Head.

The interior is equally impressive. The ascending gallery leading to the King's Chamber, where Cheops's sarcophagus is still to be seen, is over 150 feet long. When you are in it, the sense of the thousands of tons of super-incumbent stone deliberately piled up above your head is more oppressive than the sense of overlying rock-masses in the galleries of a natural cave. On the walls of the upward-sloping limb of the passage there are projections, against which the royal sarcophagus was rested on its final journey; and in the central chamber is the enormous object itself. It is hard enough for the visitor to crawl up the narrow ramp: what it must have been like for the workmen struggling to move the huge box of stone upwards, is difficult to conceive.

Here in the gallery and chamber the fine workmanship of five thousand years ago makes its full impact. There is no mortar: the blocks of granite and limestone fit to a hair's breadth: and all this was done with only copper and stone tools. The masonry of the ancient Incas (so much superior to that of their Spanish conquerors) gave me the same impression.

Most of the gallery is surmounted by a remarkable corbel vault (the true arch was still unknown), comprising seven overlapping courses, with a final roof-span of over a metre.

To climb the Great Pyramid is to receive the same impression of size in yet a third fashion. It is a real piece of rock-scrambling, in the course of which most visitors are grateful for the help of the guides. When I was on the summit, the sun was getting low in the sky. Suddenly I realized that it was casting the shadow of the pyramid far out on to the fertile valley-floor in a huge inverted V. Only once in my life had I had a comparable experience, of a man-made structure intruding into the realm of physical geography. That was when I saw the Empire State Building, a structure nearly 5000 years later in date, losing itself in a layer of cloud well above the tops of the common ruck of skyscrapers.

The Great Pyramids
Harriet Martineau, 1848

We set out for Geezeh at half-past eight, on fine handsome asses, so spirited as to be almost as good to ride as horses. Today we once more came in sight of that curious sign of civilisation, – shaven donkeys. Dark rings were left round the legs, and the neck and hind-quarters were shaven. The scarlet housings and gay rider made a set-out very unlike what one sees of donkey-riding at home. I was not aware till I came to Egypt how dependent a donkey is on dress.*

Our first adventure was being carried on men's shoulders over a muddy pond which stopped the way. We knew that our plague today would be from the multitude of country people who would obtrude their services upon us. At this pond the teasing began. Our dragoman met it vigorously, by trying to throw a pertinacious fellow, bigger than himself, into the water. It was a desperate scuffle, such as would make ladies shriek and fly in England: but it came to nothing, as usual. All the rest of the way, men joined us from the fields on either hand, till, when we arrived at the sand, our train was swelled to forty.

I was surprised to find myself disappointed in the Pyramids now, when it had been precisely the reverse at a distance. Instead of their growing larger as we approached, they became less and less wonderful, till at last they exactly met one's preconception, except in being rougher, and of a brighter tint. The platform on which the largest stands is higher than our reading had given us to suppose; and the Second Pyramid, which at a distance looks as large as the other, here sinks surprisingly. This was to me the strongest evidence of the magnitude of the Great Pyramid. Though I have spoken of disappointment on a near approach, these mighty objects were perfectly absorbing, as a little incident presently proved. One of our party said, on our arrival, 'When we were passing the Sphinx –,' 'O! the Sphinx!' cried I. 'You don't mean that you have seen the Sphinx!' – To be sure they had: and they insisted on it that I had too; – that I must have seen it, – could not have missed it. I was utterly bewildered. It was strange enough to have forgotten it: but not to have seen it was inexplicable. However, on visiting it, later in the day, I found I had seen it. Being intent on the Pyramid before me, I had taken the Sphinx for a capriciously-formed rock, like so many that we had passed, – forgetting that I should not meet with limestone at Geezeh. I rather doubt whether any traveller would take the Sphinx for any thing but a rock unless he was looking for it, or had his eye caught by some casual light. – One other anecdote, otherwise too personal for print, will show how engrossing is the interest of the Pyramid on

---

* Still today the donkeys are decorated in this manner.

the spot. – The most precious articles of property I had with me abroad were two ear-trumpets, because, in case of accident happening to them, I could not supply the loss. I was unwilling to carry my trumpet up the Pyramid, – knocking against the stones while I wanted my hands for climbing. So I left it below, in the hands of a trusty Arab. When I joined my party at the top of the Pyramid, I never remembered my trumpet: nor did they: and we talked as usual, during the forty minutes we were there, without my ever missing it. – When I came down, I never thought of it: and I explored the inside, came out and lunched, and still never thought of my trumpet, till, at the end of three hours and a half from my parting with it, I saw it in the hands of the Arab, and was reminded of the astonishing fact that I had heard as well without it as with it, all that time. Such a thing never happened before, and probably never will again: and a stronger proof could not be offered of the engrossing interest of a visit to the Pyramid.

On looking up, it was not the magnitude of the Pyramid which made me think it scarcely possible to achieve the ascent; but the unrelieved succession, – almost infinite, – of bright yellow steps; a most fatiguing image! – Three strong and respectable-looking Arabs now took me in charge. One of them, seeing me pinning up my gown in front, that I might not stumble over it, gave me his services as a lady's-maid. He turned up my gown all round, and tied it in a most squeezing knot, which lasted all through the enterprise. We set out from the north-east corner. By far the most formidable part of the ascent was the first six or eight blocks. If it went on to the top thus broken and precipitous, the ascent would, I felt, be impossible. Already, it was disagreeable to look down, and I was much out of breath. One of my Arabs carried a substantial campstool, which had been given me in London with a view to this very adventure, – that it might divide the higher steps, – some of which, being four feet high, seem impracticable enough beforehand. But I found it better to trust to the strong and steady lifting of the Arabs in such places, and, above every thing, not to stop at all, if possible; or, if one must stop for breath, to stand with one's face to the Pyramid. I am sure the guides are right in taking people quickly. The height is not so great, in itself: it is the way in which it is reached that is trying to look back upon. It is trying to some heads to sit on a narrow ledge, and see a dazzling succession of such ledges for two or three hundred feet below; and there, a crowd of diminutive people looking up, to see whether one is coming bobbing down all that vast staircase. I stopped for a few seconds two or three times, at good broad corners or ledges. – When I left the angle, and found myself ascending the side, the chief difficulty was over; and I cannot say that the fatigue was at all formidable. The greater part of one's weight is lifted by the Arabs at each arm; and when one comes to a four feet step, or a broken ledge, there is a third Arab behind. When we arrived at a sort of recess, broken in the angle, my guides sported two of their English words, crying out 'Half-way!' with great glee. The last half was easier than the first; and I felt, what proved to be true, that both must be easier than the coming down.

I was agreeably surprised to find at the top, besides blocks standing up which gave us some shade, a roomy and even platform, where we might sit and write, and gaze abroad, and enjoy ourselves, without even seeing over the edge, unless we wished it. There was only the lightest possible breeze, just enough to fan our faces, without disturbing us ...

Long we gazed in every direction; – most pathetically perhaps to the South, where we had seen and left so much; or over into the Delta which we should enter no more, and which lay so rich and lovely between our eyes and the horizon, that it seemed to be melting away. We began letters to friends at home, drank some water, intrepidly carried up by a little Arab girl; mounted the highest block, to get as near the sky as we could; and then found that we really must be going down.

The descent was fatiguing; but not at all alarming. Between stepping, jumping, and sliding, with full reliance on the strength and care of the guides, the descent may be easily accomplished in ten minutes: – as far, that is, as the height of the entrance to the Pyramid, which is some way from the bottom. We had bargained before starting that we should not be asked for baksheesh 'while going up the Pyramid.' Our guides took this literally, and began begging, the moment we put our feet on the summit. And all the way down my guides never let me alone, though they knew I had no money about me. They were otherwise extremely kind, giving me the benefit of their other two words of English. On my jumping down a particularly high block, they patted me on the back, crying, with approving nods, 'Ah! ah! good morning; good morning!' I joined my party at the beautiful entrance to the Pyramid, where a large assemblage of Arabs was ranged on the rising stones opposite to us, like a hill-side congregation waiting for the preacher.

Innocents in Egypt
Mark Twain, 1870

[After a prolonged tour around Europe and the Middle East, Samuel Clemens and his party reached Egypt.]

The donkeys were all good, all handsome, all strong and in good condition, all fast and all willing to prove it. They were the best we had found anywhere, and the most *recherché*. I do not know what *recherché* is, but that is what these donkeys were, anyhow. Some were of a soft mouse-colour, and the others were white, black, and vari-coloured. Some were close shaven all over, except that a tuft like a paint-brush was left on the end of the tail. Others were so shaven in fanciful landscape garden patterns, as to mark their bodies with curving lines, which were bounded on one side by hair and on the other by the close plush left by the shears. They had all been newly barbered, and were exceedingly stylish. Several of the white ones were barred like zebras with rainbow stripes of blue and red and yellow paint. These were indescribably gorgeous. Dan and Jack selected from this lot because they brought back Italian reminiscences of the 'old masters'. The saddles were the high, stuffy, frog-shaped things we had known in Ephesus and Smyrna. The donkey-boys were lively young Egyptian rascals who could follow a donkey and keep him in a canter half a day without tiring. We had plenty of spectators when we mounted, for the hotel was full of English people bound overland to India, and officers getting ready for the African campaign against the Abyssinian King Theodorus. We were not a very large party, but as we charged through the streets of the great metropolis, we made noise for five hundred, and displayed activity and created excitement in proportion. Nobody can steer a donkey, and some collided with camels, dervishes, effendis, asses, beggars, and everything else that offered to the donkeys a reasonable chance for a collision. When we turned into the broad avenue that leads out of the city towards Old Cairo, there was plenty of room. The walls of stately date-palms that fenced the gardens and bordered the way threw their shadows down and made the air cool and bracing. We rose to the spirit of the time and the race became a wild rout, a stampede, a terrific panic. I wish to live to enjoy it again.

*

Arrived at Old Cairo, the camp-followers took up the donkeys and tumbled them bodily aboard a small boat with a lateen sail, and we followed and got under way. The deck was closely packed with donkeys and men; the two sailors had to climb over and under and through the wedged mass to work the sails, and the steersman had to crowd four or five donkeys out of the way when he wished to swing his tiller and put his helm hard-down. But what were their troubles to us? We had nothing to do; nothing to do but enjoy the trip; nothing to do but shove the donkeys off our corns and look at the charming scenery of the Nile.

*

The Nile at this point is muddy, swift, and turbid, and does not lack a great deal of being as wide as the Mississippi.

We scrambled up the steep bank at the shabby town of Ghizeh, mounted the donkeys again, and scampered away. For four or five miles the route lay along a high embankment which they say is to be the bed of a railway the Sultan means to build for no other reason than that when the Empress of the French comes to visit him she can go to the Pyramids in comfort. This is true Oriental hospitality. I am very glad it is our privilege to have donkeys instead of cars.

At the distance of a few miles the Pyramids rising above the palms looked very clean-cut, very grand and imposing, and very soft and filmy as well. They swam in a rich haze that took from them all suggestions of unfeeling stone, and made them seem only the airy nothings of a dream – structures which might blossom into tiers of vague arches, or ornate colonnades, maybe, and change and change again, into all graceful forms of architecture, while we looked, and then melt deliciously away and blend with the tremulous atmosphere.

At the end of the levée we left the mules and went in a sail-boat across an arm of the Nile or an overflow, and landed where the sands of the Great Sahara left their embankment, as straight as a wall, along the verge of the alluvial plain of the river. A laborious walk in the flaming sun brought us to the foot of the great Pyramid of Cheops. It was a fairy vision no longer. It was a corrugated, unsightly mountain of stone. Each of its monstrous sides was a wide stairway which rose upwards, step above step, narrowing as it went, till it tapered to a point far aloft in the air. Insect men and women – pilgrims from the *Quaker City* – were creeping about its dizzy perches, and one little black swarm were waving postage stamps from the air summit – handkerchiefs will be understood.

[Here their party were besieged by the usual 'rabble of muscular Egyptians' who pushed and pulled them up the Pyramid.]

Twice for one minute they let me rest while they extorted bucksheesh, and then continued their maniac flight up the Pyramid. They wished to beat the other parties. It was nothing to them that I, a stranger, must be sacrificed upon the altar of their unholy ambition. But in the midst of sorrow joy blooms. Even in this dark hour I had a sweet consolation. For I knew that except these Mohammedans repented they would go straight to perdition some day. And *they* never repent – they never forsake their paganism. This thought calmed me, cheered me, and I sank down, limp and exhausted, upon the summit, but happy, so happy and serene within.

On the one hand, a mighty sea of yellow sand stretched away toward the end of the earth, solemn, silent, shorn of vegetation, its solitude uncheered by any forms of creature life; on the other, the Eden of Egypt was spread below us – a broad green floor, cloven by the sinuous river, dotted with villages, its vast distances measured and marked by the diminishing stature of receding clusters of palms. It lay asleep in an enchanted atmosphere. There was no sound, no motion. Above the date-plumes in the middle distance, swelled a domed and pinnacled mass, glimmering through a tinted, exquisite mist; away toward the horizon a dozen shapely pyramids watched over ruined Memphis: and at our feet the bland, impassible Sphinx looked out upon the picture from her throne in the sands as placidly and pensively as she had looked upon its life full fifty lagging centuries ago.

We descended, hot and out of humour. The dragoman lit candles, and we all entered a hole hear the base of the pyramid, attended by a crazy rabble of Arabs, who thrust their services upon us uninvited. They dragged us up a long inclined chute, and dripped candle-grease all over us. This chute was not more than twice as wide and high as a Saratoga trunk, and was walled, roofed, and floored with solid blocks of Egyptian granite as wide as a wardrobe, twice as thick, and three times as long. We kept on climbing through the oppressive gloom till I thought we ought to be nearing the top of the pyramid again, and then came to the 'Queen's Chamber', and shortly to the Chamber of the King. These large apartments were tombs. The walls were built of monstrous masses of smooth granite, neatly joined together. Some of them were nearly as large square as an ordinary parlour. A great stone sarcophagus like a bath-tub stood in the centre of the King's Chamber. Around it were gathered a picturesque group of Arab savages and soiled and tattered pilgrims, who held their candles aloft in the gloom while they chattered, and the winking blurs of light shed a dim glory down upon one of the irrepressible memento-seekers who was pecking at the venerable sarcophagus with his sacrilegious hammer.

We struggled out to the open air and the bright sunshine, and for the space of thirty minutes received ragged Arabs by couples, dozens, and platoons, and paid bucksheesh for services they swore and proved by each other that they had rendered, but which we had not been aware of before – and as each party was paid, they dropped into the rear of the procession.

On the Edge of Disaster
Rider Haggard, 1887

A fellow named Brownrigg and I and a lady were contemplating the second Pyramid when suddenly he announced that he was going to climb up it as far as the granite cap which still remains for something over a hundred feet at the top.

As he was a splendid athlete, with a very good head, this did not surprise us. Up he went while we sat and watched him, till he came to the cap, which at that time only eight or nine white people had ever ascended, of course with the help of guides. To our astonishment here we suddenly saw him take off his boots. The next thing we saw was Brownrigg climbing up the polished granite of the cap. Up he went from crack to crack till at last he reached the top in safety, and there proceeded to execute a war dance of triumph. Then after a rest he began to descend. I noticed from the desert, some hundreds of feet below, that although he commenced his descent with his face outwards, which is the right method, presently he turned so that it was against the sloping pyramid. Then I began to grow frightened. When he had done about thirty or forty feet of the descent I saw him stretch down his stockinged foot seeking some cranny, and draw it up again – because he could not reach the cranny without falling backwards. Twice or thrice he did this, and then remained quite still upon the cap with outstretched arms like one crucified. Evidently he could move neither up nor down.

While I stared, horrified – we three were quite alone in the place – a white-robed Arab rushed past me. He was the Sheik of the Pyramids, which without a word he began to climb with the furious activity of a frightened cat. Up he went over the lower and easy part onto the cap, which seemed to present no difficulties to him, for he knew exactly where to set his toes and had the head of an eagle or a mountain goat. Now he was just underneath Brownrigg and saying something to him. And now from that great height came a still small voice.

'If you touch me I'll knock you down!' said the voice.

Yes, crucified there upon this awful cap he declared in true British fashion that he would knock his saviour down.

I shut my eyes, and when I looked again the Sheik had got Brownrigg's foot down into the crack below, how I never discovered. Well, the rest of the sickening descent was accomplished in safety, thanks to that splendid Sheik. In a few more minutes a very pale and shaking Brownrigg was gasping on the sand beside us, while the Arab, streaming with perspiration, danced round and objurgated him and us in his native tongue until he was appeased with large baksheesh. Brownrigg, who will never be nearer to a dreadful death than he was that day, told me afterwards that, strong as his head was, he found it impossible to attempt the descent face outwards, since the thickness of the cap hid the sides of the Pyramid from his sight, so that all he saw beneath him was some three hundred feet of empty space. Therefore he turned and soon found himself quite helpless, since he could neither find any foothold beneath him, nor could he reascend. Had not the watchful Arab seen him and his case, in another few minutes he must have fallen and been dashed to pieces at our feet. The memory of that scene still makes my back feel cold and my flesh creep. I have tried to reproduce it in 'Ayesha' where Holly falls from the rock to the ice-covered river far beneath.

Lotus and Pyramid
Constance Sitwell, 1927

I am sitting on the window-sill in my room eating sugar-cane. It is so juicy and fresh one could go on nibbling at it all day. The Soudanese servant, in a green cap and full green trousers, just now brought in a basket-full cut up into pieces, and set it down on the floor with a wide smile. My window is high above the ground; beneath, the whitewashed walls of the hotel ache in the midday glare; across the sand I can see the two great Pyramids, all their colour bleached out by the fierce light. But early this morning they looked very different. Just as the sun rose I came to this window and saw them standing there drowsily splendid, a tigerish gold set on the tigerish sand.

When first I drew near the Great Pyramid it was with a feeling of real shrinking. My mind was bludgeoned and I lifted bewildered eyes; it was almost painful to realize that this was the work of men's slight hands. One wanders along the base, wondering insanely at the vast blocks so perfectly placed along the bottom courses, one stops at the corners to gaze insanely at the fabulous line that goes slanting up and up into the sapphire blue.

The sun beat down on that stupendous slope of stone, and up on it a scattering of tiny men were crawling like sluggish flies; and presently I too started to climb up; we were making for the small opening that leads downwards to the King's Chamber. We reached it at last and the Bedouin in fluttering garments who was our guide slid down the polished shaft, at the bottom of which he lit some magnesium wire which showed a narrow gleaming passage going steeply down into the core. The unnatural light played pallidly upon the smooth dark stone as we followed after him. How hot it was in the thick darkness! As we plunged deeper into that stifling fastness of stone an awful oppression seized me, and at last when we came to the solemn bat-infested chamber which contains the royal sarcophagus the sense of the weight pressing downwards became almost more than I could bear. There was something terrible in the thought of the monstrous walls that surround the little empty tomb of sombre reddish granite.

That was my first impression, but later the pyramids grew very familiar. In the evening of the day before we started up the Nile I found my way to a little pyramid, half ruined, near by, and I climbed on to a rock at its base to sit and draw there. A tiny Arab boy came along behind. He was dressed in black with an old black cloak and had a round dirty-white cap on his head. His face was round too, and his broad smile always ready. When I sat on the sand he jerked off his ragged cloak in an instant and spread it on the ground, and while I sketched he sat holding my paint-box in one hand and a paint-brush in the other.

He had some friends who joined us; a boy from Tunis with pale golden-brown skin, and a diminutive donkey-boy dressed in a stained garment of yellow who dragged the dusty donkey behind him without even one necklet of beads to adorn it. He was seven years old, he said; his donkey looked a hundred. His small wrinkled face was as yellow as his dress, and his name, he told me with some importance as he lit a cigarette, was Abbas. I thought I should never forget that preternaturally old little creature who never smiled but puffed brazenly at his cigarette.

The boy from Tunis said that he could divine the future. He stared at me and then drew the sun's disk with rays spreading all round it in the powdery sand. Stooping lower and lower over the circle of his sun with an absorbed face he kept counting these rays, and muttering words that the others tried to translate. Having reached his conclusion he straightened himself and pronounced, 'Not happy, if too much thinking.' I thanked him but replied that I did not agree. For a moment, after taking my coin, he looked at me in silence, then kicking away the traces of his sun with his hard feet, he walked off apparently heading for the empty desert.

5

Preparing to go Aboard

Introduction

The truth is, however, that the mere sight-seeing of the Nile demands some little reading and organising, if only to be enjoyed. We cannot all be profoundly learned; but we can at least do our best to understand what we see – to get rid of obstacles – to put the right thing in the right place. For the land of Egypt is, as I have said, a Great Book – not very easy reading, perhaps, under any circumstances; but at all events quite difficult enough already without the added puzzlement of being read backwards.

Amelia Edwards, 1873

Our travellers had come to Egypt to ascend the Nile and during part of their time visiting the 'lions' of Cairo they busied themselves with preparations for the journey. This meant hiring and fitting out a boat and taking on a dragoman to tend to all their needs, a *reis* to pilot and captain the boat, a crew and a cook.

Flaubert, as usual, made light of the journey in a letter to his mother. The American, Charles G. Leland, gives us more of the sense of chaos which must have accompanied these transactions. The travellers from 1847 onwards could be guided by Sir Gardner Wilkinson's exhaustive list of needs, which ranged from almond-paste to *zeers*. Harriet Martineau, ever practical, provided further useful hints – on the uses of gimlets and mackintosh sheeting, for instance. Her advice on how to look after your lady's maid was also important, for many ladies, were so accompanied. Few people mentioned the indispositions which many speak of today in Egypt, but Charles Thompson gave a warning in 1767 and Charles G. Leland had advice for the less temperate traveller.

The 'real' travellers were contemptuous of those who went by steamer and even more contemptuous of those who went on 'a Cook boat', which Charles Edwin Wilbour was strongly advised to avoid.

In Howard Hopley, who travelled in 1868 with two companions, one American and the other English, I discovered a new 'Three Men in a Boat'. He describes the taking on of that all-important person, the dragoman. In early days of Nile travel a firman or letter of introduction helped one along the way; Richard Pococke translated his in 1737. Later a contract had to be signed with one's dragoman; William C. Prime published his in 1855.

Amelia Edwards wrote a classic description of the *dahabeeyah* – the sailing boat on which most travellers ascended the river. Once aboard one's boat there were often further problems to face. In 1845, W. H. Bartlett compared his boat to an ark, but an ark with its own animal life. Sophia Poole, sister of the great chronicler of modern Egyptians, Edward Lane, and the American Stephen Olin commended the Arabs for their acknowledgement of God as they set off along the way. Howard Hopley named his boat the *Lilla* and took on her flag, a motley crew and supplies – then the three men set off up the river.

By 1886, when Samuel Manning was on the Nile, it had already been possible to go by steamer or rail for several years, but he still preferred to sail. Only a few years later 'Cook Pasha', son of Thomas, was issuing instructions for the conduct of Nile steamers – instructions which are to a great extent still followed today. He was also following every detail of their implementation. In 1898 G. W. Steevens used his journalist's wit to praise Cook Pasha and all he had done to open up the Nile to travellers.

So now, all preparations are made and the travellers are ready to set off on the journey, which, as Bayard Taylor wrote home to his mother in Pennsylvania in 1851, might be 'long and toilsome' but was sure to be most interesting.

Plans
Gustave Flaubert, 1849

Cairo, 2 December

Towards the first of January we shall board a *cange** and go up the Nile for six weeks, then drift down and return here. The entire journey to Upper Egypt is extremely easy and without the slightest danger of any kind, especially at this season when the heat is far from excessive. Therefore from now on you can change your opinion concerning the Egyptian climate. Mists come up after dark as they do anywhere else. The nights are cold (although the servants, or rather the slaves, sleep in the street, on the ground, outside the house doors), and there are clouds. To listen to some people in France, Egypt is a veritable oven: so it is, but it sometimes cools off. If you would like, darling, to have an inventory of what I wear these days (following the unanimous advice of sensible people here), this is how I dress: flannel body-belt, flannel shirt, flannel drawers, thick trousers, warm vest, thick neck-cloth, with an overcoat besides morning and evening; my head is shaved, and under my red tarboosh I wear two white skull-caps . . .

Preparations
Charles G. Leland, 1873

Well, if you have any very natural anxieties, remember this, that you will probably not go up the Nile until you have been a week at Shepheard's, or the New Hotel, or the Orient, or Nil. And if during that week you do not learn all there is afloat or a-going regarding dahabéahs, dragomans, donkeys, dirt, Denderah, damages, dancing-girls, dervishes, dampness, dollars, and deductions, may I be – dashed! The first of these *d*'s should have been dress. 'What clothes should

---

* A *cange* is a Nile boat with crossed sail.

I take to Egypt?' The answer to this is stereotyped – most people have it photographed before they leave. Plenty of good warm clothing for the cool nights, abundance of thin clothing for the warm days, and as little as possible of either, including one dress for probable dinners, opera, and festas. The truth is, that humble, plain men like you and me will do very well with one light Oxford grey *parreil partout*, or 'ditto' suit, one good stout London winter suit, and the steel-pen coat, as Tom Hood, junior, calls it, with its 'accomplices.' Should you become a Mohometan, you will of course order a turban, which should be white and made very full around the ears; but as one renegade is said to be worse than ten Turks, you had better get at least a dozen. I was told that what is called a *Circassian* or *Circassienne* would be indispensable, but on making inquiry, they informed me that a fair average article of this kind would cost at least eighty pounds, and so did not invest. I am inclined to think there must have been some misunderstanding in the matter. Perhaps I did not pronounce it correctly. Although the weather is often hot during the day in winter in Cairo, and very hot on the Nile – we had it from 95 to 100 in the shade at the First Cataract – it is still a dry heat, and not nearly so distressing as that of the hot summer days in England. At all events, make sure of some thick underclothing, and plenty of shirts – the more the better. As for money, letters of credit cost two per cent, and there is an uncomfortable discount even on Bank of England notes. Bring all the sovereigns you can come honestly by – they are always at par – but do not make a display of handfuls of them. Silver francs are good for shopping.

Things Useful for a Journey in Egypt
Sir Gardner Wilkinson, 1847

Certain things are more or less necessary in Egypt, according to the wants of each individual. I shall therefore give a list of those most useful to a traveller, marking such as should be taken from Europe with an E, those which may be obtained at Alexandria with an A, and those which need not be bought before reaching (or which are better at) Cairo, with a C. Now that the railway has been opened from Alexandria to Cairo, few or none of them will be required on that part of the journey; and while he stays at the hotel in Cairo, the traveller will have ample time for making his purchases there.

Jug and basin, C.	Towels and table-cloths, E. or C.
Carpets (Segádee), C.	Sheets, horse-hair mattrass, pillows,
Common soap, C.	and pillow-cases, &c., E., or
Lamp, or cloth fanóos, C.	cotton mattrass, *diwans*, cushions,
	sheets, &c., C.

To those who wish to be entirely protected at night from intruders, I cannot do better than recommend a contrivance of Mr. Levinge's, which he devised during his travels in the East, and which is equally adapted to a boat, a house, or a tent. It consists of a pair of sheets (*a*) about six feet long, sewed together at the bottom and the two sides, except where the piece (*c*) is attached to them, and by which you get in. To the upper end (*d*) is added a thin piece of muslin, serving as a mosquito-net (*b*), which is drawn tight at the end by a tape or string, serving to suspend it to a nail (*f*). A short way from the end (at *e*) are fastened loops, through which a cane is threaded, to form a circle for distending the net. This cane is in three pieces, about three feet long, fitting into each other by sockets. After getting in by the opening of *c* you draw the tape tight to close its mouth, and tuck it in under the mattrass, and you are secure from intruders, whether sleeping at night, or sitting under it by day. Over the part *a*, the blankets, or coverlid, are put.

Two or three blankets, E., or *buttanéeh* at C., which will fold into four.

Mosquito net, C.

Iron bedstead to fold up, E.

Giridiron, C. (if thought necessary.)

Potatoes, C.

Tobacco, C.

Pipes, C.

Wire for cleaning pipes, put into a reed, C.

Some tow for the same purpose, C.

Mouth-piece and pipe-bowls, C.

Portable soup and meats, E.

Cheese, C., or English cheese, E.

Mishmish apricots, C.

Kumredeen apricots, C.

Tea, E. (at Malta)

Wine, brandy, &c., E. or C. White wine I believe to be better in a hot climate than red.

Table with legs to fold up, and top to take off, E., or C.

Foot-tub (of tin or copper), &c., C.

Washing-tub, C.

Flag, E. or A. (for boat on Nile)

Small pulley and rope for flag, E. or C.

Small *búkray* or Turkish coffee-pot, C.

Tea-kettle, C.

Plates, knives and forks, spoons, glasses, tea-things, &c., in canteen, E. or C.

A large *búkray* might serve as tea-kettle and for boiling eggs, &c., C.

Copper saucepans, one to fit into the other (*Hellel fe Kulbe-bäd*), C.

Copper pan for stewing (*Táwa*), C.

Baskets for holding these and other things, C.

Candlesticks, C.

Bardaks (*Goollel*) or water-bottles, C.

Zeer, or jar, for holding water, C.

A fine sieve, C.

Almond-paste (*rooág* or *terwéeg*) for clarifying water, C.

Some tools, nails, and string, C.

A *Kadoom* may serve as hammer and hatchet, C.

Charcoal in mats, C.

Fireplaces (*mungud*), C. In the boat going up the Nile have a set put together in a large fireplace with a wooden back, C.

Small bellows or fan, C.

Fez caps (*tarboosh, tarabeesh*), A. or C.

Cafass, or kafass, a coop for fowls, with moveable drawer at the bottom, in order that it may be kept clean, C.

White or light-coloured boots or shoes, being cooler, and requiring no blacking, E. or C.

Biscuit, or bread twice baked, C. The bread in the villages in Upper Egypt will not please everyone: but very good bread is to be had at Thebes (*Koorneh*), and that of Sioot and some other large towns is by no means bad.

Baliási, or earthen jars for flour, rice, butter, and other things which rats might eat, are useful, C.

Candles in boxes, or in tin cases, but if in the latter not to be exposed to the sun, C. In going to the Tombs, or caves, in Upper Egypt, it is well to remember always to have candles, and the means of lighting them.

Broom called *makâsheh*, and a tin, for sweeping cabin, C.

Gun, pistols, E.

Powder and shot, &c., C.

Ink, paper, pens, &c., C.

Camp-stool and drawing table, E. or C.

Umbrella lined with a dark colour for the sun, E. or C.

Drawing paper, pencils, rubber, &c., and colours, in tin box of Windsor and Newton, E.

Side-saddle, E. It will fit a donkey also.

A light Cairene donkey-saddle, but no bridge, the asses of Upper Egypt not being accustomed to such a *luxury*, C.

Curtains for boat, of common or other cotton stuff, C.

A packing needle or two, and some string, thin ropes, needles, thread, buttons, &c., are useful, C.

A filterer is not necessary. Keneh jars and *goollel*, or earthen water-bottles, supply its place. Another precaution, when on an excursion, for *preserving* the water, is to insist on the servants not drinking it.

An iron rat-trap for the boat, C.

A small boat should also be taken from Cairo, if there be not one belonging to the *dahabéëh*; or rather, it should be part of the agreement that the *dahabàëh* should be furnished with one. It is useful for landing, for shooting, and for sending a servant ashore to make purchases on the way in Upper Egypt.

Telescope, E.

Thermometer, aneroïd barometer, if required, E.

Measuring-tape and foot-ruler, E.

For observations, a sextant and artificial horizon.

Hints to Ladies
Harriet Martineau, 1848

As to the very disagreeable subject of the vermin which abound peculiarly in Egypt, – lice, – it is right to say a few words. After every effort to the contrary, I am compelled to believe that they are not always, – nor usually, – caught from the people about one: but that they appear of their own accord in one's clothes, if worn an hour too long. I do not recommend a discontinuance of flannel clothing in Egypt. I think it quite as much wanted there as anywhere else. But it must be carefully watched. The best way is to keep two articles in wear, for alternate days; – one on, and the other hanging up at the cabin window, – if there is an inner cabin. The crew wash for the traveller; and he should be particular about having it done according to his own notions, and not theirs, about how often it should be. This extreme care about cleanliness is the only possible precaution, I believe: and it does not always avail; but it keeps down the evil to an endurable point. As far as our experience went, it was only within the limits of Egypt that the annoyance occurred at all. Fleas and bugs are met with: but not worse than at bad French and Italian inns.

The traveller should carry half a dozen gimlets, stuck into a cork, and daily at hand. They serve as a bolt to doors which have no fastening, as pins to anything he wants to fasten or keep open, as pegs to hang clothes, or watch, or thermometer upon; as a convenience in more ways than could be supposed beforehand. – Two or three squares of Mackintosh cloth are a great comfort,

– for keeping bedding dry, – for ablution, and for holding one's clothes in bathing. By substituting them for carpets, also, in Nile boats, there is a relief from danger or vermin.

As for dress, – the first consideration, both for gentlemen and ladies, is to have every possible article, made of material that can be washed: – gloves, among the rest. Cotton or thread gloves are of no use, unless of the stoutest kind. The hands are almost as much burned with these as with none. Woodstock gloves (which bear washing well) are good, though, of course, they do not look very handsome. – Brown holland is the best material for ladies' dresses; and nothing looks better, if set off with a little trimming of ribbon, which can be put on and taken off in a few minutes. – Round straw hats, with a broad brim, such as may be had at Cairo for 4*s*. or 5*s*. are the best head-covering. A double-ribbon, which bears turning when faded, will last a long time, and looks better than a more flimsy kind. – There can hardly be too large a stock of thick-soled shoes and boots. The rocks of the Desert cut up presently all but the stoutest shoes: and there are no more to be had. – Caps and frills, or lace or muslin are not to be thought of, as they cannot be 'got up', unless by the wearer's own hands. Habit-shirts of Irish linen or thick muslin will do: and, instead of caps, the tarboosh, when within the cabin or tent, is the most convenient, and certainly the most becoming head-gear: and the little cotton cap worn under it is washed without trouble. – Fans and goggles, – goggles of black woven wire, – are indispensable.

No lady who values her peace on the journey, or desires any freedom of mind or movement, will take a maid. What can a poor English girl do who must dispense with home-comforts, and endure hardships that she never dreamed of, without the intellectual enjoyments which to her mistress compensate (if they do compensate) for the inconveniences of Eastern travel? If her mistress has any foresight, or any compassion, she will leave her at home. If not, she must make up her mind to ill-humour or tears, to the spectacle of wrath or despondency, all the way. – If she will have her maid, let her, at all events, have the girl taught to ride, – and to ride well: or she may have much to answer for. To begin to ride at her years is bad enough, even at home, where there may be a choice of horses, and the rides are only moderate in length. What is a poor creature to do who is put upon a chance horse, ass, or camel, day by day, for rides of eight hours' long, for weeks together? The fatigue and distress so caused are terrible to witness, as I can testify, – though we were happily warned in time, and went unincumbered by English servants altogether.

Not a Cook Boat
Charles Edwin Wilbour, 1886

The first of Cook's new Steamers starts tomorrow for Assuan. It is really fine and looks comfortable. I asked Mrs Goadison, Ruskin's nextdoor neighbour near Lake Windermere, why she did not go in it or on one of Cook's dahabeeyehs. She said 'I could never face Mr Ruskin again if I were to go in a Cook boat.'

Indispositions
Charles Thompson, 1767

Foreigners in particular are very subject to a Pain in the Stomach, which proceeds from their going open-breasted, thereby chilling their Bowels, and sometimes brings on dangerous Fevers and Fluxes, especially in Autumn, when the River overflows the Country.

Many Persons in *May* break out into a Rash, which continues during the Heats, and is thought to proceed chiefly from drinking the Waters of the *Nile* after it begins to rise. This is so common, that it has become fashionable for the Patient to carry about with him a sort of wooden File, and to rub himself with it as he finds Occasion.

Advice
Charles G. Leland, 1873

It is not well to drink much wine, beer, or spirits in Egypt, but coffee may be far more freely indulged in than in Europe or in America. As regards smoking, most men come down to cigarettes or mild tobacco in native pipes. It is not a country for strong cigars or strong emotions. Avoid sedulously all causes of irritation or excitement – other and abler writers have preceded me in urging this on strangers in Egypt. Cultivate calmness, equanimity, and cheerfulness – few people are aware of the degree to which they *may* be cultivated here. Live for peace – it was the main temporal object of Christianity, which was founded and perfected between Egypt and Palestine, its neighbour.

Three Men for a Boat
Howard Hopley, 1868

Three people were lying at ease one bright sunny morning under the chequered shadow of a lotus tree, in the pleasant gardens of the Uzbekeeyah. They had strolled out after breakfast, to hold council as to the future. A boat was to be hired, sailors and servants taken into pay, and other preparations made for a twelve weeks' river journey. The members of this council of three so convened had each a different end in view when, in a northern city, they agreed to travel in company to the cataracts of the Nile. But slightly acquainted, they nevertheless hoped by mutual forbearance and courtesy, not only to avoid quarrels, but to arrive at an opulence of friendship ere their little commonwealth should terminate. It must be observed that a Nile voyage is no ordinary journey. There is no facility, should your companion turn fractious or sulky, or prove otherwise disagreeable, of removing to a separate hotel, or shutting yourself from his company. Neither, in the event of your taking the sulks yourself, have you a convenient chamber where in to retire, in that amiable intent. During three months, for better or for worse, for richer or for poorer, in sickness or in health, you are bound – the length of the chain being the circuit of your boat.

But to out council under the lotus-tree. It was made up first of a middle-aged Englishman, spare of build, and tall – a deliberate, mild-spoken man, wearing spectacles, and looking at you from over them: a professor. He was bent in this journey on catching rare birds, and stuffing them, on collecting insects, reptiles, and eggs, on the study of hieroglyphics in general, and particularly on cramming-up in the Theban dynasties. Then there was a stout and enterprising American, bent on getting thin by exercise, and on otherwise accomplishing his own pleasure; and lastly, the reader's humble servant, in search of health and relaxation of mind.

'Choose a dragoman at once, and let *him* hire a boat for us. That is my advice,' said the professor, a little testily. *We* had inclined to the opposite order of proceeding; namely, the boat first, and the dragoman after. We reasoned that, as the latter gentlemen notoriously form profitable alliances with boat-owners, it would be prudent to strike a bargain with each separately. The professor, however, demurred to this, and carried the day.

'You could not,' he argued, 'outmanoeuvre a dragoman; he would inevitably circumvent you in the attempt, and make it worse for you in the end. Better at once make a semblance of giving in.'

Our choice of these gentlemen this fell between three, equally recommended, who were hereupon summoned to appear – a Maltese, a Greek, and an Egyptian. We chose the latter. Why, I can hardly tell; perhaps it was from the gorgeousness of his attire. He stood before us, sounding his own trumpet so dexterously, and looking withal so truthful and honest, that there was no resisting him. We were quite bashful as to being seated in so imposing a presence.

*

Let us look at the man as he stood there.

A handsome, bronze-skinned fellow of five-and-twenty, lithe and lusty, with a finely chiselled face – a face much akin in its present mode of placidness and repose to that of the sculptured Rameses at Thebes, whose descendant you might almost figure him to have been. A broad forehead, slightly curved nose, full pulpy lips, and large dark, lustrous eyes, of whose depths, as of wayside wells, you can never make quite sure. He wore a gorgeous turban, perfect in its twists, with multitudinous silk tassels tangling about the neck. Trowsers of purple, falling halfway down the legs, exceedingly ample, and girt in at the waist by a sumptuous Damascus scarf of many colours, a gold embroidered vest, and a braided jacket of green, completed his attire.

Such in outward appearance was Haroun, whom we engaged. We took him in spite of the uncertainty in his eyes, and found him – as dragomans go – a good servant; or perhaps it were better to say a considerate master. Haroun was a man who knew full well that we infidel islanders were delivered into his hands as a prey, to be squeezed as a sponge – only not too dry. He did not in the least shrink from this arrangement, but chose to do it in a gentlemanly way, by which means the squeezing was not over-keenly felt. In after-times he argued on it very touchingly.

The Contract
The Americans and Mohammed Abd-el-Atti, 1855

We, the undersigned, J. Hammond Trumbull, and W. C. Prime, with Mrs Trumbull and Mrs Prime, have this day agreed with Mohammed Abd-el-Atti for a trip up the Nile, on the following conditions:

1. Mohammed Abd-el-Atti engages to provide a comfortable boat, with awning and jolly boat; to furnish said boat with beds, bedding, tables, china, glass, water filters, and all and every requisite necessary for the convenience and comfort of first-class passengers.
2. Mohammed Abd-el-Atti agrees to provide all stores, provisions, candles, lights, etc., as shall be necessary for the entire voyage. Also to provide as many courses for breakfast, dinner, etc., as shall be required by the above parties.
3. Mohammed Abd-el-Atti agrees to provide and pay for one cook, one servant, and one assistant, to wash clothes, etc., during the entire voyage.
4. Under the above conditions Mohammed Abd-el-Atti agrees to take Messrs Prime and Trumbull, and party, to Es Souan, and back again to Cairo, for the sum of two hundred and twenty-five pounds in gold, giving them fifteen days' stoppage on the voyage, at any place or places they may wish to stop or remain at, and providing donkeys and guides for visiting any such places.
5. For the first fifteen days of stoppage, exceeding the above period, that they may wish to remain below the first cataract, they will pay to Mohammed Abd-el-Atti the sum of three pounds fifteen shillings per diem.
6. For any period they may wish to remain below the first cataract, after the expiration of the above provided period, they shall pay Mohammed Abd-el-Atti the sum of three pounds per day for each day.
7. Should the above parties, after their arrival at the first cataract, wish to proceed to the second cataract, Mohammed Abd-el-Atti agrees to take them on in the same boat, and same style, and they shall then pay him the sum of sixty-seven pounds ten shillings for the trip between the two cataracts and back, and they shall have three days stoppage, for visiting such places as they may desire. And if they shall desire to stop more than three days above the first cataract, then, for every day of stoppage above three, they shall pay him at the rate of three pounds per day.
8. It is, moreover, fully understood that Mohammed Abd-el-Atti is to pay all presents on the voyage; to pay all donkey hire, guides, guards, etc.; to pay the expenses of taking the boat up and down the cataracts, and all and every present to crew, sailors, reis, pilot, or persons on shore, during, and at the end of the voyage.
9. It is understood that, if the party should go to the second cataract, then the provision for days of stoppage over fifteen days below the first cataract is altered, and they shall pay Mohammed Abd-el-Atti, in that case, only three pounds per day over the first fifteen days provided for, for every day more than such fifteen that they may wish to stop.

Dated, at Cairo, this 27th day of October, 1855.

N.B. The boat is to be procured and equipped, and the trip to commence as soon as possible.

The Firman
Richard Pococke, 1737

[Many of the earlier travellers sought a firman or letter of introduction from an important person in order that they should be able to travel safely along the river. Pococke translated two of his firmans.]

A letter to the Sheik of Saccara, in order to see the Pyramids.

To Ahmed, Sheik of Saccara
    May the great God protect you! AFTER saluting you. There comes one of the nation of Franks to the pyramids, having a desire to see them. And I recommend him unto you, that no one may molest him, or give him any sort of trouble. Take all possible care of him, because he is under our protection. I again recommend him to you; and may the great God be your defence!
Ali Kekiah
Hazaban Gelfi

To Emir Mahomet Kamali
What I order.
    The person that brings this letter is an Englishman, going into Upper Egypt, to see whatever is curious there; so when he delivers this letter take care to protect him from all harm; and I command you again to take care of him. I desire you not to fail of it, for the love you bear us.
Osman Bey Merlue

The *Dahabeeyah*
Amelia B. Edwards, 1873

A dahabeeyah, at the first glance, is more like a civic or an Oxford University barge, than anything in the shape of a boat with which we in England are familiar.* It is shallow and flat-bottomed, and is adapted for either sailing or rowing. It carries two masts; a big one near the prow, and a smaller one at the stern. The cabins are on deck, and occupy the after-part of the vessel; and the roof of the cabins forms the raised deck, or open-air drawing-room already mentioned. This upper deck is reached from the lower deck by two little flights of steps, and is the exclusive territory of the passengers. The lower deck is the territory of the crew. A dahabeeyah is, in fact, not very unlike the Noah's Ark of our childhood, with this difference – the habitable part, instead of occupying the middle of the vessel, is all at one end, top-heavy and many-windowed; while the fore-deck is not more than six feet above the level of the water. The hold, however, is under the lower deck, and so counterbalances the weight at the other end. Not to multiply comparisons unnecessarily, I may say that a large dahabeeyah reminds one of old pictures of the Bucentaur; especially when the men are at their oars.
    The kitchen – which is a mere shed like a Dutch oven in shape, and contains

---

* A *dahabeeyah* was being restored at Luxor in 1990, so Nile visitors may once again meet one on the river.

only a charcoal stove and a row of stewpans – stands between the big mast and the prow, removal as far as possible from the passengers' cabins. In this position the cook is protected from a favourable wind by his shed; but in the case of a contrary wind he is screened by an awning. How, under even the most favourable circumstances, these men can serve up the elaborate dinners which are the pride of a Nile cook's heart, is sufficiently wonderful; but how they achieve the same results when wind-storms and sand-storms are blowing, and every breath is laden with the fine grit of the desert, is little short of miraculous.

Thus far, all dahabeeyahs are alike. The cabin arrangements differ, however, according to the size of the boat; and it must be remembered that in describing the *Philae*, I describe a dahabeeyah of the largest build – her total length from stem to stern being just one hundred feet, and the width of her upper deck at the broadest part little short of twenty.

Our floor being on a somewhat lower level than the men's deck, we went down three steps to the entrance door, on each side of which was an external cupboard, one serving as a storeroom and the other as a pantry. This door led into a passage out of which opened four sleeping-cabins, two on each side. These cabins measured about eight feet in length by four and a half in width, and contained a bed, a chair, a fixed washing-stand, a looking-glass against the wall, a shelf, a row of hooks, and under each bed two large drawers for clothes. At the end of this little passage another door opened into the dining saloon – a spacious, cheerful room, some twenty-three or twenty-four feet long, situate in the widest part of the boat, and lighted by four windows on each side and a skylight. The panelled walls and ceiling were painted in white picked out with gold; a cushioned divan covered with a smart woollen reps ran along each side; and a gay Brussels carpet adorned the floor. The dining-table stood in the centre of the room; and there was ample space for a piano, two little bookcases, and several chairs. The window-curtains and portières were of the same reps as the divan, the prevailing colours being scarlet and orange. Add a couple of mirrors in gilt frames; a vase of flowers on the table (for we were rarely without flowers of some sort even in Nubia, where our daily bouquet had to be made with a few bean blossoms and castor-oil berries); plenty of books; the gentlemen's guns and sticks in one corner; and the hats of all the party hanging in the spaces between the windows; and it will be easy to realise the homely, habitable look of our general sitting-room.

Another door and passage opening from the upper end of the saloon led to three more sleeping-rooms, two of which were single and one double; a bathroom; a tiny back staircase leading to the upper deck; and the stern cabin saloon. This last, following the form of the stern, was semicircular, lighted by eight windows, and surrounded by a divan. Under this, as under the saloon divans, there ran a row of deep drawers, which, being fairly divided, held our clothes, wine, and books. The entire length of the dahabeeyah being exactly one hundred feet, I take the cabin part to have occupied about fifty-six or fifty-seven feet (that is to say, about six or seven feet over the exact half), and the lower deck to have measured the remaining forty-three feet. But these dimensions, being given from memory, are approximate.

For the crew there was no sleeping accommodation whatever, unless they chose to creep into the hold among the luggage and packing-cases. But this they never did. They just rolled themselves up at night, heads and all, in rough brown blankets, and lay about the lower deck like gods.

The Reïs, or captain, the steersman, and twelve sailors, the dragoman, head cook, assistant cook, two waiters, and the boy who cooked for the crew, completed our equipment.

Bugs and Beatings
W. H. Bartlett, 1845

The boat, when fitted up, was quite a snug little ark, a world in itself. I went on board, proud of my floating home. I was monarch of all I surveyed, and amused myself with arranging every thing in the nicest order; and what with books, pistols, matting carpets, and green blinds, it looked so pretty and so cheerful, and when I lay down on my bed in the cabin, the breezes were so delightful and refreshing, and I heartily rejoiced I was out of the stifling heat of Cairo and fairly embarked on my cruise.

But, alas for all human anticipations! the morning opened most inauspiciously; the boat proves to be full of bugs, and I passed a restless, a savage night; in addition, Salem has a violent attack of ophthalmia, and has been rolling about on deck in agony; fortunately, we had with us sulphate of zinc and copper, and after obtaining from the city some rosewater, I mixed them, and applied as per prescription in Sir G. Wilkinson's Hand-book, and had the satisfaction of seeing Salem rapidly improve. The extermination of the bugs was a matter of more difficulty; the scoundrel of a Reis had neglected to sink the boat as he had promised, and from every chink and crevice in the old planks hundreds came forth, scenting the blood of an Englishman; books, matting, and clothing were all in a swarm with the disgusting vermin, from the swollen old patriarch to the youngest of his descendant fry. We threw the mats overboard to begin with, removed all the furniture, and by dint of sundry pails of water, furious scrubbing, ferreting out of the nests with an iron pike, stuffing the chinks with camphor, and then subjecting every separate article to a rigid investigation, we routed the main body the first day, and by a watchful look-out till the second evening, and cutting off stragglers, had fairly gained the victory; the rest, if there were any, retreating forward to their fitting quarters near the person of the Reis and his men, and coming no more about the quarter-deck. Salem was indignant at the Reis, who turned out a lazy, dirty, worthless rascal, and wanted to beat him; but this discipline of the stick, though very ancient, highly necessary, and perfectly well understood in Egypt, revolts at first one's English prejudices, and I forbade him to resort to it. He shrugged his shoulders, and assured me, that as I should at length be driven to it in spite of myself, it was better to begin at once by producing a wholesome impression, which would be an ultimate saving in the amount required, declaring that, but for my injunction, he would begin by breaking the Reis's head at once.

Nile-boat Prayers
Sophia Poole, 1842

A custom which is always observed by the Arab boat-men at the commencement of a voyage much pleased me. As soon as the wind had filled our large sail, the Reyyis (or captain of the boat) exclaimed, 'El-Fat-'Hah'. This is the title of the opening chapter of the Kur'an (a short and simple prayer,) which the Reyyis and all the crew repeated together in a low tone of voice. Would to Heaven that in this respect, the example of the poor Muslim might be followed by our countrymen, that our entire dependence on the protecting providence of God might be universally acknowledged, and every journey, and every voyage, be sanctified by prayer.

Give Us Strength
Stephen Olin, 1843

The disposition to acknowledge the Divine agency in everything, appears in a great variety of instances. The boatmen call on God and Mohammed for help when they attempt to raise a heavy burden, or to shove the boat off from a bank of mud or sand. They pull the towline and ply the oar to the time of a song or chorus which implores the divine aid: 'We are men of God. O Prophet, give us strength. Allah, help us!' The song is often divided, one part of the boat's company, more commonly a single person, uttering a sentiment, to which the rest make a response – 'We are the men of God!' *Response.* – 'O Prophet, give us strength. Allah, help us!' The effect is not unpleasant, and if one could hope there was anything of the spirit of piety in the performance, it would be delightful. I am, of course, indebted to others for the sense of the boatmen's song, though it is so often repeated as to impress itself upon the memory of those who do not understand the language.

On Board the *Lilla*
Howard Hopley, 1868

While our sailors were absent on leave, bidding good-bye to their wives and children (or hareems, they called them, the domestic circle goes by that name: Hareem means sacred), we were busily at work provisioning the boat. It took us nearly a week. The Professor and I, laden with sacks, baskets, and boxes, were beating between Boulac and the bazaars all the day long, as industrious as ants. The donkeys had a heavy time of it. Our American – for brevity's sake I will in future call him Smith – as chief of the commissariat, took kindly to it. Not insensible to good living himself, he understood better than we how to lay in of that which was toothsome and good.

'What are your flesh-pots?' he one day asked, 'without the savoury addition of leeks and onions?' Accordingly, a sack of these succulent vegetables was added to our load.

We engaged a Nubian cook with one eye – a wonderful fellow for stews – who suggested what, and how much, in the way of stores, to buy. This was rather a ticklish matter; for to run short would be little less than ruin. Nothing could be got up the river save fresh meat, poultry, eggs, and milk. All else must be laid in before starting. 'Surely this and that are unnecessary,' we pleaded. But the fellow was inexorable, and we gave in. Flour for bread-making, macaroni, mustard, charcoal, candles, coffee, we could understand; but such luxuries as one tambourine, one darabouku, two pairs of cymbals, two flutes – musical instruments for the delectation of the sailors – puzzled us fairly. Haroun, however, said it was all right. We confided the difficulty to him. He was always affable in these matters, and argued with you persuasively; he would pose himself gracefully, his head well back, one hand on the hip, the other gently raised to give eloquent effect, and dazzle you with his rings. 'You see, sare,' he explained, 'sailor he sing to you; he make *fantasia* by moonlight. You listen, you no be sad: you laugh, sare. All gentlemen pay darabouku music quite regular.' Of course there was no appeal; so the fiddler went on board.

As soon as the last load was laid in, we prepared to hoist sail. An afternoon came in which we paid our bills, buckled our straps – portmanteaus, boxes, and the like – on to the back of the peevish camel, and watched him swagger out of the shadowy courtyard of our 'inn' into the light, bound for Boulac. Merry enough were we to get away. We jumped on our donkeys, and followed in state in the wake of the camel. Haroun was in his glory, a conscious centre of admiring eyes. We surnamed him the caliph, in virtue of his stately bearing, and in remembrance of his namesake of Baghdad, Haroun-al-Raschid the Magnificent. Like a general on the battle-field, he rode about, restraining, directing. Perpetually he was lingering to waft adieu to one or another of his Cairene friends who hung about our path; dignity forbade further display. Unluckily, at a critical moment, the caliph's donkey failed from beneath him, and he bit the dust. Then, and not till then, he relaxed; for determining, like Sancho Panza, to profit by his humiliation, he jauntily remade his turban, and positively sang a song as we passed through the sycamore avenue leading to Boulac.

When a great man thus unbends, singing is contagious. Sailors and donkey-boys now took up the strain, and even Hassan from his perch on the camel looked down, and droned out a chorus. It was like an Italian festa – all holiday. We joined boldly in the mirth. *Que voulez vous?* Had we not all Egypt before us? Great indeed is the witchery of Egyptian travel, and the beginning of a journey is more jocund than the end. Who could resist the infection? Even the Professor flourished his stick and hummed a stave.

Steam or Sail
Samuel Manning, 1886

The delicious sense of repose, the Oriental *Kièf*, the Italian *dolce far niente*, which constitutes so large a part of the enjoyment of the Nile trip, is impossible on board a steamer. Though the rate of progress be slow as compared with that on European or American waters, it is yet far too rapid to let us abandon ourselves to the lotus-eating indolence which is so refreshing to the wearied frame and over-wrought brain of the traveller in search of health. Then, too, it is impossible to linger where we please. We must hurry on. Two hours may be enough for the tombs of Beni Hassan, three hours for the temple of Esneh, four days for Luxor and Karnak; but it is distressing to feel that we cannot stop if we like. Haunted by the fear of being too late, we complete our survey, watch in hand, to be sure of catching the steamer before she leaves her moorings in the river. The risk of finding uncongenial company on board is likewise not inconsiderable. In a public conveyance it is not possible to choose one's fellow-travellers, and it may happen that our meditations on the grand memories of the past are being perpetually broken in upon by 'men whose talk is bullocks.' A very serious objection to the old steamers used to be their scandalously dirty condition, and the swarms of vermin with which they were infested. This, of course, does not now apply; the new vessels being as clean and as comfortable as the most fastidious can desire. Nevertheless, for those who have ample means and leisure, and who have resources within themselves, or in their party, to bear the monotony of some days or weeks on board a boat with nothing to do and little to see, the Nile trip in a dahabiyyeh is one of the most delightful excursions in the world. To others the steamer offers a very fair substitute.

But what is a dahabiyyeh? The dahabiyyeh, gentle reader, is a boat in form and outline not unlike the barges of the City Companies in the days when the Thames was to Londoners what the Nile is to the Egyptians. Its saloons and cabins are on deck. Some are luxuriously fitted up, room being found even for a piano. They differ in size, affording accommodation for from two to six or eight passengers. For the crew no sleeping accommodation whatever is provided. They roll themselves up in their *burnouses* and lie down on the fore-deck like bundles of old clothes, for which I have not infrequently mistaken them. The boat is worked by two large triangular sails fitted to masts fore and aft, and there are benches for rowers when needed. The resemblance between the Nile boats of the present day and those of the ancient Egyptians, as depicted on the monuments, has been often noticed.

'Instructions to the Managers of Cook's Nile Steamers'
John Mason Cook, 1892

[This flimsy little booklet was issued to each manager and had to be returned 'to the Chief Office in Cairo at the end of the season, or whenever the holder of it is called to some other position.' One hears the voice of John Mason Cook as one reads. Examples of instructions include:]

II   Captain and Pilot (*Reis barroni*) must know the exact draught of the boat on which they are working.

IV   Boats coming down the river must always take the Summer Channel, or the best Channel, and meet, on the western side, boats going up.

IX   Steamers coming down and meeting another steamer or sailing boat going up and being in a strong current, must decrease her speed, but if the channel is very narrow she must, if necessary, turn round south again and go to shore.

XIV   Steamers on starting from the shore must go slow.

XXII Steamers must anchor, stop or go on shore if there is a thick fog which prevents the Reis seeing the way, and the whistle, must blow at intervals.

XXXI Should one steamer be following another, she must, at a distance of about ¼ mile, give two long whistles by way of warning.

[The Manager is then reminded that:]
... he is the responsible person on board the steamer; he has full control of every department, and he is also responsible for every description of servants on board, but must not interfere either with the navigation or the working of the engine.

[In addition to the 'Instructions', there were certain 'Rules'. Among these were:]

IV   In case of steamers going aground the Captain must work in harmony with the Reis as to the best means of getting off.
XIV   Steamers to salute all Government steamers and Khedival yachts they meet or pass, with the whistle three times.
XV   To salute our own steamers by dipping the Egyptian flag.
XVIII In *returning* the salute to a competitive steamer our steamer to dip the Egyptian flag three times.

[The italics are explained by a note later in the 'Instructions':]
Saluting steamers: Under no circumstances are our steamers to salute a steamer of a competing company; but should the competing steamer salute ours first, we must return the salute out of respect for the Egyptian flag.

[Further guidance is given about the use of flags:]

Signal flags:
Code for using them.
Blue: Make to shore or drop anchor mid-stream for important communication.
Green: Go easy or stop mid-stream, and wait for our felucca. (This signal will be explained when you read on and find who might be in the felucca.)
Yellow/white/blue and green is a code for where mail has been left.
Yellow and white: Can you spare provisions? If so, give one long whistle and wait for our felucca.
Two long whistles means 'No'.

[There is one further rule about the conduct of steamers on the river:]
Under no circumstances are our steamers to stop, even if called upon to do so by the Reis in charge of any competing steamers, even if they are badly stuck and require special assistance. The only case under which our steamers can be allowed to assist would be in the event of there being any danger to the passengers on board; but under no other circumstances are our steamers to stop or render the slightest assistance to them.

[There then follows a list of instructions about the 'housekeeping' side of the manager's duties. Interestingly among these is the following:]
A book must be kept by the Manager to enter all the menus of both luncheon and dinner every day. Such books are still kept by Nile steamers today.

[Now comes the warning:]
Mr J. M. Cook will most likely be on the river during the season. Managers to keep a look out for him signalling any boat to stop at any point on the river, and when he comes on board, to report to him any special matter of importance that may have arisen during the voyage.

On the Boats
Deborah Manley, 1990

Today, unless you are adventurous enough to sail down the Nile by felucca, your journey will be in one of the 200 or so river boats that act like floating hotels between Luxor and Aswan. Hemmed in by the barges and the 'British' dam at Aswan, they move up and down between the two all year long, although a few boats are now designed to go all the way from Cairo to Aswan. They glory in great classical names like *Rameses*, *King of the River*, or *Nefertari*, *King Tut*, *Ra* even, or have names which compete for today's dreams like *Moon River* or *Nile Splendor* (note the US spelling). Our boat was the MV *Atlas*, one of the smaller, less grandiloquent crafts, but comfy, well run and of a pleasing size. Sadly for the company which owned it (these floating hotels are owned by tourist companies or by the hotel chains who own the land-based hotels too), but pleasantly for us, it was hardly more than half full. Going down river from Aswan most of the boats seemed to be even more empty. When at capacity the *Atlas* would hold eighty-five passengers and a crew of sixty. These crew members would encompass a manager and two assistant managers (the manager is effectively the captain and chief executive, purser and PR manager rolled into one); a pilot and two assistants, an engineer and five assistants, a *maître d'* and ten stewards, a housekeeper with ten staff, three barmen and nine sailors who doubled as porters, and ten service staff. In addition each language group is accompanied by its own tour guide.

At any one time about a fifth of this hierarchy will be on ten days' leave after six weeks on the river. Many of them are able to visit their homes when the boats dock at Luxor or Aswan, but others come from as far away as Cairo.

How do all these people come to their jobs on the boats? For all except the manual workers there are various forms of apprenticeships. Some will have gone to hotel-management school; the guides will have done a university tourist course; the stewards come from long lines of Nubian servants with experience passed down through the families. The pilots learn the river on feluccas and graduate up through work boats to the helm of a floating hotel, learning as they go. There is a lot of camaraderie among the pilots, who wave and shout across to one another from boat to boat as they pass – and give blasts of their horns.

We joined the helmsman one morning as he zig-zagged along past a village at the bend of the river. Despite his pointing them out to us, we could barely discern the slight ripple that warned of a sandbank below the surface, and guided the assured skill of his actions. Nowadays, since the High Dam, the river at least stays in one place. No longer do unexpected shoals catch unwary boats as they frequently did in the past.

At Aswan each company has its own anchorage. The Nile side of what is delightfully described on the signposts as Corneesh Road is lined by arches on which are listed each company's boats, with steps dropped down the steep bank to the mooring. In Luxor and along the river it is a free for all, but the *Atlas* appears to have clout and seniority and often moors beside Luxor temple.

The boats may be lined up two or more deep. We briefly were boat eight on the outer edge. All the boats have a wide central reception area, and to reach an outside boat you walk straight through all of them from the shore.

The problem is that the inner boats do not appear to know who is moored outside them.

In the evening the pack will be shuffled so that the boats that plan to leave earliest are on the outer edge of the pack. We watched with pleasure one evening as four of these huge floating hotels moved around on the Nile in a grand but graceful minuet as they waited for an inner boat to get its act together and depart. Our pilot, who did not have a loudspeaker, shouted instructions across the water which were relayed to the loiterer by another boat's loudspeaker. Among all this the local people's ferry chugged its way back and forth, like a mongrel dog that had wandered into a ballroom.

My Dear Bert
John Mason Cook, 1888

[John Mason Cook's minute attention to detail and determination to have everything just so is summed up in this letter to his son T. A. Cook (known in the family as Bert).]

From SS *Rameses*
Cairo, 22 December 1888

My Dear Bert,
Soap for the Tourist Steamers
On the *Rameses* I see Yardley's Windsor Soap instead of Franks soap – how is this? 2 years ago I ordered Franks soap to be supplied, which I considered the best and I have never authorised the change – have you?
Your affect. Father

In Praise of Cook Pasha
G. W. Steevens, 1898

To the general English mind Cook represents a sort of machine which sits in Ludgate Circus and punches little holes in tickets. It never occurred to me, somehow, that Cook might be a man. But he is. I have seen him, and spoken, with him, and eaten with him, and voyaged with him four days, and he is very much a man indeed.[*]

Is it not a wonderful chance to meet with Cook in the flesh? It would hardly be more stirring to meet the Attraction of Gravitation in a Terai hat standing solidly at Assouan Railway Station.

*

A man like this was just the man for Egypt. He knew what he wanted, and he meant to get it: he did get it, and, what was as much to the point, it was the right thing to want. Up and down the Nile he went; he knew all the dragomans and the boat-captains – and they came to know him. For a small thing, just to show you, the early steamers were steered by a tiller: as the pilot had to sit right forward, so as to see the channel, the tiller became unearthly

[*] John Mason Cook, son of Thomas Cook.

110

long and infernally clumsy. But the pilots wouldn't hear of steering by a wheel – it had never been done on the Nile, they pointed out, and therefore it never could be done. So Mr Cook built his boat with a wheel, and steered her himself. Now the steamer pilots look down on their unfortunate brethren who have no wheel, and wonder how they can possibly do with that clumsy tiller.

At first he ran the Egyptian Government's steamers: then he built the *Prince Abbas*. A high-built, flat-bottomed boat like that, though, said the wise men of Egypt, would capsize in the first gale. And when she lay for days in his arsenal at Bulac, without going out for her trials, they opined that the madman Cook was punished for his rashness at last. 'But I was waiting for a gale of wind,' explains Mr Cook, and when the barometer promised one he went down to the arsenal and ordered everything ready for the trial. 'Better wait,' said the manager; 'there's a gale coming.' 'That's just why I'm taking her out,' said Mr Cook; and out he took her, and she was steady as a rock. No more whispering about the stability of Cook's Nile steamers after that.

And what does he look like? He looks as you would expect him to look. Tall and strongly knit, he stands erect and firm on his legs to-day, though his beard is snow-white and his round forehead is bare. His white eyebrows bristle resolutely over just the eyes that such a man ought to have – eyes that look out of their sockets like a gun out of a port, blue eyes that seem to have a backward surface looking at the brain, eyes that think as well as see. His movements and gait, I am afraid, are a little stiffer, but they are strong, and it is the gait of a man who knows whither he is going and intends getting there. Altogether a man of force – a man also of humour, of much kindness, but primarily a man of force. I would sooner have him for my friend than for my enemy. Yet I would sooner have him for my enemy than most men; for he would hit straight, and expect to be hit straight back.

Apply this kind of man to a country like Egypt and you will get results. The results in Mr Cook's case are, first, his own success, the establishment of the largest British business in Egypt; second, the opening up of Egypt as a holiday-land to all the world; third, a vast benefit to Egypt herself. Of the private prosperity of Thomas Cook & Son (Egypt), Limited, it is not my business to tell you: but I can give, and have given, you a few hints about the wonderful organisation which deserves and commands success. Perhaps you think I have said too much. But you wouldn't if you were in Egypt, for in a land of wonders I do not know but that the ramifications of Cook & Son are the most wonderful feature. In Egypt he who puts himself into the hands of Cook can go anywhere and do anything. Whether it be the transport of an army or the regulations for the use of a steamer's bathroom, you will find every point thought of, and every point thought out.

Tourists poured in from every land. In the season of 1898 some people talked of 50,000 visitors.

British and American predominate, but perhaps what strikes you most is the swarm of Germans. Ten years ago you would have said they had neither the money nor the enterprise to take them farther afield than Naples. Today you meet them everywhere. We had a sing-song on one of the tourist steamers coming up, and a German, being asked to play being some practical joker, gave us forty-five minutes of the 'Nibelung's Ring'. There was nothing, given your German, extraordinary in that: the striking point was that there were enough

Germans round to give in a hand. The German in Egypt gets himself up exactly in the manner of the comic Englishman of the Continental circus. Men in huge helmets, with huge puggary, huge blue goggles, knickerbockers, and chess-board stockings; women in the same helmets and goggles, vast blue veils, sunshade, short skirts, and vast hands and feet; both sexes crested with Meyer or Baedeker rampant – they make a picture at which native Egypt gapes in undisguised delight.

... when 'the Governor' is pleased to travel up and down his Nile, you may see the natives coming up to him in long lines, salaaming and kissing his hand. When he appears they assemble and chant a song with refrain, 'Goood-mees-ta-Cook.' Once he took Lord Cromer up the Nile, and they went to visit a desert sheikh somewhere at the back of Luxor. The old man had no idea that the British had been possessing Egypt all these years – barely knew that the late Khedive was dead.

'Haven't you ever heard of me?' asked Lord Cromer. No; the sheikh had never heard of Lord Cromer.

'Have you heard of Mr Cook?'

'Oh, yes; Cook Pasha – everybody knows Cook Pasha.'

Do Not Worry, Mother
Bayard Taylor, 1851

Cairo, Egypt, 14 November 1851

... You need be under no apprehension about my trip into the interior. I am not going to the Niger, nor to the source of the Nile, nor where nobody else has ever been. I am going to Khartoum in Nubia, as I expected to do on leaving home, and as I assured you all. Put no faith in newspaper reports from people who don't understand geography. The journey is long and toilsome, but here, where the people ought to know something about it, they tell me there is no danger from the Arabs and that the trip will be most interesting... I engaged a dragoman yesterday... The American consul assures me that he is one of the best in Egypt... He speaks English and Italian very well. I am going to don the red cap and sash, and sport a sabre at my side. Today I had my hair cut within a quarter of an inch of the skin, and when I look in the glass I see a strange individual. Think of me as having no hair, a long beard, and a copper-colored face. My throat gives me no trouble. I wear no cravat, and shall get an Egyptian shirt which is open at the neck and has no collar...

6

Cairo to Asyut

Introduction

Dahabeah 'Sesostris', 8 January

James (my brother) and I dress for dinner, as getting ready gives us a little diversion, keeps us from slumping and certainly will have no bad effects upon servants and crew.
William Jarvie, 1904

Frederick Norden made a slow start in 1737 and Dr Richardson was delayed by the loss of the jolly boat in 1816, but on the whole, once travellers left Cairo, they were really on their way. Amelia Edwards's heart sang as she set off with a fair breeze on a brilliant afternoon in 1873. Howard Hopley's understanding of Egypt grew with each day, although Catherine Grey and the Prince and Princess of Wales seem to have been more interested in their own surroundings and in the possibility of there being something for the Prince to shoot. William Golding in 1984 used a small boat – though admittedly one with a motor – to make his trip upriver; little seemed to have changed in a century apart from a few looming industrial sites.

Florence Nightingale in 1849 settled into life on the Nile with great pleasure, and carefully stitched a pennant to hang from the yardarm. Lucie Duff Gordon was a resident when she travelled from Cairo in 1863; she did not have her own boat but paid her passage on a steamer, as had the indomitable Austrian traveller Ida Pfieffer in 1852.

Now there were guidebooks to introduce places of interest along the way and indicate distances travelled. Sir Wallis Budge, Keeper of Egyptology at the British Museum, wrote the guidebook that was given to every Cook's traveller, which probably brought him greater income and wider fame than his academic career. Baedeker was, of course, in many travellers' luggage.

The enjoyment of the journey rings through all the records, with Howard Hopley delighting in the harmony, Flaubert glorying in the colours and Pierre Loti listening to the Nile sounds, for example. But some people still faced problems. James Bruce in 1768 warned of swimming robbers, Stephen Olin's crew was full of night fears in 1843 and George Melly suffered other problems in 1851. There was much to see along the shores as Egypt unfurled. Howard Hopley recorded religious observation and in 1913 Rudyard Kipling eavesdropped on capitalists. Eliot Warburton, the well-loved Irishman, revelled in the Nile dawn – it is a very special part of the day. William Golding wrote as the morning progressed. The travellers reached the 'bird mountain' of Gebel-at-Ter and W. H. Bartlett described the diving Coptic monks in their nakedness, which even the Victorian ladies seem to have taken in their stride. Near Biba, Villiers Stuart waited for a wind in 1879 and a fat dervish supplied it. The national flags and personal pennants were very useful to let other Nile travellers know who you were and from where you came. Each boat also had to register in Cairo, so travellers like Eliot Warburton in 1845 could watch out for their acquaintance along the river. The Howard Hopley trio met up with friends to celebrate New Year 1869 with some unattractive companions. As Harriet Martineau said, with all this there was so much to see that she was seldom in her cabin.

Henry Light in 1814 came close to the people. Sophia Poole explained the backsheesh system and Charles Thompson and Frederick Henniker made comment. William Jarvie, a delightful American who travelled in a family party in 1904, watched his dragoman wrangling for fish. Frederic Eden described the passing boats; W. H. Bartlett and others wrote disapprovingly of the slave boats, but Eden spoke more sympathetically of a harem boat.

When the wind blew north all was well and the sail boats sped up the river, but when the wind dropped there was nothing for it but 'tracking'. Amelia Edwards described this painful business. But when the wind came there could be other problems. Florence Nightingale was caught in the khamsin, the storm wind of the desert. But even after days like these the Egyptian evenings are delicious, as Samuel Manning makes clear.

Sir Wallis Budge and Dean Stanley introduce the tombs at Beni-Hassan, and Howard Hopley brings them to life.

The travellers were also collectors. Some, like Belzoni, were officially sent out by Henry Salt, the British Consul, on the instructions of William Hamilton at the Foreign Office; others, like William C. Prime, were in business. There was much to discover, collect and buy. E. D. Clarke found Roman coins still in circulation in 1801; Jeremiah Lynch purchased a centuries-old cat in 1889, and in 1818 Thomas Legh and in 1855 William C. Prime describe the horrors faced by collectors in the crocodile pits of Manfalut. Villiers Stuart adds to the descriptions of the mummy trade in 1879, and Eliot Warburton explains how live crocodiles were being hunted off the Nile.

Hardly Starting
Frederick Norden, 1737

[After an illness of three months in Cairo, Norden recovered at last and set off up the Nile.]

We agreed with a barge master to carry us to Essuaen for money and a new coat, on condition that he should not take in a person more than our company consisted of, which had been lately augmented by a Coptic priest and two missionaries from Rome: one of whom was a valuable acquisition in as much as he understood the Arabian language very well.

We insisted on another condition with the reys (spelt reis by others) or master of the barge, to wit, to take no merchandize on board, lest the trafficking thereof should delay our navigation. But he had been beforehand with us, and got secretly on board whatever things he had a mind to carry, so that after some debate we were obliged to desist on that head. All preparative for our travelling expedited, we embarked on the afternoon of Sunday 17 of November ... but for the remainder of the afternoon we did not make much more way than the length of a cannon shot, because our goodly reys was not on board with us, so that properly speaking our inended course began not till the following day ...

Delay
Dr Richardson, 1816

[Travelling as physician to the party of Lord Belmore, with the British Consul Henry Salt accompanying them, Dr Richardson set off from Cairo.]

... when it had become dark, the feluca, or jolly-boat, whether from accident or design, broke away from the vessel on which I was aboard. This produced a dreadful uproar. The reis abused the sailors, and the sailors retaliated upon the reis, and the greatest disorder prevailed. The old reis, for we had two of them on board, father and son, pranced about like one demented, calling out, 'El feluca! el feluca!' If he had lost the dearest object upon earth, he could not have uttered more horrifying shrieks of despair. We got off our course, ran aground, stove in our prow, and by ten o'clock were obliged to make fast to the bank for the night ... This was rather discouraging at the outset. However, we recovered our feluca that night, and by eight o'clock next morning had repaired the injury done to the prow and proceeded in pursuit of the other two *maashes*, which had got considerably ahead. We came up with them about ten, opposite the Pyramid of Sakareh, and all in company proceeded joyfully on our voyage.

The Esprit du Nil
Amelia B. Edwards, 1873

And now we are on board, and have shaken hands with the captain, and are as busy as bees; for there are cabins to put in order, flowers to arrange, and a hundred little things to be seen to before the guests arrive. It is wonderful, however, what a few books and roses, an open piano, and a sketch or two, will do. In a few minutes the comfortless hired look has vanished, and long enough before the first comers are announced, the Philæ wears an aspect as cozy and home-like as if she had been occupied for a month.

As for the luncheon, it certainly surprised the givers of the entertainment quite as much as it must have surprised their guests. Being, no doubt, a pre-arranged display of professional pride on the part of dragoman and cook, it was more like an excessive Christmas dinner than a modest midday meal. We sat through it unflinchingly, however, for about an hour and three quarters, when a startling discharge of firearms sent us all running upon deck, and created a wholesome diversion in our favour. It was the French boat signalling her departure, shaking out her big sail, and going off triumphantly.

I fear that we of the Bagstones and Philæ* – being mere mortals and Englishwomen – could not help feeling just a little spiteful when we found the tricolor had started first; but then it was a consolation to know that the Frenchmen were going only to Assuân. Such is the *esprit du Nil*. The people in dahabeeyahs despise Cook's tourists; those who are bound for the Second Cataract look down with lofty compassion upon those whose ambition extends only to the First; and travellers who engage their boat by the month hold their heads a trifle higher than those who contract for the trip. We, who were going as far as we liked and for as long as we liked, could afford to be magnanimous. So we forgave the Frenchmen, went down again to the saloon, and had coffee and music.

*

At last all is ready. The awning that has all day roofed in the upper deck is taken down; the captain stands at the head of the steps; the steersman is at the helm; the dragoman has loaded his musket. Is the Bagstones ready? We wave a handkerchief of inquiry – the signal is answered – the mooring ropes are loosened – the sailors pole the boat off from the bank – bang go the guns, six from the Philæ, and six from the Bagstones, and away we go, our huge sail filling as it takes the wind!

Happy are the Nile travellers who start thus with a fair breeze on a brilliant afternoon. The good boat cleaves her way swiftly and steadily. Water-side palaces and gardens glide by, and are left behind. The domes and minarets of Cairo drop quickly out of sight. The mosque of the citadel, and the ruined fort that looks down upon it from the mountain ridge above, diminish in the distance. The Pyramids stand up sharp and clear.

And now, as the afternoon wanes, we draw near to a dense, wide-spreading forest of stately date-palms on the western bank, knowing that beyond them, though unseen, lie the mounds of Memphis and all the wonders of Sakkârah. Then the sun goes down behind the Libyan hills; and the palms stand out black and bronzed against a golden sky; and the Pyramids, left far behind, look grey and ghostly in the distance.

Presently, when it is quite dusk and the stars are out, we moor for the night at Bedreshayn. Such was our first day on the Nile.

Egyptian Harmony
Howard Hopley, 1868

There is a profound charm in this landscape; a beauty that grows slowly upon you. The climate also indisposes you for violent contrasts or excitement, you fall in with the prevailing tendency to the tranquil and solemn. All seems to harmonize with the inner impression of *Egypt* on your mind. And although as to mere size there exists nothing here to emulate the majesty of Alpine scenery, there is nevertheless a pervading sentiment and admixture of the sublime. A feeling of mystery may explain this. Looked upon from that point of view, no scenery, save perhaps the awful group of Sinai, can be grander or more severe

---

* The names they and another couple of ladies gave their boats. The boats came to their hirers unnamed and were given names for each journey.

than this; for the element of mystery tinctures everything in Egypt. Every vestige of its architecture, too, that you meet adds to the feeling. A great critic speaks of structures characterized by 'a severe and, in many cases, mysterious majesty, which we remember with an undiminished awe, like that felt at the presence and operation of some great Spiritual Power.' That is eminently true of the great piles of Egypt. Somehow you instinctively speak low when the Great Pyramid looms into sight. I have seen laughter hushed in an instant by that unexpected apparition.

Gradually, as you travel on, you come to perceive whence spring the first glimmerings of Egyptian art. The relation of art to nature is nowhere so strongly marked as here. It was the landscape, ever rich in tropic beauty, the sweep of the majestic river, the eternal silence of the desert hills, that engendered in the minds of the early Egyptians feelings which were developed in their art. Most of what you now discover of mysterious yearning, of calm power, of pathos, of stability, as suggested in the paintings, sculpture, and architecture of Egypt, was first mirrored on the artist's soul by a contemplation of what he saw around him. This is manifest even in respect of outward form. The grand ideal of the Egyptian temple is to be found in the stratified cliff. On that fantastic wall you may define pylons, porticoes, pillared arcades without number. A very dull imagination might there build up temples grander than Karnak and more colossal than the pyramid. A chamber cut in the rock, vaulted as the heavens are vaulted, and sown over with golden stars on a field of azure – that was the beginning of all architecture. The very earliest column known is a twisted sheaf of water-lilies, of which the closed flowers form the capital. Then came combinations of all manner of flower-like forms, the paper-reed, the lotus, the palm for the capital, while the shaft was wreathed with paintings of the same. Lastly, by the pillar side, the artist placed Man, the master – or rather his representative, Osiris – shrouded and silent, bearing in his folded arms the symbols of power and judgment, but speechless. Nature could tell no more.

You can never in your thoughts detach the Egypt of the past from the Egypt of to-day; neither, indeed, can you ever quite exclude it from sight. Temples, scattered ruins on the plain, tombs sown thick along the mountain cliff on either hand, arrest your eye in succession. And with every thoughtful mind this undercurrent of feeling, as regards the past, must tincture the landscape with colourings of its own. It is a background never lost sight of. The incidents of the near landscape, those change, but that travels on with you. From the pyramids – which stand as man's handwriting upon Egypt, his autograph which Time cannot obliterate – onward to far Syene,* it is there.

Royal Fleet
Catherine Grey, 1868

6 February

At two o'clock we left our Palace and embarked on board the boats which had been prepared for us, to commence our voyage up the Nile. Our party was

* Aswan.

117

large, and the number of vessels provided for us formed really a little fleet, of which the following was the order of sailing:– A large and very smartly fitted-up steamer, the *Federabanee*, Captain Achmet Bey, heads the squadron, and is occupied by Prince Louis of Battenberg, Major Teesdale, Captain Ellis, equerries in waiting, Lord Carrington, Mr. O. Montagu, Dr. Minter, Sir Samuel Baker, and Mr. Brierly. On deck there is a large saloon all fitted up with silk, and looking-glasses, and every description of luxury, and here we are always to have our meals. Outside this again there is a small open saloon with a large looking-glass at the back, so that wherever one sits one sees the scenery behind one.

This steamer tows a most beautiful dahabeah, as they call these Nile boats, which has been named the *Alexandra*, in which the Prince and Princess and myself are to live. It is all fitted up in blue and gold, with a great deal of taste, and the cabins are all large and most comfortable. The Prince and Princess have a very nice sleeping cabin, with a bath-room and dressing-room apiece. There is a large sitting-room with a piano and very pretty furniture; and then come my two cabins, small, about seven feet square, but very comfortable, and outside these, a large cabin for the dresser, Mrs. Jones, and my excellent Fina [her maid]. We are, indeed, very well off, except that we must go on board the big steamer for every meal – breakfast at ten, luncheon at two, and at seven, dinner. This is rather troublesome, and will, I fear, often oblige us to remain all day on board the big boat, a thing we do not fancy much, so the Princess means to try and get back to the small boat after breakfast every day, in order to have some hours' quiet for useful occupations.

After these boats comes the kitchen-steamer with four French and one Arab cook on board. It carries all the kitchen apparatus and tows a large barge full of provisions, dead and alive – turkeys, sheep, chickens &c. Another steamer conveys Colonel Stanton, our Consul-General at Cairo, with our two Egyptian gentlemen, Mourad Pasha and Abdel Kader Bey; and also tows a barge containing three horses and two donkeys, as well as a poor unfortunate French washer-woman, who, with her husband and child on board, is to go with us as far as the First Cataract, and to wait for us there till we return. Another smaller steamer, which draws very little water, also follows, in case we should not be able to get on in our big boat, the water this year being lower than they think it has been for these last hundred years. All this shows how the Viceroy has spared no trouble, and no expense to provide his royal visitors with everything, and with every luxury that could possibly contribute to their comfort and pleasure.

I think we shall have a very happy and quiet time, for all the party seem likely to agree, and to be disposed to make the best of everything. The weather is still bitterly cold, only 10° Centigrade in my cabin.

At six o'clock stopped for the night, and some of the Duke's party joined us after dinner.

The Journey Starts
William Golding, 1984

We wrapped up even more warmly and went on deck and stood, chillily in the cold north wind. On the left, a mountain of white stone lay perhaps half a mile from the eastern bank of the river. There was much machinery, smoke and clouds of dust. This was Tura with its quarry for fine limestone. Chephren faced his pyramid with it, all blinding white. Five thousand years of quarrying had put half a mile between the mountain and the river. It was something to have seen after all and consolation for not being able to see the pyramids from the river. After Tura the banks became a bit more countrified and even Egyptian. There were plantations of date palms and lines of delicate green trees – tamarisks, I think. We passed a huge dovecote built in the distinctively Egyptian manner, massive mud walls then domes and minarets with niches for nesting. There were donkeys, untethered and grazing on the bank where it was clear of reeds. It seemed odd to see a donkey doing what it liked and not laden to death. But this was February, the Egyptian winter, and a relatively lazy time for man and beast, unless your business happened to be with the water traffic or you were a woman. The Nile was very low and women were washing clothes on the mud beaches. A solitary man moulded mud brick and women processed up the bank with huge water jugs on their heads. The palms, I thought, looked like bottle brushes – but then did I know what bottle brushes looked like? Here and there brickyards or brickfields obtruded more rawly into the Nile with great screens of red fragments. There were sailing boats moored alongside the screens taking in loads of red brick. Rarely the interruption to the mud bank was not red brick but stone foundations of some vanished building which might have been any age.

At Home on the Nile
Florence Nightingale, 1849

9 December

We shall have been on board a week tomorrow, and are now thoroughly settled in our house: all our gimlets up, our divans out, our Turkish slippers (mezd) provided, and everything on its own hook, as befits such close quarters. Now, if you ask how I like the dahabieh life, I must say I am no dahabieh bird, no divan incumbent. I do long to be wandering about the desert by myself, poking my own nose into all the villages and running hither and thither, and making acquaintances *où bon me semble*. I long to be riding on my ass across the plain, I rejoice when the wind is foul, and I can get ashore. They call me 'the wild ass of the wilderness, snuffing up the wind,' because I am so fond of getting away. I dearly love our dahabieh as my home, but if it is to stay in it the whole day, as we are fain to do when the wind is fair, that is not in my way at all. However, I must tell you what walks I have had. This morning I went ashore with one of the crew at sunrise; it was cold, as cold as an English morning in October, and there was even a touch of hoar frost. But when I got under the shelter of the palm trees it was warmer. We went inland to a village, the situation of which was marked to us by its fringe of palms. Whenever you see these, you are sure of finding houses. We met a woman leading out her flock to water at a pool left by the inundation of the Nile, her black goats and white sheep. A little further on, we came to a brick-field, mud bricks laid out to bake in the sun, and full of chopped straw to make them adhere. It made one think of Rebekah and the Hebrews' task, at every turn. Then we walked round the village. But no European can have the least idea of the misery of an African village; if he has not seen it, no description brings it home. I saw a door about three feet high, of a mud hut, and peeping in, saw in the darkness nothing but a white-horned sheep, and a white hen. But something else was moving, and presently crawled out four human beings, three women and a child; they made a miserable pretence of veiling their faces before my Efreet. The only reason why they had not their camel with them was because he could not get in, next door was a maize enclosure, which differed from the first only by being cleaner, and having no roof. I looked over, and saw him. My Efreet is so careful of me that he won't let anybody come near me. If they do, he utters some dreadful form of words, which I don't understand, and they instantly fall back.

All the houses in the village were exactly like this, the mud walls very thick, nearly three feet. There appeared to me to be only one den inside, but I did not go in because I had promised not. Some little things were setting out to fetch water from the Nile, each with his amphora on the head, each with a rag which scarcely descended over the body, but shrouded the head (the Arab always covers his head). The dogs, who are like foxes, descended from the roofs at sight of me and my Efreet, but, awed by a similar charm, fell back.

The village, which seemed a considerable place, with a governor and a governor's house, possessed a khan. I peeped in. Strings of camels lay round the walls – a few inner cells behind them, roofless and floorless, showed tokens of travellers. But I was afraid of a commotion: so veiled my face and passed on. A tray covered with the Turkish thimblefuls of coffee (which we also drink) was coming out – the only refinement the Arab possesses. In every village you see a coffee-house; generally a roofless cabin built of maize stalks, with mud benches round the inside, but always the thimblefuls of coffee, made, not like ours, but pounded, boiled for a moment, and poured off directly and drunk black. You cannot drink our coffee in this climate with impunity; it is too heating. We walked round the village, the huts all tumbled together up and down, as animals build their nests, without regularity or plan. The pigeons seemed better lodged: they had round mud cones provided for them, taller than the houses, stuck full of pots at the top for them to build in, and sticks for them to perch on. There was not much curiosity about me, though they (the Arabs, not the pigeons) could never have seen a European woman before; but they looked on with the same interest which the dogs did, – no more. By the time I came back and overtook the dahabieh, which had been tracked meanwhile for some distance (there was little wind, and that was south), the sun was high, but it was still too cold to breakfast on deck, as we have done once.

After breakfast we all five went ashore together for the first time. Paolo and Mr B. took their guns to shoot us our dinner and soon killed seven quails. We meanwhile wandered about in a desert place, or sat under what shelter we could find beneath a tuft of grass (the grasses grow as high as reeds), for the sun had by this time risen with a burning heat. A troop of mounted police, fine looking fellows, rode past us, turbaned and trousered, with guns and pistols.

It is rather tiresome always to have an Efreet with one on land, which I am never allowed to go without, and to be dogged by him everywhere, but it is a most courteous Efreet, and almost too afraid of my coming to harm. It will not let me even climb the dyke without helping me.

All my work since I came on board has been making the pennant (the flag and name of every boat are obliged to be registered at Cairo), blue bunting with swallow tails, a Latin red cross upon it, and ΠΑΡΘΕΝΟΠΗ* in white tape. It was hoisted this morning at the yardarm, and looks beautiful. It has taken all my tape and a vast amount of stitches, but it will be the finest pennant on the river, and my petticoats will joyfully acknowledge the tribute to sisterly affection, – for sisterly affection in tape in Lower Egypt, let me observe, is worth having. The Union Jack flies at the stern, Mr. B,'s colours half-way up the rigging, all made by ourselves. For two days we had no wind, and tracked or rowed or pushed all day. On the third day the north wind rose and we stood away for Benisouef.

On Board a River Steamer
Lucie Duff Gordon, 1863

After infinite delays and worries, we are at last on board, and shall sail tomorrow morning. After all was comfortably settled, Ismail Pasha sent for all the steamers up to Rhoda, near Minieh, and at the same time ordered a Turkish General to come up instantly somehow. So Latif Pasha, the head of the steamers, had to turn me out of the best cabin, and if I had not come myself, and taken rather forcible possession of the forecastle cabin, the servants of the Turkish General would not have allowed Omar to embark the baggage. He had been waiting all the morning in despair on the bank; but at four I arrived, and ordered the *hammals* to carry the goods into the fore-cabin, and walked on board myself, where the Arab captain pantomimically placed me in his right eye and on the top of his head.

Once installed, this has become a hareem, and I may defy the Turkish Effendi with success. I have got a good-sized cabin with good, clean divans round three sides for Sally† and myself. Omar will sleep on deck and cook where he can. A poor Turkish lady is to inhabit a sort of dusthole by the side of my cabin; if she seems decent, I will entertain her hospitably. There is no furniture of any sort but the divan, and we cook our own food, bring our own candles, jugs, basins, beds and everything. If Sally and I were not such complete Arabs we should think it very miserable; but as things stand this year we say, *Alhamdulillah* (it is no worse.)

Luckily it is a very warm night, so we can make our arrangements unchilled. There is no door to the cabin, so·we nail up an old plaid, and, as no one ever looks into a hareem, it is quite enough. All on board are Arabs – captain,

---

* Parthenope, her sister's name.
† Her maid.

engineer and men. An English Sitt* is a novelty, and the captain is unhappy that things are not *alla Franca* for me. We are to tow three dahabiehs – M. Mounier's, one belonging to the envoy from the Sultan of Darfur, and another. Three steamers were to have done it, but the Pasha had a fancy for all the boats, and so our poor little craft must do her best. Only fancy the Queen ordering all the river steamers up to Windsor!

At Minieh the Turkish General leaves us, and we shall have the boat to ourselves, so the captain has just been down to tell me. I should like to go with the gentlemen from Darfur, as you may suppose. See what strange combinations of people float on old Nile. Two English women, one French (Mme Mournier), one Frenchman, Turks, Arabs, Negroes, Circassians, and men from Darfur, all in one party; perhaps the third boat contains some other strange element. The Turks are from Constantinople and can't speak Arabic, and make faces at the muddy river water, which, indeed, I would rather have filtered.

I am quite surprised to see how well these men manage their work. The boat is quite as clean as an English boat as crowded could be kept, and the engine in beautiful order. The head-engineer, Ahmad Effendi, and indeed all the crew and captain too, wear English clothes and use the universal, 'All right, stop her – fooreh (full) speed, half speed – turn her head', etc. I was delighted to hear, 'All right – go ahead – *el-Fathah*' in one breath. Here we always say the *Fathah* (first chapter of the Koran, nearly identical with the Lord's Prayer) when starting on a journey, concluding a bargain, etc. The combination was very quaint.

There are rats and fleas on board, but neither bugs nor cockroaches. Already the climate has changed, the air is sensibly drier and clearer and the weather much warmer, and we are not yet at Assiut. I remarked last year that the climate changed most at Keneh, forty miles below Thebes. The banks are terribly broken and washed away by the inundation, and the Nile far higher even now than it was six weeks earlier last year.

Beni Suef
E. A. Wallis Budge, 1906

73 miles from Cairo, the capital of a province bearing the same name. In ancient days it was famous for its textile fabrics, and supplied Upper Egypt with flax.

On the Nile
Gustav Flaubert, 1849

The water of the Nile is quite yellow; it carries a good deal of soil. One might think of it as being weary of all the countries it has crossed, weary of endlessly murmuring the same monotonous complaint that it has traveled too far. If the Niger and the Nile are but one and the same river, where does this water come from? What has it seen? Like the ocean, this river sends our thoughts back almost incalculable distances, then there is the eternal dream of Cleopatra, and the great memory of the sun, the golden sun of the Pharaohs. As evening fell,

* Lady.

the sky turned all red to the right, all pink to the left. The pyramids of Sakkara stood out sharp and gray against the vermilion backdrop of the horizon. An incandescence glowed in all that part of the sky, drenching it with a golden light. On the other bank, to the left, everything was pink; the closer to the earth, the deeper the pink. The pink lifted and paled, becoming yellow, then greenish; then the green itself paled, and almost imperceptibly, through white, became the blue which made the vault above our heads, where there was the final melting of the transition (abrupt) between the two great colours.

Dance of the sailors. Joseph at his stoves. The boat heeling. The Nile in the middle of the landscape; and we in the middle of the Nile. Tufts of palm-trees grow at the base of the pyramids of Sakkara like nettles at the foot of graves.

Visiting the Consul
Jeremiah Lynch, 1889

[Visiting the Consul was a normal courtesy among Victorian travellers, but Mr Lynch, being US Consul-General in Egypt, got a special welcome.]

At Beni-Sooef we were welcomed by the American consul, who is a Copt or native Christian. He and his fathers before him have been our agents for thirty-two years, and the family is quite rich. He received us in a large, roomy, lumbering old house, with white-washed ceilings and sides, and a clay floor covered with matting. A pleasant-faced, cheery old gentleman, with an immaculate white robe and neat tarbush. He invited us to dinner, having at first sent to the *Vittoria* for wine. Beni-Sooef had no wineshops, and the consul's cellar was bereft of that sinful commodity. The dinner was very good, with rice pilaf, turkeys, chicken, mutton, and several dishes of sweets. The dessert is half the banquet in Egypt. The people are inordinately fond of sugared dates and figs. There were two kinds of pudding, and a cake with soft candy scattered through it, as we have raisins. I wonder how their teeth are so fine and white.

The banquet lasted nearly three hours, and to the end the consul-general and myself ate of every course. There were several local notables present, yet, save the mudir, or governor, not one of them, including the consul, spoke any other language than Arabic. One might have supposed that, after representing America for thirty-two years, some one of the family would have learned a little English, but all the consul and his sons could say was 'Yes' and 'No'.

The American flag waved from the roof, and portraits of several Presidents ornamented the principal apartment, including a large medallion picture of General Grant, to which his autograph was attached. It will be remembered that he visited Egypt and went up the Nile to Luxor in 1879.

Dangers
James Bruce, 1768

A certain kind of robber, peculiar to the Nile, is constantly on the watch to rob boats, in which they suppose the crew are off their guard. They generally approach the boat when it is calm, either swimming under water, or, when it is dark, upon goat skins, after which they mount with the utmost silence, and take away whatever they can lay their hands on. They are not very fond it seems meddling with vessels whereon they see Franks, or Europeans; by them some have been wounded by firearms. The attempts are generally made when you are at anchor, or under weigh, at night, in very moderate weather, but oftenest when you are falling down the stream without masts; for it requires strength, vigour and skill, to get aboard a vessel going before a brisk wind, though indeed they are abundantly provided with all these requisites.

Night Fears
Stephen Olin, 1843

Our men refused to stop for the night on the eastern side of the river. They have the utmost horror of the Bedouins of the Desert; and wherever their sterile domains press close upon the Nile, we are entertained with stories of robbery and bloodshed, and warned of the danger of mooring in a suspected neighbourhood. This tale of danger has been in the mouths of our crew from the commencement of our voyage. They seldom fail to let us know by the time the sun has disappeared, or before, that we are in a safe and proper place to spend the night, and faithfully forewarn us of the imminent peril to be encountered from sleeping in proximity to the lawless villagers who infest the banks of the river a little farther on. When we compel them to go on, as we usually do, without respect to the dangers of the voyage, which always prove chimerical, they seldom fail to assure us that we owe our safety to their vigilance. They have not slept a moment during the night, so intense has been their desire to guard the Howagas from danger and depredation. We had reason for believing to-night that their fears were real. They rowed the boat across the river voluntarily. This act of violence done to the *vis inertiæ* which seems the ruling element of their nature, was good evidence of the reality of their apprehension.

One evening we stopped for the night at 7 pm and were much annoyed by the cry of hyenas, which had taken refuge in the long grass and reeds that abound in this locality.

Melancholy and Invaders
George Melly, 1851

The huge sails were loosed, and expanded to a mild evening breeze, with just strength enough to blow out the folds of our Union-Jack, which flew proudly over us. It was an exciting moment, but I cannot say that it was wholly free from melancholy; for while we looked up the mighty river with eager impatience for the wonders it was to disclose, we could not but feel that, when our anchor was hauled up, we threw off our last hold of society, completely severed ourselves from all communication with our friends, and crossed the confines of barbarism. But this impression was not allowed to deepen, and speedily gave way before our earnest longings for new objects and other regions.

It was late before I went to bed, and I had scarcely fallen asleep, when I was aroused by a pressure on my feet. At first, I thought some one must be sitting upon me, and was about to remonstrate, but a sudden squeaking undeceived me, and I discovered that the intruders were three enormous rats, who had stretched themselves very comfortably on the coverlet. Fortunately my boots were at hand, and I flung one into the midst of them, on which they scampered off in great dismay, vehemently protesting against such uncourteous treatment. I then got up, and barricaded the door, which I was assisted in doing by one of our servants, all of whom, as rare specimens of their class, now claim from me a word of notice.

Notes along the Nile
Pierre Loti, 1910

A monotonous chant on three notes, which must date from the first Pharaohs, may still be heard in our days on the banks of the Nile, from the Delta as far as Nubia. At different places along the river, half-nude men, with torsos of bronze and voices all alike, intone it in the morning when they commence their endless labours and continue it throughout the day, until the evening brings repose.

Whoever has journeyed in a dahabiya up the old river will remember this song of the water-drawers, with its accompaniment, in slow cadence, of creakings of wet wood.

It is the song of the 'shadûf', and the 'shadûf' is a primitive rigging, which has remained unchanged since times beyond all reckoning. It is composed of a long antenna, like the yard of a tartan, which is supported in see-saw fashion on an upright beam, and carries at its extremity a wooden bucket. A man, with movements of singular beauty, works it while he sings, lowers the antenna, draws the water from the river, and raises the filled bucket, which another man catches in its ascent and empties into a basin made out of the mud of the river bank. When the river is low there are three such basins, placed one above the other, as if they were stages by which the precious water mounts to the fields of corn and lucerne. And then three 'shadûfs', one above the other, creak together, lowering and raising their great scarabæus' horns to the rhythm of the same song.

All along the banks of the Nile this movement of the antennæ of the shadûfs is to be seen. It had its beginning in the earliest ages and is still the characteristic manifestation of human life along the river banks. It ceases only in the summer, when the river, swollen by the rains of equatorial Africa, overflows this land of Egypt, which it itself has made in the midst of the Saharan sands. But in the winter, which is here a time of luminous drought and changeless blue skies, it is in full swing. Then every day, from dawn until the evening prayer, the men are busy at their water-drawing, transformed for the time into tireless machines, with muscles that work like metal bands. The action never changes, any more than the song, and often their thoughts must wander from their automatic toil, and lose themselves in some dream, akin to that of their ancestors who were yoked to the same rigging four or five thousand years ago. Their torsos, deluged at each rising of the overflowing bucket, stream constantly with cold water; and sometimes the wind is icy, even while the sun burns; but these perpetual workers are, as we have said, of bronze, and their hardened bodies take no harm.

These men are the fellahs, the peasants of the valley of the Nile – pure Egyptians, whose type has not changed in the course of centuries. In the oldest of the bas-reliefs of Thebes or Memphis you may see many such, with the same noble profile and thickish lips, the same elongated eyes shadowed by heavy eyelids, the same slender figure, surmounted by broad shoulders.

Devotions
Howard Hopley, 1868

It is the mid-day hour of prayer. Wayfarers here and there are halting in the silent noon to go through their devotions. A rigid Moslem – be he in his shop, or under sail, or on a journey – is ever scrupulous as to his prayers. This is no closet worship. He makes no secret of it. You would not be uncharitable, perhaps, in considering it rather an ostentatious proceeding. This is why, on my journey, I took note of many so occupied. Some had spread their carpets by the wayside, others in the flickering shadow of a palm. There were also such as, having no carpet to spread, being poor, knelt down on their garment laid in the dust. One good man had cast his donkey adrift. The ass, cunning fellow, quickly found pleasant pasture amid the tender corn in an adjacent field; and there he stood, with one eye on his prostrate master, nibbling in hot haste, and doubtless approving most highly of the Prophet's institution. I watched a grandee about to commence his prostrations. Two horsemen – his servants – sumptuously attired, with pistols and dirks stuck in their silken girdles, dismounted, and were laying out their master's carpet. It seemed a royal road to heaven this; and in my mind I was taking that dandy son of Islam to task, when a sudden remembrance checked me. I thought of a church in a certain parish I knew, where gorgeously-liveried footmen might be seen on Sunday mornings escorting their mistresses up long aisles into snug pews, laden with piles of prayer-books to deliver at the door. The cases were so parallel, the distinctions of class so ostentatiously paraded at a moment when all should be and are equal, that I was driven off into a sidelong train of thought, and began to wonder what a pious Moslem's opinion might be on more than one of our fashions and observances in the matter of religious worship.

It is not pleasant to be interrupted in any occupation, but to disturb a Mussulman at his prayers is a very serious thing. For if he speaks in answer to you, or his attention is withdrawn, either by turning the head or otherwise moving his position, the prayer goes for nought; he must begin again.

Up the River
Rudyard Kipling, 1913

Once upon a time there was a murderer who got off with a life-sentence. What impressed him most, when he had time to think, was the frank boredom of all who took part in the ritual.

'It was just like going to a doctor or a dentist,' he explained. '*You* come to 'em very full of your affairs, and then you discover that it's only part of their daily work to *them*. I expect,' he added, 'I should have found it the same if – er – I'd gone on to the finish.'

He would have. Break into any new Hell or Heaven and you will be met at its well-worn threshold by the bored experts in attendance.

For three weeks we sat on copiously chaired and carpeted decks, carefully isolated from everything that had anything to do with Egypt, under chaperonage of a properly orientalised dragoman. Twice or thrice daily, our steamer drew up at a mud-bank covered with donkeys. Saddles were hauled out of a hatch in our bows; the donkeys were dressed, dealt round like cards: we rode off through crops or desert, as the case might be, were introduced in ringing tones to a temple, and were then duly returned to our bridge and our Baedekers. For sheer comfort, not to say padded sloth, the life was unequalled, and since the bulk of our passengers were citizens of the United States – Egypt in winter ought to be admitted into the Union as a temporary territory – there was no lack of interest. They were overwhelmingly women, with here and there a placid nose-led husband or father, visibly suffering from congestion of information about his native city. I had the joy of seeing two such men meet. They turned their backs resolutely on the River, bit and lit cigars, and for one hour and a quarter ceased not to emit statistics of the industries, commerce, manufacture, transport, and journalism of their towns – Los Angeles, let us say, and Rochester, N.Y. It sounded like a duel between two cash-registers.

One forgot, of course, that all the dreary figures were alive to them, and as Los Angeles spoke Rochester visualised. Next day I met an Englishman from the Soudan end of things, very full of a little-known railway which had been laid down in what had looked like raw desert, and therefore had turned out to be full of paying freight. He was in the full-tide of it when Los Angeles ranged alongside and cast anchor, fascinated by the mere roll of numbers.

'Haow's that?' he cut in sharply at a pause.

He was told how, and went on to drain my friend dry concerning that railroad, out of sheer fraternal interest, as he explained, in 'any darn' thing that's been made anywhere.'

'So you see,' my friend went on, 'we shall be bringing Abyssinian cattle into Cairo.'

'On the hoof?' One quick glance at the Desert ranges.

'No, no! By rail and River. And after *that* we're going to grow cotton between the Blue and the White Nile and knock spots out of the States.'

'Ha-ow's that?'

'This way.' The speaker spread his first and second fingers fanwise under the big, interested beak. 'That's the Blue Nile. And that's the White. There's a difference of so many feet between 'em, an' in that fork here, 'tween my fingers, we shall – '

'I see. Irrigate on the strength of the little difference between the levels. How many acres?'

Again Los Angeles was told. He expanded like a frog in a shower. 'An' I thought,' he murmured, 'Egypt was all mummies and the Bible! *I* used to know something about cotton. Now we'll talk.'

Nile by Night and Dawn
Eliot Warburton, 1845

This sailing on the moon-lit Nile has an inexpressible charm; every sight is softened, every sound is musical, every air breathes balm. The pyramids, silvered by the moon, tower over the dark palms, and the broken ridges of the Arabian hills stand clearly out from the star-spangled sky. Distant lights, gleaming faintly among the scarce seen minarets, mark the site of Cairo, whose voices come at intervals as faintly to the ear. Sometimes the scream of a startled pelican, or the gargle of some huge fish as he wallows in the water, may disturb the silence for a moment, but it only makes the calm that follows more profound.

All nature seems so tranced, and all the world wound in such a dream, that we can scarcely realize our own identity: vainly we try to think of Europe, and gas-lamps, and new police, and politics. Hark! to the jackal's cry among the Moslem tombs! See where the swarthy pilot sits, statue-like, with his turban and flowing beard: those plains before us have been trod by Pharaohs; these waters have borne Cleopatra; yonder citadel was the home of Saladin! We need not sleep to dream.

The night is gone – gone like a passing shadow; the sun springs suddenly into the throne of purple and rose-coloured clouds that the mist has left for him. There is scarcely a dawn – even now it was night – then day – suddenly as a cannon's flash.

Our boat lay moored to the bank. Mahmoud started to his feet, and shouted yallough! like a trumpet. Till then the deck seemed vacant; the crew were sleeping in grave-like apertures between the planks, wrapped in their white capotes. These were very shroud-like, and gave their resurrection a rather ghastly appearance. All nature seems to waken now; flocks of turtle-doves are rustling round the villages; dogs are barking the flocks to pasture, cocks are crowing, donkeys are braying, water-wheels are creaking, and the Moslems prostrate themselves in prayer, with their forehead to the ground, or their hands crossed upon their bosoms, their eyes motionless, and their lips quivering with the first chapter of the Koran.

For my own part, a plunge into the Nile constitutes the principal part of a toilette in which razor or looking-glass are unknown. Re-dressed, re-turbaned, and re-seated on my carpet, Abdallah, with a graceful obeisance, presents a chibouque of fragrant latakeea, as different from our coarse English tobacco as a pastile is from burnt feathers; and Mahmoud offers a little cup of coffee's very essence. In the meantime, the crew are pitching the tent upon a little lawn beneath some palm-trees, for yonder forest shadows the ruins of Memphis, and the gardens wherein Moses used to wander with Pharaoh's daughter. Here then I shall wait for my good friend and fellow voyager, who lingers at Grand Cairo, while I haunt the ancient city of the Pharaohs, shooting quails, and questioning the past.

Ascent of the Great Pyramid!

The Pyramids, 1845.

Sleeping tent, from Sir Gardner Wilkinson's
Things Useful for a Journey in Egypt, *1847.*

To those who wish to be entirely protected at night from intruders, I cannot do better than recommend a contrivance of Mr. Levinge's, which he devised during his travels in the East, and which is equally adapted to a boat, a house, or a tent. It consists of a pair of sheets (*a*), about six feet long,

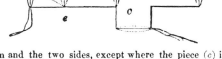

sewed together at the bottom and the two sides, except where the piece (*c*) is attached to them, and by which you get in. To the upper end (*d*) is added a thin piece of muslin, serving as a mosquito-net (*b*), which is drawn tight at the end by a tape or string, serving to suspend it to a nail (*f*). A short way from the end (at *e*) are fastened loops, through which a cane is threaded, to form a circle for distending the net. This cane is in three pieces, about three feet long, fitting into each other by sockets. After getting in by the opening of *c* you draw the tape tight to close its mouth, and tuck it in under the mattrass, and you are secure from

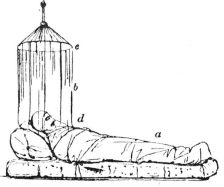

intruders, whether sleeping at night, or sitting under it by day. Over the part *a*, the blankets, or coverlid, are put.

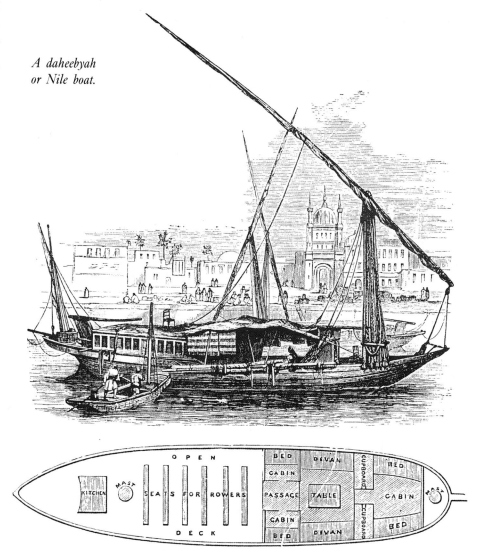

*A daheebyah
or Nile boat.*

Plan of a daheebyah for four persons, sixty feet long.

Kitchen on a Nile boat.

Cangias moored at the river bank, 1873.

The crew of Samuel Manning's boat.

The shadoof, 1845.

A slave boat at Girgeh, 1845.

Women coming to the river to fill their water jars, 1868.

Crocodiles – Timseach! Timseach!

Aboard a Nile steamer, 1868.

Gwawazee, *or dancing girls, 1836.*

A performer on the nay, *1836.*

Dendera temple, half buried.

Obelisk and Propylon of the Temple at Luxor, 1845.

Nile Morning
William Golding, 1984

I surfaced – probably from sleep though I couldn't be sure at the time – at about a quarter to six. It was still dark outside and cold. I looked out. Strange! There were robed people about, some in boats, some on the bank but no one was moving. The water was so flat that the current was not visible. The stillness of the scene was such that the figures of robed men seemed to brood as if contemplating some inevitable and awful tragedy before which movement and noise were useless and irrelevant. Had they, I asked myself, sat, crouched, leaned or stood thus all night? Were they – were *we* since the night had left me diminished – like lizards, which require the sun's warmth before their muscles can operate? I watched them as the dawn lightened swiftly and the faintest trace of mist drew away from the water. A fisherman was crouched in his rowing boat, his ridiculous oars (two unshaped baulks of timber) lying idle along the thwarts, his head closely wrapped against the chill of dawn. He was moored only ten yards from us. He never moved, wrapped elaborately in a thick galabia. It was as if the night was a time for grief from which men had to recover daily.

The east lightened all at once. A woman crept out of a house with a tin water vessel on her head. She came slowly down the mud bank and the tin flashed as the first grain of the sun struck it. The fisherman lifted his head. Figures began to move on the bank. It was theatrical in that it led from the first tableau of grief to the common preoccupations of day in two minutes flat. A woman led a donkey. The fisherman shipped him ridiculous oars and rowed slow strokes. Two men spread their robes and squatted by the water. The rising sun grabbed the hill of straw and at once turned it to the gold woven for the girl in the fairy story. The pigeons started to peck, the rats rustle. A big sailing boat, her torn sails wrinkled like ancient skins came with a just perceptible movement as the current brought her towards us. She was empty, going north. A smaller boat stood south towards us but did little more than stem the current. She was loaded deep with raw, red brick and seemed to have no more than six inches of freeboard.

[Soon the engineer came aboard. Golding asked that he be told that he hoped they would go further than they had on the first day.]

Alaa translated. Shasli continued to writhe, answered, then swung himself up into the glass box which housed our wheel. Alaa translated. I could not believe what I heard.

'*What!*'

' "He who rides the sea of the Nile must have sails woven of patience." '

I was speechless. The philosopher of the Nile started our engine and we moved off.

Gebel at-Ter
E. A. Wallis Budge, 1906

136 miles from Cairo, on the east bank of the Nile, is Gebel at-Ter or the 'Bird mountain' so called because tradition says that all birds of Egypt assemble

here once a year, and that they leave behind them when departing one solitary bird, that remains there until they return the following year to relieve him of his watch, and to set another in his place.

Diving Copts
W. H. Bartlett, 1845

Next day the breeze sprung up and we ran together under Gebel e Tayr, or the 'mountain of the birds', a range of precipitous cliffs coming down sheer to the water, broken into ledges which afford shelter to a vast number of water-fowl. On the bleak exposed level above is a Coptic convent, or rather enclosed village, which is famous for a race of aquatic Christian mendicants, who, darting down the steep cliffs from their aerial perch, plunge into the river, and beset the boats of travellers with importunate clamour. My red cross* made me a palpable mark, and accordingly it was not long ere I beheld one of the fraternity rapidly cleaving the waves, shouting 'Christiano Howaga,'† though how he could have descended the perpendicular precipice I sought in vain to discover. Striking out most vigorously, he soon came up with the boat; brandy was his first entreaty, then bread, bottles, and above all, beckshish. He was a stalwart rogue, and as he stood, *in puris naturalibus*, upon the deck, I thought that had there been any on board to whom it would have signified, I would have had him soundly switched with the corbash and kicked into his favourite element, notwith-standing our Christian brotherhood: as it was, the incident was amusing enough, and we gave him a little of all he asked for: the brandy he took internally, the bread he balanced on his head, the piastres he put into his mouth, and holding a bottle in one hand he contrived, though thus encumbered, to steer his course with the other into a cranny of the rocks, and scrambled up, the Lord knows how, to his abode, amid the loud shouts of the admiring boatmen. A recent traveller, Mr. Curzon, has solved the mystery of the ascent, having climbed up to the convent by a very curious natural tunnel which perforates the precipice.

Biba
Karl Baedeker, 1929

145 miles from Cairo. A district capital, the junction of a secondary line running parallel with the main railway line (two trains daily in either direction). At Biba is a Coptic church with a tall bell-tower.

Blessings for a Wind
Villiers Stuart, 1879

December 9. – At noon on December 5, the owner of the good boat *Gazelle*, having seen us comfortably settled on board, wished us a good voyage and took his leave; and we shook out our great white sails, and started for the Second

* England's flag of St George.
† Christian foreigner or traveller.

Cataract. The first day we made a splendid run, accomplishing sixty miles without a check, and anchoring for the night a little below Zeiteon. The wind then failed us; thus for three days we lay becalmed like the 'Ancient Mariner,' a painted ship upon a painted river. The spell was at last broken in the following manner: A rickety boat put off from shore containing a fat man who sat in the stern doing nothing, and a thin youth who struggled hard against the swift current to reach us. We were for refusing the ragged strangers admission – not so the reis and crew; they explained to us that this was a holy man, a saint, who must be propitiated, or no luck could attend our voyage. Thus admonished we made the fat dervish welcome. He mounted the deck, his turban his only garment; he would have kissed us had we encouraged him; failing that he kissed the reis, the steersman, the sailors, the cook, and cabin boy, singly and individually, then blessed them collectively along with the boat, and having popped their united contributions into his mouth, returned to shore the way that he came. The curious thing is that, immediately on his departure, the wind, which had for three days mocked our hopes, sprang up in good earnest, filled our flagging sails, and whipped us along at a pace that made the water murmur under our bows, gladdened our hearts, and stereotyped for ever the faith of the crew in the holy man.

Late in the afternoon we reached an ancient village called Bibè, where I landed with the dragoman to post a letter. In this we failed, for the simple reason that there was no post office; but the place itself was as curious a specimen of an Egyptian village as I have yet visited. I found myself among a multitude of mounds from forty to fifty feet high, on the top of which were perched the mud huts in which the present generation of Bibites dwell. The winding valleys that meandered in and out among these mounds were the original streets, retaining their first level pretty nearly, while their steep sides presented sections of all the successive generations of dwellings which had gone on accumulating, each built on top of the last; these sections exhibited strata of broken pottery and the *débris* of mud bricks. In the deepest part of one of these valleys, where some excavations had recently been made, I came upon a bed of mummies cropping out like a coal seam at the lower part of a high mound. The mummies were packed together as closely as they could be stowed; their clothes so fresh and recent that I hesitated at first to believe in their antiquity until I remembered – first, that the making of mummies in Egypt ceased at least 1500 years ago; and, secondly, that the vast accumulation of *débris* beneath which these were buried, some fifty feet below the present surface, bore silent but conclusive testimony to the long ages during which they had reposed there. The villagers had dragged out and broken up many of them, hoping to find ornaments or jewellery, but they were the mummies of poor persons, and contained nothing but the remains of mortality, which littered the surface in the shape of skulls, ribs, thigh-bones, rags, and mahogany-coloured masses of what had once been human flesh, but was now reduced to dried fibre, saturated with bitumen. The work of destruction having yielded nothing more valuable, the remainder of the slumbering dead were left in peace. The mystery is how the mummies came there, for the Egyptians were not in the habit of burying them within the precincts of their cities, but, on the contrary, far away from them. It is evident, therefore, that Bibè must have been the site of an ancient cemetery before it became a town.

Among the mounds, and in and out through the valleys already described, careered naked boys and girls with pot-bellies, and shining nut-brown skins; mixed up with them were big buffaloes and funny little buffalo calves, donkeys, turkeys, fowl, shaggy sheep, and lean mangy dogs, quiet enough now, but who by-and-by will begin a concert of fiendish sounds which will make night hideous. On the summits of the mounds towered up battlemented walls of mud, crowned with embrasures, which consisted, however, of nothing more warlike than dove-cots, for the battlements were built of earthen jars, within which were the domestic establishments of countless pigeons. The houses enclosed court-yards, out of most of which grew tall date-palms; clusters of these decorated the summits of the mounds, their long graceful fronds drooping over them and redeeming them from utter ugliness and squalor. I came also upon a couple of bushes of Hibiscus, covered with gorgeous crimson blossoms. Having threaded my way through this strange scene, I reached the outskirts of the town, where stood the Railway Station and telegraph posts, to add to the curious medley of things ancient and modern, of life and of death.

Visiting
Eliot Warburton, 1845

Before leaving Cairo for the Nile voyage, each traveller registered his name, with that of his boat, and the colour of his private flag; so that every person arriving in Egypt could find out what friends were 'up' the river, and knew what flag to look for. I found the names of two of my old friends among those who were wandering about Upper Egypt, and we had been for some days, after leaving Siout, eagerly watching for their well-known signal-flags. One morning, just at dawn, I was awakened by the cry of 'Bindera Ingeeleez'; and, looking out from my dormitory, I saw the flutter of a red ensign among some palm-trees at a bend of the river. A few minutes more, and the boat emerged from the grove, and on her tall spars floated the blue and white flag we were in search of.

A shot brought her to, and she was soon moored astern of our boat; and M— was not a little surprised to see, standing by his bedside, one whom he believed to be three thousand miles away.

Our tent was soon pitched upon the shore; and it did not require the contrast of the lonely life we had been leading so long to give zest to our long-lost conversation. I recollect few more pleasurable hours than those we passed in the shadow of the tent, looking out upon that strange wild scenery, with the Arabian hills, and all their wonders, and the Nile, where lay our two little boats before us, so strangely met, and soon to sever for the north and south.

Two days afterwards, we again caught sight of a familiar flag fluttering over a sandy promontory. By the time it approached, our tent was pitched upon the shore, and carpets and cushions spread for the reception of Lady L. T. and her party, who found a greeting in that tent as warm as the sunshine that shone over it. The fair traveller spoke with pleasure and enthusiasm of all that they had seen; and I do believe that, with all its drawbacks, Egypt is the most interesting and convenient country that a lady can travel over. After dinner, the group in the tent would have surprised the fashionable world, that know nothing of adventure beyond a fête champêtre at Fulham. Four turbaned and bearded men sat round a fair and noble lady, whose graceful-looking and fragrant *nargileh** puffed and bubbled in harmony with their long *chibouques*.† The complexions of the whole party were almost as dark as those of our crews, and the lady might have passed for Cleopatra, in a tableau ...

New Year on the Nile
Howard Hopley, 1869

It was seven o'clock. The old year was fast dying; nevertheless five hours remained to us. What should we do? It happened, while we were thus debating by candlelight, that the mellow sound of voices, as from a chorus far away, came floating in through the open passage. 'What's that?' cried Smith, lazily poking the end of a long chibouke across from his lounge on the divan into the candle to relight his tobacco; 'is it a boat?'

The caliph at that moment, pushing back the curtain, showed his important face, beaming like a full moon, at the door. 'Traveller, his boat, sar, walking down river; too dark to see flag. Him hang blue light to mast.'

We got our guns ready for saluting, and mounted on the upper deck. It was one of those nights you never see but in the East. The broad face of the river lay stilled as in deep slumber, still – without a ripple. Each single star from the firmament above mirrored itself distinctly in that sea of glass. You almost feared to look down into the awful abysses of that second semisphere, high over which you felt yourself to be floating as in some airy ocean. I had never seen so perfect an illusion before, nor do I believe any other river or lake could show it but the Nile. Far away over the water, as yet, glowed a row of little lights from the cabin windows of the approaching dahabeeyah. We could hear the dip of their oars in the intervals of the boatmen's song. As for the ship, a shadowy mass, it loomed bigger and bigger on the stream, until the Arab oarsmen – twelve in rank – rowing and singing with all their might, took indistinct shape in the flickering light of a little lantern hung above them.

Bang! Bang! Six shots in quick succession went pealing across the water, – and the sound came back to us in echo from the Lybian hills. There was a momentary lull. We saw the Arabs resting on their oars. The dark mass came floating nearer and nearer, and the reflected window-lights showed already athwart our bows. We could perceive a stir on board – then a flash. Our salute was returned. The ship's course now changed. It was evident that an order had been given to pull in for shore.

The meeting of friends or countrymen is quite an event on the Nile. It is about the only break in your journey which reminds you of nationality or home. Thus, when we presented ourselves on board the newly-arrived craft, and found its owner to be an Englishman, and, more, an acquaintance of our Professor's, we fraternized as they only do who meet thus in far distant lands. Our host, Mr. Doubledash – a man well known in scientific circles and conversaziones, where he shines as a great light, and where he has undergone many a stiff

---

* Hookah.
† Long-stemmed pipe

tussle with the Professor – had started early this season for the Cataracts. But, finding, as he expressed it, things rather dull, he determined to make the best of his way back, and get across the long desert into Palestine, taking Petra (if the fates, or rather, Bedouins, were propitious) in his track. 'I rejoice to have fallen in with you,' he said, when we were duly installed on his divans, and a Nubian boy had handed the inevitable coffee and chiboukes; 'I was so anxious for a chat about home news. Have you any papers?'

We had '*The Times*', a month old, and we, of course, ran over all we knew of the world's later history, for our host's edification. 'Ah, well!' he replied, 'I need not have worried myself. Not much is lost by my absence. Life up here, you know, is like that lake in the Land of Roses, half-sweet, half-bitter. You are ever fancying something will go wrong at home because you are away, and thus you muddy the pleasant waters of travel. But it doesn't; and that takes the conceit out of you. May I entreat you, sir, to be careful?' – this was delivered to Smith, who, swinging his legs off the divan, was kicking unconcernedly at something hidden beneath – 'there is a mummy under there.'

'A mummy!' ejaculated Smith, springing up in horror, 'I hope I have not hurt him!'

'No, I think not; he is pretty tough. There are a couple more on deck, too – women, in boxes: but this fellow is unrolled. If you will lend a hand we will have him out.'

Whereupon, while one of us held a pair of candles, the Thing in question was dragged from beneath the divan and laid on the table. It was the perfect body of a man mummified in youth, stiff and unyielding, as if accumulated ages had hardened it into iron. Every sinuous line of muscle and ligament flanking the rigid limbs could still be traced. The brown face had become distorted into a sinister grin, half exposing the upper teeth; while folds of thick clustering hair matted with bitumen wreathed about the brow.

'I bought him at Thebes,' said Mr. Doubledash, pulling off tenderly some threads of mummy cloth, which still adhered to the body. 'Mustapha Aga hit upon a fresh tomb while I was there, and he took me to see it. I purchased the three tenants *in situ*. It was quite a speculation, you know. "They might happen to turn out well or they might not," Mustapha told me. So I took my chance. The outer coffins were magnificent,' continued our friend enthusiastically. 'As big as that table, and crowded as thick with paintings as the walls of the Academy. But I left them behind me, for I hadn't room. Even as it is,' he added, with a sigh, 'my Arabs are always stumbling over the women up-stairs, and wanting to burn them. They are very good for making fires, they say.'

'Did you find anything in them?' the Professor asked.

'No; merely a scarabeus or two knotted to a net of beads over the breast, and a ring; but no jewels. As for the ladies, they are not yet thoroughly unrolled, for I wanted to save them for England. In fact, I broke the head of one in tearing away her painted mask, and trying to unclasp a necklace she had on. I fancy the head had been hurt by the embalmers. There it is behind you, sir, on the shelf.'

This last was levelled at Smith, who, taken in flank, and now thoroughly horrified, turned sharp round to look; and there, truly enough, propped up by a powder-flask, stood the ghastly thing grinning hideously at him!

'I think,' stammered Smith, 'I should like, if you will excuse it, to go on to your upper deck and have a look at those – those not yet unrolled mummies.'

So Much to See
Harriet Martineau, 1848

And when on board, there was so much to be seen on the ordinary banks that I was rarely in the cabin. Before breakfast, I was walking the deck. After breakfast, I was sewing, reading, or writing, or idling on deck, under the shade of the awning. After dinner, we all came out eagerly, to enjoy the last hour of sunshine, and the glories of the sunset and the after-glow, and the rising of the moon and constellations. And sorry was I every night when it was ten o'clock, and I must go under a lower roof than that of the dazzling heavens. All these hours of our first days had their ample amusement from what we saw on the banks alone, till we could penetrate further.

There were the pranks of the crew, whose oddities were unceasing, and particularly rich in the early morning. Then it was that they mimicked whatever they saw us do, – sometimes for the joke, but as often with the utmost serious-ness. I sometimes thought that they took certain of our practices for religious exercises. The solemnity with which one or another tried to walk the deck rapidly, to dance, and to skip the rope, looked like this. The poor fellow who laid hands on the skipping-rope paid (he probably thought) the penalty of his impiety. At the first attempt, down he came, flat on his face. If Mr. E. looked through his glass, some Ibraheem or Mustafa would snatch up an oar for a telescope, and see marvellous things in the plain. If, in the heat, either of the gentlemen nodded over his book, half the crew would go to sleep instantly, peeping every moment to see the effect. – Then, there were the veiled women coming down to the river to fill their water-pots. Or the men, at prayer-time, performing their ablutions and prostrations. And there was the pretty sight of the preparation of the drying banks for the new crop; – the hoeing with the short, heavy antique hoe. And the harrow, drawn by a camel, would appear on the ridge of the bank. And the working of the Shadoofs (pole and bucket for raising water) was perpetual, and always interesting. Those who know what the shadoof is like, may conceive the picture of its working:– the almost naked Arabs, – usually in pairs, – lowering and raising their skin buckets by the long lever overhead, and emptying them into the trough beside them, with an observ-ance of time as regular as in their singing. Where the bank is high, there is another pair of shadoofs at work above and behind: and sometimes a third, before the water can be sent flowing in its little channels through the fields.

Then, there were the endless manoeuvres of innumerable birds, about the islets and rocks: and a buffalo, here and there, swimming from bank to bank, and finding it, at last, no easy matter to gain the land. – Then, there was the ferryboat, with its ragged sail, and its motley freight of turbaned men, veiled women, naked children, brown sheep, frightened asses, and imperturbable buf-falo. – Then, there were the long palisades of sugar canes edging the banks; or the steep slopes, all soft and bright with the springing wheat or the bristling lupins. Then, there were the villages, with their somewhat pyramidal houses, their clouds of pigeons, and their shelter of palms: or, here and there, a town, with its minarets rising out of its cincture of acacia. And it was not long before we found our sight sharpened to discern holes in the rocks, far or near, – holes so squared at the entrance as to hint of sculpture or painting within. – And then, as the evening drew on, there was the sinking of the sun, and the coming out of the colours which had been discharged by the glare in the middle of the day. The vast and dreary and hazy Arabian desert became yellow, melting into the purple hills; the muddy waters took a lilac hue; and the shadows of the sharp-cut banks were as blue as the central sky. As for the moon, we could, for the first time in our lives, see her the first night; – the slenderest thread of light, of cup-like form, visible for a few minutes after sunset; the old moon being so clearly marked as to be seen by itself after the radiant rim was gone. I have seen it behind a palm, or resting on the ridge of a mountain like a copper ball. And when the fuller moon came up from the east, and I, forgetting the clearness of the sky, have been struck by the sudden dimness, and have looked up to watch her passing behind a cloud, it was delicious to see, instead of any cloud, the fronds of a palm waving upon her disk.

Communications with the People
Henry Light, 1814

In some villages I was able to assist the sick by medicines and advice; in others, I added to the catalogue of charms by writing Arabic sentences in praise of God and the Prophet at the request of the villagers [he notes that Mungo Park had on parts of his journeys earned his keep by writing such charms]. These, placed in the turban or hung round the neck, were to preserve the wearer from the evil angel. In one village, called Abou Gaziz, I was requested by a party of women to hold my drawn sword on the ground, whilst they went through the ceremony of jumping across it, with various ridiculous motions, to correct the well known Eastern curse of barrenness, and was rewarded by blessings and offerings of Durra cake.

Baksheesh
Sophia Poole, 1842

The system of giving a present at the conclusion of an engagement with an Arab is a good one; because the hope of baksheesh has the effect of preserving civil manners, and often fair dealing, and such hope ought not to be disappointed.

Comment
Frederick Henniker, 1822

Met a fellah carrying onions, a few of which he gave to us, I offered him money and he refused it; for the onions did not belong to him – how unchristian-like and uncivilised . . .

Comment
Charles Thompson, 1767

Leeks and onions, which were once deified in Egypt, still abound there, but are not held in that extravagant veneration.

A Fishy Transaction
William Jarvie, 1904

22 January

This morning I suggested that some fresh fish would be nice – native fish – so later on we hailed a fisherman who had just hauled in his line and he came alongside and held up two nice looking fish, weighing, I should think, about three pounds each. He came on board and Yango [the dragoman] turned him over to the captain. Fisherman named a price at which the captain was amazed and named a sum a quarter of what had been asked. Fisherman insulted, returned to his boat, threw down fish and ordered his boat cast loose, which was partially done when Yango took a hand in – told the fisherman that he was a swindler and ordered him off, and to take his extremely ugly face with him. Fisherman retorted, and for some minutes the air was blue with verbal explosions. Finally fisherman relented a little and grew less demonstrative. Yango same, and the incident terminated by the fisherman handing the fish on board with a smile and Yango opening his bag and giving half the sum first demanded; boats separated and kisses were exchanged at long range. So you see that interest never lags.

Passing Boats
Frederic Eden, 1862

Constantly coming up to the same place, were native boats, of all forms and build. There is one towing up the river bank, full of brown-garmented fellaheen. As they come to the point where the creek re-enters the river, and cuts across their path, three or four, slipping out of their clothes, and into the water, wade through, and push their boat across. One's eye has become so accustomed to all shades of brown and black skin, that it scarce notes whether they are clothed or not.

Close behind them comes a boat that would be more round than long, if it were not more square than either. The timbers of the roughest logs are held together by wooden pegs, whose heads, not driven home, project an inch or more from out of the sides. It is caulked with mud, and manned by three from eight to ten year old clotheless urchins. The protuberance of their stomachs is balanced behind, and their whole shape suggests the idea, that it can be but a few generations since their family went on all fours. Then passes another boat. The after-part is filled with the canopy and posts of an old English four-post bedstead; under this covering, the proprietor sits in state, solemn, sedate, and proud, in much clothing, and with an amber mouth-piece. Above his head, a negro boy squats on the canopy steering, and the sail, a sheet of holes and patches, is managed by a gaunt Arab, clad in what seems to be the last sail worn out, when the present one was new. But the boats are endless in variety. One more, the most incongruous of all, and I have done. It holds an Arab boatman, a boy whose only covering is the scalplock on the top of his shaven crown, and a Jew, in red fez, black frock coat, white umbrella, and photographic apparatus. But the ferry boat *must* be added to the list. It is exactly the shape of a Turkish slipper, and is supposed by antiquaries, to have been the felucca of Noah's ark. More probably it was built about the same time as the temple of Karnak. Great as are the preservative powers of this climate, it is scarcely possible that any of the original timbers remain. No doubt as the ages wore on, a beam would occasionally decay, and be replaced; but there still remains the boat, a wondrous specimen of joiner's power, and of wood mosaic. Into it goes a donkey, and another, and another. Does anybody know the use of a donkey's tail? An expert, say a costermonger, would answer 'for a crupper.' No such thing. From the beginning was Egypt and the Nile. The Nile never wanted a boat, nor Egypt an ass; and the tail was given to help the one into the other. See how quickly it is done! First his forelegs are lifted in, then a man from above in the boat, gives a single haul at the tail, and in goes the donkey like a shot.

A native boat on a market day resembles the last-to-be-filled carpet-bag of a family luggage. The amount it holds is only equalled by the variety of the contents; however full it may be, there is always room for one thing more. In such a boat are packed away men, women, and boys; donkeys, sheep, goats, and a camel; turkeys, chicken, and geese; cucumbers, onions, lettuce, and trusses of white clover. I had almost forgotten sugar-canes, butter and eggs, palm ropes, mats and netting, water-jars, fleas, and flies – for such things are there as a matter of course. The first thing generally seen getting out is the bare leg of an impatient lady. She soon follows, with two chickens under her arm, and a score or so of eggs in the skirt of her clothing, which is too much occupied with its brittle charges to have due regard for any regular duty. Then out rush the crowd: a number of brown-coated fellaheen stagger away under their onions or clover, or half push, half carry their donkeys on shore. Turbans of all degrees of cleanliness follow; their wearers, too sedate to hurry, each with his long pipe, and many with a servant to carry it. Perhaps a greater man still, with red tarboosh, amber mouthpiece, three or four followers, and a donkey caparisoned with a red saddle, and even a bridle. Only the very distinguished '*brics*' are bridled. Small people content themselves with a cudgel, and direct their donkey by a blow on the cheek, or a kick with the foot. Last of all comes the camel, rolling, grunting, complaining, anything but the docile animal our early education, with its usual accuracy, described him to be.

Slave Boat
W. H. Bartlett, 1845

We found several boats moored at the landing-place [at Girgeh] without the town; from the next to our own proceeded loud chattering, and the light caught upon the naked dusky skins and woolly heads of a number of negroes. I went ashore and found this to be a Djerm descending the river laden with female slaves for the Cairo market, the major part negro girls of little value, with some few more delicate specimens, however, of Abyssinian beauty, much esteemed, as Mr. Lane informs us, by the voluptuaries of the capital.

I went on shore very early the next morning; it was a dead calm on the river. The principal Jellab, or slave-dealer, was seated on the shore, apparently waiting the chance of a purchaser. A number of the negro girls were lounging about upon the sunny shore, revelling in the grateful heat; while others sat upon the boat. They were fine, well-made creatures, glossy as satin, and in excellent condition; for the most part lively, careless chatterers, and rather bearing out the accounts of some travellers of warm imaginations, who represent them as purely sensual, and always anxious to attract a purchaser as soon as possible. Whatever suffering they might have endured in the circumstances of their original capture, they were to all appearance taken very great care of. A fat, flabby old Turk now came waddling down from Girgeh, and the Abyssinians were produced and shown. They did not, however, answer his expectations, in fact, I had myself seen far handsomer in the slave bazaar at Cairo, and he fell back upon the negro girls. A group was now formed round one whom I had not noticed before, and who presented in her reluctant, downcast manner, a singular contrast to the rest. Her dress consisted merely of a string of leathern thongs around the loins, but a large wrapper was thrown loosely over her. The Jellab placed her, like a connoisseur, and proceeded to dwell upon her 'points,' but she did not somehow tell upon the sensual fantasy of the old Turk, he was provoked by her air of dejection, and rudely thrust up her declining head; next, with a cautious manipulation from head to foot, proceeded, in jockey phrase, to ascertain her soundness; and, finally, hastily whipping off the scanty covering from the poor shrinking creature, he proceeded to satisfy, with a hasty glance, the last and most important particulars of his curiosity. The Jellab looked up and smiled with an unanswerable air, but the old Turk looked dubious and unsatisfied, the crowd of callous and laughing spectators were, as usual, divided in opinion, while the defenceless subject of their gaze and controversy stood cowering before them with an air of abject, hopeless despondency. One might see that, although of a race supposed to be comparatively destitute of feeling, nature had made her of a mould too fine for such rude handling; perhaps some home remembrance came across her mind, for a more melancholy expression I never witnessed in a human creature. Finally, the old Turk declined to purchase her, and she walked listlessly back again to her corner in the hold of the Djerm.

Nile Harem
Frederic Eden, 1862

It was spring time. The birds knew it, and made the most of it. The wagtails had gone; but that cosmopolitan, whom we are apt to call the London sparrow, hopped about, and at one time we had eight or ten on our deck, repeating that they were well aware of the season, till the energy of their assertions forced them to sit in the heat with their beaks gaping. A pair of doves took possession of the rigging, and chased each other with cooing and wooing till getting in our cabin, as we sat at breakfast, they were frightened at their own impudence. And another sign of the times was seen in the departure of the 'families' of the Cairene pashas on their annual trip up Nile.

The great men's wives apparently require a change of air in spring, for we met about this time several families on the river. There was the procession of three or four steamers, each towing dahabeahs, covered with guards and flags. The whole turn out was most magnificent, and at the same time dull, severe, and proper. But very amusing was the family of a mudir. A single dahabeah contained it, but with such difficulty that the decks were covered with women and children, and the cabins were so crowded, that a beauty, more or less fat, more or less old, but all more than less painted, was bursting full-blown out of every window. Dressed as they would be at home, with their faces and throats uncovered, we had, as we passed close by, an uncommon opportunity of seeing a harem. One strikingly pretty woman wore a most gorgeous dress of scarlet and gold, another had a very pretty gown of red and white stripes; all ate, all talked, all laughed, and there was a general rush to look at C.

So great was the attraction of a European woman that the younger ones seemed for a moment to forget their sweetmeats, and one older lady even stopped in the peeling of a banana. The eunuch in charge was occupied, as we came up, in what appeared to me to be a flirtation in the stern cabin, but the general silence, the hushed voices, and non-cracking of nuts, recalled him to a sense of the situation. He made some gentle remonstrance at the small care shown by the family in the concealment of their charms; at which the oldest and plainest drew a veil over her face, but the others plainly said 'bother,' and we looked at each other with mutual gratification until the wind and stream separated us.

Tracking
Amelia B. Edwards, 1873

The good wind continued to blow all that night; but fell at sunrise, precisely when we were about to start. The river now stretched away before us, smooth as glass, and there was nothing for it, said Reïs Hassan, but tracking. We had heard of tracking often enough since coming to Egypt, but without having any definite idea of the process. Coming on deck, however, before breakfast, we found nine of our poor fellows harnessed to a rope like barge-horses, towing the huge boat against the current. Seven of the M. B.'s crew, similarly harnessed, followed at a few yards' distance. The two ropes met and crossed and dipped into the water together. Already our last night's mooring-place was out of sight, and the Pyramid of Ouenephes stood up amid its lesser brethren on the edge of the desert, as if bidding us good-bye. But the sight of the trackers jarred, somehow, with the placid beauty of the picture. We got used to it, as one gets used to everything, in time; but it looked like slaves' work, and shocked our English notions disagreeably.

Thus the morning passes. We sit on deck writing letters; reading; watching the sunny river-side pictures that glide by at a foot's pace and are so long in sight. Palm-groves, sandbanks, patches of fuzzy-headed dura* and fields of some yellow-flowering herb, succeed each other. A boy plods along the bank, leading a camel. They go slowly; but they soon leave us behind. A native boat meets us, floating down side-wise with the current. A girl comes to the water's edge with a great empty jar on her head, and waits to fill it till the trackers have gone by. The pigeon-towers of a mud-village peep above a clump of lebbek trees, a quarter of a mile inland. Here a solitary brown man, with only a felt skull-cap on his head and a slip of scanty tunic fastened about his loins, works a shâdûf, stooping and rising, stooping and rising, with the regularity of a pendulum. It is the same machine which we shall see by and by depicted in the tombs at Thebes; and the man is so evidently an ancient Egyptian, that we find ourselves wondering how he escaped being mummified four or five thousand years ago.

By and by, a little breeze springs up. The men drop the rope and jump on board – the big sail is set – the breeze freshens – and, away we go again, as merrily as the day we left Cairo.

The Khamsin
Florence Nightingale, 1849

About three, the khamsin increased; it was a wind like this which destroyed six years ago a caravan of 300 camels belonging to Mehemet Ali. The air became filled with sand. The river seemed turned upside down, and flowing bottom upwards, the whirlwind of sand from the desert literally covering it. We could not see across the river; and when we could stand upon deck, which was not often, our eyes were completely filled and our faces covered with sand. As to the critic making Thames *not* to walk between his banks, he does not deserve the credit of originality for that idea, for Nile invented the plan first, and today, instead of walking between his banks, his banks walked between him. I saw the sand blown up into a *ridge* upon the water, and it looked as if you could have passed the river on dry ground, only the dry ground was on the top. I am glad to have seen it, for I should never have believed in it if I had not, and I give you leave not to believe. By this time Nile seemed to be walking with his bed on his head; but it was no beneficent miracle, like the paralytic man's, for it looked as if earth, air, and water had been blasted together into one whirlwind of sand. We could not wash, for it was no use fishing for water in the Nile: instead of water he gave us a stone, i.e. a sand-bank. The waves were as high as when there is a moderate sea in the Channel, and the wind was hot. It grew dark, and the blast increased so, that we drove a stake into the bank and fastened a rope to it for the night.

Presently Paolo rushed in for one of the guns, which was always kept loaded. He said he saw a strange boat coming in sight. I ran out on deck after him, and sure enough, in the pitchy darkness, I saw one of the dahabiehs which had overtaken us in the afternoon, floating past us, bottom upwards; nothing to be seen of her passengers. She struck in the sand just astern of us, and remained fast there. By this time the wind had increased so much, and we bumped so

* Sorghum.

incessantly, that we were afraid the rope would not hold, and we put out another. I could not help laughing, in the middle of all this, at the figure of our Reïs, who had squatted himself at the bottom of our little boat (which was between the dahabieh and the bank), and sat there smoking his pipe, and taking no further interest in the question. If the rope wouldn't hold it wouldn't, and why should he be disturbed?

I did not go to bed – we bumped incessantly, and at the stern especially so hard that we thought we must spring a leak. It was so dark that we could see nothing, but in the morning we found that our boat had been astride of the poor wreck all night, which had been whirled round by the eddy under us. At dawn I looked out, she had entirely gone to pieces – nothing was left of her but a few of the cabin planks, which our boat picked up, a chest of clothes which we saved, and her oranges floating in the whirlpool. I never saw anything more affecting than those poor oranges, the last luxury of their life in the midst of death. Torrents of rain were falling – our cabin roof was completely soaked through – the sky was still one heavy mass, but the wind had a little fallen, and we struggled on, towed by the wretched crew, their teeth chattering, dripping with wet, and evidently thinking the Day of Judgment, the end of the world, was come (for to them rain is much what to us English an earthquake might be), to Manfaloot, which we reached about twelve. There we learnt that of the five boats which passed us yesterday to windward four had gone down, and of their passengers, twenty (including women and children) had been lost. Almost all their relations were in Manfaloot. We gave up the chest of clothes to the governor, to the great displeasure of our crew, who fully intended to keep it for themselves.

Nile Evening
Samuel Manning, 1875

We watch the banks glide past us as in a dream. With the drawing on of evening a glory of colour comes out in the light of the setting sun. Purple shadows are cast by the mountains. The reds and greys of sandstone, granite, and limestone cliffs blend exquisitely with the tawny yellow of the desert, the rich green of the banks, and the blue of the river, giving combinations and contrast of colour in which the artist revels. The cold grey twilight follows immediately upon sunset; but in a few minutes there is a marvellous change. The earth and sky are suffused with a delicate pink tinge, known as the after-glow. This is the most fairy-like and magical effect of colour I have ever seen. Swiss travellers are familiar with something like it in the rosy flush of the snowy Alps before sunrise and after sunset. The peculiarity in Egypt is that light and colour return after an interval of ashy grey, like the coming back of life to a corpse, and that it is not confined to a part of the landscape, but floods the whole. I have seen no explanation of this most beautiful phenomenon, and can only conjecture that it is connected with the reflection and refraction of the light of the setting sun from the sands of the Libyan Desert. Then comes on the night – and such a night! The stars shine with a lustrous brilliancy so intense that I have seen a distinct shadow cast by the planet Jupiter, whilst his satellites were easily visible through an ordinary opera-glass. Orion was an object of indescribable splendour. Under which of her aspects the moon was most beautiful I cannot say – whether the first slender thread of light, invisible in our denser atmosphere, or in her growing brightness, or in her full-orbed radiance.

Beni Hassan
E. A. Wallis Budge, 1906

167 miles from Cairo, on the east bank of the Nile, is remarkable for the large collection of fine historical tombs. The famous tombs ... are hewn out of the living rock, and are situated high up in the mountain ... each tomb ... consists of a hall for offerings and a shaft leading down to a corridor, which ends in a chamber containing the sarcophagus and the mummy.

Tombs of Beni Hassan
Dean Stanley, 1852

These tombs of Beni Hassan are amongst the oldest monuments of Egypt ... yet exhibiting, in the most lively manner, hunting, wrestling, and dancing – and curious as showing how gay and agile these ancient people could be, who in their architecture and graven sculptures appear so solemn and immoveable. Except a doubtful figure of Osiris in one, and a mummy on a barge in another, there is nothing of death or judgment here.

Fashionable Past
Howard Hopley, 1868

We passed the famous grottoes of Beni Hassan – a terrace of tombs high on the shelving Arabian ridge, overlooking a two miles' breadth of fertile land between mountain and river. In them, as in some vast gallery – hall after hall painted in graphic wall-picturings, and glowing in yet unfaded tints – you may wander at will, and study the familiar everyday life of men who walked the land before the days of Joseph. In these mansions ... mimic men and women are wrestling, fishing, ploughing and reaping, trapping birds, giving dinner parties, being flogged, *cutting their toe-nails*, treading the wine-press, dancing, playing the harp, weaving linen, playing at catch-ball, being shaved by the barber, *playing at draughts*. Verily there is nothing new under the sun! What say you to an elderly lady robed in a dress having *three flounces*? And there are stranger things than that! Yes; the old, old story of human life is there, told as in a picture-book. Though seen through a gap of four thousand years, your eye moistens over it still. Here are life's festive scenes and revels – the wine-cup and the garland; and here its scenes of sorrow – mourners are weeping over their dead. Nothing is lacking. And so, by a mystic sympathy – that touch of nature which links man with man – you reach out a hand across the ages, and feel the throbbings of a humanity kindred with your own.

We passed that long wooded shore where, under the eastern mountains, the ruins of the Roman Antinoe lie scattered. Young Antinous, friend of Hadrian, bathing in the Nile hard by, was drowned, and the emperor built this city in honour of his favourite. Palm-trees now grow in the forum, and flocks of goats browse over the ruined amphitheatre. Many a Christian martyr suffered at Antinoe in the fiery persecution under Diocletian. That mountain wall behind the city, and the rocky ravine to southward, are pierced thick with grottoes (ancient Egyptian tombs), bearing the marks of our early ancestors in the Faith. There has been a Laura of monks in that ravine; and rough stairways were cut on the crags to afford easier access from ledge to ledge. These haunts of the persecuted early Church, multiplied all through the land of Egypt, possess an interest of their own, and furnish an attestation to the truth of Christianity and to the full-heartedness of belief actuating its early followers, which is worthy of note.

Through the cool green reaches of Manfalout – past those picturesque terraces and gardens by the water side – along a range of flowery slopes swelling from the water's edge, and by crested minarets and fretted domes, we floated on to where the Arabian desert again closes in and mountain crags frown precipitous over the stream.

Ancient Coins
E. D. Clarke, 1801

Who would have believed that ancient *Roman* coins were still in circulation in any part of the world? Yet this is strictly true. We noticed *Roman* copper medals in *Cairo* given in exchange in the markets among the coins of the city, and valued at something less than our halfpenny. What is more remarkable, we obtained some of the large bronze medals of the *Ptolemies*, circulating at higher value, but in the same manner.

Buying a Cat
Jeremiah Lynch, 1889

On the return to the boat, we went a little out of the road in the desert to see the cat mummies and select some examples. Right in the sandy level plain, not more than four or five feet from the surface, were numerous uncovered circular holes, about eight feet in diameter. Each pit was full of the mummied bodies of cats, carefully swathed in bands and folds of linen. The pits were close together, and the sands around were strewn with the broken bones, mummies, and bandages of these animals. Not only cats and kittens rested peacefully in their last sleep, but dogs, jackals, and even pigs had found in their great sorrow dear ones who, with delicate hands and deep emotion, had carefully laid them in their linen shroud to their eternal rest. This solemn necropolis of those whose virtues and deeds have never yet been fully related was unearthed thirty years ago, and, by the vandal hands of the natives, is being fast emptied of its precious remains. I surmise that the value of these relics may not always be the same, and that the time approaches when a varied assortment of domestic animals with appendages complete and three thousand years old, will not be furnished for the small sum of one dollar. One funeral procession, on its way to the *Vittoria*, encountered the Bishop of Truro and several other clergymen bound for Beni-Hassan, astride of red-saddled donkeys. Though aware of the sacred character of our *cortège*, they did not arrest their rapid progress, but simply smiled and passed on.

Manfalut
E. A. Wallis Budge, 1906

220 miles from Cairo on the west bank of the Nile, occupying the site of an ancient Egyptian town. Leo Africanus says the town was destroyed by the Romans, and was rebuilt under Muhammadan rule ... Quite close on the east bank is Ma'abdah, in the hills of which was found a burial place full of mummies of crocodiles.

Recycling Mummies
Villiers Stuart, 1879

I enquired how it came that the mummies had all been disturbed and scattered about; they told me that a great number had been taken away by the Viceroy, but that the greatest destruction had been caused by a German speculator, who, about three years ago, came and employed men to bring out the mummies wholesale; he stripped off their bandages, and freighted a large barge with them as rags for the paper mills; the bones of men and reptiles alike he carried off to make superphosphate of, so that the poor Egyptians who took such pains to find a resting-place where they might never be disturbed, have been applied as manure to the ground, and will be eaten in the shape of bread grown from this strangely compounded superphosphate. Such is life and such is death!

They told me also that many of the human mummies so abstracted had their faces and feet gilded thickly, others merely had the mummy cloth that covered their faces painted with their likenesses. The wonder is how this strange mausoleum was ever discovered amid the wild naked peaks of the Egyptian Sierra. While I was resting, I offered the guides a dollar if they would re-enter the caverns, and bring me out another crocodile. They disappeared into the bowels of the earth, and after the lapse of half an hour we heard them below, and then there slowly arose through the fissure the grisly apparition of a human mummy stripped of its bandages and therefore naked, but quite perfect, mounting bolt upright from the depths beneath, as if through the trap-door of a theatre, without any visible motive power. A ghastly spectacle, strangely at discord with the bright sunshine. How many centuries had elapsed since the sun last shone upon that form?

When I had sufficiently recovered, we packed the mummies we had collected upon our donkeys. One of the Arabs carried the large crocodile at right angles across his saddle-peak. I wish I could have had the group photographed: the turbaned rider – the shaggy little beast he bestrode, and the grim reptile that shared his saddle – a four-footed Lazarus come forth from the grave it had occupied for at least twenty-five centuries. One of the Arabs made a bundle of mummy legs and arms, threw them over his shoulders, and marched on ahead.

We thus proceeded along the mountain plateau for several miles till we reached a steep ravine, down which we scrambled into the plain below, and were presently received on board with much curiosity as to the adventures we had undergone and the trophies we had brought back.

The Crocodile Pits
Thomas Legh, 1816

[At Maahbeh, seven miles from the river beyond the eastern mountains, are the crocodile pits which caused such problems to travellers. Thomas Legh recorded his experience at length. A guide with a torch led the way, and they crept through a tunnel at the bottom of the pit. They came out into a large chamber where there were mummies of crocodiles and a great number of bats. After advancing through low galleries for more than an hour, their way was interrupted by a ditch. They leapt over it and then crawled along a low passage. It was dark and hot and Legh began to find breathing extremely difficult.]

My head began to ache most violently, and I had a most distressing sensation of fullness about the heart. We felt we had gone too far, and yet were almost deprived of the power to return. At this moment the torch of the first Arab went out; I was close to him and saw him fall on his side; he uttered a groan; his legs were strongly convulsed, and I heard a rattling noise in his throat – he was dead. The Arab behind me, seeing the torch of his companion extinguished, and conceiving he had stumbled, passed me, advanced to his assistance, and stooped. I observed him appear faint, totter and fall in a moment: he also was dead. The third Arab came forward, and made an effort to approach the bodies, but stopped short. We looked at each other in silent horror. The danger increased every instant; our torches burned faintly; our knees tottered under us, and we felt our strength nearly gone. There was no time to be lost.

[Legh, Smelt and their guide turned and fled, leaving the third Arab behind. They managed to find their way back to the open air. It was excessively hot but their sailors were waiting there with water, and, unfolding their turbans 'and slinging them round our bodies drew us up to the top of the pit.' They dare not admit the disaster which had occurred and pretended the Arabs were following after. They hurried back to the boat on the Nile and escaped the immediate wrath of the local people, although they reported the matter officially soon after.]

The Crocodile Pits
William C. Prime, 1855

[Despite having read Legh's account, William C. Prime, with the magnetic draw of a storeful of mummy crocodiles, was determined to go into the crocodile pits in 1855. On their way he and his friend, Trumbull, met two English gentlemen and their dragoman and they joined forces. Following the same route as Legh, they reached the large cavern, from which a cloud of bats met them, 'dashing into my face, wounding my forehead and cheeks, clinging by scores to my hair and beard, like so many thousand devils disputing the entrance to hell'.

When the others clambered out into the cavern and relit their candles they found Prime 'begrimmed with dirt, and seven bats (they counted them) hanging on my beard, with a perfect network and Medusa-coil of them in my hair.' The air in the cavern was 'foul, vile, terrible', filled with ammonia from the bat droppings. The danger was now that with many openings from the cavern, they would not choose the right one through which to return. When they found the onward passage, the air was even worse. 'The lungs operated freely, but took no refreshment from it, while the heat was awful, and perspiration rolled down our faces and bodies, soaking our clothes and making mud on our features and hands, with the fine dust that filled the atmosphere.' Prime forced his large frame on through the narrowing passage and eventually out into a more open space (where an earlier French expedition had carved their names).]

The walls were covered with a jet black substance, like the purest lamp black, which the point of a knife would scratch off, exposing the white rock. Numerous stalactites hung from the ceiling, all jet black, and some grotesque stalagmites at the sides of the passage startled me at first with the idea that they were sculptures. This black sooty matter I can not account for unless it be the exhalations in ancient times from the crocodiles which were laid here, for we were at last in the depository.

The floor was covered with crocodile bones and mummy cloths. A spark of fire falling into them would have made this a veritable hell. As this idea was suggested, my English friends, whose experience in the narrow hole had been sufficiently alarming, vanished out of sight. They fairly ran. Having seen the mummies, and seized a few small ones in their hands, they hastened out, and left me with Abdallah and my two guides. Advancing over the mummies and up the hill which they formed, I found that I was in one of a number of large chambers, of the depth of which it was of course impossible to get any idea, as they were piled full of mummied crocodiles to the very ceiling. There was no means of estimating the number of them. When I say there were thousands on thousands of them, I shall not be thought to exaggerate after I describe the manner in which they were packed and laid in.

Climbing to the top of the hill, and extinguishing all lights but one, which I made Abdallah hold very carefully, I began to throw down the top of the pile to ascertain of what it was composed, and at length I made an opening between the mummies and the ceiling, through which I could go on further, descending a sort of hill of these dead animals, such as I had come up. In this way I progressed some distance, in a gallery or chamber that was not less than twenty feet wide and probably twenty or thirty feet deep.

The crocodiles were laid in regular layers, head to tail and tail to head. First on the floor was a layer of large crocodiles, side by side, each one carefully mummied and wrapped up in cloths. Then smaller ones were laid between the tails and filling up the hollows between these. Then, and most curious of all, the remaining interstices were packed full of young crocodiles, measuring with remarkable uniformity about thirteen inches in length, each one stretched out between two slips of palm-leaf stem, which were bound to its sides like splints, and then wrapped from head to foot in a strip of cloth, wound around, commencing at the tail and fastened at the head. These small ones were made up in bundles, usually of eight, and packed in closely wherever they could be stowed. I brought out more than a hundred of them, of which my friends in Egypt seized on the most as curiosities, but I succeeded in getting some twenty or thirty of them to America with me.

This layer completed, a layer of palm branches was carefully laid over it, spread thick and smooth, and then a second and precisely similar layer of crocodiles was made, and another of palm branches, and thus continued to the ceiling. These palm branches, stems, and mummies like here in precisely the state they were in two thousand years ago. No leaf of the palm had decayed. There could have been no moisture from the mummies whatever – or if any it had no effect on the palm branches.

Among these crocodiles I found the mummies of many men.

Sitting down on the hill, by the dim candle light, I overhauled gods and men with sacrilegious hand. It was a strange, wild, and awful scene. Among all the pictures that my memory has treasured of wandering life, I have none so fearful and thrilling as this. It was hell – a still, silent, cold hell. All these bodies lay in rows, in close packages, like so many souls damned to eternal silence and sorrow in this prison. Five bodies of men that I drew out of the mass lay before me, and cursed me with their hideous stillness and inaction. I dared them to tell me in words the reproaches of which their silent forms were so liberal; reproaches for penetrating their abode and disturbing the repose of twenty or forty centuries.

These were of the poorest and most common sort, destitute of any box, wound in coarse cloth and laid in the grave with the beasts that were sacred to their god. One I found afterward in a thin plain box, but it contained no indication of its period, and bore no mark of its owner's name or position, much to my disappointment.

'Let us go further,' I said to the guides, at length.

'There is no further.'

[Prime eventually 'crawled out as I had crawled in' and 'never saw light so clear and beautiful as was the daylight that fell in the entrance to the cavern.' Returning to the boat, he plunged immediately into the river, for 'until this was accomplished, it was useless to hope to be recognized ... my complexion was dead crocodile, my odour was dead crocodile, my clothes were dead crocodile ... I was but little removed from being a dead crocodile myself.']

Timseach! Timseach!
Eliot Warburton, 1845

The first time a man fires at a crocodile is an epoch in his life. We had only now arrived in the waters where they abound, for it is a curious fact that none are ever seen below Mineyeh, though Herotodus speaks of them as fighting with the dolphins at the mouths of the Nile. A prize had been offered for the first man who detected a crocodile, and the crew had now been for two days on the alert in search of them. Buoyed up with the expectation of such game, we had latterly reserved our fire for them exclusively, and the wild duck and turtle; nay, even the vulture and the eagle had swept past, or soared above us in security.

At length, the cry of 'Timseach, timseach!' was heard from half a dozen claimants of the proffered prize, and half a dozen black fingers were eagerly pointed to a spit of sand, on which were strewn apparently some logs of trees. It was a Covey of Crocodiles! Hastily and silently the boat was run in shore. R. was ill, so I had the enterprise to myself, and clambered up the steep bank with a quicker pulse than when I first levelled a rifle at a Highland deer. My intended victims might have prided themselves on their superior nonchalance; and, indeed, as I approached them, there seemed to be a sneer on their ghastly mouths and winking eyes. Slowly they rose, one after the other, and waddled to the water, all but one, the most gallant or most gorged of the party. He lay still until I was within a hundred yards of them; then, slowly rising on his fin-like legs, he lumbered towards the river, looking askance at me with an expression of countenance that seemed to say, 'He can do me no harm; however, I may as well have a swim.' I took aim at the throat of the supercilious brute, and, as soon as my hand steadied, the very pulsation of my finger pulled the trigger. Bang! went the gun; whizz! flew the bullet; and my excited ear could catch the *thud* with which it plunged into the scaly leather of his neck. His waddle became a plunge, the waves closed over him, and the sun shone on the calm water, as I reached the brink of the shore, that was still indented by the waving of his gigantic tail. But there is blood upon the water, and he rises for a moment to the surface. 'A hundred piastres for the timseach,' I exclaimed, and half a dozen Arabs plunged into the stream. There! he rises again, and the Blacks dash at him as if he hadn't a tooth in his head. Now he is gone, the waters close over him, and I never saw him since.

7

Asyut to Luxor

Introduction

Now, 249½ miles from Cairo, the travellers reached Asyut (or Siout or Assiout) and its barrage, which was described in 1984 by William Golding. Here Sir Gaston Maspero was to enjoy a calèche ride in the town and G. W. Steevens, with those Cook's passengers who had recovered from Pharaoh's revenge, looked on to the minarets.

On to Girgeh and Edward Lear writing to his sister Ann in 1854. Then Kena (or Qena), near the temple of Dendera and the villages of William Golding's crew. There is a celebration for Eliot Warburton's crew and entertainment for Gustave Flaubert, Sir Gaston Maspero and the Lord Curzon.

At last, at Abydos we come to the first of the great temples. Strabo introduces it in 24 BC and Douglas Sladen, in 1908, describes this very special place. William Jarvie picnics there in 1904 and a few years later the French traveller Pierre Loti was horrified by the tourists feasting in the temple, and by their very existence. Edward Lear felt unsympathetic to other tourists there in 1867.

Next comes Nag Hammadi, where many of the boats from Luxor moor today. From here you visit Dendera, as Frederick Henniker did in 1822, when donkeys were already easily available for tourists. Sir Gaston Maspero as Director of Antiquities must have visited Dendera often; he describes it in 1902.

We end this stretch of the Nile journey with Miss Riggs, a lady who travelled with Thomas Cook himself on the very first excursion up the Nile and to the Holy Land in 1868–9.

Asyut
E. A. Wallis Budge, 1906

249½ miles from Cairo. The capital of the province of the same name; and the seat of the Inspector-General of Upper Egypt ... the Greeks called the city Lycopolis, or 'wolfcity', probably because the jackal-headed Anubis was worshipped here. Asyut is a large city with spacious bazaars and fine mosques; it is famous for its red pottery and its market, held every Saturday, to which wares from Arabia and Upper Egypt are brought.

The Asyut Dam is what is called an open Barrage, and consists of 111 bays or openings ... each bay is provided with regulating gates. The total length of the work is 2,691 feet, and a lock has been built on the west bank, large enough to pass the largest tourist boat plying on the river.

The Barrage at Asyut
William Golding, 1984

We went on deck and waited for the barrage at Asyut to come in sight. It was impressive. It is essentially a road stretching across the river with one hundred sluice gates ranged side by side below it. At one end there is a kind of travelling crane made of what looks like gigantic meccano. This machine is the size of a four-storey house, the bottom storey of which straddles the road, while leaving a hole in itself big enough for any truck to pass. The whole huge contraption travels on railway lines set on either side of the road and running from one end of the barrage to the other. So the crane can move from sluice to sluice and adjust each of the hundred massive gates as required. As we approached it was plain that the river had not yet been ponded for the replenishment of the irrigation system for all the gates were letting plenty of water foam through. On the righthand side of the barrage as we faced it, were lock gates with trams and sandals waiting for them to open. Getting through into that lock, and getting out of it waterwards was a slow business. The in-between business was terribly slow. That whole operation took us about three hours. 'He who rides the Nile must have sails woven of patience.' The word that proverb uses for 'Nile' means 'Sea' so perhaps the whole thing is mock-heroic. How can you tell, in a language you don't know?

Once clear of the lock we went roaring up the river at our top and smoky speed and were chased at once by a police launch. I had just the same nervous reaction you feel, however virtuous your conduct, if the police stop your car. But Alaa's letter from the Chief of Police was now working its magic more potently the further we got away from Cairo. The police launch merely wanted to know if we required anything. Shasli, never missing an opportunity, got water and fuel with a quick tie-up at the police station.

The Nile is notably broader above Asyut. Most rivers get a bit wider as they approach the sea, since tributaries increase their flow. But the Nile has no tributary to join it anywhere north of Khartoum. So the flow, what with more than a thousand miles of evaporation and irrigation, decreases all the way to the Delta. To say thus is to simplify a process that is vastly complex and, be it said, not yet fully understood by the people who study the water or administer its distribution.

A Cab Drive in Siout
Sir Gaston Maspero, 1899

The first thing we notice in getting alongside are the cabs prowling about round the landing-places. They are the little Parisian victorias with movable hood, leathern apron, and flap-seat at the back, two lean horses, and a numbered driver.*

Donkey-boys still abound, pushing and shouting, but they no longer assume the haughty insolence of a former day: they feel that their reign is ending, and they are humble in the hope of carrying off a customer despite the competition. But usually nothing comes of their efforts at civility. A cab is called, four people crowd into it, holding on as best they can, and the equipage sets out by the grace of God. At first you drive by the river along the towing-path between the edge of a field of ragged dourah and the sloping embankment. There is a prospect of a fall of 6 or 9 feet at every jerk made by the horses, and for ten minutes the carriage rolls, pitches, jumps over the irrigation posts and trenches, has a narrow escape of losing a back wheel, heels over, is about to upset, when by the grace of the unknown saint who presides over the safety of cabs in Egypt, it escapes for that time. After five or six minutes of this preliminary exercise we turn to the left and proceed towards the town at a trot through the boatmen's quarter, a row of houses in process of building, two or three bacals piled up with preserves, petroleum, and cotton goods, a *Sudanese* bar dripping with raki and adulterated spirits, painted, unveiled women in loud-coloured garments, an open-air cookshop where stews of doubtful appearance simmer with a seasoning of dust. Next comes an empty space, the haunt of wandering dogs and hens, then a wealthy suburb with blue, pink, apple-green, or yellow villas inhabited chiefly by Copts, gardens, cafés, restaurants, hotels with French, Greek, or Italian names, and at last the railway. Two goods trains are manoeuvring on a siding by a caravan of camels loaded with sugar-canes, and the 5.55 train for Minieh whistles loudly as it departs.

Beyond there are more villas, more restaurants, more hotels, and of a sudden we come on the entry to Old Siout, disfigured by European embellishments. One side of the canal is dry, the gateway of the Moudirieh has been pulled down to make way for the traffic, but the courtyard remains as before, and the town has changed very little. The sloping street that fits on, as it were, to the back of the Moudirieh is exactly as I knew it in 1881, and if the alleys to the left in the direction of the hill have been widened, the new buildings are in the usual Arab style and do not clash with the old ones.

On Tour with Cook's
G. W. Steevens, 1898

The Cook's tourist steamer Rameses the Great had pulled up at Bedrechein, and our pilgrimage had begun. There were exactly eighty of us – English, French, Germans, Belgians, South Africans, Americans, and Australians, from the uttermost ends of the earth. There were many elderly men, a great host of young women, five men under thirty, and three children under ten. Our mood was devotional. We regarded the dragoman with respect, and the great tomb of Thi with awe. Our trusty cameras were slung at our backs: our diaries lay in our cabins with our stylographs at half-cock beside them: the two hours since we left Cairo had been given to the diligent study of a book full of queer

---

* These cabs, called calèches, are still widely used today.

pictures of circles and hieroglyphic ducks and hares couchant, with which Mr Cook had presented each of us on leaving. And now we were about to see all these things. Up and down the long dining-tables every face was set with high purpose.

Already Mohammed* was on the sandy beach, selecting donkeys. Out we streamed after him into a sea of waving brown arms and legs surging furiously over the little island of beasts. Some of the elder ladies mounted chairs, and were borne off, palanquin fashion, on the shoulders of four boatmen. The rest climbed with delicious quavers on to donkeys, the donkey-boys screamed, and yelled, and whacked, and we were off.

By now we had passed under a grove of dusty palms, over the railway embankment, threaded the mud-walled alleys of the village, and were out, a straggling column a couple of miles long, among fields of young clover and springing corn. We had not waited to hear Mohammed lecture on the great statue of Rameses. We came on it suddenly among palm trees; but it has tumbled down and got broken, and hieroglyphics are crawling all over it.

The party reaches its tomb. The dragoman, Mohammed, catches up, dismounts with dignity and orders the doors of the tomb to be thrown open.

Except for the sheer delight and impertinence of being in the tomb of somebody else very much older than yourself, I am not sure there is very much in it after all. It is half-a-dozen chambers hewn in the rock which underlies the desert sand, and our company quite fills it up. There are some rudimentary carvings on the wall still splashed with faint red and yellow, and there is a statue of the entombed himself – an angular person of a brick-red colour attired in what Mohammed tactfully calls a kilt.

The tourists' days were regulated much as they are today, although their starting times seem to have been later.

The keynote of the Nile life is peace; it is an existence placid, regular, reposeful. There is just enough variety in it to keep your mind awake, and just enough sameness to keep it off the stretch. There is just enough excursioning ashore to persuade you that you are not lazy, and just enough lazing aboard to assure you that you are enjoying rest. You pick up letters on the way, enough to remind you that you are of the world, and to convince you blessedly that for the moment you are not in it. A vision of half-barbarous life passes before you all day, and you survey it in the intervals of French cooking. You are not to worry, not to plan, not to arrange about anything; you are just to sit easy and be happy.

You come up in the morning, and there, steel-blue in the sun, shines the benevolent Nile. You forget how many days you have been looking at it; you could look at this miracle for ever. Just now we are under a bank of low, brown cliff, the frontier of the desert. On the other side is a flat green plain – so flat that you can see no end to it, though the transparent blue film of another distant line of hills reminds you that on that side also the desert presses. Over the green rim rise groves of palms, the silhouette of a man with a mattock, of a woman striding erect beneath her water-jar, of a fat, turbaned sheikh on a donkey. Now we are swinging across from under the bluffs past an eyot of yellow sand towards the fertile side; already the navigable channel is narrow

* Cook's dragoman.

and devious, even at this season, and the long-gowned pilot on the bridge seldom has his hand off the wheel. Now the solitary palms thicken into groves with a clump or two of denser acacias: here is a village. Mud huts pierced by loop-hole windows, rush firewood stacked on the roofs, black veils carrying water, young boys, half blue shirt, half brown nakedness, paddling in the river. Rural Egypt at Kodak range – and you sitting in a long chair to look at it.

Then those of us that are feeling very well – and the proportion rises day by day – pound on up to the very top of the rocks, and look down. Below us in the haze basks Assiout, with its minarets. At our very feet, on the edge of the belt of cultivation, is another city – a city of mud walls, and whitewash, and domes. It seems as large as Assiout, but quite empty – only it is not, for it is a thickly-peopled cemetery. On our right is the valley of the Nile – a steely thread through broad acres of glowing, living green. This is already the second crop of clover since the flood reached its heights in September: three weeks back it was just sprouting; to-day it covers the earth like a carpet. And leftward and behind us is the desert, the cruel, haunting, yellow desert, with camel-trains trailing over it like ants. In that one view you see all Egypt – the river, the life of the valley, and the death of the desert; the city of the living in the one, the city of the dead with its foot on the threshold of the other.

Then back to our welcoming steamer. Cast off, and then more Nile, more Egypt daily more familiar, daily more fascinating. We are in the region of sugar-refineries now; for every minaret there rises a tall stack vomiting black smoke. But close beside them was a grove of drooping palms and a dome and minaret – black, too, but clear black tracery against the blazing gold of sunset. The gold faded, and the white moon lit to silver; the tender blue curtain of darkness brooded down over the floating blue Nile; the minarets suddenly dwindled into slender columns of fire, with the hanging lanterns of Ramadan. Close at their side the chimneys belched and belched, griming the moonlight. It was yet another paradox of Egypt – the old and the new.

Girgeh
Karl Baedeker, 1929

[It was from Girgeh that travellers started for Abydos.]

341½ miles from Cairo. A district capital at which a large market is held on Tuesdays. Many of the houses are built of burnt brick and decorated with glazed tiles. There are numerous mosques. Outside the town lies a Roman Catholic monastery (presided over by a Brother of the Holy Sepulchre), which is one of the oldest in Egypt.

Abydos
Strabo, 24 BC

Above Ptolemais [now El-Manshah] lies Abydos the site of the Memnonium, and wonderful palace of stone, built in the manner of the Labyrinth, only somewhat less elaborate in its complexity. Below the Memnonium is a spring, reached by passages with low vaults, consisting of a single stone and remarkable for their extent and mode of construction. This spring is connected with the Nile by a canal, which flows through a grove of Egyptian thorn-acacias, sacred to Apollo. Abydos seems once to have been a large city, second only to Thebes, but now it is a small place.

The Love of Abydos
Douglas Sladen, 1908

[Twice we asked our guides in 1990, 'If you could choose one temple to visit as your last wish, which would it be?' Both times they answered Abydos.]

When we left the convent we rode past the fortress and a sandy waste of half-buried, mud-brick tombs and houses of the Middle and New Empires, to the Temple of Rameses II, which has, unfortunately, had the upper parts of its walls and its roofs destroyed. It has, as my Cincinnati friend observed, been scalped, or it would be one of the finest temples in Egypt, for its sculptures and paintings are very fresh and beautiful, and the stones and marbles employed in its construction are more precious than those employed elsewhere by the Pharaohs.

It was clear that our dragoman loved Abydos better than any other place he took us to. He bubbled over with information and high spirits. This is the sort of dialogue to which he treated us. He clapped his hands and began: 'This way, this way, ladies, see procession round the walls – men carrying can-shaped vessels of beer – Mohammed knows the numerals – 106 barrels. Each column have a figure of Osiris bearing the name of Rameses the Great.'

While I was examining the lovely black granite door-jambs, he began to spell out the cartouches in the way he had: 'Rameses beloved of Amen – the great son of Ptah elected by Ra – the son of the sun – Amen beloved of Ra.'

And while I was examining the gay colours on the smooth, fine limestone he bubbled on: 'Ramese beloved of Amen.'

The colours and the paintings were delightful, and there were such pretty people in the processions. I liked everything about this sumptuous temple. While I was photographing the place where the minor Abydos tablet, now in the British Museum, was cut off, in the way they had in the good old days when finding was keeping and anybody who liked could help himself to ancient monuments, Mohammed began again.

'Ladies, ladies and gentlemen, here is Osiris in the Hades accompanied by Isis, Nephetes, and Amnte – one, two, three – receiving the homage. The homage is of a rather practical kind.'

'I, your son Seti the First, am burning incense before you, and I pray you to give me a good Nile.' The figure of Seti was gloriously dignified and beautiful. Mohammed was witheringly sarcastic to a lady who ventured to suggest that Seti's hands were in rather a strained position. 'Madam – hands not wrong – if artist makes any mistakes Seti will cut his head off.'

A Picnic Lunch
William Jarvie, 1904

22 January

After visiting the second temple we went back [to Abydos] and in the Hypostile Hall found our dragoman had arranged a most sumptuous repast, which he had brought from the 'Sesostris'.* He had one of our tablecloths spread upon a table, around which were our chairs. The first course was sardines, olives, bread and butter; second, eggs; third, cold tongue and ham; fourth, chicken and salad; fifth, pudding; sixth, oranges, bananas, dates and figs; seventh, coffee. With this were various condiments, such as Cross and Blackwell's mustard pickles, chutney, etc., wine for Mrs. Thayer and myself, Poland water and vichy celeste for James and Maggie. A fine spread, was it not?

We made quite a caravan coming back, for in addition to our four, there were our dragoman, our head waiter and three of the crew. We had also a dashing Egyptian cavalryman mounted on a superb horse. He had been on duty at the temple and seemed to take a fancy to us, for he rode with us all the way back to Belianeh, and occasionally would clear the way of camels, which he sometimes thought were taking up too much of the road and might squeeze us as we passed.

Luncheon with Osiris
Pierre Loti, 1910

But what is the noise in this sanctuary? It seems to be full of people. There, sure enough, beyond the second row of columns, is quite a little crowd talking loudly in English. I fancy that I can hear the clinking of glasses and the tapping of knives and forks.

Oh! poor, poor temple, to what strange uses are you come ... This excess of grotesqueness in profanation is more insulting surely than to be sacked by barbarians! Behold the table set for some thirty guests, and the guests themselves – of both sexes – merry and lighthearted, belong to that special type of humanity which patronises Thomas Cook & Son (Egypt Ltd.). They wear cork helmets, and the classic green spectacles; drink whisky and soda, and eat voraciously sandwiches and other viands out of greasy paper, which now litters the floor. And the women! Heavens! what scarecrows they are! And this kind of thing, so the black-robed Bedouin guards inform us, is repeated every day so long as the season lasts. A luncheon in the temple of Osiris is part of the programme of pleasure trips. Each day at noon a new band arrives, on heedless and unfortunate donkeys.

The tables and the crockery remain, of course, in the old temple! Let us escape quickly, if possible before the sight shall have become graven on our memory.

But alas! even when we are outside, alone again on the expanse of dazzling sands, we can no longer take things seriously. Abydos and the desert have

* 8½ miles!

ceased to exist. The faces of those women remain to haunt us, their faces and their hats, and those looks which they vouchsafed us from over their solar spectacles ... The ugliness associated with the name of Cook was once explained to me in this wise, and the explanation at first sight seemed satisfactory: 'The United Kingdom, justifiably jealous of the beauty of its daughters, submits them to a jury when they reach the age of puberty; and those that are classed as too ugly to reproduce their kind are accorded an unlimited account at Thomas Cook & Sons, and thus vowed to a course of perpetual travel, which leaves them no time to think of certain trifles incidental to life.' The explanation, as I say, seduced me for the time being. But a more attentive examination of the bands that infest the valley of the Nile enables me to aver that all these good English ladies are of an age notoriously canonical: and the catastrophe of procreation, therefore, supposing that such an accident could ever have happened to them, must date back to a time long anterior to their enrolment. And I remain perplexed!

To Ann Lear
Edward Lear, 1854

17 January. 10 miles from Haon on the Nile.

My dear Ann

It almost seems absurd to begin another letter to you so soon, seeing I sent one yesterday from Girgeh, but as we are now only 40 miles from Khenneh, (the next post town,) & as I promised to write at every opportunity, I will not lose a single one, although you may possibly get 2 or 3 of my notes all in a lump.

I did not stay [above] half an hour at Girgeh yesterday – only just to put your letter into the post people's care; – I hope they [the letters] go safely! Girgeh, a large town, is a tumbly down place, & so dusty!! – but I shall see it better in returning; there seem some pretty mosques in it, & as I sailed away, we thought it looked well reflected in the water. But 12 miles beyond, a town called Belliannh is charming! such exquisite palms, – such curious towers, built for pigeons!! – I hope to draw it on my return.

I think the sunset last night was the most astonishingly beautiful I ever saw; – it is not so much *the sunset* itself, – as the sun here is so very bright; – but the half or ¾ of an hour afterwards, which is so amazing. The sky was all in broad stripes of lilac, green, rose, & amber, & it is impossible to describe the effect of this, which only lasts a short time. Before the moon rises – (which here looks *round* like a ball, & not flat like a plate) all the sky become light, & when it comes above the mountains, I see to read or draw, just the same as by day! This morning I have had a delicious walk – through never ending corn fields; at times the ground was all blue & grey with CLOUDS of pigeons; & the most beautiful little plovers & kingfishers hop just before my feet. But what pleased me very much, was to find a real vulgar old English *toad*! waddling in the field! – as for crocodiles, none have been seen yet; of course you know, that *crocodiles* are not dangerous like *alligators*; the crocodile is very timid, & is only to be seen basking on sand islands at a distance. The broad-bean fields are a great pleasure to me now; they are all in full bloom; – the Arab name for beans is Fool, – & at first the sailors used to puzzle me very much when they pointed to the fields & said – 'fool! fool!'

Nag Hammadi
Karl Baedeker, 1929

373 miles from Cairo. A district capital with a large sugar factory. The railway crosses the Nile here by a large iron bridge, (1362 feet long).

Donkeys to Dendera
Frederick Henniker, 1822

Donkeys and saddles *ready made* are always forthcoming for an 'Engilitz'. In a few minutes we were in sight of the temple, and use our outmost exertions to reach it. My obstinate animal has been there often enough, and now runs into a corn field, where I leave him and trust to my own legs . . .

On a flat plain of beautiful verdure rises a small dark mound, covered with ruins, in the centre of which appears the celebrated temple of Dendera. On nearer approach, the surrounding fragments, which had given the principal features of the picturesque, vanish into the mud walls of an Arab village.

Dendera has been so often described in large square books that to repeat what has already been said would be wearisome to us both . . . but [on arrival at the Portico] I am lost in admiration, even though the concomitant filthy hill is nearly on a level with the top of the portal – . . . the beauties of Egyptian architecture are here in full perfection.

Approaching Denderah
Sir Gaston Maspero, 1902

The ordinary way of reaching Denderah is so devious that, if pressed for time, it is better to avoid it. So we go down among the sugar-canes to find a short cut, and proceed in Indian file along the irrigation trenches as best we can. The donkey-boys have their work cut out for them in preventing their beasts from slipping in the mud or stumbling over the fallen canes. The harvest began a fortnight ago, to the benefit of the sugar refineries of Nag-Hammadi. Vast spaces are already cleared. In spite of the approaching darkness two or three gangs of labourers were still at work cutting down the canes and tying them on to the growling camels. But the day's task is over almost everywhere, and the reapers are wending homewards chattering as they go. As we meet them, they suspend their conversation and assail us with the usual request for bakhshîsch, but in so good-humoured a tone that it is almost a friendly greeting.

We have already left them far behind when we still hear the women's laugh and the shrill tones of the children. The ground soon rises, and the sebakh diggers have dug into it so terribly, that it is necessary to be very careful not to fall into some hole. Rows of ruined walls show the positions of the ancient streets and mark on the ground the grouping of the buildings: here the ruins of a vaulted house, there a half-overturned basilica, its pillars of grey stone, its architraves broken, its mortar in black basalt, the whole submerged in incredible masses of broken glass and reddish potsherds. On the top of the eminence is a thick, heavy gate, the sides cut about and covered with mediocre hieroglyphics in praise of the Emperor Domitian and of the Antonines. We enter, and suddenly at the end of a kind of dusty avenue see a dozen yards above us in the air an army of large, calm, smiling faces sheltered by a stiff, hard cornice. It is as if the temple was starting from the ground to go to meet the visitor.

Mariette and his successors tried to disengage it completely, but they only succeeded in emptying the interior, and the exterior remained buried half-way up. The descent was made by a modern staircase, instead of entering on the flat through the ancient gateway. The banisters and the steps were worn away; it seemed as if we were going down into a cellar. But for some years now the rubbish which disgraced the façade has been cleared away, and entrance is gained just under the portico.

The old staircase is destroyed, and the sort of iron ladder that replaces it is disquietingly fragile, but the view is one of the most extensive in Egypt. In the distance the grand yet simple lines of the hills extend in somewhat monotonous fashion. The Nile, its shining surface dotted with white sails, flows among the trees. The country stretches green and pleasant, with tufts of acacias and palms scattered about it. Here and there a village on a hill stands out grey amid the greenness. The evening mists begin to be visible above the houses. The wind brings in gusts the scent of flowering beans, and so penetrating a sweetness breathes from everything that we can do nothing but look vaguely at what is before us in a sort of voluptuous languor. The sun has just gone down; at the edge of the horizon a ripple of flame and liquid gold marks its course and lends colour to the growing twilight. The tones change and follow each other unceasingly, become lighter, melt into each other, graduate from flaming red to purple, amethyst, golden yellow, soft pink, faded green, pale blue. For three-quarters of an hour there is a play of colour of inexhaustible strength and richness; then as darkness gains on the world the tints grow confused and melt away, the reflections vanish, the air thickens, the sky becomes a uniform dark blue. We must break the charm and go down.

The temple is undoubtedly beautiful in the daytime when the sun shines on it and brings out all the details. But to see it as it used to be, and to recapture something of the emotions it roused in the souls of the faithful, it should be visited at night. The guards have lighted their lantern, but its feeble glimmer by contrast rather emphasises than dissipates the darkness in which we move. It seems as if the air has hardened and refuses to take the light. The building seems to have disappeared. Here and there a door-post, the shaft or the base of a column, a panel of a wall with its decoration of figures only half visible, rises and floats before our eyes for a moment, then suddenly fades away and is reabsorbed in the darkness. A flight of bats envelops us in a circle of short, rapid cries, the pattering of swift claws resounds at our approach, the echoes awake with a hollow noise which does not seem to coincide with our footsteps. A kind of vague presence seems to hover in the gloom, and to pursue us from chamber to chamber. Should we be really greatly astonished if at the turn of a corridor we met a priest come back to his post after centuries of absence, or if the sound of distant timbrels which announced the theophanies of the goddess began to vibrate in the depths of the sanctuary? In the open air and under the starry vault of heaven the feeling of religious awe remains with us. Silently and almost fearfully we take the road to the river. When, at the end of the avenue, we turned round for a last look, the grand heads of Hathor seemed to become alive, and reply with kindliness to our farewell greeting. A moonbeam lit a spark of life in their eyes, and accentuated on their lips the melancholy smile that gives the Egyptian statues a mysterious attraction.

Standstill
Gustave Flaubert, 1849

... Every time I visited a monument I had my photographic apparatus carried along and took with me one of my sailors, Hadji Ismael, an extremely handsome Nubian, whom I had climb up on the ruins which I wanted to photograph. In this way I was always able to include a uniform scale of proportions. The great difficulty was to get Hadji Ismael to stand perfectly motionless while I performed my operations; and I finally succeeded by means of a trick whose success will convey the depth of naïveté of these poor Arabs. I told him that the brass tube of the lens jutting from the camera was a cannon, which would vomit a hail of shot if he had the misfortune to move – a story which immobilized him completely, as can be seen from my plates.

The day I was returning from Dendera I overheard the following conversation between him and Raïs Ibrahim – a curious account of a photographic expedition:

'Well, Hadji Ismael, what news?' asked the *raïs* as we boarded the *cange*.

'None,' the sailor answered. 'The Father of Thinness ('Abu Muknaf,' as I was always called by my crew) ordered me to climb up on a column that bore the huge face of an idol; he wrapped his head in the black veil, he turned his yellow cannon towards me, then he cried: "Do not move!" The cannon looked at me with its little shining eye, but I kept very still, and it did not kill me.'

'God is the greatest,' said Raïs Ibrahim, sententiously.

'And our Lord Mohammed is his prophet,' replied Hadji.

Keneh
E. A. Wallis Budge, 1906

405½ miles from Cairo, on the east bank of the river, is the capital of the province of the same name. The city is famous for its dates, and for the trade which it carries on with the Arabian peninsula, and for its manufactories of the drinking bottle called 'Kullah', commonly pronounced 'gullah'. A short distance from the river on the west bank, a little to the north of the village of Denderah, stands the Temple of Denderah.

At the Bend of the River
William Golding, 1984

Akhmet the engineer came rushing up on deck. He was, I thought, about to announce some catastrophe. But he reached into the wheelhouse and sounded our siren. I did not grasp the significance of this and wondered what signal it was. Perhaps those who ride the sea of the Nile have the equivalent of 'get out of my way because I can't get out of yours'? But why the engineer?

Alaa explained in due course. Akhmet has been passing 'his' village and was letting them know he would be home soon. Then, with the suburbs of Qena stretching along the bank on our left Shasli did the same thing only more prolonged, a blast. The two others, Saïd and Faroz, were up on the fo'c'sle staring ahead at the Theban Hills which sheltered Faroz's village and suggested the long way up to Saïd's. Saïd came back to the centre cabin. Before he went below I asked him if he was feeling better. Oh yes, he said, he was nearer home. Shasli slowed then manoeuvred us against some broad steps above which there were trees with fairy lights and loudspeakers and people looking down curiously at our little boat; for this was a place where four-decker tourist boats were accustomed to tie up. It was a park and religious music was being broadcast from all the loudspeakers in the trees. Shasli was ashore, up the steps and out of sight before I could ask him anything.

The engine, which had been idling, now stopped. Faroz and Akhmet appeared in bathing trunks. Before my startled eyes they waded from the steps into the soup, then swam round our stern. I looked to see them collapse, die at once, or bloat and shrivel, or scream then sink, bubbling. But nothing happened. Faroz seized the propellor and shook it. You could hear the shaft knocking about in the stern gland. I went below. Saïd had a floorboard up and there was water in the bilges. I asked Alaa where the best boatyard was and how soon we could get new white metal bearings or at least have the defects assessed by an expert.

He laughed. 'You are planning again.'

Shopping and Feasting
Eliot Warburton, 1845

At each village where we halt for supplies, a little market is *improvised* round about us. The old men squat in a circle in the front places, smoking their pipes, and discussing us as coolly and gravely as if we were mere abstractions. The men offer spears, or crocodiles, or antiquities, for sale; the women, butter, eggs, milk, and poultry – the latter cost about twopence each; eggs about threepence a hundred; butter, seven pence a pound; a sheep costs about four and sixpence.

On arriving at Keneh, we gave a feast to the crew, consisting of an old ram, which they preferred to younger mutton, because it 'stood more chewing.' The creature was alive, killed, boiled, and devoured, within an hour: his very eyes, feet, intestines, and, I do believe, his horns, were swallowed, and nothing remained but his skin. This, in the first moment of digestive leisure, was stretched, while warm, over the drum, dried almost immediately by the hot sun; and, in the dance and song which followed, it actually contributed to the festivities consequent on its proprietor's devourment, and, like Zitzka's skin, was beaten with thrilling associations of its owner.

Entertainer at Keneh
Sir Gaston Maspero, 1895

It would seem as if all the animals of an Egyptian farm had assembled on the shore by the side of the dahabieh. A whining camel is exchanging surly reflections with a disconsolate donkey, two buffaloes bellow in two different keys, dogs crawl, barking loudly, turkeys cluck, a half-dozen cocks challenge one another loudly and shrilly, and now and again an Arab flute, snuffling and shrill, accompanies the cadence of a lamentable melopoeia. The noise increases and at length becomes so bad that I can stand it no longer, and go up on deck to send the menagerie to finish its serenade elsewhere. But neither camel, nor ass, nor dog is to be seen, only on the shore a sort of turbaned juggler, who, puffing out his cheeks and waddling along, is making the uproar all by himself, imitating the cries of animals in the hope of bakhshîsch. He is respected for twenty leagues round, and pointed out to tourists as one of the wonders of Keneh.

The Dancing Girls at Keneh
Marquess Curzon of Kedleston, 1895

The dance was over. We had looked on at the contortions and wrigglings, the undulations and oscillations of the bodies of the girls as they performed on the deck of the boat. So violent had been their movements that the coins which hung on their gauzy dresses rattled and rang. The usual accompaniment had been furnished by the castanets of the dancers, the two-stringed cocoa-nut fiddle of the seated musicians, and the thrumming of the *darabookah*, or native drum. One of the girls, more agile than her companions, had laid down on the carpet and rolled over and over with a champagne bottle on her head containing a lighted candle stuck in its neck.

The company, departing for their native village of Keneh, famed for its school of dancers, had to cross a narrow plank between the steamer and the steep bank of the Nile. Suddenly a cry was raised that one of them, either jostled as she stepped ashore, or slipping on the plank, had fallen overboard. Looking over the side of the boat and listening to the confused noise in the bows, I saw something black float by on the surface of the water a few feet away. Little as I guessed at the moment, this was the head and hair of the drowning girl, who had gone without a struggle or a sound to her doom.

Quickly lowering a boat, we pulled down stream and lifted out the body 150 yards farther down.

On the muddy bank, lit only by the flicker of a solitary lantern and the remote glitter of the stars, lay the poor child's body, the head thrown back, the brown bosom bare, the bedraggled finery clinging round the limbs that half an hour before had tripped and twisted and turned. For three-quarters of an hour we endeavoured in vain to restore respiration amid the piercing cries of the other members of the troupe. It was of no use. One more unfortunate had gone to her death, and the Nile – a very fatal current into which to fall – had claimed another victim. I collect £10 on board and sent it to the *Mudir* of Keneh for distribution to the girl's relatives. But so handsome was the price, or so tempting the bribe, that when we came down stream again a deputation from Keneh awaited us to implore the favour of another performance.

To Lady Waldegrave
Edward Lear, 1867

Cairo, 8 March

Dear Lady Waldegrave

Nubia delighted me; it isn't a bit like Egypt, except that there's a river in both. Sad, stern, uncompromising landscape – dark ashy purple lines of hills – piles of granite rocks – fringes of palm – & ever and anon astonishing ruins of oldest Temples: – above all wonderful – Aboo Simbel which took my breath away. The 2d. Cataract also is very interesting – & at Philae & Denderah I got new subjects – beside scores & scores of little atomy illustrations all the way up & down the river. An 'American' or Montreal cousin was with me above Luxor, but he was a fearful bore; of whom it is only necessary to say that he whistled all day aloud – & that he was 'disappointed' in Abou Simbel. You cannot imagine the extent of the American element in travel here! They are as 25 to one English. They go about in dozens & scores – one dragoman to so many – & are a fearful race mostly. One lot of 16 – with whom was an acquaintance of my own – came up by steamer – but outvoted my friend, who desired to see the Temple of Abydas, – because 'it was Sunday, & it was wrong to break the Sabbath to inspect a heathen church.' Whereon the Parson who was one of the party preached 3 times that day, & Mr— my friend shut himself up in a rage. Would it be believed, the same lot, Parson & all, went on arriving at Assouan – on a *Sunday* evening – to see some of those poor women whose dances cannot be described, who only dance them by threats & offers of large sums of money? As all outer adornment of the person – except noserings & necklaces, are dispensed with on these occasions, the swallowing of camels & straining at gnats is finely illustrated. At Luxor I frequently saw Lady Duff Gordon – but on my return she had broken a blood vessel – & is now reported very ill indeed. She is doubtless a complete enthusiast, but very clever and agreeable.

Meanwhile it is getting very hot here, & the flies are becoming most odious & unscrupulous. As a whole the Shepheard's Hotel (or Zech's as it is called now,) is more like a pigstye mixed with a beargarden or a horribly noisy railway station than anything I can compare it to. To add to my difficulty in writing I have a miserable toothache or neuralgia – so I must stop.

My kindest regards to the Mimber, & with many thanks; believe me, Yours sincerely, Edward Lear

Nile Morning
Deborah Manley, 1990

A white donkey gambols excitedly as it is let out of its stable into the morning. A small boy in a brilliant-yellow tracksuit makes his way to school along the river bank swinging his bright-red plastic schoolbag. Fishermen rocked in our wash in their red and green boats. Wagtails come aboard for crumbs. A heron, known to the Egyptians as the sad owner, stands in the reeds, silent waiting. The luminous yellow-green ragged leaf-heads of the ripe sugar-cane – the green of the palms turned grey by the dusty air in which the hill ranges are lost – the wheat still bright green and young. A patchwork of small fields in green, yellow and dark rich brown soil. Jellabahed figures in deep and mid-blue. Trainloads of sugar cane piled higher and yet higher. A village hot, dusty and untidy, full of unravelling ventures. The beans, the fula, are in flower. Water buffalo with their badly stuffed shapes, all lumpy and angular and then smoothly fat according to their posture.

The mosques stand out in new paint, ochre, cream, eau de nil, and at night are strung with Christmas tree lights, brilliant in Egypt's cheap electricity. Two geese parade along the road. Always children. Friezes of children waving at us from a levée like brilliant fruit drops in orange, lemon, lime, apricot and cerise.

The First Excursionists: A Private Diary
Miss Riggs, 1869

Diary Jan 25 1869
Cook's 1st Grand Tour to the Nile and Palestine.

[In this way Miss Riggs, one of the first party to go to the East with Thomas Cook, headed her diary. Here are excerpts from that diary, giving a picture of a typical tourist which in most ways could have been written today.]

Left Hampstead 5:30 p.m. for London Bridge to join Mr Cook Senior, found him there with his wife, son and daughter . . . [In Paris Miss Riggs broke her blue parasol, but had it mended, and her luggage proved to a little over '60 lb weight guaranteed by Mr Cook on account of her saddle'.] There was great excitement in the Alps owing to the difficulty the engine had in working us up the winding and precipitous incline, sometimes stopping entirely and gasping dreadfully. . . [On into Italy where they were delayed after Rome because Victor Emmanuel had just passed on his way to Brindisi . . . which, Miss Riggs noted, in 1,420 miles from London. She admired the ship for Alexandria, which is 850 miles from Brindisi. On arrival in Alexandria, Miss Riggs described the problems which all travellers faced, but Mr Cook held his party back to the end. In Alexandria she went on tour and reported all she saw and was told, and commented on the thick mud everywhere. She bought smoke-coloured glasses and went to the English church.

The 150-mile journey to Cairo took five hours, but undeterred she went sight-seeing that very afternoon. Among her visits in Cairo she visited an American Mission school – 'most touching and interesting little girls, all gentle and soft-looking – not the vivacity and brightness of English children but the langour and submission showing itself in the child which the mothers' possess in a land where all is tyranny and oppression'. She learned more and more about Cairo, which they had 'unfortunately reached a week too late for the grand departure of pilgrims for Mecca', but she describes all that she was told about the pilgrimage.

At last, on 10 February they left Cairo in carriages for the two boats where some time was spent 'arranging cabins according to precedence'. A Miss Porter shared hers, but did not like her berth close to the boiler. . . The berth was about half a yard wide and there was about the same space for dressing.

She lists in advance the stoppages up to the 1st Cataract 'which included 8 hours at Keneh and Denderah, 3 days at Luxor, 6 hours at Edfou, and 2 days at Assouan . . . but as nothing is certain in Egypt many changes will no doubt take place'. One can hear the warning of today's tour guide in those words.

At Sittina the party passed the convent where Christian Coptic monks swam offshore to the passing boats for backsheesh . . . 'one got up on our steamer, collection made – quite naked.' She passes quickly on.

Their first donkey ride was at Beni Hassan, where their saddles were put on badly because their own dragoman did not see to it properly. At Assouit they again visited a mission school . . . At Gouhag they met up with an engineer, Abdel Effendi, who was very hospitable, bidding them all to dine . . . but Miss Riggs found him too hospitable for he 'returned with us to steamer and then sat again . . . wine brought up for him . . . tired of him – he did not leave until quite late'.

At Keneh the people on the other boat indicated that they did not 'quite approve of Mr Cook being on our boat . . . the young Americans helping to increase the feeling . . . and the commissariat too was not so good and taking wine of their own on board gave offence too, I think' . . . in addition a pipe burst and made one of the cabin's useless as 'Mr Webb had to turn out and sleep on deck'. To their dismay, soon after a paddlewheel broke . . . the other boat wanted 'a written order from Mr Cook to proceed to Thebes without us' and 'a disagreement arose'. However next morning the boat was mended and both boats started together for Thebes . . . 'though we ran aground often on our way'. Because of the delay they missed 'the grand illumination at Karnac which took place in honour of the Prince and Princess of Wales'.

The British and American consul in Luxor read them the list of the names of the Royal party from his visitors' book. She notes that Hamied, dragoman to the Prince, was 'Hippopotamus Johnny at the Zoological Gardens who came to England with the first river horse'.]

8

Luxor: Royal Thebes

Introduction

Royal Thebes,
   Egyptian treasure-house of countless wealth, Who boasts her hundred gates, through each of which, With horse and car, two hundred warriors march.

Homer's *Iliad*, Book IX
Lord Derby's translation

What spires are to a modern city, – what the towers of a cathedral are to its nave and choir, – that the statues of the Pharaoh were to the streets and temples of Thebes.

Dean Stanley, 1852

Alone of the cities of Egypt, the situation of Thebes is as beautiful by nature as by art.

Reaching Luxor, Royal Thebes, was a high point in the journey up the Nile. The Victorians knew their Homer and looked unsuccessfully for the hundred gates, but as Rose Macaulay and Diodorus Siculus say, it is all enormously huge and enormously old. Vivant Denon, Napoleon's savant, describes the French arrival in 1799 and while David Roberts scoffed at the French, he too was impressed, as were the Indian sepoys of Henry Light's acquaintance. Frederick Norden had problems there with his fellow travellers in 1737, but Amelia Edwards's *reis* brought her there with great excitement.

The sheer size of it all astonishes us today, as it did Henry Light and Frederick Henniker, despite the fact that in their day the temples were half filled with rubble and village houses, and that, according to Pierre Loti, it was all spoiled anyway. Douglas Sladen loved it all and in 1908 describes as exquisite gardens which nowadays would hardly rate such praise.

Alan Pryce-Jones saw it from a felucca. Mrs Colonel Elwood, who went from Luxor across the desert in a palanquin to the Red Sea and India in 1830, was entertained with great courtesy, and Florence Nightingale in 1850 found the social life almost too abundant, while Vivant Denon must have prayed for time at Karnak in 1799, overwhelmed as he was, like Amelia Edwards, by its grandeur and solemnity. Howard Hopley in 1868 had more leisure at Karnak.

Luxor is famed for its forgeries, some of which are now antiques themselves, with a value of their own. William C. Prime sought out the forgers and Princess Marta Bibescû danced on Karnak's pylons under the moon and stars.

Thebes
Rose Macaulay, 1953

450 miles from Cairo.

Thebes: enormously huge, enormously old, so old that no one knows its beginning; the massive, magnificent sprawl, lying along both banks of the Nile with its temples and palaces, prehistoric halls, great avenues of sphinxes, colossal statues, obelisks and sculptures, miles of immemorial tombs, Pharaohs and treasures, is outside the coverage of imagination. The scale is too vast, the antiquity too prehistoric, the gods and the Pharaohs too mysteriously of the Nile.

Great Diospolis
Diodorus Siculus, 60 BC

The Great Diospolis, by the Greeks called Thebes, was six leagues in circumference ... The fame of her power and of her riches, celebrated by Homer, filled the universe. Her gates, and the numerous vestibules of her temples, induced this poet to bestow on her the name ... the city of a hundred gates. Never did city receive so many offerings in gold, in silver, in ivory, in colossal statues, and in obelisks of a single stone. Above all were to be admired, her four principal temples. The most ancient was surprisingly grand and sumptuous ... The richness and finishing of the ornaments corresponded with its grandeur. Several Kings contributed to embellish it. It still subsists, but the gold, the silver, the ivory and the precious stones, were carried off, when Cambyses set fire to all the Egyptian temples.

Arrival of the French at Luxor
Vivant Denon, 1799

At nine o'clock, in making a sharp turn round a projecting point, we discovered all at once the site of the ancient Thebes in its whole extent. This celebrated city, the size of which Homer has characterised with the single expression of the *hundred-gated*, – a boasting and poetical phrase which has been repeated with so much confidence for so many centuries; – this illustrious city ... enveloped in the veil of mystery and the obscurity of ages, whereby even its own colossal monuments are magnified to the imagination, – still impressed the mind with such gigantic phantoms that the whole army, suddenly and with one accord, stood in amazement at the sight of its shattered ruins, and clapped their hands with delight, as if the end and object of their various toils, and the complete conquest of Egypt, were accomplished and secured by taking possession of the splendid remains of this ancient metropolis.

Another View
David Roberts, RA, 1836

[Roberts laughed at the 'affected enthusiasm of the French army', as narrated by Denon – stopping *en masse*, and clapping their hands in ecstasy of delight.]

In the vast plain of Thebes these ruins, enormous as they are, are mere patches, and nothing could have been distinguished at a distance whence these are first seen to create such enthusiasm, or make this show of it a praiseworthy *performance* . . . It is only on coming near that you are overwhelmed with astonishment.

Recognition
Henry Light, 1814

When the hindo Sepoys, who came into Egypt by the Red Sea, at the close of the former war, to assist our army there, were introduced to the ruined temples of the Nile, and beheld the figures of the Egyptian deities, they immediately worshipped them. Here was a light brought to dispel the gloom of some thousands of years . . .

The Struggle for Luxor
Frederick Norden, 1737

14 December

It was four o'clock in the afternoon, when I began to perceive, on the eastern side, an obelisk: little after I discovered a great number of peristils, some portals and antique structures, confusedly scattered up and down the plain.

From these signs I immediately concluded that I saw the ruins of ancient Thebes; but I could not prevail upon our reys to put me ashore, by fair words, promises or menace. He did not here plead his fear of the Arabians; his only excuse was the impossibility of landing, on account of the islands and sandbanks that obstructed. He swore, moreover, by his beard, that there was no going thither, without making a great round of land.

[The next day they crossed the Nile to the west side. Norden landed and:]

. . . did not go far before [he] met two great colossuses. Encouraged by this first discovery, I returned for my arms, and the company of those whom curiosity might incite to be of the party. The reys perceiving our design, spared no pains to thwart it, nay employed all his eloquence to intimidate us. But when he found his representations had no weight with us, he had recourse to another stratagem, which he thought would prove more effectual to deter us, which was to swear, that if we went ashore, he would go homeward with his bark, and not wait for our return. But he was made to understand our fixed determination, and that if he dared to sail off, as he threatened, that we would certainly overtake him and make him pay dearly for his insolence. This threat had the desired effect upon him; and he changed his note, humbly conjuring us not to land, for the sake of him; (saying that if misfortune befell the party, he would be blamed).

[Eventually Norden and some others went ashore. He then saw the temples at Luxor, which he knew nothing of in any detail, and measured and described all he saw.]

Good Morning – Luxor!
Amelia B. Edwards, 1873

Coming on deck the third morning after leaving Denderah, we found the dahabeeyah decorated with palm-branches, our sailors in their holiday turbans, and Reïs Hassan *en grande tenue*; that is to say in shoes and stockings, which he only wore on very great occasions.

'Nehârak-sa'ïd – good morning – Luxor!' said he, all in one breath.

It was a hot, hazy morning, with dim ghosts of mountains glowing through the mist, and a warm wind blowing.

We ran to the side; looked out eagerly; but could see nothing. Still the Captain smiled and nodded; and the sailors ran hither and thither, sweeping and garnishing; and Egendi, to whom his worst enemy could not have imputed the charge of bashfulness, said 'Luxor – kharûf* – all right!' every time he came near us.

We had read and dreamed so much about Thebes, and it had always seemed so far away, that but for this delicate allusion to the promised sheep, we could hardly have believed we were really drawing nigh unto those famous shores. About ten, however, the mist was lifted away like a curtain, and we saw to the left a rich plain studded with palm-groves; to the right a broad margin of cultivated lands bounded by a bold range of limestone mountains; and on the farthest horizon another range, all grey and shadowy.

'Karnak – Gournah – Luxor!' says Reïs Hassan triumphantly, pointing in every direction at once. Talhamy tries to show us Medinet Habu and the Memnonium. The Painter vows he can see the heads of the sitting Colossi and the entrance to the Valley of the Tombs of the Kings.

We, meanwhile, stare bewildered, incredulous; seeing none of these things; finding it difficult, indeed, to believe that any one else sees them. The river widens away before us; the flats are green on either side; the mountains are pierced with terraces of rock-cut tombs; while far away inland, apparently on the verge of the desert, we see here a clump of sycamores – yonder a dark hillock – midway between both a confused heap of something that may be either fallen rock or fallen masonry; but nothing that looks like a Temple, nothing to indicate that we are already within recognisable distance of the grandest ruins in the world.

Presently, however, as the boat goes on, a massive, windowless structure which looks (Heaven preserve us!) just like a brand-new fort or prison, towers up above the palm-groves to the left. This, we are told, is one of the propylons of Karnak; while a few whitewashed huts and a little crowd of masts now coming into sight a mile or so higher up, mark the position of Luxor. Then up

---

* 'Kharuf', pronounced 'hanoof', is the Arabic for English sheep.

capers Engendi with his never-failing 'Luxor – kharâf – all right!' to fetch down the tar and darabukkeh. The captain claps his hands. A circle is formed on the lower deck. The men, all smiles, strike up their liveliest chorus, and so, with barbaric music and well-filled sails, and flags flying, and green boughs waving overhead, we make our triumphal entry into Luxor.

The top of another pylon; the slender peak of an obelisk; a colonnade of giant pillars half-buried in the soil; the white houses of the English, American, and Prussian Consuls, each with its flagstaff and ensign; a steep slope of sandy shore; a background of mud walls and pigeon-towers; a foreground of native boats and gaily-painted dahabeeyahs lying at anchor – such, as we sweep by, is our first panoramic view of this famous village. A group of turbaned officials sitting in the shade of an arched doorway rise and salute us as we pass. The assembled dahabeeyahs dozing with folded sails, like sea-birds asleep, are roused to spasmodic activity. Flags are lowered; guns are fired; all Luxor is startled from its midday siesta. Then, before the smoke has had time to clear off, up comes the Bagstones in gallant form; whereupon the dahabeeyahs blaze away again as before.

People and the Temple
Henry Light, 1814

. . . I contented myself with one short visit to the temple at Luxor, on the east bank of the Nile, which at first disappointed me; its vast dimensions being hidden amongst the numerous modern huts erected within its extent, and the height lost in the accumulation of rubbish. It was not until I began to compare its columns with the human figure, that I was sensible to their magnitude.

The Temple at Luxor
Frederick Henniker, 1822

At Lougsor – This temple swarms with dogs, Arabs, houses, and other filth, by the accumulation of which the entrance of this magnificent fabric, which is thought to be 50 foot in height, will not now admit a man without stooping; part of the building has been converted into a Greek church, now into a cinder hole – the obelisks though half buried are the finest in the world.

Palace not Temple
Pierre Loti, 1910

[Pierre Loti moored over night near Luxor and then moved nearer to the temple – he thought.]

An hour later we arrived at Luxor, and what a surprise awaits us there!

The thing which dominates the whole town, and may be seen five or six miles away, is the Winter Palace, a hasty modern production which has grown on the border of the Nile during the past year: a colossal hotel, obviously sham, made of plaster and mud, on a framework of iron. Twice or three times as high as the admirable Pharaonic temple, its impudent façade rises there, painted a dirty yellow. One such thing, it will readily be understood, is sufficient to disfigure pitiably the whole of the surroundings. The old Arab town, with its little white houses its minarets and its palm-trees, might as well not exist. The famous temple and the forest of heavy Osiridean columns admire themselves in vain in the waters of the river. It is the end of Luxor.

And what a crowd of people is here! While, on the contrary, the opposite bank seems so absolutely desertlike, with its stretches of golden sand and, on the horizon, its mountains of the colour of glowing embers, which, as we know, are full of mummies.

Poor Luxor! Along the banks is a row of tourist boats, a sort of two or three storeyed barracks, which nowadays infest the Nile from Cairo to the Cataracts. Their whistlings and the vibration of their dynamos make an intolerable noise. How shall I find a quiet place for my dahabiya, where the functionaries of Messrs Cook will not come to disturb me?

We can now see nothing of the palaces of Thebes, whither I am to repair in the evening. We are farther from them than we were last night. The apparition during our morning's journey had slowly receded in the plains flooded by sunlight. And then the Winter Palace and the new boats shut out the view.

*

In a line with the Winter Palace a number of stalls follow one another. All those things with which our tourists are wont to array themselves are on sale there; fans, fly flaps, helmets and blue spectacles. And, in thousands, photographs of the ruins. And there too are the toys, the souvenirs of the Soudan: old negro knives, panther-skins and gazelle horns. Numbers of Indians even are come to this improvised fair, bringing their stuffs from Rajputana and Cashmere. And, above all, there are dealers in mummies, offering for sale mysteriously shaped coffins, mummy-cloths, dead hands, gods, scarabæ – and the thousand and one things that this old soil has yielded for centuries like an inexhaustible mine.

Along the stalls, keeping in the shade of the houses and the scattered palms, pass representatives of the plutocracy of the world. Dressed by the same costumiers, bedecked in the same plumes, and with faces reddened by the same sun, the millionaire daughters of the Chicago merchants elbow their sisters of the old nobility. Pressing amongst them impudent young Bedouins pester the fair travellers to mount their saddled donkeys. And as if they were charged to add to this babel a note of beauty, the battalions of Mr Cook, of both sexes, and always in a hurry, pass by with long strides.

Beyond the shops, following the line of the quay, there are other hotels. Less aggressive, all of them, than the Winter Palace, they have had the discretion not to raise themselves too high, and to cover their fronts with white chalk in the Arab fashion, even to conceal themselves in clusters of palm-trees.

And finally there is the colossal temple of Luxor, looking as out of place now as the poor obelisk which Egypt gave us as a present, and which stands today in the Place de la Concorde.

Bordering the Nile, it is a colossal grove of stone, about three hundred yards in length. In epochs of a magnificence that is now scarcely conceivable this forest of columns grew high and thick, rising impetuously at the bidding of

Amenophis and the great Rames. And how beautiful it must have been even yesterday, dominating in its superb disarray this surrounding country, vowed for centuries to neglect and silence!

But today, with all these things that men have built around it, you might say that it no longer exists.

A City of Giants
Giovanni Belzoni, 1816

On the 22nd, we saw for the first time the ruins of great Thebes, and landed at Luxor. Here I beg the reader to observe, that but very imperfect ideas can be formed of the extensive ruins of Thebes, even from the accounts of the most skilful and accurate travellers. It is absolutely impossible to imagine the scene displayed, without seeing it. The most sublime ideas, that can be formed from the most magnificent specimens of our present architecture, would give a very incorrect picture of these ruins; for such is the difference, not only in magnitude, but in form, proportion, and construction, that even the pencil can convey but a faint idea of the whole. It appeared to me like entering a city of giants, who, after a long conflict, were all destroyed, leaving the ruins of their various temples as the only proofs of their former existence. The temple of Luxor presents to the traveller at once one of the most splendid groups of Egyptian grandeur. The extensive propylon, with the two obelisks, and colossal statues in the front; the thick groups of enormous columns; the variety of apartments and the sanctuary it contains; the beautiful ornaments which adorn every part of the walls and columns, described by Mr. Hamilton; cause in the astonished traveller an oblivion of all that he has seen before. If his attention be attracted to the north side of Thebes by the towering remains, that project a great height above the wood of palm trees, he will gradually enter that forest-like assemblage of ruins of temples, columns, obelisks, colossi, sphynxes, portals, and an endless number of other astonishing objects, that will convince him at once of the impossibility of a description. On the west side of the Nile, still the traveller finds himself among wonders. The temples of Gournou, Memnonium, and Medinet Aboo, attest the extent of the great city on this side. The unrivalled colossal figures in the plains of Thebes, the number of tombs excavated in the rocks, those in the great valley of the kings, with their paintings, sculptures, mummies, sarcophagi, figures, etc. are all objects worthy of the admiration of the traveller; who will not fail to wonder how a nation, which was once so great as to erect these stupendous edifices, could so far fall into oblivion, that even their language and writing are totally unknown to us.

In Love with Luxor
Douglas Sladen, 1908

Luxor is an unimaginably beautiful place. There are houses in Luxor with exquisite riverside gardens, from which you look down upon Luxor's mighty temple, aggrandised by Egypt's rulers from Rameses the Great to Alexander the Great, and across the river at all the temples of Thebes, with the rim of the Sahara behind them.

Those riverside gardens of Luxor! I know of nothing quite so beautiful in their way. Take the garden of the Savoy Hotel, for instance. Green lawns and flowering shrubs of tropical luxuriance are divided from the river by a high terrace to guard them from the annual inundation. Along this terrace runs a snow-white pergola, roofed from the sun, and with its white columns curtained by a crimson bougainvillea. On the other side broad steps lead down from the terrace to the Nile, running many feet below. Across the water is Thebes, spread out for the eye. At the foot of the steps lie two or three Nile galleys, as classical in outline as if they had belonged to the ancient city, with their white-robed crews lazily executing Nubian dances, or plaiting fantastic fly-switches of palm-leaves, to lure piastres from the pockets of the visitors, till some one wishes to cross to Thebes or go for a sail on the Nile.

But it is hard to leave that terrace. I could sit all day long, all the winter through, at the openings of that pergola, watching the fishermen plying their primitive craft and the huge *gyassas* which carry on the trade of the Nile drifting down the swift current or running before the strong north wind, with their cargoes of golden grain or piled-up pitchers of white clay.

Once in a way one of Cook's tourist steamers comes merrily up from Cairo – a thing of beauty, with its gleaming white hull and its decks as gay as a garden-party, with men in light flannels and women in summer splendour.

I shall not easily forget our first hour in Luxor. Our steamer ran alongside just as the last rose of sunset was flushing the marvellous procession of lotus-headed columns reflected in the Nile. At such a moment the great temple of Luxor looks almost unearthly in its splendour and its long array of giant columns.

When the business of landing was over, we found ourselves in that contest of afterglow and darkness which in Egypt passes for dusk, walking past the temple, and a little hill which had a temple underneath, and a mosque on the top of it, and blatant antiquity dealers, along the lofty shore to the cool dark palm groves which envelop Karnak. As we returned from the mysteriousness of seeing that wilderness of ruins for the first time, in the deepening dusk, we compared it with our vision of Thebes – a wide plain, with the Temple of Der-el-Bahari cut in the bulwarks of the Sahara, which we had seen beyond the Nile canopied by the green-and-golden afterglow on which our eyes had been fixed for the first ten minutes of our walk. Which was to hold our hearts – Karnak, or Thebes, or Luxor?

We came back a different way, threading the winding bazar of Luxor, with its poor little curio shops lit by a single feeble lamp, and its garish Greek groceries. We had barely time to dress for dinner, and promised ourselves an early retirement to rest from our labours, for we were to rise at dawn to begin a long day at Thebes. But when we stepped ashore after our coffee to make merry over the banalities of the shops, which followed various trades, but all lived by selling postcards, we found night almost turned into day by the southern moon. In Egypt, one acts upon impulse, as there is no rain to make one reflect. In a few minutes half the passengers – the men in evening dress, the ladies in décolleté dresses and delicate slippers – were galloping on donkeys towards Karnak. The most anybody did in the way of preparation was to spread a dust cloak over the donkey and his saddle to keep off the dirt.

The effect of the flying white dresses in the moonlight was charming, especially as we neared Karnak, and rode into the palm groves with the soft sand of the road glittering like snow wherever the moon could reach it through the trees.

As the cavalcade rode up to Karnak there were more fairy-tale effects than ever. Little black dogs ran along the dark walls of the village on the left, and barked defiance. Over the wall rose the fantastic outlines of the houses and their mosque. Sometimes at the end of a street was a little group of white-robed men and black-shrouded women. Once a belated camel came swaying past; and more than once an old sheikh, almost veiled in white, ambled past on a gaily comparisoned ass.

Then the Sphinxes of the avenue, at first looking like gnawed bones, and then like wild animals pretending to be asleep, made their appearance, and then the gay pylon of the Ptolemies, a square-headed, richly figured arch, with the sealed temple of Khonsu behind it, burst upon our view.

We made no attempt to enter Khonsu's temple, but whipped up our donkeys past it, on to the great square of Karnak to see the moon strike the heaven-pointing finger of Queen Hatasu's obelisk and the mountainous temple of Amon-Ra.

We took this in as we rode across the square to the pleasant Eastern bungalow of the curator of the temples, the learned and affable Legrain. Here the night struck a different note. For the lights of a human dwelling gleamed out of the odorous masses of tropical creepers, and the loggia on the roof was delicately outlined against the moonlit sky; while our white asses, as we dismounted, went and stood in the shadows under the dark lebbeks, where it was their wont to shelter from the fierceness of the Egyptian day.

We soon forgot both, for right before us were the perfect Sphinxes of the avenue, which led from the Temple of Amon-Ra to the quay, now far from the river, where the Pharaohs took galley for Thebes. The polished granite of these monsters, as perfect as the lions in Trafalgar Square, gleamed like silver. They looked with great benevolence on the dainty women with the trains of their evening dresses over their left arms, who paused to look into their faces and parade a pretty ignorance.

From a Felucca
Alan Pryce-Jones, 1931

... I went out as often as I could with Fuly in our orange and blue felucca, to taste the wind and comprehend the town. Nothing is more enchanting than the Nile under a wind ... I liked to stand in the bows of the bumping, clumsy boat, to look down at the water which in the wind curls like a sheep's back, or to look up at the curved and pregnant sail darkening, on the far side of its fullness, into a soft shadow full of light and energy, tugging towards me on my narrow triangle of wood. I lay on the edge making ridge and furrow with my fingers in the water, cutting through the curls of the water, with half an eye to a wire or a rope to seize when the boat gives right over to a new wind. Perhaps I stood up, arranged a triumphant story to suit the attitude, remembered Jason as my hair came down into my eyes and I was able to flatter myself with beauty and courage denied, taking the fruit before the test out of joy in the light. But then affectations thought out are bowled over by wonder at the shapes of sails, the long sinewy triangles caught with the apex down in a muscular wind, sometimes the wings that facile poetry cares to call them, sometimes so like leaves that you can see the veins standing out in the grip of the wind, and the wooden bough making through the water, scattering it and throwing it up as though it were spilling its own sap in the effort.

When the wind ended and we were only moving on the current, I could hear the damp wood creaking on the bank, of water-wheels which plodded round to bring up a trickle of water into the fields, incessantly, for the water was no sooner out of the river than it was drunk up by the sun. And quickly we came in sight of the town – of the river steamers and the ferries, the photographer's shop on the bank and the bands of men who sold the *New York Times*, or beads, or whisks, or fortunes, or virgins, or donkeys, to the unhardened traveller.

Soirée at Luxor
Mrs Colonel Elwood, 1825

Charles ascended the top of one of the Propyla [of Luxor temple], whilst I remained in the court below, upon which my friend, the courteous Cacheff, most politely brushing the dust off from a low wall with the skirt of his own robe, waved to me, and made signs for me to come and sit down by him whilst waiting for Charles' return. He then invited us into his house, built of, and amongst the ruins; and very like an owlet's retreat it proved. Ascending a rude staircase, we entered an apartment of tolerable size, the walls and floor of which were composed of beaten mud, but at the superior and elevated part of the room were carpets and sofas, upon which the Cacheff placed us, myself on his right, and Charles on his left hand, whilst our respective attendants seated themselves on the ground. He then asked us several questions in a very polite manner; coffee in the usual beautiful little China cups was brought, and pipes: but I had some difficulty to keep my countenance, when, after smoking one of the latter for a short time, he most courteously offered it to *me*. Repressing a strong inclination to laugh, I declined it, observing that 'the English ladies did not smoke:' upon which he presented it to Charles, and then to our head servant, Sheik Chaund, who however very properly refused it, 'as being too great an honour for him.' An ewer and basin of water were then brought in, and we took our leave, highly amused with our *soirée* at the house of the Cacheff of Luxor.

Returning to our boat, we passed several female figures of granite, sitting gazing pensively on the Nile, the ceaseless flow of whose waters they had been watching for probably more centuries than I had lived years. The Cacheff very generously offered any, or all these statues to Charles, but fortunately for the future traveller and antiquary, they were too cumbrous and ponderous to be pleasant travelling companions across the Desert, although I certainly should have liked to have had a female friend with me occasionally. Could we have animated these said statues, what an agreeable gossip we might have had with them concerning King Sesostris, and other heroes of the olden time, when Thebes, like London, was populous, and animated, and great, and powerful:

but we were forced to leave these granite ladies to their meditations upon the Nile . . .

Life at Thebes
Florence Nightingale, 1850

11 February

Dear People,

Do you want to know how we pass our days? We rise up early in the morning, and are breakfasted perhaps by eight o'clock. Then we cross the water in the 'sandal', which is a small 'dingee', to western Thebes; the asses rush into the water to meet us, or the crew carry us ashore; we mount the asses, and with a great multitude – for in Egypt every attendant has his ass, and every ass his attendant – we repair (preceded by a tall man with a spear, his wild turban coming undone in the wind), like a small army, to a tomb; the tomb instantly fills – we suffocate for two or three hours, the guides having, besides, lighted fires and torches therein. When nature can sustain no more, we rush out, and goollehs, bread and dates are laid upon a stone. Those who have strength then begin again, till dark; those who have not, lie on stones in the valley.

Then begins the delightful ride home, the quiet, the silence (except that no Arab is ever silent – the donkey men and the guides talk without one moment's interruption, if it is ten miles or if it is one, the whole way home), the sunset tints, the goats coming home, the women spinning at the head, the gamous (the great Nile buffalo) crossing the little branches of the Nile in large herds on their way home, two little children perhaps riding on the neck of the largest, a stray jackal coming out, and the Pair looking golden in the western sunlight; the evening picture is all beautiful. Our asses enter the river and slide us into the sandal, and home we come to the little fleet of European boats moored under the colonnades of Luxor, which really from the river are almost beautiful.

We dine, and after dinner, when we are all hung up by the tails, like the chameleons, pretending to be dead, and waiting for half-past seven, or at latest eight, to bury us, lo! a dreadful plash of oars, or Paolo puts in his head, with an abominable grin at our mute misery, and say, 'The Hungarian count!' or 'the German professor!' and so on. Mr. B— immediately retires to his own room, whence he is generally heard to snore. We unwillingly, but nobly, sacrifice ourselves to our duty, sit up (in the brown Holland dressing gowns we are sure to have on, having been much too tired to dress), and talk; but we never give one drop of tea, which has greatly limited these visitations, for, in our street, the doors stand always open, and the people have nothing to do but to spend their evenings on board each other's boat. One night, and one night only, we were got out. Capt.—, good-natured man, came himself in his sandal, and positively carried us off; and one day the —'s dined with us, and with all the devotion of Arab hospitality which distinguished us, we killed – was it not beautiful of us? – no, not our horse, we had none, but our dog, for dinner. I think I told you of our dog – a turkey, 'as big as donkey', as Paolo said. Oh what a loss was there, how he used to walk majestically up and down the beach in front of the boat, which he believed it his duty to guard, bastinadoing the chickens when they made a noise. He killed two cocks the day he died. No man could get him into a coop (the crew were afraid to go near him), yet he never strayed. No dog ever ventured near our boat while he lived; the moment he was dead, the hungry Luxor dogs used to come on board every night, till Mustafa, like Cuddie's lady, greeted them with boiling water; and after his death, we never could keep a quail a single night, though our numerous acquaintances kept us well in quails, for our four cats had parties every night, and bared the larder, and we killed him!

As soon as our guests were gone, sometimes before, we went to bed. Don't think us grown quite savage and uncivilised. It is very hard to be all day by the deathbed of the greatest of your race, and to come home and talk about quails or London.

Karnak at Last
Vivant Denon, 1799

[The French army returned through Karnak and halted there.]

Unable, by myself, to take the plan of Karnak temple, or make large views of this mass of ruins, which, at first sight resembles the saw-yard of a quarry, or rather piled mountains, my design was to employ the two hours there in making draughts of the historical low-reliefs . . .

[This he did.]

. . . The day advanced, and the soldiers had not yet obtained anything to eat: travellers are not like Roman heroes, they sometimes feel the want of refreshment: the sun gained upon them, and it was resolved to sleep at Karnac . . .

[Even so, Denon decided that he would need eight days to take a plan, 'in the least degree satisfactory'.]

I was unable to measure the surface of this group of edifices; but, in encompassing it several times on horseback, at a full trot, I always performed the rise in twenty-five minutes.

[Denon worked on the next day until heat overcame him.]

It was so hot that the sun had burned my feet, through my boots; I could remain in one place only by causing my servant to walk between the sun and myself, that the rays might be interrupted, and a little shade thrown upon me by his body; the stones had acquired so much heat, that, in picking up some cornelean agates which are found in great number even within the enclosure of the town, I was so burnt by them, that, in order to carry them, I was obliged to throw them on my handkerchief, as I would have touched hot coals.

Worn out with fatigue, I threw myself down in a little Arabian tomb, which had been prepared for me for the night, and which appeared a delicious chamber, till I was told that, at the time of our passing Karnac before, the throat had there been cut of a Frenchman who had lagged behind the column: the marks of this assassination, still imprinted on the walls filled me with horror; but I was laid down, I was sleepy, and so weary that I believe I should not have risen off the dead body itself of the unfortunate victim.

Karnak in Silence
Amelia B. Edwards, 1873

An immense perspective of pillars and pylons leading up to a very distant obelisk opened out before us. We went in, the great walls towering up like cliffs above our heads, and entered the First Court. Here, in the midst of a large quadrangle open to the sky stands a solitary column, the last of a central avenue of twelve, some of which, disjointed by the shock, lie just as they fell, like skeletons of vertebrate monsters left stranded by the Flood.

Crossing this Court in the flowing sunlight, we came to a mighty doorway between two more propylons – the doorway splendid with coloured bas-reliefs; the propylons mere cataracts of fallen blocks piled up to the right and left in grand confusion. The cornice of the doorway is gone. Only a jutting fragment of the lintel stone remains. That stone, when perfect, measured forty feet and ten inches across. The doorway must have been a full hundred feet in height.

We went on. Leaving to the right a mutilated colossus engraven on arm and breast with the cartouche of Rameses II, we crossed the shade upon the threshold, and passed into the famous Hypostyle Hall of Seti the First.

It is a place that has been much written about and often painted; but of which no writing and no art can convey more than a dwarfed and pallid impression. To describe it, in the sense of building up a recognisable image by means of words, is impossible. The scale is too vast; the effect too tremendous; the sense of one's own dumbness, and littleness, and incapacity, too complete and crushing. It is a place that strikes you into silence; that empties you, as it were, not only of words but of ideas. Nor is this a first effect only. Later in the year, when we came back down the river and moored close by, and spent long days among the ruins, I found I never had a word to say in the Great Hall. Others might measure the girth of those tremendous columns; others might climb hither and thither, and find out points of view, and test the accuracy of Wilkinson and Mariette; but I could only look, and be silent.

A Phantom City
Howard Hopley, 1868

Before we left – for we found it impossible to penetrate much farther – we determined to climb on to some roof, and look over the wilderness of temple. For a time we blundered about along piles of ruin, guided by capricious lights, let in through crevices and sculptured doorways. Now a long vista of indistinct splendour would unfold itself: now a mournful avenue of pillars opening out into light: now a moonlit glade of columns, across which the slanting shadows fell. All around was so breathlessly hushed that the silence fell chill on the heart. The chirrup of bats scared from their gloomy haunts in secret chamber or chapel made a welcome diversion. The distant wail of jackals also, those grim wanderers of the desert, came to our ears, but not one crossed our path. An old vulture, asleep on the rim of a lotus capital, woke up in great consternation as we went by; he winged his way along a dark colonnade into the light, and finally settled on the peak of a glossy obelisk that ascended through deep shadow into a loftier region where the moonlight dwelt. We stood underneath, and shouted

178

at him in vain. The creature, vexed at his momentary fear, would not condescend to ruffle himself further, and neither of us could fling high enough to reach him. Sulky and motionless as the painted gods on pillar and wall, he stood, fixed, as if he had been a statue, to that splendid pedestal.

We hit upon a secret stairway crowded with sculptured forms, leading up through the thickness of a wall to a rather dangerous standpoint on some architraves binding the pillars of an inner sanctuary. From hence we gained a tolerably commanding view of the whole scene. The view was naturally limited by the light, and its effect by the same cause exaggerated. Space and distance are not to be grappled with under the gleam of a southern moon. To us it seemed as if a vast city lay before us, reposing in a breathless trance. We could picture to ourselves its streets, its squares, its palaces, its arcades, its domes – populous with a myriad shadowy beings, held for ever in stony silence. Massive patches of black shade scarred that broad expanse of temple, for the most part flooded in the moon's soft splendour. We could discern the radiating lines of more than one sphinx avenue in the distance, mapped out on the sand. Nearer, slanting rows of shadows marked the presence of some colonnade. A phalanx of Osiride pillars stood in high relief in the forefront of the sanctuary beneath us, each with its colossal human form appended, tipped with light – a shrouded figure, erect, serene, with arms folded over the breast, as in the hushed repose of death.

But, indeed, all lesser incidents were lost in the overwhelming effect of the whole – an effect that it would be difficult to overstate. It would be difficult, also, to analyze the mingled feelings that moonlit scene called up in the mind.

*

We cast a lingering look beyond the river to the girdling mountains in the west, and to the eastern plain which stretched calm before us like some boundless sea of sand, and then descended from our height. The shadows had lengthened sensibly, and the moon was dipping low into the river as we made our way homewards across the plain.

Antique Makers
William C. Prime, 1855

I left the *Phantom* and walked around the village [Luxor], my footsteps dogged by twenty donkey-boys, and as many donkeys, each of the former hoping that I would grow tired and patronize one of them. At every corner and turn a Coptic scoundrel would produce a lot of antiques for sale, and I amused myself by asking prices. At Luxor rates, Dr. Abbott's collection is worth a million.

Oh! confident Howajji, beware in Luxor of Ibrahim the Copt, and on the western shore of Achmet-el-Kamouri, the Mussulman. Skillful manufacturers of every form of antique are plenty in the neighbourhood, and these men have them in their employ, and sell to unwary travellers the productions of the modern Arabs as veritable specimens of the antique. Achmet is the chief manufacturer himself, and has a ready hand at the chisel.

The manufacture of antiques is a large business in Egypt, and very profitable. Scarabi are moulded from clay or cut from stone, with close imitation of the ancient, and sold readily at prices varying from one to five dollars. At Thebes is the head-quarters of this business. Still, no antiquarian will be deceived; and it requires very little practice to be able in an instant to determine whether an article is ancient or modern. When the Copt finds that you do know the distinction, he becomes communicative, and readily lets you into the secret of his business; and while he is confidentially informing you of the way in which the Arabs do it, and how this is modern and that is not, beware lest you become too trusting, and he sells you in selling a ring, or a vase, or a seal. He is a wily fellow and sharp, and he knows well how to manage a Howajji.

Dining at Karnac
Princess Marta Bibescû, 1930

Arab musicians sing:

> Gardener, give me a rose,
> If you give me no rose,
> Then a kiss –
> A kiss and a bite.

It is light music, but it lasts.

*

We follow in the night the sandy avenue of sacred rams, that series of 'paternosters'. The perfume of mimosa from the abandoned house of Legrain, a little French dwelling shadowed by the great pylons, comes to us on the Nile breeze.

Prince I.D. points out certain lights which move on the pylons up near the stars.

'Your dinner awaits you there,' he said.

We went up to the lofty terrace by a half-ruined spiral staircase, like the ones in cathedrals. The handsome serving-men, black shadows against the sky, stood mute and motionless around a small laden table. They must have been jinn out of the air to have carried such a large meal to this place.

At my right, the Nile and mountain Assasif with its strawberry and cream tint. At my left, the prodigious ruin of the eighth wonder of the world. The moon hangs high above the table exactly in the center of the found candles enclosed in glass globes.

*

The Prince has brought a phonograph.

Some American tourists, attracted by the familiar sounds of *Old Man River* in that great solitude, appear, like jacks-in-the-box, at the head of the stairway. The Jinn have to drive them away with great flappings of napkins.

When our meal is finished, a jinni who comes to carry out the coffee cups brings me the moon on a silver salver.

9

The Other Side

Introduction

Saturday 20 February

Breakfast at 6:30 so as to make an early start for the tombs of the Kings. We had to cross in little boats to the other side of the Nile; our other party had the start of us by half an hour so they took the first donkeys and we had to wait some time for ours. . . Our dragoman and steward of the boat brought our lunch and spread it out at the mouth of one of these subterraneous caverns that once held so many dead . . . very hot day. . . Mr Dennett quite knocked up . . . on our return . . . found little boats ready and glad we were to sit and enjoy the deck after the fatiguing day.

Miss Riggs, 1868

No visit to Luxor is complete without crossing to 'the other side' and the Valleys of the Kings, Queens and Nobles. W. G. Browne had to be brave to go there in 1792, and in 1799 Vivant Denon felt himself in danger. Amelia Edwards climbed the Colossus and William Hamilton, who was to arrange a lot of the funding of British collections in Egypt, was amazed by the great fallen Rameses, just as we are today, although we do not clamber on it as he did. Dean Stanley brings Rameses upright in the mind. Shelley had been quoted on that spot from the year he wrote his sonnet. Belzoni started work on the young Memnon, which was to be carried to London. William Jarvie, a great proponent of the picnic, picnicked this time in a tomb.

People entered the tombs with interest and varying levels of reverence. Constance Sitwell in 1927 looked at a bunch of flowers in a mummy's hand. The artist E. W. Merrick knew of a footprint in the sand; Dr Richardson was met by swarms of bats; Belzoni could not avoid tasting mummies. Mrs Elwood disliked mummy-seekers in 1830; H. V. Morton in 1938 recalled witnessing the greatest mummy-hunt of all; and William C. Prime was a mummy-seeker himself. Even Amelia Edwards found herself dealing with grave robbers, and H. V. Morton inadvertently held a mummy's hand. Annie Quibbell, closely linked with the Department of Antiquities, could stay on the other side in 1925 after the tourists had departed for the hotels in Luxor, and she has the last, regretting words.

Protectors of the Tombs
W. G. Browne, 1792

On landing with my Greek servant at Kourna [or Kurnu], no male inhabitant appeared; but two or three women were standing at the entrance of their dens. As we passed, in quest of the sheck-el-bellad, to request a guide, one of the women said, in Arabic, 'Are you not afraid of crocodiles?' I replied in the negative. She said, emphatically, 'We are crocodiles;' and proceeded to depict her own people as thieves and murderers. They are indeed a ferocious clan, differing in person from other Egyptians. Spears twelve or fourteen feet in length are deadly weapons in their hands.

In the temple at Medinet-Abu we observed a large quantity of blood, and were told by the peasants of Beirat that the Kournese had there murdered a Muggrebin and a Greek, travellers passing from Assuan to Kahira, who had strayed thither from mere curiosity, or perhaps with a view of finding treasure, in which the Muggrebins pretend to superior skill.

Medinet-Abu and the Tombs
Vivant Denon, 1799

I galloped forward to catch some features of the ruins of the temples of Medinet-Abu, where the troop would take me up in passing. I arrived an hour before it. I saw that on the right of the temple which adjoins the village there was a square edifice which had been a palace, very small indeed, but to which the neighbouring porticoes would have served for additions, in a climate where galleries of columns and terraces are apartments. This little palace has a character which differs very much from that of all other edifices, both in its plan, in its double storey of square windows, and in a sort of balconies, each of which are sustained by four heads, in the attitude of caryatides. It is to be regretted that this private edifice is in so great a state of destruction, especially in its interior, and that that which remains of its exterior decoration has been so much injured: the sculptures which decorate the exterior walls, as in that part of the temple of Karnac which I suspect to have been a palace, represent the figures of kings, threatening groups of prostrate captives.

Still going before the troop, and pressed onward by its march, I hastened to the two colossuses, and saw them with the effect of the rising sun, at the hour in which it is customary to go and hear that of Memnon speak: after this, I went to the insulated palace called the *memnonium*.

While I had forgotten to observe, my companions had forgotten to warn me, and I perceived that the detachment had left me half a league in its rear: I galloped to rejoin it. The troop was fatigued, and it was again become a question whether the expedition to the tombs should take place. I swallowed in silence the anger I felt; and I believe that this silence gained more than any words my discontent could have dictated, for, in the end, the route was proceeded on without further discussion. We first crossed the village of Kùrùn, the ancient Necropolis: on approaching these subterranean abodes, the inhabitants, for the third time, saluted us with several discharges of musketry. This was the only spot in upper Egypt in which it was refused to acknowledge our government;

secure in their sepulchral retreats, like larves, they left them only to terrify mankind: guilty of many other crimes, they hid their remorse, and fortified their disobedience, in the obscurity of these excavations, which are so numerous that they alone attest the immense population of ancient Thebes. It was through these humble tombs that the kings were carried two leagues from their palace, into the silent valley that was to become their final dwelling-place: this valley, to the north-east of Thebes, straitens insensibly; flanked by steep mountains, time can have effected but trivial changes in its antique forms, since, towards its extremity, the opening of the rock still scarcely affords space for a passage to the tombs, especially for the sumptuous trains which doubtlessly accompanied ceremonies like these, and which must have produced a striking-contrast with the austere asperity of these wild rocks: nevertheless, it is to be believed that this road was taken only for the sake of grander display, for the valley, from its entrance to its end, tending wholly to the south, the point at which are the tombs, can be but a very short distance from the memnonium and yet it was not till after three quarters of an hour's march in this desert that, in the midst of the rocks, we suddenly found the openings, even with the ground. These openings at first present no other architectural ornament than a door, with plain chambranles, of a square form, decorated on the superior part with a flattened oval, on which are inscribed in hieroglyphics a *scarabæus*, a figure of a man having the head of a sparrow-hawk, and, out of the oval, two figures on their knees, in the attitude of adoration: as soon as the sill of the first door is passed, there are found long galleries of twelve feet in width, by twenty in height, lined with stucco, sculptured and painted; the roofs of the vaults, formed in elegant elliptic arches, are covered with hieroglyphics, disposed with so much taste, that, in spite of the uncouthness of their forms, and though there be neither middle-tint nor aerial perspective in these paintings, the ceilings present an agreeable whole, and an assortment of colours of which the effect is rich and grateful.

It would require a stay of some weeks in order to seek and establish a system on the subjects of pictures so numerous, and moreover so mysterious, and I was allowed only a few minutes, and these with a bad grace.

It had been sounded to horse, when I discovered some little chambers, on the walls of which were painted the representations of all sorts of arms, such as maces, coats of mail, tiger-skins, bows, arrows, quivers, pikes, darts, sabres, helmets, goads, and whips; in another, a collection of household utensils, such as cabinets, commodes, chairs, elbow-chairs, stools, and folding mattresses, of an exquisite form, and such as we have these many years admired as the productions of our cabinet-makers, when they have been guided by skilful designers: as painting only copies that which exists, we must suffer ourselves to be convinced that the Egyptians employed indian wood, sculptured and gilt, for their furniture, and brocaded silks for the coverings; to these were added various vessels, as vases, coffee-pots, a ewer, with its salver, a tea-pot,* and a basket. Another chamber was devoted to agriculture, and decorated with its implements and labours; as, a plough similar to that used at present, a man sowing grain on the brink of a canal, from the banks of which the inundation

---

* If the vessel which M. Denon has here called a teapot is really entitled to that name, it is a circumstance which remarkably affects the history of both tea and the tombs of the kings.

has retired, a reaping, performed with the sickle, and rice-fields, in the act of being tilled. In a fourth is a figure in white clothing, playing on a harp of eleven strings; the harp sculptured with ornaments of the same tint and the same wood as those at this moment used by ourselves.

How could I, thus hastily, leave these precious curiosities? I begged with earnestness for a quarter of an hour; and, watch in hand, I was allowed twenty minutes: one person lit the way, while another held a torch to each particular object to which I directed my attention.

With the Colossus
Amelia B. Edwards, 1873

Of all Theban ruins, the Ramesseum is the most cheerful. Drenched in sunshine, the warm limestone of which it is built seems to have mellowed and turned golden with time. No walls enclose it. No towering pylons over-shadow it. It stands high, and the air circulates freely among those simple and beautiful columns. There are not many Egyptian ruins in which one can talk and be merry; but in the Ramesseum one may thoroughly enjoy the passing hour. [Miss Edwards described the scene and then turned to the great fallen statue.]

The one wholly unmistakable point in the narrative is however, the colossal statue of Syenite, 'the largest in Egypt'. The siege and the river, the troops of captives are to be found elsewhere; but nowhere, save here, a colossus which answers to that description. This statue was larger than even the twin Colossi of the Plain. They measure eighteen feet and three inches across the shoulders; this measures twenty-two feet and four inches. They sit about fifty feet high, without their pedestals; this one must have lifted his head some ten feet higher still. 'The measure of his foot,' says Diodorus, 'exceeded seven cubits'; the Greek cubit being a little over eighteen inches in length. The foot of the fallen Rameses measures nearly eleven feet in length by four feet ten inches in breadth. This, also, is the only very large Theban colossus sculptured in the red Syenite of Assûan.

Ruined almost beyond recognition as it is, one never doubts for a moment that this statue was one of the wonders of Egyptian workmanship. It most probably repeated in every detail the colossi of Abou Simbel; but it surpassed them as much in finish of carving as in perfection of material. The stone is even more beautiful in colour than that of the famous obelisks of Karnak; and is so close and hard in grain, that the scarab-cutters of Luxor are said to use splinters of it as our engravers use diamonds, for the points of their graving tools. The solid contents of the whole, when entire, are calculated at 887 tons. How this astounding mass was transported from Assûan, how it was raised, how it was overthrown, are problems upon which a great deal of ingenious conjecture has been wasted. One traveller affirms that the wedge-marks of the destroyer are distinctly visible. Another, having carefully examined the fractured edges, declares that the keenest eye can detect neither wedge-marks nor any other evidences of violence. We looked for none of these signs and tokens. We never asked ourselves how or when the ruin had been done. It was enough that the mighty had fallen.

Inasmuch as one can clamber upon and measure these stupendous fragments, the fallen colossus is more astonishing, perhaps, as a wreck than it would have been as a whole. Here, snapped across at the waist and flung helplessly back, lie a huge head and shoulders, to climb which is like climbing a rock. Yonder, amid piles of unintelligible débris, we see a great foot, and nearer the head, part of an enormous trunk, together with the upper halves of two huge thighs clothed in the usual shenti or striped tunic. The klaft or headdress is also striped, and these stripes in both instances, retain the delicate yellow colour with which they were originally filled in. To judge from the way in which this colour was applied, one would say that the statue was tinted rather than painted. The surface-work, wherever it remains, is as smooth and highly finished as the cutting of the finest gem. Even the ground of the superb cartouche, on the upper half of the arm, is elaborately polished. Finally, in the pit which it ploughed out in falling, lies the great pedestal, hieroglyphed with the usual pompous titles of Rameses Mer-Amen. Diodorus, knowing nothing of Rameses or his style, interprets the inscription after his own fanciful fashion:– 'I am Osymandias, King of Kings. If any would know how great I am, and where I lie, let him excel me in any of my works.'

The Great Figure
William Hamilton, 1801

. . . the temple between Medinet-Abou and El-Ebeh was called the Memnonium by the French, on account of the broken colossal statue of red granite within its precincts. Among other dimensions of this colossus, I found that it measured six feet ten inches over the foot, and 62 or 63 feet around the shoulders. This enormous statue has been broken off at the waist, and the upper part is now laid prostrate on its back. The face is extremely obliterated, and next to the wonder excited at the boldness of the sculptor who made it, and the extraordinary powers of those that erected it, the labour and exertions that must have been used for its destruction are most astonishing. It could only have been brought about with the help of military engines, and must then have been the work of a length of time. Its fall has carried along with it the whole wall of the temple which stood within its reach.

It was not without great difficulty and danger that we could climb on its shoulder and back; and in going from thence upon its chest, I was assisted by my Arab servant, who walked by my side, in the hieroglyphic characters engraven on the arm.

The Great Statue of the Ramesseum
Dean Stanley, 1852

By some extraordinary catastrophe this statue has been thrown down, and the Arabs have scooped their millstones out of his face; but you can see what he was, – the largest statue in the world. Far and wide his enormous head must have seen, – eyes, nose and ears. Far and wide you must have seen his hands resting on his elephantine knees. You sit on his breast and look at the Ostride statues which support the porticos of the temple, and they seem pigmies before him. Nothing that now exists in the world can give any notion of what the effect

185

must have been when he was erect ... Rameses was resting in awful majesty after the conquest of the whole known world.

Preparing to Collect
Giovanni Belzoni, 1817

After having taken a cursory view of Luxor and Carnak, to which my curiosity led me on my landing, I crossed the Nile to the west, and proceeding straight to the Memnonium, I had to pass before the two colossal figures in the plain. I need not say, that I was struck with wonder. They are mutilated indeed, but their enormous size strikes the mind with admiration. The next object that met my view was the Memnonium. It stands elevated above the plain, which is annually inundated by the Nile. The water reaches quite to the propylon; and, though this is considerably lower than the temple, I beg leave to observe, that it may be considered as one of the proofs, that the bed of the Nile has risen considerably higher since the Memnonium was erected; for it is not to be supposed that the Egyptians built the propylon, which is the entrance to the temple, so low as not to be able to enter it when the water was at its height. There are other proofs of this opinion, which I shall have an opportunity of introducing in this volume. The groups of columns of that temple, and the views of the numerous tombs excavated in the high rock behind it, present a strange appearance to the eye. On my approaching these ruins, I was surprised at the sight of the great colossus of Memnon, or Sesostris, or Osymandias, or Phamenoph, or perhaps some other king of Egypt; for such are the various opinions of its origin, and so many names have been given to it, that at last it has no name at all. I can but say, that it must have been one of the most venerated statues of the Egyptians; for it would have required more labour to convey such a mass of granite from Assouan to Thebes, than to transport the obelisk, commonly known under the appellation of Pompey's Pillar, to Alexandria.

As I entered these ruins, my first thought was to examine the colossal bust I had to take away. I found it near the remains of its body and chair, with its face upwards, and apparently smiling on me, at the thought of being taken to England. I must say, that my expectations were exceeded by its beauty, but not by its size. I observed, that it must have been absolutely the same statue as is mentioned by Norden, lying in his time with its face downwards, which must have been the cause of its preservation. I will not venture to assert who separated the bust from the rest of the body by an explosion, or by whom the bust has been turned face upwards. The place where it lay was nearly in a line with the side of the main gateway into the temple; and, as there is another colossal head near it, there may have been one on each side of the doorway, as they are to be seen at Luxor and Carnak.

All the implements brought from Cairo to the Memnonium consisted of fourteen poles, eight of which were employed in making a sort of car to lay the bust on, four ropes of palm leaves, and four rollers, without tackle of any sort. I selected a place in the porticoes; and, as our boat was too far off to go to sleep in it every night, I had all our things brought on shore, and made a dwelling house of the Memnonium. A small hut was formed of stones, and we were handsomely lodged. Mrs. Belzoni had by this time accustomed herself to travel, and was equally indifferent with myself about accommodations.

To the Valley of the Kings
William Jarvie, 1904

28 January

We rode through a valley which wound about hills and giant rocks for about four miles up to the place known as the 'Tombs of the Kings'. You cannot imagine a more appropriate way to these tombs, for it is truly a way of the dead. Not a tree, not a shrub, not a blade of grass, not even a human being lives in this valley. Yet it is marvellously beautiful in its impressiveness, and the grand tombs at the end are a fitting termination and a most fitting place for the burial of these great men.

We went into the tombs of Sethos I, Ramses I, VI and IX, and afterwards had lunch in a tomb, which had been prepared for that purpose.

Entering a Tomb
E. W. Merrick, 1888

We were told of a tomb in which, when first opened, the footprints of the slaves who carried the corpse in thousands of years before could plainly be seen on the sand.

On the Other Side
Constance Sitwell, 1927

We lingered a little where the Colossi stonily sit, gazing out over the land with strange battered calm, their shadows stretching far over the corn that grows thickly to the very base of their thrones. Not far beyond them is the limit of the irrigated ground, and here we found a camel and an ox yoked together ploughing up the caked soil along the last line of living green. Arid and dusty, the earth flew up behind them. In front of us now was a scorched strip of desert, a stone-strewn waste backed by the tawny precipices of the Libyan mountains, and in that mountain face are the Tombs of the Kings.

It was too hot to hurry the donkeys and slowly we rode up towards the ravine which leads to the tomb where Amenhotep still lies. In the ravine itself the heat and glare grew even more intense. The sun beat down with gathering strength upon the crags of yellow and orange limestone, whose jagged edged quivered above us against the blazing sky. Our narrow path was walled in by ribs of rock which threw out all the heat. At last, in the bare face of the cliff we came to a small door. I thanked heaven, saying to myself that we should find darkness inside; surely, too, inside it would be cool? But I was wrong, for after jumping off our donkeys and leaving the guide behind, we plunged into a yet heavier heat. Deeper we went and deeper into an oven of stone, – down long sloping

187

corridors and down steps, past an empty painted chamber and past a well, then down another stretch of stifling dark until right in the heart of the rock we reached the crypt where the king lies.

The tomb has been lit by electricity, and a harsh light now strikes down on the long-dead face. I looked at it with astonishment; it is wonderful that the mummied flesh, the withered tendons, the brittle bones, should have kept so royal an air. Yes, in spite of time and our desecrations, Amenhotep reposes with kingly calm in his ponderous sarcophagus of sandstone. The silent centuries have come and gone and he has lain alone in the sweltering darkness, suffering no change that seems of any account. How noisily the years have passed by outside, how peacefully for him! No change! Only his stained wrappings have become rags, and some one has put in his folded hands a tiny bunch of flowers that have become skeletons. 'Well,' they made me think, 'flowers were the same, I suppose, in Thebes and Babylon. Poppies in Ninevah and jonquils in Tyre! Solomon saw the bright anemones of Judea growing scarlet and purple amongst the stones; and here are Amenhotep and I each with our little bunch.' I looked at the flagging handful which I still held; the dying fragrance of the clover hung heavily in that stagnant air. Maybe, I thought, as we walked back along the soundless passage, this king liked the honey smell of warm clover too when he was outside in the sun.

Entering a Tomb
Dr Richardson, 1816

[Lord Belmore and his party were the first Europeans to be shown into the tomb which Belzoni had discovered. Here Dr Richardson visits other tombs.]

All these tombs have been open for many years to the passing intruder; they are much injured, filled with broken fragments of what formerly constituted their greatest pride and ornament, and polluted by swarms of bats, which occupy them in such legions that the visitor is frequently obliged to stand with his eyes shut, and bear their stormy flight for five or six minutes at a time. If he can save his torch the attack is soon over, if not, as often as he lights it with his flint and steel it is again renewed; when the storm is over, he may continue his researches. But the walls are so contaminated with the filth of these abominable vermin that in general they end in disappointment. With all his impatience to examine the walls, he must not forget to look at his feet, lest, as we found in one of them, a snake should be lurking, which he may find it his interest to avoid.

Deep in Mummies
Giovanni Belzoni, 1817

A traveller is generally satisfied when he has seen the large hall, the gallery, the staircase, and as far as he can conveniently go: besides, he is taken up with the strange works he observes cut in various places, and painted on each side of the walls; so that when he comes to a narrow and difficult passage, or to have to descend to the bottom of a well or cavity, he declines taking such trouble, naturally supposing that he cannot see in these abysses any thing so magnificent as what he sees above, and consequently deeming it useless to proceed any further. Of some of these tombs many persons could not withstand the suffocating air, which often causes fainting. A vast quantity of dust rises, so fine that it enters into the throat and nostrils, and chokes the nose and mouth to such a degree, that it requires great power of lungs to resist it and the strong effluvia of the mummies. This is no all; the entry or passage where the bodies are is roughly cut in the rocks, and the falling of the sand from the upper part or ceiling of the passage causes it to be nearly filled up. In some places there is not more than a vacancy of a foot left, which you must contrive to pass through in a creeping posture like a snail, on pointed and keen stones that cut like glass. After getting through these passages, some of them two or three hundred yards long, you generally find a more commodious place, perhaps high enough to sit. But what a place of rest! surrounded by bodies, by heaps of mummies in all directions; which, previous to my being accustomed to the sight, impressed me with horror. The blackness of the wall, the faint light given by the candles or torches for want of air, the different objects that surrounded me, seeming to converse with each other, and the Arabs with the candles or torches in their hands, naked and covered with dust, themselves resembling living mummies, absolutely formed a scene that cannot be described. In such a situation I found myself several times, and often returned exhausted and fainting, till at last I became inured to it, and indifferent to what I suffered, except from the dust, which never failed to choke my throat and nose; and though fortunately, I am destitute of the sense of smelling, I could taste that the mummies were rather unpleasant to swallow. After the exertion of entering into such a place, through a passage of fifty, a hundred, three hundred, or perhaps six hundred yards, nearly overcome, I sought a resting place, found one, and contrived to sit; but when my weight bore on the body of an Egyptian, it crushed it like a bandbox. I naturally had recourse to my hands to sustain my weight, but they found no better support; so that I sunk altogether among the broken mummies, with a crash of bones, rags, and wooden cases, which raised such a dust as kept me motionless for a quarter of an hour, waiting till it subsided again. I could not remove from the place, however, without increasing it, and every step I took I crushed a mummy in some part or other. Once I was conducted from such a place to another resembling it, through a passage of about twenty feet in length, and no wider than that a body could be forced through. It was choked with mummies, and I could not pass without putting my face in contact with that of some decayed Egyptian; but as the passage inclined downwards, my own weight helped me on: however, I could not avoid being covered with bones, legs, arms, and heads rolling from above. Thus I proceeded from one cave to another, all full of mummies piled up in various ways, some standing, some lying, and some on their heads.

Resurrection-men
Mrs Colonel Elwood, 1825

It is said, the Egyptians had a tradition that they were to rise again at the end of three thousand years, but it may be presumed they anticipated a more glorious resurrection from the grave than the being thus ignominiously torn from their tombs, and exposed and examined in a manner so revolting to humanity, to satisfy the curiosity of the traveller. For my part, I see little difference between the resurrection-men in London, who steal the bodies of the dead for the purposes of science, and the mummy-seekers in Egypt, who exhume them for curiosity. Why are not the corporeal frames of the ancient Egyptians to be considered as sacred as those of Europeans? And why should not those who disinter the Egyptians expect to be haunted by the ghosts of Amenophis or Rameses of Thebes, as soon as by those of Mr. Smith and Mr. Johnson of London? Most of these mummies were wrapped in cloth of a saffron hue, and a quantity of it, their former habiliments, was scattered about, but we were so pressed for time that we could spare but little for the investigation of objects so curious and so interesting: and, oh! how did we wish for some of those hours of frivolity and ennui, which, from the conventional forms of society, are necessarily often spent in civilized company, to devote to the wonders that surrounded us; but we saw so much in so short a period, that neither my physical nor my mental powers were competent to appreciate properly all I beheld. In comparison with what we had just viewed, Pompeii appeared modern, and bread out of the Tomb of King Sesostris made that in the Italian ovens of no curiosity.

We breakfasted with Mr Hay and Mr Bonomi* in their tent, and were favoured by them with a sight of some very spirited and correct sketches of the paintings and sculpture on the different temples, particularly those lately discovered by themselves, and which I imagine and believe will one day be given to the public. After which, the thermometer being at 105°, you may conceive I was not sorry to lie down upon my couch, being half dead with fatigue, for it was then near noon, and we had been in constant exertion of body and mind ever since daybreak.

The Valley of the Kings
H. V. Morton, 1938

It is a pity that the donkeys that once took you there have almost disappeared, because the slow ride into the Valley of the Dead, the gradual approach to that

---

* Robert Hay (1799–1863) was a Scottish traveller, antiquarian and collector. A one-time naval officer, he left his ship to travel up the Nile in 1824, and revisited Egypt on several occasions over the next dozen years, accompanied by different scholars and artists. Joseph Bonomi (1796–1878) was an English sculptor who went to Egypt with Hay in 1824 and remained there working with him and Edward Lane for several years. Gardner Wilkinson used him as a draughtsman. Back in England, he set up the Egyptian Court at the Crystal Palace in London in 1853 and created the first hieroglyphic printers' fount. He was the curator of Sir John Soane's Museum in London, where Belzoni's sarcophagus was in his care, from 1861 until his death.

fiery cleft in the hills, every yard becoming more grim and more desolate, was, I think, a better approach than the rush in a car over a bumpy road.

The Valley widens, the road ends, and the orange-yellow mountains become higher and the rise more steeply on every side. Their lower slopes are covered with small limestone chips, the refuse flung out three thousand years ago, when the tombs were tunnelled. In the sunlight this limestone is as white as snow.

Sixty-one tombs have been found, but only about seventeen are open to inspection. How many more remain to be discovered no one can tell. Most of the existing tombs were rifled in ancient times, and the only untouched royal burial which has ever been found is the tomb of Tut-ankh-Amûn.

There is no sound in the valley but the insistent stutter of a small petrol engine which makes electric light for the tombs. Gaffirs paid by the Government, and armed with guns and buck-shot, guard the tombs day and night. There is a certain poetic justice in the fact that these guardians are descended from the tomb robbers who until recent times spent their lives searching for mummies, ready to tear them limb from limb for the gold which they hoped was concealed about them.

The entrances to the tombs are all the same: a flight of limestone steps leading down into the mountain, and a black opening hewn in the face of the rock, protected by a grille like the door to a safety deposit vault. One of the first tombs on the right is that of the young Pharaoh Tut-ankh-Amûn, the smallest and the plainest tomb in the valley. That its position had been forgotten when the architects tunnelled the later tomb of Rameses VI, immediately above, is well known. Had their tunnels deviated only a yard or so in some places, they must have broken down into the golden treasury which, all unknown to them, was lying below.

As I descended the sixteen shallow steps into this tomb, I remembered the last time I had done so fourteen years ago, when the burial-chambers were piled almost to the ceiling with the treasures which are now in Cairo.

It was a queer experience to stand beside the two guardian statues of the king and to know that when Alexander the Great was born they had already been there for over a thousand years, grasping their thin wands of office, and that their incredible vigil had lengthened to more than two thousand years by the time William the Conqueror set foot in England. The awe which dawns in the mind at such a moment is partly due to the feeling that Time, whose inexorable demands cease not even when we sleep, had somehow spared this hidden cave under the mountain. That the gold and the wood had not perished did not seem so wonderful to me as that wreaths of flowers, brown with age and tender as ash, had still retained their shape; and from these I turned to thoughts of the hands which had plucked the flowers and had cast them in the places where they still lay.

I remembered, too, how I had sat waiting on the wall outside and had heard, muffled by the rock, the sound of hammers and chisels breaking in upon the king's silence. Bit by bit the wall which separated the ante-chamber from the tomb-chamber was broken sufficiently for those who were watching to see, in the darkness beyond, the tall, gleaming tabernacle which rose over the nest of coffins in which the mummy of the king was found.

I stood again in the tomb of Tut-ankh-Amûn. By the pale radiance of an electric light I mounted a wooden platform and looked down into another chamber, where I saw a beautiful sarcophagus of red granite. Inside is a gold coffin shaped to the human figure, which encloses the badly preserved mummy of a youth of eighteen; for that was the age at which death overtook Tut-ankh-Amûn.

The gold face gazes calmly with open eyes towards the roof of the tomb. The king is portrayed wearing a close-fitting war-helmet of gold, with the symbols of his country, the Vulture and the Cobra, rising from his forehead. His gold hands are crossed on his breast; in the right he grasps the Flail, in the left the Crook, emblems of royalty. Tall figures painted on the wall show him, followed by his Ka, or spirit, embracing the mummied figure of Osiris, the God of the Dead.

In this silent tomb, where many thoughts crowd into the mind, one thought perhaps comes first: gladness that the discoverers have not taken the mummy of the king away to Cairo, but have left it in tomb where it was placed over three thousand years ago.

Purchases from Goornou
William C. Prime, 1855

Abd-el-Atti had been making a purchase of an antique, on his own account, from an Arab of Goornou. He had learned that a mummy of the most ancient, rare, and valuable kind, had been found, and he had negotiated for and bought it. It belonged to a company of more than thirty of the Goornou resurrectionists, and they would not consent to bring it over to Luxor to the boat, lest they should be caught with it by some government officer and lose mummy and some of their own skin besides, a not unusual occurrence. Therefore the dragoman was puzzled on the subject, not liking to lose the opportunity for speculation, and not knowing how to avoid it. At length he was relieved by this plan. He directed the Arabs to bring down the daughter of Pharaoh to the shore of the Nile, three miles below on the west bank, near a tree which we all knew, at midnight on the night of our starting. He went down early with the small boat and four men to receive the freight. On our appearance with the *Phantom* he was to board us.

Mustapha and Houssein Kasheef came down in the evening, and sat and talked till nearly midnight. Mustapha had a small cannon, presented him by some traveller who had carried it for saluting purposes, to which he zealously applies it, and he had loaded it to the muzzle for a grand discharge on our departure. But I determined to send him off quietly to bed with the idea that we would not go till morning, and let him save his gunpowder.

Midnight was at hand. The moonlight lay like a dream of beauty on the river and on the ruins. Through the vast corridor of the temple a broad pathway of silver light came down, that made Mustapha's house seem like another Bethel at the foot of a heavenward way.

I sat alone in the cabin of the *Phantom*, the others were sound asleep, dreaming, I doubt not, of home.

When I came out on deck, the crew were lying here and there like so many piles of cloth, giving signs of animation only in the long regular heaving of each mass.

Tourists, about 1880.

The temple at Karnak.

The two colossi at the time of the inundation, 1845.

The colossal fallen statue of Rameses the Great, 1845.

Medenet Habou, 1845.

The entrance court of the temple at Edfou, 1845.

The Valley of the Tombs of the Kings, 1845.

The market place at Esneh, about 1880.

Frontier of Egypt and Nubia, 1845.

A group of Nubians.

Approaching Philae, 1845.

The Sheikh, Rais and pilot of the Cataract.

View from Philae, 1845.

Abu Simbel temple, 1845.

Scarab.

I stirred them up gently, making as little noise as possible, and ordered them to be as quiet. I did not wish to wake Mustapha's cannon. They moved about like ghosts on the moonlit shore, casting off the fasts. I took my place on the upper deck as usual, and gave my orders in pantomime, for the lowest utterance of the human voice echoed from the magnificent corridor in which Mustapha was sleeping.

The *Phantom* drifted slowly out into the current of the river. As she went out of the bight or bay in which we had been lying, the current took her and she shot downward.

All was still. Moonlight lay on the temple and on the shore. The tall group of palms, nearest to the mound on which we had buried poor Tonge, lifted their branches calmly into the glory of the moonlight. There my eye was fixed longer than elsewhere, and looking there I forgot to look at the temple, and so before I knew it we were away from Thebes, and all danger of rousing the echoes of the palace with Egyptian gunpowder was gone.

'Shil!'

They were ready, every man at his oar, and at the word the fourteen oars struck the splashing water together, and the *Phantom* flew down the river.

We coasted the western shore. Near the large tree that was the old landing place on that bank, they lay on their oars, and I looked ahead on the moonlit shore for some indication of Abd-el-Atti with his companion of Pharaonic days. There was a small grove of trees not far below us which was the appointed place of meeting, and here I saw something which looked like the small boat. The shore was three hundred feet broad, and the moonlight lay across it, making it appear as white as snow, while on the bank above there was a grove of trees. From this, as we approached, a group of fifteen men suddenly emerged into the moonlight, bearing something heavy, with which they hastened across the open beach to the boat. Then, retiring a few paces, they stood in a row; while the boat pushed off and joined us as we drifted by.

'Now – all together, men. Lift carefully and slowly. So she comes!' and the princess or priestess was hoisted to the cabin deck and laid on one of our vacant sofas, covered with canvas and blankets to hide her from curious eyes, and the men again lay down to their oars.

We swept close to shore by the row of silent Arabs; the Goornou resurrectionists guttural 'Salaam Aleikoum,' came to us as we went along, and they retired into the grove.

So the daughter of the Pharaoh (who dares say she was not the daughter of Amunoph himself?) commenced her voyage from her ancient resting place and the graves of her fathers. Three thousand years of repose – then, the Nile-boat of a wandering Howajji – then, a curiosity-room in Cairo – and then the sea, the Pillars of Hercules, the Fortunate Islands, and a new world! There is verily no rest even in an Egyptian grave. This royal lady slept quietly on our cabin deck during the voyage down the river, and Abd-el-Atti transferred her to Dr Abbott at Cairo, who, I suppose, will ship her to enrich the collection in New York.

Treating with Grave Robbers
Amelia B. Edwards, 1873

There were whispers about this time of a tomb that had been discovered on the western side – a wonderful tomb, rich in all kinds of treasures. No one, of course, had seen these things. No one knew who had found them. No one knew where they were hidden. But there was a solemn secrecy about certain of the Arabs, and a conscious look about some of the visitors, and an air of awakened vigilance about the government officials, which savoured of mystery. These rumours by and by assumed more definite proportions. Dark hints were dropped of a possible papyrus; the M.B.'s babbled of mummies; and an American dahabeeyah, lying innocently off Karnak, was reported to have a mummy on board. Now, neither L, nor the Writer desired to become the happy proprietor of an ancient Egyptian; but the papyrus was a thing to be thought of. In a fatal hour we expressed a wish to see it. From that moment every mummy-snatcher in the place regarded us as his lawful prey. Beguiled into one den after another, we were shown all the stolen goods in Thebes. Some of the things were very curious and interesting. In one house we were offered two bronze vases, each with a band of delicately-engraved hieroglyphics running round the lip; also a square stand of basket-work in two colours, precisely like that engraved in Sir G. Wilkinson's first volume, after the original in the Berlin Museum. Pieces of mummy-case and wall-sculpture and sepulchral tablets abounded; and on one occasion we were introduced into the presence of – a mummy!

All these houses were tombs, and in this one the mummy was stowed away in a kind of recess at the end of a long rock-cut passage; probably the very place once occupied by the original tenant. It was a mummy of the same period as that which we saw disentombed under the auspices of the Governor, and was enclosed in the same kind of cartonnage, patterned in many colours on a white ground. I shall never forget that curious scene – the dark and dusty vault; the Arabs with their lanterns; the mummy in its gaudy cerements lying on an old mat at our feet.

Meanwhile we tried in vain to get sight of the coveted papyrus. A grave Arab dropped in once or twice after nightfall, and talked it over vaguely with the dragoman; but never came to the point. He offered it first, with a mummy, for £100. Finding, however, that we would neither buy his papyrus unseen nor his mummy at any price, he haggled and hesitated for a day or two, evidently trying to play us off against some rival or rivals unknown, and then finally disappeared. These rivals, we afterwards found, were the M.B.'s. They bought both mummy and papyrus at an enormous price; and then, unable to endure the perfume of their ancient Egyptian, drowned the dear departed at the end of a week.

The Mummy's Hand
H. V. Morton, 1938

When I came out of the tombs at Qurna, and before my eyes had become used to the light, I was aware that people were running towards me. One of the first to arrive thrust something into my hand. I looked down and saw that I was holding the hand of a mummy. I did not wonder to whom it had belonged, or whether it had once been a beautiful hand or an ugly one; I was anxious only to get rid of it. It was dry, black, and claw-like, and was even more hideous than it need have been by the loss of one finger.

The man to whom it belonged refused to take it back, believing that as long as I held it there was a chance that I might give him the shilling he was asking in preference to all the other things that old and young were thrusting on me. While I was wondering what to do, I saw a man who looked as old, as brown, as dried up, and as horrible as any mummy, coming slowly in my direction, leaning on a staff. Although his eyes were closed and he seemed to be blind, he found his way nimbly over the stone-scattered ground, and when he came near he cleared a way for himself by making savage swings with his staff at the legs of the crowd. Several children ran away howling, but I noticed that not one of those who received his blows showed any resentment, for such is the respect for age in the East.

The old man evidently had something important to say to me. When a few yards away, he slowly opened his eyes; and they were white. A desire to get away from this terrible old man came over me, but I waited to see what he wanted. Slowly he thrust his hand into the body of his shirt and drew forth a piece of coffin. It was horrible to see this old man, himself a walking mummy, trying to sell me a bit of coffin, and a nausea for this disgusting trade in tomb relics swept over me until I was ready to put distinguished archaeologist and all others who have dug up Egypt's dead on the same level with this dreadful apparition.

I looked down at the mummy's hand, which I was still holding, and decided to buy it for a shilling and bury it, or get rid of it somehow to put it out of its misery. My purchase seemed to astonish the crowd, and especially the man who had sold it, and they all disappeared shouting into the sandhills, leaving only the terrible old man standing in a bewildered, half-witted way, holding a piece of yellow coffin wood.

I had no newspaper in which to wrap the mummy's hand, and when I tried to put it in my pocket it clawed at the edge of the cloth and refused to go in. I began to feel sorry that I had bought it. To have buried it where I stood, or to have slipped it behind a rock, would have been futile, for it would have been re-discovered within a few hours and offered to some other visitor. There was nothing to do but to walk about hand in hand with it until I could find a safe place to bury it.

After a few bizarre hours of ownership, H. V. Morton managed to sink the hand in the depths of the Nile.

Time in the Valley
Annie Quibell, 1925

Most of us feel the need of quietness in the Valley, above all other places, and often it is very difficult to get it. If one goes with a large party and must stick to them, it is hopeless, but more independent travellers can do better. I would give earnest counsel to make a day of the royal tombs and not to go back for lunch, either to Luxor, or over the hill to the rest house at Der el Bahri. People will probably remonstrate and think us mad to stay on after the electric light is

195

taken off at one o'clock, but by that time we have seen the tombs and we want to see the Valley. When the carriages have all clattered down the road and the last of the donkeys has jingled up the slope to Der el Bahri, let us seek out a place under the shadow of a great rock and settle down for an hour or two of peace among the solemn cliffs. There is shade at midday and in the early afternoon at the head of the Valley.

After we have rested and filled our souls with the great scene around, there is a choice of ways by which to return. Down the Valley is the dullest; over the cliff to Der el Bahri is fine and lets us have a beautiful view from the top, but there is better to be done. There are few good walks in Egypt, but there are some, and perhaps the best of them is the path from the Bibân el Muluk to Der el Medineh. It is quite easy for tolerably good walkers, starting from the valley to the right of the path to Der el Bahri and going upwards above the tomb of Thothmes III.

At the top of the pass are the remains of the shelters where the sentinels of old used to be posted to guard the royal cemetery. From this point onwards the view is glorious. All the line of temples lies below us, Seti's the farthest south, in a clump of palms, Der el Bahri, lying right under the precipice, the Ramesseum, and the big bulk of Medinet Habu to the north. On the desert, in a valley to the right of Medinet Habu are the Tombs of the Queens. On the low desert over the hill of the Sheikh Abd el Gurneh and in the surrounding cliffs, is the cemetery of Thebes, of the nobles and the commonalty.

Beyond Medinet Habu, lines on the desert surface show us the palace of Amenhotep III and the big oblong, just on the edge of the cultivated land, enclosed by high mounds, was once a lake, where he took his pleasure boating. Across the Nile are the temples of Luxor and Karnak and the green country, with three distant peaks closing the prospect.

It is too obvious, perhaps, to say that the more often we can cross to the West Bank the better we shall like it. There is more to see than anywhere else in Egypt and the beauty of the surroundings is so remarkable that every day we spend among them leaves a memory that does not fade in after years.

About six hundred years after Mentuhotep's time, and after another period of darkness and chaos had come and gone, Hatshepsut chose the same magnificent surroundings for her temple. She, too, made a causeway, which covered a considerable part of the older one, and, incidentally, preserved for us a good many of the tree roots. Her temple is much larger and is built in terraces, each of which was decorated with splendid coloured reliefs under porticoes of fluted columns. At the foot of her ramp, on either side, is a small T-shaped pool, in which some papyrus roots and a boomerang were found. The boomerang was used for catching birds, but in this tiny pool it is quite impossible there could have been any form of sport; it must have been used in some of the many ceremonials held in this temple. It is rather better to go to Der al Bahri in the afternoon if possible, as it is in shade, and the view over the sunlit valley to Luxor and Karnak when the tints of the distant hills are violet and rose is really inexpressibly beautiful.

To those who stay long enough in Luxor to cross over often and to acquire what I may call the tomb habit, the Sheikh Abd el Gurneh hill offers endless entertainment. The modern village itself is a most curious sight. All the population used to live in tombs and many still do. Most of the daily life goes on in a small courtyard in front, which is generally enclosed by a brick wall and contains the children and other live stock belonging to the family, some articles of furniture and two or three odd mushroom-shaped mud tables raised upon mud pedestals, which serve the double purpose of storing grain and making sufficiently safe sleeping places for the children, out of the way of scorpions.

Much has been done to rescue the painted and inscribed tombs from the long devastation they have suffered, but when I knew Gurneh nearly thirty years ago, the state of matters was not very unlike what Belzoni describes it in 1817, and, though it is really amazing that anything should have survived, it is appalling to think how much that was beautiful and absolutely unique, must have perished for ever.

10

Luxor to Aswan

Introduction

On the 7th of May, I began to look for the beauties of Elephantina, and soon was gratified, when we sailed among the masses of blue granite, which at this low season of the year, rose high above the water: this had now lost its rapidity. I was presented with a scene composed of water, rocks and buildings, which latter had the additional effect of being formed of cupolas, minarets, mosques and ruins, interspersed amongst plantations of lofty palm-trees, and surrounded by mountains of deep red and sandy hue, on the tops and sides of which were other ruins of convents, churches and mosques.

Henry Light, 1814

After travelling so far, the next stage of the journey, from Luxor to Aswan (or Elephantina), held fewer excitements for the travellers, although it made a pleasant interlude. Winston Churchill in 1898 was on his way to war and hardly stopped. Esneh is introduced by Annie Quibell in 1925 – its barrage was being built in front of Douglas Sladen's eyes in 1907. William Golding, there in 1984, reported on its thriving camel market. On to Edfu, where William Jarvie covered his nose in 1904, and where in 1864 the great Egyptologist Mariette Bey had uncovered the temple so greatly admired by Constance Sitwell in 1927. Stephen Olin in 1843 found the Egyptians more congenial than the other travellers.

The temple of Kom Ombo, described by Michael Haag in 1987, is one of the few that still dominates the river, and was much admired by Harriet Martineau.

Thence to Aswan – a sparkling place to which William Hamilton was mistakenly given the keys in 1801. Lucie Duff Gordon settled there happily among the people in 1863 and Villiers Stuart too found them pleasing in 1879. Sir Gaston Maspero reminisced. Samuel Manning recognized that he had reached a boundary – one that George Hoskins had had to negotiate in 1833. Mr W. E. Kingsford recommended the Cataract Hotel, the splendour of which makes it still one of the great sights of Aswan.

Vivant Denon found in 1799 that the solitude of the desert monastery stirred him with alarm. The people of Egypt change when you reach Aswan, as Charlie Pye-Smith observed; Lucie Duff Gordon particularly recommended the charm of the girls. The 'excursionists' were unpopular with travellers like the artist Emma Merrick in 1888, Olin's dragoman was unpopular with the locals in 1843, who were themselves unpopular with Hercule Poirot! Constance Sitwell was simply oppressed by her Nubian day.

Up the River with the 21st Lancers
Winston Churchill, 1898

Here we are on the Nile. The railway is left, and progress is by steamer. One was already waiting. The versatile and ubiquitous Cook had undertaken the arrangements, as his name painted on everything clearly showed. The horses had to be moved from the trucks and persuaded, in spite of their protests, to enter two great barges. On these they were tightly packed – so tightly, indeed, that they could not kick, and biting was the sole expression they could give to their feelings. The baggage was then shipped, and when this task was finished the steamer took the barges in tow, and pushing out into the stream began its journey to Assuan. The barges were heavy, the currents adverse, and hence the progress was slow and tedious.

For four days and four nights the steamer plodded up the Nile. At Luxor we stopped for a couple of hours, almost moored to the temple. I paid it a flying visit. Something in the strange shapes of the great pillars appeals to the human love of the mystical. It requires no effort of imagination to roof the temple and fill its great hall with the awe-struck worshippers, or to occupy the odd, nameless chambers at the far end with the powerful priests who crushed the body and soul out of ancient Egypt. Now that the roof is off and the sun shines into all the nooks and corners, we may admire the beauty of the work without fearing its evil purposes. It is also a favourite place for tourists to be photographed in. The science and the triumph of the living century are displayed in vivid contrast with the art and repose of the century long dead. We are reminded of the bright butterfly on the tomb. The truth of the simile, however, vanishes when the photographs of the tourists are proudly shown by the local photographer. We were not without Philistines on board.

'Have you been to see the temple?' I asked an officer. 'No, certainly not; supposing I am killed, I shall have dragged all round there for nothing.'

We reached Assuan at last, and the business of disembarkation began again. The First Cataract of the Nile opposed the further passage of the original steamer; but above the rapids another waited. From Assuan to Shellal is a march of six miles. The horses, delighted to stretch their limbs, enjoyed themselves. The heat and the dust moderated the enthusiasm of their riders. The baggage went by train, with a sufficient escort.

The scene when we arrived at Shellal was indeed strange. In the foreground, under the shade of the palm-tree, whose sombre tints were brightened by the glow of the evening sun, lay the fresh steamers which were to carry us to Wady Halfa. The shore was lined with barges and *gyassas*. On the banks piles of military stores were accumulated. Great stacks of shovels, of small-arm ammunition in boxes with red labels, of Maxim-gun ammunition in boxes painted green, of medical stores, of all the varied necessaries of an army, rose on every side. The train which had conveyed us from Assuan drew up in the midst of this. An array of coolies and of convicts – of the same appearance as the coolies, but for heavy chains on their legs – was drawn up to assist the soldiers in unloading the trucks and loading the boats. The work began. The spectacle, so far as the foreground was concerned, was one of singular animation. Blue-clothed brown men and brown-clad white men bustled about in a busy whirlpool. Whistles blew, trumpets sounded, the horses fought and squealed, officers shouted: and behind, among the dark rocks of the river gorge, the broken pillars and walls of the Temple of Philæ were outlined against the sunset sky.

Esneh
Annie Quibell, 1925

The high red cliffs recede on the West side, soon after we leave Luxor, and, on both sides of the valley, low hills of sandstone, much strewn with boulders, come into view. At Esna, 484½ miles from Cairo, a town of some importance, the cultivation is wide for this part of Egypt and the hills are rather far away. There is a great Temple here, but most of it is still underneath the houses, as Luxor and Edfu used to be.

The Barrage at Esna
Douglas Sladen, 1908

Esna, as we approached it in 1907, was all in a ferment; it was beside itself with importance. A fourth of the great Nile barrages was in the full swing of construction. Already a monster viaduct, long and high, was advancing upon the river from the eastern bank; and scores of huge *gyassas*, the Nile merchant-men, laden with earth, were running upstream with their vast wings of sails blown out stiff, to dump their cargoes on the advancing dam. The presence of all these native craft, of an army of fellahin navvies, and a posse of English engineers made business in the little town brisk. It reminded the Esnites of the palmy days when Esna had a governor, and was the chief town of a province, which was quietly cut in two and handed over to Kena and Assuan in 1889. Its government offices were moved to Assuan; the staff at any rate must have been pleased, since Assuan in winter is the most fashionable place in Egypt.

Most of the thirteen thousand five hundred inhabitants of Esna, who were not earning wages at barrage-building, were assembled on the shore for the arrival of our steamer. A barber was doing a thriving trade by the water's edge, and you could have any number you wanted of leather water-bottles, decorated with shells. But the principal feature of the alfresco market which was accommodating itself to the steep slopes of the bank, was the display of baskets, about four feet high, shaped like oil-jars, and woven of purple, green, and white cane splints, arranged in rows.

Until the barrage was commenced, travellers only regarded Esna from one point of view – as a place with a temple; and until the time of Mohammed Ali this was buried up to the capitals of its façade, and over head and ears every-where else. He had one chamber of it – the hypostyle hall, cleared out in 1842; the rest of the temple, which is said to be still complete, was underground when I was there, and half the city of Esna was built on the top of it. As it had formerly stood at the top of the town, this was naturally the airiest situation.

Camels
William Golding, 1984

At Esna we saw the famous camel market. Hundreds of camels were being sold, some for work but most for slaughter. There were trucks waiting from as far away as Cairo and Alexandria. In common with all Third World peoples these traders and their customers had little thought for the camel's comfort. The worst sight I saw this time was two camels roped down in a truck too small for them so that they could neither stand nor kneel. However, I suppose the feeling, or view rather than feeling, was that they were meat already.

A little further on we came across a huge herd (if that is the appropriate collective noun) of camels being driven north. They had made one of the longest herding treks left in the world, all the way through the desert from south of Khartoum. The escorts were a number of genuine-seeming Sons of the Desert, who could have ridden straight into a story by P. C. Wren. They all rode camels and flourished long sticks as a substitute for the long rifles which had been taken from them at the border. Their leader was a really magnificent sight. He and the camels were enough to stop the traffic though they were off the road. Soon there was a row of car-people busy photographing camel-people. At this, the magnificent leader rode forward, shouting insults at the photographers. He was a noble savage, and he scared everyone back into their cars.

Edfu
E. A. Wallis Budge, 1906

515½ miles from Cairo, on the west bank of the Nile . . . The Temple of Edfu, for which alone both ancient and modern towns were famous, occupied 180 years three months and fourteen days in building (237–57 BC).

Riding through Edfu
William Jarvie, 1904

2 February

The noses, ears, mouths and eyes of our party, carried away enough of Egypt, which had been held suspended in the air, to found an oasis in the desert.

The Temple at Edfu
Constance Sitwell, 1927

The massive outer walls of the temple are still whole at Edfu; one can look right down the open passages that run all the length of the building; one can walk unseen along those mighty corridors between calm golden walls incised with histories of gods and warriors and kings. There is no painting here, no colour but the scorched bright amber of the stone, and the pure cobalt of the sky above. I wandered about by myself without the fear of being alone, which haunts one beneath the monstrous columns of Karnac. This building is neither stupendous nor strange, and centuries of quiet burial beneath the drifting sand have kept it from falling into ruin. It stands now as it stood then, its beauty, unchanged, its shadow clear-cut and distinct under the fierce insistent sunlight as they were of old.

As I passed between the towers of the gateway which lift their splendid sloping sides high into the blue I tried to imagine the scene on a feast day when decorated poles were fixed to the walls, and the coloured banners streamed fluttering against the sky. In the court the arrogant painted priests assembled in their brightly fringed robes of fine linen. I suppose they had the same proud mouths and delicate oval faces that one still sees here and there among the living as well as in the sculptured dead. Did they stand in solemn order, their shadows sharp upon the ground, with the vivid walls behind, all fresh with tints of daffodil, turquoise, and pale vermilion?, and the King, would he be there with the leopard-skin thrown over his shoulder and the sun striking dazzling on the golden cobra, with lifted head that made his royal headdress? Yes, and his arms are heavy with bracelets and ornaments set with lapis-lazuli and emeralds.

The stones of the stairs leading on to the roof are worn by the feet of men who walked there thousands of years ago. I climbed them now, going in the steps of those who carried offerings to the sun-god, and stood looking down on the wide empty view. There is no town here now; nothing moves at this somnolent hour, only down a path through the doura and the maize a man in a yellow-striped burnous walks slowly along carrying a squawking turkey blue with rage.

Salutations
Stephen Olin, 1843

February 2. We stopped for the night off Edfou, the wind failing us about 9 o'clock. Our sleep was interrupted by the arrival of a downward bound boat, which moored just above us. We were told by our crew that the party were Americans, and on this account were more eager in our inquiries, as we expected to meet a gentleman from Boston about this time on his return from the cataracts. It is usual with Americans, when they meet abroad, to dispense with formalities that, even in the United States, where society is less embarrassed with etiquette than it is in most other countries, attend the formation of a new acquaintance; and one has seldom to regret having approached a country-man in this frank, unceremonious style. Our manners in this respect are seldom imitated by foreigners, though they commonly respond to such advances courteously. The exceptions to this remark are most numerous among the English. The strange boat belonged to two gentlemen of that nation and a German, and all our inquiries this morning did not provoke a word of reply, though one of the gentlemen sat in the door of his cabin in full view, and must have perceived our difficulty in communicating with his rais in Arabic. This peculiar, and, I must regard it, unamiable, reserve of our English brethren, is often justified by them on the score of prudence. They are not disposed to admit into sociable relations improper persons, who may afterward prove troublesome acquaintances. There can at least be little danger on that ground in the interior of Africa, and in such interviews as the meeting of two boats for a few minutes will allow.

One is perpetually struck with the different and more hospitable manners of the Arabs, who never pass each other without a profusion of salutations and compliments, couched in the most courteous language, and always expressive of benevolent and pious sentiments. Our crew kept up this interchange of greetings with that of the unsocial Englishmen till we were obliged to interpose in order to procure a little quiet for sleep.

The rais, or some other person, cries, on the meeting of two boats, 'Peace be upon you.' The most common answer is, 'On you be peace.' Other forms of salutation are often heard. 'God be with you.' 'May God strengthen you.' 'May God receive you into paradise.' To my taste, nothing could be more beautiful, and no language could be chosen more appropriate for the purpose. How much more grateful to the ears of a friend, or a weary traveller, is a simple prayer for his happiness, then the meager inquiries and compliments that pass between us on similar occasions? There is no hope of a change in manners in this respect; but I think every person of unsophisticated taste and pious feeling must appreciate the deeper import and more touching influence of the Oriental salutations.

Kom Ombo
Michael Haag, 1987

556½ miles from Cairo. The temple stands on a low promontary overlooking the Nile. Its elevation, its seclusion, the combination of sun and water flowing past as though in slow but determined search for the Mediterranean, at last suggests something of Greece. It has ruined well, and there is something in its stones of that Hellenic response to light, the uncompromising noonday glare, the soft farewell of the setting sun without fear of night.

Observed at Kom Ombo
Harriet Martineau, 1848

One curious architectural device of the Egyptians, which we found almost everywhere by looking for it, is here apparent at a glance, when one stands on the great circuit wall which incloses the whole group of edifices; – their plan of regularly diminishing the size of the inner chambers, so as to give, from the entrance, an appearance of a longer perspective than exists. They evidently liked an ascending ground, the ascent of which was disguised as much as possible by the use of extremely shallow steps. The roof was made to descend in a greater degree, the descent being concealed inside by the large cornices and deep architraves they employed. The sides were made to draw in; and thus the Holy Place was always small; while to those who looked towards it from the outer chambers, (and it was entered by the priests alone) it appeared, not small, but distant. I had observed this in some of the Nubian temples, when looking at them sideways from a distance; but here it was particularly evident; the roof descending in deep steps from the portico to the pronaos; from the naos to the corridors; and from the corridors to the adyta; which last were level with the sand.

When I was in the portico, looking up at the architraves, I saw into another ancient secret, which I should have been sorry to have overlooked. Some of the paintings were half-finished; and their ground was still covered with the intersecting red lines by which the artists secured their proportions. These guiding lines were meant to have been effaced as soon as the outlines were completed; yet here they are at the end of, at least, two thousand years! No hand, however light, has touched them, through all the intervening generations of men; – no rains have washed them out, during all the changing seasons that have passed over them: – no damp has moulded them: no curiosity has meddled with them. It is as if the artist had lain down for his siesta, with his tools beside his hand, and would be up presently to resume his work: yet that artist has been a mummy, lying somewhere in the heart of the neighbouring hills, ever since the time when our island was bristling with forests, and its inhabitants were dressed in skins, and dyed their bodies blue with woad, to look terrible in battle. In another part of this temple, the stone is diced in small squares, to receive the hieroglyphic figures.

Aswan
E. A. Wallis Budge, 1906

587 miles from Cairo, the southern limit of Egypt proper, on the east bank of the river, with over 13,000 inhabitants ... The town obtained great notoriety among the Greeks from the fact that Ptolemy considered it to lie on the Tropic of Cancer, and to be the most northerly point where, at the time of the summer solstice, the sun's rays fell vertically; as a matter of fact, however, the town lies 0'37'23" north of the Tropic of Cancer.

At Aswan
Lucie Duff Gordon, 1863

11 February

At Aswan I had been strolling about in that most poetically melancholy spot, the granite quarry of old Egypt and burial-place of Muslim martyrs, and as I came homewards along the bank a party of slave merchants, who had just loaded their goods for Senaar from the boat on the camels, asked me to dinner, and, oh! how delicious it felt to sit on a mat among the camels and strange bales of goods and eat the hot tough bread, sour milk and dates, offered with such stately courtesy. We got quite intimate over our leather cup of sherbet (brown sugar and water), and the handsome jet-black men, with features as beautiful as those of the young Bacchus, described the distant lands in a way which would have charmed Herodotus. They proposed to me to join them, 'they had food enough', and Omar and I were equally inclined to go.

It is of no use to talk of the ruins; everybody has said, I suppose, all that can be said ... The scribbling of names is quite infamous, beautiful paintings are defaced by Tomkins and Hobson, but worst of all Prince Pückler Muskau has engraved his and his *Ordenskreuz* in huge letters on the naked breast of that august and pathetic giant who sits at Abu Simbel. I wish someone would kick him for his profanity.

Assouân
Villiers Stuart, 1879

18 December

On awaking, and taking a bird's-eye view from our cabin window of the outer world, a very amusing scene occupied the foreground. A number of Nubian men, women, and children were squatting on the sandy shore with their wares arranged on mats before them, patiently awaiting our appearance, smoking and chatting with our crew the while; but no sooner did we step forth, than the greatest excitement prevailed, they started up with one accord and took to brandishing their merchandize over their heads, advertising them by power of lung, and deafening us with a perfect Babel of sounds. They held out at arms' length towards us, ostrich eggs, Nubian spears, armlets, necklaces, bracelets, porcupine quills, bows and arrows, ebony clubs, daggers, ostrich feathers, leopard skins, hippopotamus-hide whips, cunningly made baskets, and Egyptian antiquities; our dragoman took very good care not to let them come on board. Their wares were handed in for our inspection, they themselves were made to keep their distance; and when we went on shore, we landed under escort of a body-guard of our crew, who kept the Nubian merchants off with their sticks.

A little higher up the beach were the goods of a caravan, bound for Khartoum; boxes and bales arranged in a circle formed a sort of camp; their saloon, reception-room, and dining-room was the home of the travellers by day, and their dormitory by night. We visited them at the hour of breakfast; their wants were being ministered to by a number of Nubian girls, some having milk to sell, others cheese, butter, new-baked cakes, cucumbers, buttermilk, and other delicacies. Some were smoking, some were cooking, some were bargaining with the vendors of eatables; in the middle was a sort of trophy supported on three poles, and consisting of water skins; jars covered with goats' hide with the shaggy hair still on, lanterns, pots, and other camp equipage. Outside the magic circle squatted some camels; it was a very picturesque and amusing scene.

Looking Backward from Assouân
Sir Gaston Maspero, 1902

Where is the Assouân of twenty years ago, the half-Nubian village, its originality as yet unspoilt by a European admixture? No railway disgorged every evening carriage-loads of dusty tourists: four or five dahabiehs at most rode at anchor far apart in the height of the season. The post-boat, brought up a few dozen tourists in the week, and twice a month Cook's parties arrived in a big steamer. Then for two or three days there was going and coming of small boats between

Elephantine and the mainland, donkeys galloping along the road to Philæ, warlike reviews of Barabras at ten francs a dance, ballets of almehs, endless bargainings for Nubian swords and weapons, ostrich feathers, raw ivory, Soudanese stuffs, or jewellery. One fine morning the whistle announced departure, and amid a sound of paddle-wheels civilised man set out for the north as noisily as he had come. The town, delighted with its gains, but tired of the confusion, uttered a sign of relief and lazily sank to sleep again to the lullabies of the *sâkiych*.

But now from the middle of December to the middle of March Assouân never sleeps. It has become a winter resort, like Nice or Sorrento, and has had to transform itself to satisfy the demands of its passing visitors. The embankment, formerly so picturesque, though rough and dirty, has been replaced by a regular quay, with decorations in brick, adorned with palms already high and with lebakhs which will grow if Heaven pleases. The whole front is almost European in appearance, with its banks, post-office, hospital, fountain, chapel, cafés, hotels, taverns, shops with glass windows and covered with advertisements. A Dalmatian photographer invites you in composite French not to buy your films anywhere except at his shop. His neighbour, a Greek tobacconist, offers you the best to be had in cigarettes and silks, all English, but if you need eau de Cologne you must go on farther to the Italian bookseller, who will supply you. As you pass obliging Parsees cry their cloths, printed in loud colours, and their coarse Indian silver-work. At the southern end two or three cabs of the most correct pattern await custom with resignation, at the head of a rank of numbered donkeys, and then the railway station with its level entrance marks the end of the esplanade.

Here, then, the quay ends, and the shore reappears, capricious, scattered over with all kinds of breakneck objects, bristling with heaps of broken stones, piles of wood, of barrels or of sacks, but also with booths and tents that betray a fair in which toys and popular cakes are offered for sale, where there is cooking in the open air, and even an itinerant circus under the French flag, whence a freshly shorn ass's foal and a superb white camel come forth to the tune of a polka to drink at the river. It is time to turn aside if we wish to escape these suburban attractions, and we strike into a silent street which, turning its back to the town, seems to plunge south into a desert of granite and sand. The site has the wretched aspect of the outskirts of cities, houses in ruins, unproductive gardens, vague plots of ground disfigured by filth, through which the road winds and climbs. A portion of a mosque totters on the right, a trench is hollowed where the road sinks down, and suddenly, as in Perrault's fairy tale, the ground half opens and a courtyard appears at the bottom framed on two sides by long, new buildings. A troop of young people on donkeys come out of the gateway and strike into the country. Groups of people walking about stop their chatting to watch them, and then begin to talk again faster than ever. Two dragomans dispute in a corner and mutually curse their father. A cook, dressed in white, his cap on one side and his knife in his waistband, chases a boy who has stolen a pigeon from his kitchen. It is the Cataract Hotel, which is the beginning beyond Assouân of a second Assouân, more European than the first. Exactly opposite, the English Church rears its cupola, finished last year, and a little to the south the reservoir, finished this year, stands on the height.

At Assouân
Samuel Manning, 1874

The approach to Assouan is very picturesque, and affords a pleasing contrast to the scenery of the Lower and Middle Nile. Instead of flat monotonous banks of sand and mud, we have masses of rock, broken up into grotesque and fantastic forms. Groves of palm, mimosa, and castor-oil plant come down to the water's edge. The limestone and sandstone ranges which hem in the Nile Valley from Cairo to Silsilis, give place to granite, porphyry, and basalt. The islands in the stream are no longer shifting accretions of mud, alternately formed and dissolved by the force of the current, but rocks and boulders of granite, which rise high above the river and resist its utmost force. The ruined convents and towers which crown the hills might almost cheat us into the belief that we were afloat on the Rhine or the Moselle, but for the tropical character of the scenery.

This altered aspect of the scenery is in accordance with the political geography of the district. We have reached the southern boundary of Egypt and are about to enter Nubia. The kingdom of the Pharaohs lies behind us, and we are on the borderland from which they marched for the conquest of Ethiopia. To this fact Ezekiel refers when, denouncing the Divine vengeance against Egypt, he says: 'Behold, therefore, I am against thee, and against thy rivers, and I will make the land of Egypt utterly waste and desolate, from Migdol to Syene, even the border of Ethiopia.'*

Assouan is a great centre for traffic with the interior. Caravans arrive from the desert, the camels are unloaded, and in a few days start again with consignments of manufactured articles – prints, beads, guns, powder – for barter with the native tribes. Dhows from Nubia and the Soudan, too heavily laden to descend the cataract, discharge their cargoes near Philæ, to be borne overland to this point for transhipment to Cairo or Alexandria. A broad open space outside the town, on the bank of the river, serves at once as warehouse and exchange. Arabs, Turks, Negroes, Nubians, Abyssinians meet here on a footing of perfect equality. Trade levels all distinctions. Many of them are camped in native fashion. Bales of goods are arranged in a circle, so as to form a rampart against attack.

A Turkish Divan
George A. Hoskins, 1833

5 February

... we arrived at Assuan, and immediately I waited on the Nazr to procure camels [Hoskins was intending to cross the desert southwards to Ethiopia]. On entering a Turkish divan, the traveller is merely required to make a grave bow, placing his right hand to his left breast, and to seat himself on the divan in the Turkish style, which for the information of those readers who have not been

---

* Ezekiel 30:10. Migdol was the frontier town at the north-east and Syene, or Assouan, was to the south.

in the country, I should say is exactly that easy position which it seems in Europe tailors only are privileged to assume. When seated, he usually salutes the great man again in the same manner as before; but if the latter be of very high rank it is better to show respect by placing the right hand, first, to the lips, and then, above the forehead. A few complementary speeches are now exchanged, such as:

'How do you do?'
'What a tall man you are!'
'What a fine beard!'
'You are like one of us!'

Welcome and thanks. Coffee is then presented to the traveller.

The Pasha gives pipes to noblemen at his own divan only; but every English gentleman has the right to expect one, or to smoke his own at the divan of any of his subordinate officers.

The Turk, if he is only a Katschef or Nazr, ought to make a kind of half rise from his seat when the traveller enters; but it is very seldom that his pride and desire of appearing a great man in his little court permits him to show this courtesy.

The Cataract and the Invalid
W. E. Kingsford, 1899

[When the Cataract Hotel opened officially in January 1900, the dining room was described in a *Daily Telegraph* review as 'unmatched even in Europe', and even today the hotel is quite splendid.]

In the construction of this Hotel, great attention has been given to the requirements of invalids – most of the rooms have verandahs, and a warm, sunny aspect; many are fitted with fireplaces, and the position and form of the building has been chosen to provide shelter from the prevailing winds.

The sanitary arrangements have been carefully studied, Moule's earth closet system being adopted, and the water being filtered through Reeves' gravity, and Berkefeld filters.

Every modern convenience is provided for in the form of electric light, hot and cold water baths, &c., and a reference to the plan will show that there are a number of private sitting-rooms to meet the requirements of invalids.

There is an English physician and nurse in Assouan, and an English housekeeper is in charge of the domestic arrangements of the Hotel.

The Monastery of St Simeon
Vivant Denon, 1799

I took the opportunity offered by a reconnoitering which was pushed into the desert on the right bank, to seek for the quarries spoken of by Pocock, and an ancient convent of Cenobites. After half an hour's march, I discovered this building, in a little valley, surrounded by rugged rocks, and by sands which their decomposition produced. The detachment, in pursuit of its route, left me to my researches in this place.

Scarcely was this gone, when I was alarmed by my solitude. Lost in long corridors the re-echoed noise of my steps under their melancholy vaults, was perhaps the only one which, for many ages, had troubled their silence. The cells of the monks resembled the cages of animals in a menagery; a square of seven feet was illumined only by a dormer-window at the height of six feet; this refinement of austerity, however, robbed the recluse only of the view of a vast extent of sky, an equally vast horizon of sand, an immensity of light as melancholy and more painful than night, and which would have but increased, perhaps, the afflicting sentiment of his solitude: in this dungeon, a couch of brick, and a recess serving for a press, was all that art had added to the bareness of the four walls: a *turning* box, placed beside the door, still proves that these solitaries took their frugal repasts apart. A few mutilated sentences written on the walls, were the only testimonies that men had inhabited these abodes. I thought I saw in these inscriptions their last sentiments, a last communication with the beings who were to survive them, a hope which time, that effaces all, had still frustrated ... Oppressed by the feelings with which these series of melancholy objects had inspired me, I went into the court, in search of space: surrounded by lofty and embattled walls, covered ways, and the embrasures of cannon, all announced that, in this dismal place, the storms of war had succeeded to the horrors of silence; that this edifice, taken from the Cenobites who had raised it with so much zeal and perseverance, had, at divers epochs, served for the retreat of vanquished parties, or the advanced post of the vanquishers. The different characters of its construction may also give the history of this edifice: begun in the first ages of Christianity, all that was built by her has still preserved its grandeur and magnificence; that which war has added has been done in haste, and is now more ruinous than the former. In the court, a little church, built with unburnt bricks, attests that a small number of solitaries has returned at a later time, and reassumed possession: to conclude, a more recent devastation gives reason to believe that it is only a few ages since the place has been wholly restored to the abandonment and silence to which it has been condemned by nature.

I was rejoined by the detachment, and, on leaving the convent, I seemed to leave a tomb.

The Other Egyptians
Charlie Pye-Smith, 1984

Wherever you go in this part of the country, the inhabitants are keen to assert their separate identity from the Egyptians of further north. They are darker in complexion, they speak Nubian as well as Arabic, and they see the border which divides Sudan from Egypt as no more than an artificial line drawn through their huge territory. They are proud of their culture and their history. A European parallel might be the Welsh in Britain or the Catalans in Spain.

The history of Aswan and Nubia has been one of trade and turbulence. For thousands of years Aswan was a meeting place for pilgrims making the trek east to Mecca, and the river provided the link between black Africa and the Mediterranean. Through Aswan would come gold, slaves, ivory, perfumes and animal products. In the marketplaces young girls from Abyssinia, from the

Upper Nile and from Nubia itself (Nubian women were highly prized as their skin was said to remain cool to the touch in the hottest weather) were bought from slavers and despatched to the harems of Cairo and the Middle East. The same merchants might buy the ostrich plumes which were used in Turkey to decorate the helmets of the janissaries and spahis, and the skin of leopard, lion and cheetah. Aswan must have been used to marauders too. It was the southerly outpost of the Roman Empire, and there have been few centuries since when some military operation was not pushing north or south through this part of the Nile Valley.

The Girls
Lucie Duff Gordon, 1865

It is worth going to Nubia to see the girls. Up to twelve or thirteen they are neatly dressed in a bead necklace and a leather fringe 4 inches wide round the loins, and anything so absolutely perfect as their shapes or so sweetly innocent as their look can't be conceived. My pilot's little girl came in the dress mentioned before carrying a present of cooked fish on her head and some fresh eggs; she was four years old and so *klug*. I gave her a captain's biscuit and some figs, and the little pet sat with her little legs tucked under her, and ate it so *manierlich* and was so long over it, and wrapped up some more white biscuit to take home in a little rag of a veil so carefully. I longed to steal her, she was such a darling. Two beautiful young Nubian women visited me in my boat, with hair in little plaits finished off with lumps of yellow clay burnished like golden tags, soft, deep bronze skins, and lips and eyes fit for Isis and Hathor. Their very dress and ornaments were the same as those represented in the tombs, and I felt inclined to ask them how many thousand years old they were. In their house I sat on an ancient Egyptian couch with the semicircular head-rest, and drank out of crockery which looked antique, and they brought a present of dates in a basket such as you may see in the British Museum. They are dressed in drapery like Greek statues, and are as perfect, but have hard, bold faces, and, though far handsomer, lack the charm of the Arab women; and the men, except at Kalabshee and those from far up the country, are not such gentlemen as the Arabs.

The Excursionists
E. W. Merrick, 1888

On one of our excursions to the temples, riding as usual on donkeys, we were overtaken by a party of Cook's excursionists, and as an American dashed past me he shouted out, 'Ain't it sport riding on a jackass?' That class of gentleman abounds up the Nile among the tourists; and I remember one, with whom we had a very casual acquaintance, remarking to me when I was feeling rather seedy at Assouan, 'Wal, you do look a worm. Guess Egypt don't suit you. You'll go home in a box likely.' American expressions sound very funny to our ears. I heard a woman on Shepheard's verandah describing a bonnet she had seen in church as being 'real lovely; nothing but a wreath of bugs (butterflies) and an osprey.'

Turmoil
Stephen Olin, 1843

This day had been full of occupation and agreeable excitement. A scene less pleasant, but still curious and interesting, because characteristic of the manners and habits of this people, was preparing for us against our return to the boat. We are accustomed to leave everything in the charge of our coptic dragoman John; and so little reason have we had for distrust, that we have seldom turned a key – clothes, books, and even money, being left with no other security than such as they may find in his fidelity. Our Arab crew we have the best possible reason to believe false and dishonest. Today John met with a tempter in the servant of the baker with whom he had been negotiating supplies for our return voyage. Grateful for his patronage, or under the influence of some baser sentiment, this man had contrived to make our faithful servant drunk. We found him barely able to stand, and quite bereft of all capacity to perform his normal duties. A drunken man is a rare spectacle in Egypt. Intoxicating drink is prohibited to Mussulmen, and whatever may be the fate of other precepts of the Koran, this, among the common people at least, seems to be pretty well observed. The climate, too, favours temperance, and our Christian dragoman is the only man I have seen intoxicated in this country. Of course this was an event of some moment, and the rumour soon brought a crowd from the town, less than half a mile distant, to witness the disgrace of the hated Nazarene. Some were evidently drawn to the spot by more selfish motives, and we found that John had been buying of their merchandise pretty freely, without discretion or economy. The vendors of all sorts of trifles were crowded about the boat. Baskets, mats, Nubian shields, barbed spears, chickens, corbashes, articles of Nubian dress, knives, ostrich eggs, antiques, &c., had been transferred from the bazaars to find vent in the expanded liberality of our unfortunate servant. The crowd on our arrival, may have consisted of one or two hundred persons. Hard words and angry feelings had risen. We found John hot with wrath at some insult, and he leapt from the boat to inflict chastisement on the real or supposed offender. The crowd shrunk back at his approach, and he pitched headlong into the sand. The sailors brought him on board, and with much difficulty we got him into the hole; but he soon sprung out again, incessantly declaring he would be avenged. The scene of tumult and confusion was undescribable. The Arabs fell to fighting among themselves. One women wept, declaring John had bought her trinkets without paying for them, and a dozen more volunteered to aid her in making good her claim. In the mean time, several were engaged in stealing the bread, which, to increase our difficulties, was just then brought by the baker. I detected one women with at least a peck of biscuits in her skirt, and another succeeded in carrying away a basketful before our eyes. Everyone seemed intent upon increasing the confusion and profiting by it. We several times drove them away from the boat by violence, but they immediately returned. The captain of the port, one of the pacha's officers, occasionally interfered, with his long Nubian spear, under the pretext of restoring order, but in effect to increase the uproar. On our departure, which we were anxious to hasten, he asked us to pay him a fee of twenty paras, about two and a half cents.

Curios in Assuan
Agatha Christie, 1937

They came out from the shade of the gardens on to a dusty stretch of road bordered by the river. Five watchful bead-sellers, two vendors of postcards, three sellers of plaster scarabs, a couple of donkey boys and some detached but hopeful infantile riff-raff closed in upon them.

'You want beads, sir? Very good, sir. Very cheap. . . .'

'Lady, you want scarab? Look – great queen – very lucky. . . .'

'You look, sir – real lapis. Very good, very cheap. . . .'

'You want to ride donkey, sir? This very good donkey. This donkey Whisky and Soda, sir. . . .'

'You want to go granite quarries, sir? This very good donkey. Other donkey very bad, sir, that donkey fall down. . . .'

'You want postcard – very cheap – very nice. . . .'

'Look, lady. . . . Only ten piastres – very cheap – lapis – this ivory. . . .'

'This very good fly whisk – this all-amber. . . .'

'You go out in boat, sir? I got very good boat, sir. . . .'

'You ride back to hotel, lady? This first-class donkey. . . .'

Hercule Poirot made vague gestures to rid himself of this human cluster of flies. Rosalie stalked through them like a sleep-walker.

'It's best to pretend to be deaf and blind,' she remarked.

The infantile riff-raff ran alongside murmuring plaintively: 'Bakshish? Bakshish? Hip hip hurrah – very good, very nice. . . .'

The Brassy Landscape of Nubia
Constance Sitwell, 1927

It had been a hateful day; some oppression lay on it since very early when from my cabin, as I was dressing, I saw a man killing a cockerel on the bank not far from the boat.

In the cool clear light of early morning he squatted there with a shawl drawn over his head, while, like a cat with a mouse, he spent as long as he could half strangling the bird, then letting it go; half cutting its throat and then letting it totter about bleeding. Moving blindly from this side to that it made feeble attempts to escape, and over and over again, after it had fluttered a little way the man idly stretched out his thin hands red with blood and caught it, and half sleepily continued his torturing game. The other chickens fed unconcernedly on amongst the rough grain that had been scattered for them; a passing boy paused to watch and laugh and poke the dying cockerel with his foot. Overhead the sky shone a soft luminous blue, the mild air blew freshness about the scene, limpidly the sun looked down on our 'light bitter world of wrong'.

Some hours later we set out, Jim and I riding in front, Philip following at a little distance behind. We were going up a mountain from which one got a distant view over the brassy landscape of Nubia. It was past noon when at last we reached our goal, a ledge on a craggy cliff facing the south. Arid was the land immediately around us, a confusion of jagged peaks and twisted ravines. It might have all been cast in some heavy metal, so hard and so massive was its surface spread out under a sky hazy with heat.

After waiting there for a while to let the donkeys have a rest we started in silence to come back. A dry wind had sprung up which blew the dust around us in eddies; it got into our eyes, the flies buzzed round our heads and we were shaken by each step the donkeys took as they jolted down the steep rock-filled defile. We passed some whitened bones by the path; we passed a dead crow lying feet upwards, and a little later I saw a hawk sitting in a cleft of a rock, its yellow eye fixed and unafraid. Beyond this there was no life to be seen till we got down to the level desert again, and here it was that we came upon the strolling players.

The last green tint of evening was still lingering in the western sky, and sharp against its strange clarity there stood out a train of camels which had halted for the night near the ancient caravan route through northern Africa. As we came nearer we heard music and singing. The evening meal was being prepared and round the fire were grouped men, camels, donkeys, and a few black goats. The grunting camels sprawled on the ground, their burdens beside them, and each time one of them moved there sounded the clank of a bell. Round the biggest fire and lit by its fitful flame the musicians had gathered and the light fell on their painted lutes, drums, and tambourines.

In the midst of them a blind man sat singing, and by his side, playing a reed pipe, was a boy with eyes set wide apart, and with a white cloth tied like a wimple round his music-haunted face. The singer was young and powerfully built but very thin, and as he sat there his wasted form wrapped round in a coarse cloth of striped yellow and crimson, he looked the embodiment of sad helplessness. His raw voice rose and fell to the odd inconclusive cadence from one of the chants of the East. Listlessly the song repeated its quavering phrases; the trembling half-tones recurred over and over again as though the music had too little heart even to cease. But darkness was creeping over the desert swiftly now; the evening meal was ready and hooded black shapes moved here and there as one fire after another blazed out in the grape-blue blur of the night.

11

Beyond Aswan

Introduction

... not only are these rocks the quarries of the statues, but it is hardly possible to look at their forms and not believe they suggested the idea. Islands, quarries, crags along the river-side, all seem either like grotesque colossal figures, sitting with their grim features carved out against the sky, their vast limbs often smoothed by the inundations of successive ages; or else like the same statues broken to slivers, like that we saw at Thebes. One can quite imagine how, in the days when power was will and will was power, Rameses, returned from his Ethiopian conquests, should say, 'Here is the stone, hard and glittering, from which my statue shall be hewn, and here is the model after which it shall be fashioned'.   Dean Stanley, 1852

Upper Egypt, near the First Cataract
11 December
I am now drawing near the point where I shall leave behind me all opportunities for sending letters home, and you will probably have to wait three months after receiving this before you hear from me again. However, you need have no fear on that account. I am already in the heart of Africa, more than five hundred miles from Cairo, and nearly half way to Khartoum, the end of my journey. The farther I go the more safe and agreeable the trip appears, and if I had any misgivings about it before leaving home I should have none now.   Bayard Taylor, 1851

Entering into Nubia begins another adventure on the Nile. For today's travellers there are all the ancient wonders of Philae and Abu Simbel and the modern wonders of the great dams. Before the dams there was the challenge of the cataract – an adventure like white-water rafting with a hundred helpers. Stephen Olin and Harriet Martineau detail aspects of the adventure, and Florence Nightingale describes it in reverse. In any case, the challenge was removed when the British built their dam. The dam is described by Douglas Sladen in 1907 and Michael Haag in 1987. It is now so overshadowed by the High Dam that we may forget what an achievement it was.

Some travellers changed to another boat above the cataract rather than face the adventure. Here, Lord Belmore's party waited for provisions and Harriet Martineau went exploring. Then Belmore's party were delayed again, and Dr Richardson must have been busy keeping an eye on his employer's blood pressure.

Now the travellers have reached Philae, with Henry Salt's friend Dr Madden

214

and Dean Stanley to introduce the enchanted island. They all speak with enthusiasm of it, as did Robert Curzon in 1837, but in 1814 Henry Light faced a plague of locusts there. David Roberts deplored the graffiti.

Above the cataract and into Nubia, Frederick Henniker unintentionally acquired a slave in 1822.

Having survived the journey up the cataract and celebrated Philae, the travellers sail on southward, where Sir Arthur Conan Doyle remarked on the contrast between the land and the passer-by. Giovanni Belzoni was there on his way to uncover the great temple at Abu Simbel in 1817.

John Lewis Burkhardt, on the eve of his great discovery, observed scarabs in 1813. Harriet Martineau was being practical again. The two delightful sea captains Charles Irby and James Mangles had trouble viewing the temple at Kalapsche in 1817, as did the Reverend Smith half a century later. Harriet Martineau thought it too modern. From Korosko Frederic Eden, who was sailing up the Nile without a dragoman in 1862, took on four other *dahabeeyahs* in a race.

On 22 March 1813 Burkhardt saw the great figures at Abu Simbel and guessed what they might be. For Rudyard Kipling in 1913, as for most visitors, this is 'the morning of mornings'. Joining up with Belzoni in 1817, Irby and Mangles assisted in the opening of the temple, but the sand constantly drifted back. When David Roberts visited in 1836 a system of removing it for visitors had been established, but in 1852, when Dean Stanley visited, the desert was flooding in again. Stanley deplored the graffiti here too – a problem which persists even today.

In 1855 William C. Prime lit up the temple with coloured lanterns. Amelia Edwards, who stayed at Abu Simbel in 1873, saw the row of giant faces each morning without lifting her head from her pillow.

The Second Cataract and Wadi Halfa was journey's end and time to go down the river. The travellers climbed the pinnacle at Abusir to look southwards towards the lands they would not see and northward back over their journey. Even Harriet Martineau inscribed her name here. Constance Sitwell looked out on the 'terrible waterless desert' in 1927, as had Sir Arthur Conan Doyle. Rudyard Kipling went walking in Wadi Halfa. Then, with Winston Churchill in 1899 and that great modern chronicler of the Nile, Alan Moorehead, it is time to return.

Bayard Taylor in 1852 spent five months on his journey, but most of us, like Michael Simmons of the *Guardian* in 1989, must travel with much more speed.

Water Sport
Stephen Olin, 1843

Our attention was soon attracted to two Nubian boys, who pursued us in quest of bucksheesh, by a species of navigation more simple and rude than our own. They had bound their scanty wardrobe in a bundle upon the top of their heads, and seated themselves astride a stick, – perhaps six inches in diameter, and five feet long, the forward end a little flattened to diminish the resistance of the water; they used their hands for paddles, and with this ticklish craft outsailed us, and ran across our track at pleasure. Sometimes they sat upright, extending their legs before them close to the log; they would lie on it at full length, one behind the other, still moving with undiminished velocity. I felt some concern for their adventure at first, but was soon relieved of my apprehension when I saw the admirable skill with which they retained their difficult position and guided their rolling bark. After amusing themselves and us for a considerable time, and receiving the bucksheesh, they returned to the shore. These boys were hardly more than six years of age. Soon after we witnessed another specimen of the aquatic skill of this amphibious race: – half-a-dozen young men and well-grown boys, who were upon the beach near us, threw off their clothes, and, running at full speed over the rocks for more than a quarter of a mile, to a bluff overlooking the falls, plunged into the foaming torrent. They were borne along by the current with fearful velocity, tossed on high and buried, alternately, by its fury; they dashed away the waves nobly, raising their hands high out of the water at every stroke; the head was carried very low, with the face apparently in the water, to avoid the greater resistance by the breast. It was a wild and exciting spectacle.

Ascent of the Cataract
Harriet Martineau, 1848

Such an event as the ascent of the Cataract can happen but once in one's life; and we would not hear of going ashore on any such plea as that the feat could be better seen from thence. What I wanted was to feel it. I would have gone far to see a stranger's boat pulled up; but I would not refuse the fortune of being on board when I could. We began, however, with going ashore at the Rapid where we failed the evening before. The rope had been proved untrustworthy; and there was no other till we joined the Rais of the Cataract, with his cable and his posse. Our Rais put together three weak ropes, which were by no means equivalent to one strong one: but the attempt succeeded.

It was a curious scene, – the appearing of the dusky natives on all the rocks around; the eager zeal of those who made themselves our guards, holding us by the arms, as if we were going to jail, and scarcely permitting us to set our feet to the ground, lest we should fall; and the daring plunges and divings of man or boy, to obtain our admiration or our baksheesh. A boy would come riding down a slope of roaring water as confidently as I would ride down a sand-hill on my ass. Their arms, in their fighting method of swimming, go round like the spokes of a wheel. Grinning boys poppled in the currents; and little seven-year-old savages must haul at the ropes, or ply their little poles when the kandjia approached a spike of rock, or dive to thrust their shoulders between its keel and any sunken obstacle: and after every such feat, they would pop up their dripping heads, and cry 'baksheesh'. I felt the great peculiarity of this day to be my seeing, for the first, and probably the only time of my life, the perfection of savage faculty: and truly it is an imposing sight.

Throughout the four hours of our ascent, I saw incessantly that though much is done by sheer force, – by men enough pulling at a rope strong enough, – some other requisites were quite as essential: – great forecast, great sagacity; much nice management among currents, and hidden and threatening rocks; and much knowledge of the forces and subtleties of wind and water. The men were sometimes plunging, to heave off the boat from a spike or ledge; sometimes swimming to a distant rock, with a rope between their teeth, which they carried round the boulders; – then squatting upon it, and holding the end of the rope with their feet, to leave their hands at liberty for hauling. Sometimes a man dived to free the cable from a catch under water; then he would spring on board, to pole at any critical pass: and then ashore, to join the long file who were pulling at the cable. Then there was their patience and diligence – very remarkable when we went round and round an eddy many times, after all but succeeding, and failing again and again from the malice of the wind. Once this happened for so long, and in such a boisterous eddy, that we began to wonder what was to be the end of it. Complicated as were the currents in this spot, we were four times saved from even grazing the rocks, when, after having nearly got through, we were borne back, and swung round to try again. The fifth time, there came a faint breath of wind, which shook our sail for a moment, and carried us over the ridge of foam. What a shout there was when we turned into still water! The last ascent but one appeared the most wonderful, – the passage was, twice over, so narrow, – barely admitting the kandjia, – the promontory of rock so sharp, and the gush of water so strong: but the big rope, and the mob of haulers on the shore and the islets heaved us up steadily, and as one might say, naturally, – as if the boat took her course advisedly.

Though this passage appeared to us the most dangerous, it was at the last that the Rais of the Cataract interfered to request us to step ashore. We were very unwilling; but we could not undertake the responsibility of opposing the local pilot. He said it was mere force that was wanted here, the difficulty being only from the rush of the waters, and not from any complication of currents. But no man would undertake to say that the rope would hold, and if it did not, destruction was inevitable. The rope held; we saw the boat drawn up steadily and beautifully; and the work was done.

Mr E., who has great experience in nautical affairs, said that nothing could be cleverer than the management of the whole business. He believed that the feat could be achieved nowhere else, as there are no such swimmers elsewhere.

The mob who took charge of us on the rocks were horribly noisy: the granite we trod on was burning hot, shining and slippery: the light, at an hour after noon, was oppressive: and the wildness of the scenery and of the thronging people was bewildering. The clamour was the worst; and for four hours there was no pause. This is, I think, the only thing in the whole affair really trying to a person of good nerves. The cries are like those of rage and fear; and one has to remind one's self incessantly that this is only the people's way: and then the clamour goes for nothing. When they do speak gently, as to us on matters of business, their voices are agreeable enough, and some very sweet. – Most of the throng to-day were quite black: some tawny. One man looked very odd. His complexion was chocolate colour, and his breast and top-knot red.

We returned to the boat heated and thirsty, and quite disposed for wine and water. The critical passage of four hours was over; but the Rais of the Cataract did not leave us till we were off Mahatta, there being still much skill and labour required to pass us through the yet troubled waters. Our boat rolled a good deal, having but little ballast as yet: and when we were about to go to dinner, a lurch caused the breakage of some soup plates and other ware: so we put off dinner till we should be at Philæ, where we were to complete our ballast. –

Meantime, we had the poor amusement of seeing a fight on shore, – the Rais and his men quarrelling about the baksheesh. The pay of the Rais and his men was included in the contract for the kandjia: but of course the Rais asked for baksheesh. He was offered ten piastres, and refused them; then a bottle of wine, which he put under his arm, demanding the ten piastres too. Then he refused both, and went off; but returned for the money; and ended by fighting about the division of it. The amount is small to contend about; but travellers should remember those who come after them, and the real good of the natives; and not give way to encroachment, to save a little trouble.

Down the Cataracts
Florence Nightingale, 1850

If the going *up* the Cataracts was strange, it was nothing to the coming *down*. We set off before sunrise, as it is necessary to have no breath of wind, with the 'bigs' and all their men on board. Our boat is the largest that has ever been up the Cataracts, and we came down a passage which is very rarely used, as the tossing rapid would swamp a smaller boat. It was widened for Ibrahim Pacha's steamer. We went on shore, but I stuck by the old boat, and truly it was a sight worth seeing how she gradually accelerated her speed as she approached the rapid, which, foaming and tossing, with scarcely two feet on either side our oars, seemed as if no boat could live in it, then took the leap like a racehorse, so gallantly, and were riding down the torrent as if she enjoyed it. Three times her bows dived under water (I don't mean that the waves broke over the boat, – that they did all the time, and half filled her with water, and all our biscuit, too, which was of more consequence), but three times she dived under water up to the kitchen, and rose again; twice she struck, but gallantly triumphed over all her enemies, and long before I have written this one line we were at the bottom, and swung round at the end of the rapid – the first time this feat has been tried, as boats are generally run ashore on the bank at the foot of the Cataract, as the only alternative. Of course, everything depends on the steering, and the oldest 'big' of all, the 'Great Father', mounted on the poop by his steersman, whence they did steer like masters. The boat obeyed, and we verged not an inch to the right or the left, Σ, who watched us from the shore, thought that we could not be going down that place, that the boat had not minded its rudder, and that they had run her down there as the only resource. I suppose such a feat of steering is without parallel in any other country. The Cataract by which we came down runs into the main stream at right angles, like water out of a cock; we were steered on the edge of the gush, on the left edge, so that when we came to the bottom, by the motion of the rudder and a vigorous pull of the oars on one side (our men were rowing with their whole might all through the descent), the bows were got out of the current on the left, which caught the stern, and the boat turned on her centre like a pivot, and swung round into still water; this is a new feat.

Mr. B— and I sat on the pantry, embracing our water jar, on the top of which we received the congratulations of all the 'bigs' and of all their men, who all shook hands with us, and cried 'Salaam!' the moment it was over. There was but one more little rapid to pass, and when we arrived at Syene, and were

218

quietly at breakfast, the great 'big' came in, and then the pilots, and solemnly applied my hand to his lips and forehead, and kissed Mr. B— on the top of his head, and then asked for Baksheesh. The dignity with which an Arab shakes hands with you and begs is charming.

The Great Dam at Assuan
Douglas Sladen, 1907

The Assuan Dam has been called the eighth wonder of the world – a famous American scientist has pronounced it a greater engineering feat than the Pyramids. It looks more than anything else like the wall of a Japanese castle thrown across the bed of the Nile: it looks like enough to the vast bastions, with which the engineers of the Renaissance fortified Italian cities, the principle being a sloping wall of immense thickness.

But no castle or city ever had such a fortification as the Dam of Assuan, which was ninety feet thick at the base and twenty-one feet thick at the top, and has now been made fifteen feet thicker all the way up. It is built of granite from the well-tried quarries which supplied nearly all the monuments of the Pharaohs; its foundations are sunk deep into the granite rock below the bed of the Nile; its ends are built deep into the granite cliffs on each side of the Nile. It is a mile and a quarter long, and was a hundred and fifty feet high in places before the recent elevation of fifteen feet extra began. It has a hundred and eighty sluices arranged at four different levels, which are opened and closed by electricity.

When the new works are finished and the dam is full, its level will be not much short of a hundred feet above the bed of the river, and another million acres will be irrigable in addition to the half million already gained. The value of this reclaimed million acres is estimated to be £30,000,000 sterling. At the beginning of July, when the Nile begins to rise, all the sluices are opened till about the first of September.

About the beginning of December, when the mud-charged water ceases to run and the water becomes relatively clear, the sluices are closed in a certain order, and the reservoir gradually fills till the first of February. About the end of April, when the water begins to be exhausted, the reservoir discharges the quantity necessary, which goes on till the river rises again.

The river-bed below the dam is divided by cross-walls, so that any portion of it can be drained if it is necessary to examine or repair the dam. The escape of water through the masonry has been infinitesimal. The thickening will make it immensely stronger. It was built six inches apart from the original dam, this interval being left open for two years till the new masonry became as cool as the old, when stones and cement were to be thrown in to fill it up. The new masonry is bolted to the old with thick steel rods.

At the western end of the dam is a navigable canal two kilometres long, which contains a series of four locks, that allow the native craft, and even steamers of considerable size, like the stern wheelers of the Sudan Government, to go up and down. These locks are more than two hundred feet long and about thirty feet wide; their doors are respectively sixty, forty-five, thirty-six, and thirty-three feet high.

219

The heat at the dam is alarming. It haas been known to rise to 130° in the shade by day and 100° by night. When the new works are completed the waters of the Nile will be driven back for nearly three hundred kilometres, and the water will be twenty feet deeper, though the dam is only fifteen feet higher.

An elaborate system of charts is kept in the offices. From Assuan the height of the river is reported every hour, and also at various stations up the river as far as Roseires on the Blue Nile. It takes the flood ten days to travel from Roseires to Khartûm.

Provisioning for Nubia
Dr Richardson, 1816

[Lord Belmore's party transferred to smaller boats above the cataract.]

We had laid in plenty of bread, which at Assouan is excellent, both better flour and better baked than any we had met with in the whole course of our journey . . . Plenty of livestock, sheep, poultry, and two milch goats; eggs, and melons, were among our stores. Lentils we could always procure . . . and a pleasant leguminous vegetable can always be had in any part of Egypt or Nile . . . We always succeeded in our attempts to secure a little butter as we passed on, and the noble traveller [Lord Belmore] had taken care to be well provided with a due assortment of the juice of the grape, before we left Cairo.

Into the Desert
Harriet Martineau, 1848

[Looking for boats above the Cataract, Harriet Martineau had breakfast early and set off on asses for Mahatta, – the village at the head of the Cataract.]

. . . This, our first ride in the Desert, was full of wonder and delight. It was only about three miles: but it might have been thirty from the amount of novelty in it. Our thick umbrellas, covered with brown holland, were a necessary protection against the heat, which would have been almost intolerable, but for the cool north wind. – I believed before that I had imagined the Desert: but now I felt that nobody could. No one could conceive the confusion of piled and scattered rocks, which, even in a ride of three miles, deprives a stranger of all sense of direction, except by the heavens. These narrow passes among black rocks, all suffocation and glare, without shade or relief, are the very home of despair. The oppression of the sense of sight disturbs the brain, so that the will of the unhappy wanderer cannot keep his nerves in order. I thought of poor Hagar here, and seemed to feel her story for the first time. I thought of Scotch shepherds lost in the snow, and of their mild case in comparison with that of Arab goat-herds lost in the Desert. The difference is of death by lethargy and death by torture. We were afterwards in the depth of Arabia, and lived five weeks in tents in the Desert: but no Arabian scene impressed me more with the characteristics of the Desert than this ride of three miles from Aswan to Mahatta. The presence of dragon-flies in the Desert surprised me; – not only here, but in places afterwards – where there appeared to be no water within a great distance. To those who have been wont to watch the coming forth of the dragon-fly from its sheath on the rush on the margin of a pool, and flitting about the mountain watercourse, or the moist meadows at home, it is strange to see them by dozens glittering in the sunshine of the Desert, where there appears to be nothing for them to alight on; – nothing that would not shrivel them up, if they rested for a moment from the wing. The hard dry locust seemed more in its place, and the innumerable beetles, which everywhere left a net-work of delicate tracks on the light sand. Distant figures are striking in the desert, in the extreme clearness of light and shade. Shadows strike upon the sense here as bright lights do elsewhere. It seems to me that I remember every figure I ever saw in the Desert; – every veiled woman tending her goats, or carrying her water-jar on her head; – every man in blue skirting the hillocks; every man in brown guiding his ass or his camel through the sandy defiles of the black rocks, or on a slope by moonlight, when he casts a long shadow. Every moving thing has a new value to the eye in such a region.

When we came out upon Mahatta, we were in Nubia, and found ourselves at once in the midst of the wildness of which we had read so much in relation to the First Cataract. The Mississippi is wild: and the Indian grounds of Wisconsin, with their wigwam camps, are wild: but their wildness is only that of primitive nature. This is fantastic, – impish. It is the wildness of Prospero's island. Prospero's island and his company of servitors were never out my head between Aswan and the next placid reach of the river above Philoe. – The rocks are not sublime: they are too like Titanic heaps of black paving-stones to be imposing otherwise than by their oddity: and they are strewn about the land and river to an excess and with a caprice which takes one's imagination quite out of the ordinary world. Their appearance is made the more strange by the cartouches and other hieroglyphic inscriptions which abound among them; – sometimes on a face above the river; sometimes on a mere ordinary block near the path; – sometimes on an unapproachable fragment in the middle of the stream. When we emerged from the Desert upon Mahatta, the scene was somewhat softened by the cultivation behind the village, and the shade of the spreading sycamores and clustered palms. Heaps of dates, like the wheat in our granaries for quantity, lay piled on the shore; and mounds of packages (chiefly dates) ready for export. The river was all divided into streamlets and ponds by the black islets. Where it was overshadowed, it was dark grey or deep blue; but where the light caught it, rushing between a wooded island and the shore, it was of the clearest green. – The people were wild, – especially the boys, who were naked and excessively noisy: but I did not dislike their behaviour, which was very harmless, though they had to be flogged out of the path, like a herd of pigs.

Delayed Again
Dr Richardson, 1816

[Lord Belmore's party had been delayed leaving Cairo when the felucca of one boat broke loose. They faced another delay after leaving Aswan.]

It was our intention to have sailed at an early hour next morning; but on giving directions for that purpose, it was discovered that the colours had been left behind at Assouan, and it was impossible to sail without them; they were our national banners, the badge and ensign of our country, which we were determined to display wherever wind or wave would carry us ... A trusty British tar* was despatched with a guide back to the vessels [which they had left below the cataract, transferring to smaller local boats to sail into Nubia], to bring the flag which he had often defended ... The next day ... we spread our sails and banner to the wind, and with a favourable breeze began to stem the current of the north.

Philae
Dr R. R. Madden, 1827

There are four recollections of a traveller, which might tempt him to live forever: the sea view of Constantinople, the sight of the Coliseum by moonlight, the prospect from the summit of Vesuvius at dawn, and the first glimpse of Philæ at sunset.

Philae
Dean Stanley, 1852

And now, it is immediately above the roar of these rapids – but still in the very centre of these colossal rockeries – that emerges into sight an island lying in the river – fringed with palms, and crowned with a long line of temples and colonnades. This is Philae.

The Island of Philoe
Robert Curzon, 1833

Excepting the Pyramids, nothing in Egypt struck me so much as when on a bright moonlit night I first entered the court of the great temple of Philoe. The colours of the paintings on the walls are as vivid in many places as they were the day they were finished: the silence and the solemn grandeur of the immense buildings around me were most imposing; and on emerging from the lofty gateway between the two towers of the propylon, as I wandered about the island, the tufts of palms, which are here of great height, with their weeping branches, seemed to be mourning over the desolation of the stately palaces and temples to which in ancient times all the illustrious of Egypt were wont to resort, and into whose inner recesses none might penetrate; for the secret and awful mysteries of the worship of Osiris were not to be revealed, nor were they even to be spoken of by those who were not initiated into the highest orders of the priesthood. Now all may wander where they choose, and speculate on the uses of the dark chambers hidden in the thickness of the walls, and trace out the plans of the courts and temples with the long lines of columns which formed

* Sailor accompanying Captain Corry, the Earl's brother.

the avenue of approach from the principal landing-place to the front of the great temple.

I have been three times at Philoe, and indeed I had so great an admiration of the place, that on my last visit, thinking it probable that I should never again behold its wonderful ruins and extraordinary scenery, I determined to spend the day there alone, that I might meditate at my leisure, and wander as I chose from one well-remembered spot to another, without the incumbrance of half a dozen people staring at whatever I looked at, and following me about out of pure idleness. Greatly did I enjoy my solitary day, and whilst leaning over the parapet on the top of the great Propylon, or seated on one of the terraces which overhung the Nile, I in imagination repeopled the scene with the forms of the priests and worshippers of other days, restored the fallen temples to their former glory, and could almost think I saw the processions winding round their walls, and heard the trumpets, and the harps, and the sacred hymns in honour of the great Osiris. In the evening a native came over with a little boat to take me off the island, and I quitted with regret this strange and interesting region.

Graffiti
David Roberts, RA, 1836

[At Philae Roberts noted that an American traveller had written his name on the inscription of Desaix recording the visit here of Napoleon's army in 1799, and that it had been crossed out and the words added, '*La page de l'histoire ne doit pas être salie.*' Roberts goes on to complain:]

How is it that an Englishman, with the scribbling propensities of which he is so often accused, has not yet added to this record: 'Expelled from the land of Egypt by an English army, September 2nd 1801'?

To Philae after the Dam
Sir Gaston Maspero, 1908

We must take half an hour's journey by train, first through one of the native suburbs of Assouân, then in sight of a horde of Bicharis encamped on the outskirts of the suburb so as to give the tourists an impression of life in the desert, and lastly along a monotonous slope of rocks and reddish sand. The train is a real Paris suburban train, with its carriages too old for the service of the long-distance lines, with an old-fashioned locomotive, a great boiler stuck on wheels, which will resolutely do its fifteen miles an hour if the driver will let it. It goes painfully panting over the slope until at last straight in front of it, above the line of sandstone that just now bounded the horizon, there slowly come into view mounds of blackish granite and a blue-grey plain flooded with light in which the currents thread their way and cross each other. Groups of dying palms or withered acacias are set in the water in front of the embankment itself, marking the outline of the ancient banks, and a mass of submerged buildings of different heights seems as if fallen into the middle of the basin – pylons, colonnades, kiosks, tops of temples – exactly what is to be seen of Philæ between December 15th of one year and May 15th of the following year. We get out of the train and embark, and coast successively the sanctuary of Isis, the propylæa of Hadrian, the Quay Wall on the east, and doubling at the spot where the obelisk of Nectanebo formerly marked the landing-stage of the ancient place of disembarkation, we arrive between the two porticoes of Augustus and Tiberius. We go through the monumental door, almost at the level of the inscription engraved by the French soldiers of Desaix, and passing through the courtyard reach the top step of the grand staircase. The water flows noisily from the house of the priests of Isis to the chapel of Hathor, then it runs to the right of the pronaos through the postern that opened on to the propylæa of Trajan and Hadrian. We seem to be transported unawares into one of the fantastic havens bordered with watch-towers and palaces that the Romans of the Imperial epoch were fond of painting on the walls.

Tourists may still go dryshod over the place of disembarkation, the hypostyle, the Holy of Holies, the courtyard and Chamber of the New Year, the portions of buildings grouped in front or on the sides of the naos, and the corridors that form communications between them. At least the Nile only wets them exceptionally when the north wind, stirring the water, raises waves which flow through the halls. But if the water only seldom flows over the pavements, its presence is felt everywhere in the veinings and under the outer layer of the stone. Without possibility of preventing its progress, it has silently filtered through from bottom to top, by rills as fine as hairs, and between two inundations has impregnated the entire fabric. The walls look damp to the eye and are damp to the fingers if they are touched. The sandstone has shed the grey granulated covering the dryness of which had clothed it for centuries, and it slowly resumes the yellowish colour it had in the quarry. The faded and dirty colours which here and there clothe the figures of the gods or the architectural ornaments are strengthened and revived by the damp. Even the celebrated capitals of the pronaos have less dry and inharmonious tones than formerly. The reds, blues, yellows, and greens have insensibly run into each other at the edges under the persistent influence of the dampness acting behind them in the stone: and while this interior work softens and shades them, the reflections of the ever-moving water which light them from below through the bay of the pylon make the colours vibrate delightfully.

Their beauty should be enjoyed while it remains entire, for work is still going on at the barrage on that side. The granite causeway is being enlarged, since it no longer offers a sufficiently firm base for new courses of masonry, and the rocks of the Cataract, blasted every day, provide the material which will allow the engineers to raise the present plan of the reservoir six or seven yards. And in five or six years nearly all that was spared in 1902 will be delivered up to the flood. It will flow over the threshold of the doors, it will invade without hindrance the parts provisionally guarded from it, it will deliberately attack the walls, and will not desist until it has reached the prescribed level. The figures of divinities and kings who meet or pursue one another from the plinth to the frieze, presenting and accepting the offering, prostrated, bowed, ranged in ceremonious rows, will be gradually drowned – the feet one day, then the knees, the loins, the bust, the head – so that nothing of them more will be seen, and the mystery of the worship of Isis will be for ever hidden. A sort of rectangular balustrade will mark the site of the kiosk of Trajan.

A Purchase near Aswan
Frederick Henniker, 1822

At Derahry we were informed that a caravan had just arrived, with gum, ostrich features, and slaves; the latter are registered in this place as soon as they are brought into Egypt, and a poll-tax is paid to the Pasha; it is one of the largest and cheapest human Smithfields* in the kingdom . . . the slaves are allowed to bask during the day in a walled courtyard, and at night they are distributed among the cottages like a subscription pack of hounds. The whipper-in carried a caravash or thong, made of rhinoceros hide, an instrument too cruel to beat a donkey with, and swishing this about in a masterly manner he accompanied me to the kennel: here we found a squattee of young ladies seated in a circle; in the centre was a broken bowl, and into this they were all dipping their fingers with as much greediness as if it was a hasty-pudding. My nose soon informed me that it was grease; and I am told that it is a luxury of women, and consolation even to a slave; with this they besmear themselves from head to toe, and glisten in the sun like a newly varnished picture; they were so pleased with the fat, that they paid little attention to the dealer as he pointed out the peculiar beauties of each . . .

There was one of the party who, though she took her share of this finery, a plaything of a savage, seemed but little pleased with it. She was pretty, sorrowful and uninteresting – her price seventeen guineas.† With the hope of finding an opportunity to send her home, I paid the money and gave the maiden her liberty . . . The girl came forward, kissed my hand, and without saying a word to anyone, she ran to hide herself in the boat. There was something perfectly unaccountable in her silence: she went away without speaking to those who spoke her own language, and were natives of her own country; and without even bidding farewell to those companions of misery that had been her associates in the most tedious journey that is known in the vale of tears, those whom she left chained, and whom she might never behold again!

[On the boat Henniker explained to the girl that he was giving her freedom. She burst into tears and said she would rather die than go back. Eventually he promised that she would remain a *slave*.]

Instead of Canoes
Frederick Norden, 1738

Thursday, 2 January

It is as difficult to get canoes hereabouts as at the First Cataract. We observed that day a comical manner of the natives crossing the Nile. Two men sat on a pack of straw preceded by a cow that swam before them. One of them held the tail of the cow with one hand, and with the other he managed a rope fastened to her horns. The man behind steered with a little oar, by means of which he preserved the equilibrium. We saw likewise that day laden camels

---

* The London meat market.
† A guinea was one pound and one shilling.

cross the river in the following manner. A man swims before, having the bridle of the first camel in his mouth; to whose tail the second is tied, the third to his; a man seated on a pack of straw forms the rear guard, whose care is that the second and third camels follow in a line.

Nile Evenings
Frederick Henniker, 1822

Among the amusements [in Nubia] are rope-dancers and story-tellers: of the former I saw a strolling company at Dehr, and of the latter there is one at every village; he is the oracle of the conversazione, and goes about like a circulating library. Frequently when we moored for the evening, one of these entertainers used to come on board to amuse the crew. The most popular subject is a history of the adventures and miracles of Mohammed . . .

Nubia
Sir Arthur Conan Doyle, 1897

Between these two huge and barren expanses [of desert], Nubia writhes like a green sand-worm along the course of the river. Here and there it disappears altogether, and the Nile runs between black and sun-cracked hills, with the orange drift-sand lying like glaciers in their valleys. Everywhere one sees traces of vanished races and submerged civilisations. Grotesque graves dot the hills or stand up against the skyline, – pyramidal graves, tumulus graves, rock graves, – everywhere graves. And, occasionally, as the boat rounds a rocky point, one sees a deserted city up above, – houses, walls, battlements, – with the sun shining through the empty window squares. Sometimes you learn that it has been Roman, sometimes Egyptian; sometimes all record of its name or origin has been absolutely lost. There they stand, these grim and silent cities, and up on the hills you can see the graves of their people, like the port-holes of a man-of-war. It is through this weird, dead country that the tourists smoke and gossip and flirt as they pass up to the Egyptian frontier.

Beyond Assuan
Giovanni Belzoni, 1817

A few miles above this place the Nile turns towards the north-west, and as the wind blew mostly from that quarter, we had it right against us, besides a very strong current, for the Nile was nearly at its height. Though the day was very hot, the night was exceedingly cold, considering the climate we were in. At this place we found it very difficult to advance, for the wind still continued strong ahead, and the sailors could not track the boat by ropes on the shore, as the bank was covered with thorns and acacia-trees, so that it took us two days to reach the territory of Deir, where the river resumes its course again to the south. From the trees I have mentioned we gathered a little gum-arabic; and the Reis of the boat caught some chameleons, which we intended to keep alive.

They feed on flies and boiled rice, and drink water; but they did not agree together in confinement, for they bit off the tails and legs of each other. If put into water, they swell like bladders, and swim faster than they can crawl. They generally live on palm-trees, and descend in the evening to drink. We caught about thirty, but they all gradually died. I saw a female full of eggs, of the size of large peas, eighteen in number, all attached to the matrix.

The Sacred Scarab
John Lewis Burkhardt, 1813

On the sandy shore, on the west side of the Nile, are numberless beetles (*Scarabæi*), of great variety in size and shape; I often found the sandy road on that side completely covered with traces of their feet. The Nubians who call them Kafers, or Infidels, dread them from a belief that they are venomous, and that they poison whatever kind of food they touch.

Their colour is generally black, and the largest I have seen were of the size of a half crown piece. The worship paid to this animal by the ancient Egyptians may probably have had its origin in Nubia; it might well be adopted as a symbol of passive resignation to the decrees of Providence; for it is impossible, from the sandy mound which they inhabit, that these beetles can ever taste water, and the food they partake of must be very scanty; they are however always seen busily and wearidly toiling their way over the sands.

Good Housekeeping
Harriet Martineau, 1848

I was ironing till dinner-time, that we might carry our sheets and towels in the best condition to the kandjia. No one would laugh at, or despise this who knew the importance, in hot countries, of the condition of linen; and none who have not tried can judge of the difference in comfort of ironed linen and that which is rough dried. By sparing a few hours per week, Mrs. Y. and I made neat and comfortable things washed by the crew; and when we saw the plight of other travellers, – gentlemen in rough dried collars, and ladies in gowns which looked as if they had been merely wrung out of the wash-tub, we thought the little trouble our ironing cost us well bestowed. Every body knows now that to take English servants ruins every thing, – destroys all the ease and comfort of the journey; and the Arabs cannot iron. They cannot comprehend what it is for. One boat's crew last year decided, after a long consultation, that it was the English way of killing lice. This was not our crew: but I do not think ours understood to the last the meaning of the weekly ceremony of the flat-iron. The dragoman of another party, being sounded about ironing his employer's white trowsers, positively declined the attempt; saying that he had once tried, and at the first touch had burnt off the right leg. If any lady going up the Nile should be so happy as to be able to iron, I should strongly advise her putting up a pair of flat-irons among her baggage. If she can also starch, it will add much to her comfort and that of her party, at little cost of time and trouble.

Kalabsha
Karl Baedeker, 1929

618 miles from Cairo and 31 miles from Aswan. A large commune on both banks of the Nile ... Hard by the river as we proceed south, lie the ruins of the ancient town of Talmis. Closely hemmed in by the modern houses, appears the large and picturesque Temple of Kalabsha.*

Guardians at Kalapsche
Charles Irby and James Mangles, 1817

In the evening we landed at Kalapsche [on their return from Abu Simbel] and went up to see the temple. Here we found all the natives assembled, and armed with their daggers to dispute the entrance; we asked the reason for their being assembled in such numbers, and what they wanted: they said they must be paid before we entered the temple. We asked the speaker if he meant he was to be paid himself, or who it was that we were to give money to? They all cried out that we must pay every one of them. Now, as there were about sixty of them, and many others arriving, we thought this a bad speculation, and were, therefore, proceeding to explain to them that it was not any great object for us to see the temple a second time, since we had already inspected it; and if they chose to let us enter, we would give them a reasonable present when we came out, otherwise that it was immaterial to us whether we saw it or not, and that we should go without seeing it.

While this was going on their janissary picked a quarrel with some of the people and they had to extricate him in haste and go back to the boat 'being well hooted as we went down'.

Guardians of Kalabshe
Reverend A. C. Smith, 1868

That same day we reached Kalabshe, where we were amazed to see the shore lined with a multitude of as veritable savages as one could find in any part of the continent of Africa; men and boys, many of them without a vestige of clothing, and others with the smallest apology for dress, armed with guns and long spears, and all gesticulating with out-stretched arms, and screeching at us with shrill voices, seemed prepared to dispute our landing. This was something more violent than we had expected; though every traveller, from the days of Belzoni down to the present time, speaks of the insolent and savage demeanour of these rude barbarians, and not a few have in consequence thought it more prudent to continue the voyage than to encounter such uncivilised ruffians. However as we swung round to our anchor, we discovered that all this noise of brandishing of weapons was but another form of demanding 'backsheesh,' while they offered their spears, antelopes' horns, and ornaments for barter, and

---

* Now removed to the island of New Kalabsha, immediately up river from the High Dam, some 32 miles from its original position.

demanded 'bereut,' or powder, in exchange; thrusting forwards their long guns as a tangible proof that if we complied with their requests our liberality would not be thrown away. As we went ashore, the hubbub from so many voices increased, while every man tried to attract our attention exclusively to himself; and then, accompanied by some dozens of these naked niggers, still screaming for backsheesh at every step, aided by a crowd of women in the most scanty costume, offering their trinkets at twenty times their value, we passed on to the two famous temples, both of which are deserving of close attention.

The Temple of Kaláb'-sheh
Harriet Martineau, 1848

I was glad to go over it, and admire its magnificence, and the elegance of many parts; and be amazed at its vastness: but it is too modern to interest us much here. It was founded and carried on, – (not quite to completion) – by one after another of the Cæsars: and it is therefore not truly Egyptian. The most interesting circumstance to me was that here we could form some judgment of the effect of the Egyptian colour-decoration: for here there were two chambers in fine preservation, except where water had poured down from the massive lion-head spouts (Roman) and had washed away the colours. The relief to the eye of these strips of pure sculpture was very striking. My conclusion certainly was, from the impression given by these two chambers, that, however valuable colour may be for bringing out the details, and even the perspective, of sculptured designs, any large aggregate of it has a very barbaric appearance. – Still, we must not judge of the old Egyptian painting by this Roman specimen. The disk of Isis is here painted deep red, – the colour of the ordinary complexion. The pale green and brilliant blue of the ancient times are present; and I saw here, and here only, a violet or plum-colour.

As for the rest, this temple is a heap of magnificent ruin; magnificent for vastness and richness; but not for taste. One pillar standing among many overthrown, – rich capitals toppled down among rough stones; and such mounds of fragments as make us wonder what force could have been used to cause such destruction, – these are the interests of this temple. It may be observed too, that the adytum has no figure at the end, and that it appears never to have been finished. It is a singular spectacle, – the most sacred part unfinished, while the capitals of the outer columns, with their delicate carvings of vine-leaves and tendrils twining among the leaves of the doum palm, are overthrown and broken!

Competition
Frederic Eden, 1862

We found assembled at Korosco a fleet of Barabra boats, and no less than four other dahabeahs. The early morning was dead calm, and we sent our cook ashore for meat. But at 8 a gentle breeze sprang up, a breeze from the southwest, as unusual as it was welcome. Great was the noise and confusion; the whole fleet at once got under weigh, we with our accustomed tardiness last of all. Everybody's all sail was set, and away we went. Everybody's cook was ashore, for rumours, this time true (the words of truth, banished from Egypt, still exist in Nubia), had reached us of beef. Beef, a thing undreamt of since Cairo was left below us!

So as we ran along the shore, we saw the *chefs* of the fleet, meat-laden, running too; and the Barabras' also, disturbed on their various errands or idlings, seeking in crowds to catch up their respective boats. At first the boats easily beat the men, but soon an awkward bend brought us up so close hauled that we could hardly stem the stream. Then much jockeyship ensured, and every reis sought to coax his boat clear of the rocks and his companions. Some took to their tow-ropes, and these we slipped. Rejoicing in our better luck, or as we called it judgment, we had passed half the fleet, when a large dahabeah ran aground in front and inside of us. It was impossible for us to pass her, and equally impossible for anything to pass us. Being in shallow water, we were able to hold our position with the punting-poles; but we could not pole against the stream, it was too strong; we could not tow, for she lay between us and the bank, and the wind was not favourable enough to allow of our running by: so our sails were furled. There she stuck, and there we stuck, and everybody else in a line stuck behind us. Soon we saw a darker ruffle coming over the surface of the river. 'Make sail!' was cried. It was well done and handily done, and we sailed by the impeding boat, and right up the river at the head of the dahabeahs.

Emboldened by success, we then took advantage of the slant of wind to cross the river to the windward side. It held good till we had reached the slack water under the towing-bank, and we looked across to see every boat of the fleet to leeward of us, and on the wrong side of the swift Nile. It was great fun to all. We were delighted, after Western fashion, to win a race, to beat anything or anybody; the crew, as men of the East, to enjoy the fruits of victory in lessened toil. But enthusiasm is contagious; our high spirits infected the whole crew, and when, immediately afterwards, the wind died away, the men, with the old reis at their head, jumped ashore with the tow-rope, and spite of trees and thorns we reached that evening the end of the dreaded reach, and stopped the head boat of the whole fleet.

Nubia
Dean Stanley, 1852

... you feel you are now beyond the reach of history.

Desert and Temple
Rudyard Kipling, 1913

There was a morning of mornings when we lay opposite the rock-hewn Temple of Abu Simbel, where four great figures, each sixty feet high, sit with their hands on their knees waiting for Judgment Day. At their feet is a little breadth of blue-green crop; they seem to hold back all the weight of the Desert behind them, which, none the less, lips over at one side in a cataract of vividest orange sand. The tourist is recommended to see the sunrise here, either from within the temple where it falls on a certain altar erected by Rameses in his own honour, or from without where another Power takes charge.

The stars had paled when we began our watch; the river birds were just whispering over their toilettes in the uncertain purplish light. Then the river dimmered up like pewter; the line of the ridge behind the Temple showed itself against a milkiness in the sky; one felt rather than saw that there were four figures in the pit of gloom below it. These blocked themselves out, huge enough, but without any special terror, while the glorious ritual of the Eastern dawn went forward. Some reed of the bank revealed itself by reflection, black on silver; arched wings flapped and jarred the still water to splintered glass; the desert ridge turned to topaz, and the four figures stood clear, yet without shadowing, from their background. The stronger light flooded them red from head to foot, and they became alive – as horridly and tensely yet blindly alive as pinioned men in the death-chair before the current is switched on. One felt that if by any miracle the dawn could be delayed a second longer, they would tear themselves free, and leap forth to heaven knows what sort of vengeance. But that instant the full sun pinned them in their places – nothing more than statues slashed with light and shadow – and another day got to work.

A few yards to the left of the great images, close to the statue of an Egyptian princess, whose face was the very face of 'She,' there was a marble slab over the grave of an English officer killed in a fight against dervishes nearly a generation ago.

I Fell in with ...
John Lewis Burkhardt, 1813

[Burkhardt, nearing the end of his travels in Egypt and Nubia, was returning from Wadi Halfa and had crossed the Nile on 22 March 1817.]

At one hour and a half, ascended a steep sandy mountain ... on the west side the mountain bears the name Ebsambal, probably a Greek word ... When we reached the top of the mountain I left my guide, with the camels, and descended an almost perpendicular cleft, choked with sand, to view the temple of which I had heard many magnificent descriptions ... It stands about twenty feet above the surface of the water, entirely cut out of the perpendicular rocky side of the mountain and in complete preservation ...

[Burkhardt then described in some detail this temple.]

Having, as I supposed, seen all the antiquity of Ebsambal, I was about to ascend the sandy side of the mountain by the same way I had descended, when, having luckily turned more to the southward, I fell in with what is yet visible of four immense colossal statues cut out of the rock, at a distance of about two hundred yards from the temple, they stand in a deep recess, excavated in the mountain, but it is deeply to be regretted, that they are now almost entirely buried beneath the sands, which are blown down here in torrents. The entire head, and part of the breasts and arms of one of the statues are yet above the surface; and of the one next to it scarcely any part is visible, the head being broken off, and the body covered with sand to above the shoulders; of the other two, the bonnets only appear.

It is difficult to determine whether these statues are in a sitting or standing posture; their backs adhere to a portion of the rock, which projects from the main body, and which may represent part of a chair, or it may be merely a column for support. They do not front the river, like those of the temple just described, but are turned with their faces due north, towards the more fertile lands of Egypt, so that the line on which they stand forms an angle with the course of the stream. The head which is above the surface has a most expressive, youthful countenance, approaching nearer to the Grecian model of beauty, than of any one Egyptian figure I have seen . . .

The statue measures seven yards across the shoulders, and cannot, therefore, if in upright posture, be less than from 65 to 70 feet in height; the ear is one yard and four inches in length. On the wall of the rock in the centre of the four statues, is the figure of a hawk-headed Osiris, surmounted by a globe; beneath which, I suspect, could it be cleared away, a vast temple would be discovered . . .

Digging at Abu Simbel
David Roberts, RA, 1836

Mr Hay (the archaeologist) had the sand so far removed as to disclose entirely the two columns on the south side of the door, together with the doorway to its base, and now nine or ten Nubians can remove the sand in a few hours which may fall in, and can give ready access to the temple.

Graffiti
Dean Stanley, 1852

On the legs of the shattered Rameses at Abu Simbel . . . is the oldest Greek inscription in the world, – by a Greek soldier who came here to pursue some deserters in the last days of the Egyptian monarchy.

Celebrating at Abu Simbel
William C. Prime, 1855

Mindful of the brilliant illumination of the boat the evening previous, at Wady Halfeh, it occurred to us that we might realize somewhat of the ancient glory of Abou Simbel by lighting it with our colored lanterns.

Abd-el-Atti entered into the idea with his accustomed alacrity, and although my shoulder was exceedingly painful* I went up into the temple to advise and assist in the disposition of candles and lanterns, while the ladies, who did not go into the temple on our passage up, waited on board until the illumination was complete.

The sand hill was almost impassable. It was like climbing a snow bank fifty feet high, the feet going in deep and slipping far back at every step, so that we

---

* Prime had fallen into a pit on his entry to the rock-hewn temple at Ferayg.

had to lie down and breathe several times before we reached the top and descended into the doorway of the temple.

When our arrangements were complete we returned and brought the ladies up. The procession was picturesque. Two blazing torches led the way, and four more brought up the rear. Our English friends had arrived just after the *Phantom*, and joined us.

Never since the days of Rameses has his great temple shone so brilliantly. Every statue held bright lanterns, and for two hundred feet through the long rooms we placed them – rows of every color, shining on painted walls and lofty statues. The altar was in the shadow – for so we arranged it – hiding the lights behind it that they might shine on the faces of the gods, and not on the altar front. When all was ready we called in the ladies, and, as they entered, the sailors, who had busied themselves about the lamps, suddenly disappeared, and the temple was apparently empty. But at the moment of our re-entering, in place of the chorus of priests and attendants that was wont to arise in the hall, deep, sepulchral voices, from unknown recesses, uttered in loud and terrible unison the well-known cry, 'Bucksheesh, Hawajji!'

It was vain to resist such an appeal, and we answered it instantly; whereat the voices changed, and the men emerged from their hiding-places with shouts of thanks.

It was a gorgeous scene, worth visiting Egypt to look on that illumination; and we sat for hours in the hall, gazing with never-ceasing wonder and awe on the splendid statues and lofty walls. Then we wandered with torches through all the chambers, scaring the owls and bats from their hiding-places; and when it was nearly midnight we came out into the air, and there lay on the river and on the temple front such a moonlight as we dream of in other lands, but never see except just here. The hoary rocks looked like silver, and the grey statues gleamed in the mellow light, and seemed to know their beauty. We threw ourselves down in the sand, and drank in all the beautiful scene; and at last, when the ladies were gone down to the boat and were sleeping, I re-entered the temple, and sat down in the centre of the great hall alone, and watched the fading lights, and pondered on the old, old story of the decay of empire.

Days at Abu Simbel
Amelia B. Edwards, 1873

We came to Abou Simbel on the night of the 31st of January, and we left at sunset on the 18th February. Of these eighteen clear days, we spent fourteen at the foot of the rock of the Great Temple, called in the old Egyptian tongue the Rock of Abshek. The remaining four (taken at the end of the first week and the beginning of the second) were passed in the excursion to Wady-Halfeh and back. By thus dividing the time, our long sojourn was made less monotonous for those who had no especial work to do.

Meanwhile, it was wonderful to wake every morning close under the steep bank, and, without lifting one's head from the pillow, to see that row of giant faces so close against the sky. They showed unearthly enough by moonlight; but not half so unearthly as in the grey of dawn. At that hour, the most solemn of the twenty-four, they wore a fixed and fatal look that was little less than appalling. As the sky warmed, this awful look was succeeded by a flush that mounted and deepened like the rising flush of life. For a moment they seemed to glow – to smile – to be transfigured. Then came a flash, as of thought itself. It was the first instantaneous flash of the risen sun. It lasted less than a second. It was gone almost before one could say that it was there. The next moment, mountain, river, and sky, were distinct in the steady light of day; and the colossi – mere colossi now – sat serene and stony in the open sunshine.

Every morning I waked in time to witness that daily miracle. Every morning I saw those awful brethren pass from death to life, from life to sculptured stone. I brought myself almost to believe at last that there must sooner or later come some one sunrise when the ancient charm would snap asunder, and the giants must arise and speak.

Stupendous as they are, nothing is more difficult than to see the colossi properly. Standing between the rock and the river, one is too near; stationed on the island opposite, one is too far off; while from the sand-slope only a side-view is obtainable. Hence, for want of a fitting standpoint, many travellers have seen nothing but deformity in the most perfect face handed down to us by Egyptian art.

Viewed from below, this beautiful portrait is foreshortened out of all proportion. It looks unduly wide from ear to ear, while the lips and the lower part of the nose show relatively larger than the rest of the features. The same may be said of the great cast in the British Museum. Cooped up at the end of a narrow corridor and lifted not more than fifteen feet above the ground, it is carefully placed so as to be wrong from every point of view and shown to the greatest possible disadvantage.

The artists who wrought the original statues were, however, embarrassed by no difficulties of focus, daunted by no difficulties of scale. Giants themselves, they summoned these giants from out the solid rock, and endowed them with superhuman strength and beauty. They sought no quarried blocks of syenite or granite for their work. They fashioned no models of clay. They took a mountain, and fell upon it like Titans, and hollowed and carved it as though it were a cherry-stone, and left it for the feebler men of after-ages to marvel at for ever. One great hall and fifteen spacious chambers they hewed out from the heart of it; then smoothed the rugged precipice towards the river, and cut four huge statues with their faces to the sunrise, two to the right and two to the left of the doorway, there to keep watch to the end of time.

These tremendous warders sit sixty-six feet high, without the platform under their feet. They measure across the chest 25 feet and 4 inches; from the shoulder to the elbow, 15 feet and 6 inches; from the inner side of the elbow joint to the tip of the middle finger, 15 feet; and so on in relative proportion. If they stood up, they would tower to a height of at least 83 feet, from the soles of their feet to the tops of their enormous double-crowns.

There is but one hour in the twenty-four at which it is possible to form any idea of the general effect of this vast subject; and that is at sunrise. Then only does the pure day stream in through the doorway, and temper the gloom of the side-aisles with light reflected from the sunlit floor. The broad divisions of the picture and the distribution of the masses may then be dimly seen. The details, however, require candle-light, and can only be studied a few inches at a time. Even so, it is difficult to make out the upper groups without the help of a ladder. Salame, mounted on a chair and provided with two long sticks lashed together, could barely hold his little torch high enough to enable the Writer to copy the inscription on the middle tower of the fortress of Kadesh.

It is fine to see the sunrise on the front of the Great Temple; but something still finer takes place on certain mornings of the year, in the very heart of the mountain. As the sun comes up above the eastern hill-tops, one long level beam strikes through the doorway, pierces the inner darkness like an arrow, penetrates to the sanctuary, and falls like fire from heaven upon the altar at the feet of the Gods.

No one who has watched for the coming of that shaft of sunlight can doubt that it was a calculated effect, and that the excavation was directed at one especial angle in order to produce it. In this way Ra, to whom the temple was dedicated, may be said to have entered in daily, and by a direct manifestation of his presence to have approved the sacrifices of his worshippers.

To come out from these black holes into the twilight of the Great Hall and see the landscape set, as it were, in the ebon frame of the doorway, was alone worth the journey to Abou Simbel. The sun being at such times in the west, the river, the yellow sand-island, the palms and tamarisks opposite, and the mountains of the eastern desert, were all flooded with a glory of light and colour to which no pen or pencil could possibly do justice. At this juncture, seeing that the men's time hung heavy on their hands, our Painter conceived the idea of setting them to clean the face of the northernmost Colossus, still disfigured by the plaster left on it when the great cast was taken by Mr Hay more than half a century before. This happy thought was promptly carried into effect. A scaffolding of spars and oars was at once improvised, and the men, delighted as children at play, were soon swarming all over the huge head, just as the carvers may have swarmed over it in the days when Rameses was king.

Words from the United Nations, 1960–63

[At Abu Simbel, now lifted high above the Nile, today's travellers will read these words.]

These monuments do not belong solely to the countries who hold them in trust. The whole world has the right to see them endure.
Dr Vittorini Veronese, former Director-General of UNESCO, 1960

Through this restoration of the past, we have indeed helped to build the future of mankind.
René Maheau, former Director-General of UNESCO, 1963

Korosko
E. A. Wallis Budge, 1906

703 miles from Cairo, and 116 miles from Aswan, on the east bank of the river, was from the earliest times the point of departure for merchants and others going to and from the Sudan, via Abu Hamed, from the western bank there is a caravan route across into north Africa. A capital idea of the general

character of Nubian scenery can be obtained by ascending the mountain, which is, thanks to a good path, easily accessible.

Wadi Halfa
E. A. Wallis Budge, 1906

802 miles from Cairo and 215 miles from Aswan, and a few miles south begins the Second Cataract, a splendid view of which can be obtained from the now famous rock of Abusir on the west bank of the river. Nearly every traveller who visited Abu Simbel has been to this rock and inscribed his name upon it; the result is an interesting collection of names and dates, the like of which probably exists nowhere else.

The Farthest Point
Harriet Martineau, 1848

[Harriet Martineau's party reached 'the part properly called the Second Cataract'. It was early January 1848 – time to descend the river.]

The Nile comes sweeping down towards the rock on which we stood, dashing and driving among its thousand islets, and then gathering its thousand currents into one, to proceed calmly on its course. Its waters were turbid in the rapids, and looked as muddy where they poured down from shelf or boulder as in the Delta itself: but in all its calm reaches it reflected the sky in a blue so deep as it would not do to paint. The islets were of fantastic forms, – worn by the cataracts of ages: but still, the outlines were angular, and the black ledges were graduated by the action of the waters, as if they had been soft sand. On one or two islands I saw what I at first took for millet-patches: but they were only coarse grass and reeds. A sombre brownish tamarisk, or dwarfed mimosa, put up its melancholy head here and there; and this was all the vegetation apparent within that wide horizon, – I doubt whether a more striking scene than this, to English eyes, can be anywhere found. It is thoroughly African, thoroughly tropical, very beautiful – most majestic and most desolate. Something of the impression might be owing to the circumstances of leave-taking under which we looked abroad from our station: but still, if I saw this scene in an unknown land in a dream, I am sure I should be powerfully moved by it. This day, it certainly interested me more than the First Cataract.

I was tempted by the invitation of a sort of cairn on the top of a hill not far inland, to go there; and thence I obtained another glimpse of the Lybian Desert, and saw two more purple peaks rising westwards, soft and clear.

There is a host of names carved on the accessible side of Abboseer. We looked with interest on Belzoni's and some few others. We cut ours with a nail and hammer. Here, and here only, I left my name. On this wild rock, and at the limit of our range of travel, it seemed, not only natural, but right to some who may come after us. Our names will not be found in any temple or tomb. If we ever do such a thing, may our names be publicly held up to shame, as I am disposed to publish those of the carvers and scribblers who have forfeited their right to privacy by inscribing their names where they can never be effaced!

At the Second Cataract
Constance Sitwell, 1927

The naked black boys run panting across the sand and up the slope towards us. They have been swimming and shooting the rapids of the second cataract, and now, having each been given a coin, they fling themselves down for a rest.

I, too, lie outstretched in a patch of shade on the top of a great rock that stands high above the surrounding country. Jim and Philip, their eyes shut, are resting in the shadow of another ledge. We made our start many hours ago, at break of dawn, to avoid the heat of the day. For part of the way our boatmen rowed, and sometimes they had to tow the boat along, but there were spells when they could sit and sing while the boat beat its way up the river under sail. At last we reached these curious rocks sticking up out of the broad flood that swirls around them – black rocks, rounded and glistening like gigantic lumps of coal.

From my place here I can see our boat tied up to the bank far below; it is gaily bedecked with flags, and at the top of the mast one long pennon with the star and crescent hangs limp in the lifeless air. On deck likes a dog, asleep, with lolling tongue. As far as I can see the Nubian crew, squatting on the shore, are still as busy as ever talking. Their voices do not reach me, but I can see their gesticulations. So dead black is their skin that they look as if they had been rubbed over with blacklead and then polished like a grate; their hair is glistening with castor oil. They talk and talk, but here there is silence except for the far-off sound of the water rushing, leaping and dashing amongst the rocks.

I have to shut my eyes at last because of the glare, and when I open them again it is to watch a beetle crawling over the glittering flakes of stone. It is a shiny and fantastic creature with glassy wings and a silver body spotted with bronze. It moves slowly among a host of ants that are hurrying in and out between the hot boulders. Idly I look at them and their settlement full of stirs; ant jostles ant in the narrow ways, and they are all black – as black as those Nubian boatmen down below. Here is a city of Ethiopians – a miniature city that with one brush of my hand I could sweep away. Ethiopia! How rich and hot the name sounds; but it tells of a glory which is fled . . .

Ethiopia lies there before me; on one side of the Nile its sand is ashen grey, on the other a tawny gold. And this terrible waterless desert stretches away eastward to the coast; beyond there heaves the Red Sea. Southward and eastward it shimmers in the heat-haze, and somewhere beyond the horizon there roam dapple giraffes – fairy-tale creatures with velvety skins and liquid eyes. I wonder, are they frightened of the lions? The Kings of Ethiopia used to hunt with lions . . . Kings with lions at their side! Ethiopia, once great, your glory has indeed been swept away! Where are the emeralds and the gold, where are the gums, and resins, and fragrant woods that once you poured forth? How long ago is it since travelling companies of tall merchantmen brought their riches to Egypt over these blazing sands – their white ivory, white wool and white ostrich plumes, their abony and slaves like ebony. Bunched feathers of bright colours, and small bewildered negro boys were offered to the great ladies of Thebes and Heliopolis.

237

Looking Beyond
Arthur Conan Doyle, 1897

It was a view which, when once seem, must always haunt the mind. Such an expanse of savage and unrelieved desert might be part of some cold and burned-out planet, rather than this fertile and bountiful earth. Away and away it stretched, to die into the soft, violet haze in the extreme distance. In the foreground the sand was bright, golden yellow, which was quite dazzling in the sunshine; but beyond this golden plain lay a low line of those black slag-heaps, with yellow sand valleys winding between them. These in their turn were topped by higher and more fantastic hills, and these by others, peeping over each other's shoulders until they blended with that distant violet haze. None of these hills were of any height, – a few hundred feet at most, – but their savage, saw-toothed crests, and their steep scarps of sun-baked stones, gave them a fierce character of their own.

Hub of the Universe
Rudyard Kipling, 1913

At Halfa one feels the first breath of a frontier. Here the Egyptian Government retires into the background, and even the Cook steamer does not draw up in the exact centre of the postcard. At the telegraph-office, too, there are traces, diluted but quite recognisable, of military administration. Nor does the town, in any or place whatever, smell – which is proof that it is not looked after on popular lines. There is nothing to see in it any more than there is in Hulk C. 60, late of her Majesty's troopship *Himalaya*, now a coal-hulk in the Hamoaze at Plymouth. A river front, a narrow terraced river-walk of semi-oriental houses, barracks, a mosque, and half-a-dozen streets at right angles, the Desert racing up to the end of each, make all the town. A mile or so up stream under palm trees are bungalows of what must have been cantonments, some machinery repair-shops, and odds and ends of railway track. It is all as paltry a collection of whitewashed houses, pitiful gardens, dead walls, and trodden waste spaces as one would wish to find anywhere; and every bit of it quivers with the remembered life of armies and river-fleets, as the finger-bowl rings when the rubbing finger is lifted. The most unlikely men have done time there; stores by the thousand ton have been rolled and pushed and hauled up the banks by tens of thousands of scattered hands; hospitals have pitched themselves there, expanded enormously, shrivelled up and drifted away with the drifting regiments; railways sidings by the mile have been laid down and ripped up again, as need changed, and utterly wiped out by the sands.

Halfa has been the rail-head, Army Headquarters, and hub of the universe – the one place where a man could make sure of buying tobacco and sardines, or could hope for letters for himself and medical attendance for his friend. Now she is a little shrunken shell of a town without a proper hotel, where tourists hurry up from the river to buy complete sets of Soudan stamps at the Post Office.

Homeward
Winston Churchill, 1899

My transport duties having been satisfactorily discharged, I accompanied the Grenadier Guards down the river. Every night that week witnessed the departure of one or other of the British battalions. All day long the flotilla of broad-bottomed sailing-boats lay moored by the bank. Then, as the shadows length-ened and the evening breeze began to freshen, the lashings were cast off, and the boats pushed into the middle of the stream. The flowing white canvas was hoisted, and like a flight of enormous birds the whole fleet started for home and comfort with the warm, south wind in the shoulder of the sails and the flood Nile pressing six miles an hour at the keel. The pace was swift, yet the current was barely outstripped. As one looked at the water, the boats seemed motionless. Only the banks slipped past. How easily all the weary miles of march were covered! The strong river was impatient to be rid of the invaders who had disturbed its waters. The farewell cheers of the remaining regiments grew faint and broken. The strains of the Soudanese band playing 'The British Grenadiers' died away. The mud houses and the bivouacs on the bank were lost in the distance and in the twilight, and men turned their minds and faces towards a cooler, kinder land whither they would presently return.

It was very strange, going down the river in this pleasant fashion, to watch the camping-grounds and watering-places pass in quick succession. Already we were near the scene of the action. Here was the *khor** where all had drunk on the day itself. A little lower down the old *zeriba*† we had defended came into view. The scarlet glint of a lance-pennon under a tree near the water marked the cairn over Robert Grenfell's grave, and we paid the only tribute in our power – a mournful thought to the memory of that gallant young officer . . . And so onwards, northwards, homewards, while the night grew dark above the boats and hid them from each other, and little fires which twinkled on the stern to cook the evening meal alone showed that we drifted in company. Presently the stars came out, and by their light intensified the blackness of the moving lines of bushes on the banks, and increased the glitter of the disturbed waters of the river.

Down River
Alan Moorehead, 1960

Such life as has remained fixes itself upon the Nubian settlements on the river bank, where the brightly painted designs on the houses remind one far more of primitive Africa than ancient Egypt, and upon caravan routes winding from oasis to oasis across the desert, and the pilgrimage to Mecca which continues to cross the wastes year after year with a kind of ant-like fidelity, a determined search for grace through the awful hardships of travelling in the African heat.

At Aswan, which was a great caravan centre in its day, and the most southerly outpost of the Roman Empire, another change overtakes the river valley. For

---

* A watering point.
† Corale or cattle enclosure.

the last few hundred miles all has been stark rock and arid yellow sand, but now as one descends the last cataract past the island temples of Philae plantations of wheat and sugar-cane appear, lines of camels and donkeys move along the river bank among palms and tamarisks, and there is hardly a moment when one is out of sight of a village. On the river itself feluccas slide by with long thin coloured pennants on the masts to show the direction of the wind; and even the wind which was such a terror on the Upper Nile is now beginning to fail. It is the beginning of the softness and lushness of Egypt, and the end of the wildness of the Nile. The very birds have a tame and unhurried air, whether they be the white egrets feeding in the swamps, the pigeons on every rooftop, or the herons and storks standing in the shallows like decorations on a Japanese screen. Even that murderous thrust of the heron's beak, the quick upward jerk of the head and the swallowing of the fish, is a rhythmical and poetic movement as far removed from the image of death as is the frieze on the temple wall where the Pharaoh, with his raised arm, is about to club his cringing enemies to the ground. The buffalo, released at last in the evening from his monotonous circling round the water wheel, comes down the bank and subsides with a groan of satisfaction into the mud. Both crocodiles and hippopotamuses have now vanished from the river.

One after another the great temples next came into view: Kom Ombo dominating a bend in the river, Edfu still intact on the western bank, Luxor and Karnak, Dendera and Abydos. There is a monumental stillness in the warm air, an intimation of past existence endlessly preserved, and day after day one glides onto the north seeing the same things that every traveller has always seen. It is a process of recognition: the pyramids and the Sphinx are prefigured in the mind long before they meet the eye.

Now finally the Nile begins to drop its Ethiopian mud at Cairo, a hundred miles from the sea. Confused by flatness and its own tame pace, it spreads out through many different canals and waterways into the green fan of the delta. Little by little with its falling silt it has pushed the land out into the Mediterranean and lost itself in swamps and lakes. Of the seven mouths the ancients knew only two remain, one at Rosetta and the other at Damietta, but still at the height of its flood the river stains the sea for many miles out, and in a storm coming from the north russet waves are driven back onto the Egyptian shore.

This, then, is the end of the river, the end of a continuous chain of recreation by which the Blue Nile brings life down from the mountains to the desert and the delta. Without it the people of Egypt and of a greater part of Sudan could not exist for a single day. Even a 'low Nile' – an annual flood that has been less than average – is a disaster. This has always been so and is likely to continue for ever. It seems astonishing, therefore, that so little was known about the river to the outside world in comparatively recent times. Even as late as the closing years of the eighteenth century hardly any commerce moved along its waters, and apart from the caravan routes there were no roads. Above Cairo there were no bridges, and no city of any consequence, no government that looked beyond its own parochial affairs – and this is in an area almost the size of Europe. Lake Tana was placed with fair accuracy on the map, and so was the general course of the Blue Nile to central Sudan. But the White Nile was an utter mystery, and it was not even generally accepted that the river had not one source but two. Most of the great temples on the Lower Nile were buried in sand, and in the ramshackle mud-hut villages that perched on the river bank life went on by in a torpor of ignorance and monotony. For well over a thousand years the great civilization of ancient Egypt had been forgotten and its writings a closed book; nor did there appear to be any bright prospects for the future. The Mamelukes had made Egypt almost as inaccessible to travellers as Tibet is today, the Sudan was virtually unknown, and Ethiopia, locked away in its remote mountains, was still the land of Prester John, a region of horrendous legends and medieval myths.

In the Pharaoh's Footsteps Today
Michael Simmons, 1989

On my first postcard home, of two pyramids and the Sphinx, I wrote that Egypt was exhilarating, colourful, corrupt, religious, hopelessly dirty and noisy, impossibly charming and friendly. This left no room to record that it is also a staggering country which is almost exclusively desert. More than 50 million people are crammed on to less than 5 per cent of the land. Most are wretchedly poor and live in grotesquely overcrowded homes. A new Egyptian in born every 24 seconds.

We returned, weighed down with snaps and dodgy tummies, pale echoes of Shelley's 'traveller from an antique land'. We had seen vast monuments of stone, shattered visages of another realm, often cheek by jowl with graceless breeze-block and makeshift covers.

Once, in the desert, we stopped to watch the sunset. Total silence. Then a Chevrolet pickup, with 20 singing men crammed precariously in the back roared by. It slowed fraternally to see we were not in trouble, then went on. The voices, marvellously lusty and harmonious, trailed behind long after they had disappeared in the gloaming.

Most of the monuments, usually tombs or temples, are in or close to the desert. Almost all have been pillaged. Around 500 known collections of Egyptology dot the world; the British Museum's stash just one of 150 public displays. Howard Carter was not the only tomb robber.

The oldest site is the country's first royal city, once called Heka Ptah and founded nearly 4,500 years ago. It was renamed Memphis when it was occupied by Alexander the Great. Here, a colossal limestone statue of the warrior-pharaoh, Rameses II, lies broken and prone, enclosed by the 20th century for preservation. His ears measure 20 inches across.

Nearby, an elegant alabaster sphinx, more than 3,000 years old lies exposed to the elements. Less stunning than its cousin near the Giza pyramids, it is nevertheless beautiful. Also at the site, Zoser's so-called step pyramid is one of the oldest stone structures in the world.

As we prepared to move on, an Egyptian boy wandered by on a camel. Sensing we were English, he shouted 'Tally-ho'. When we got to the nearby village of Mit Rihana a funeral was in progress. Around 200 men, quiet and dignified in their disorder, advanced towards us, filling the narrow road. Our decrepit bus pulled to one side to let them pass.

There was no sarcophagus, of course, and no invocation of awesome gods, no lavish supplies to see the deceased through the next life – just a simple, apparently much-used wooden box draped with a carpet that could have been a prayer mat.

Where, we asked, were the women? Sayeed, our guide, replied that they would be at home sharing in the grief and sorrow. 'After all,' he said, 'at a funeral they would make a great noise.' Unlike their illustrious predecessors, Egyptians today die relatively peacefully. Islam usually allows for a safe passage from this life to the next – the need to propitiate the gods is long gone.

The pharaohs spent decades organising their own funerals. Ironic that a tourist industry, one of the country's biggest earners, should be built on the pomp and circumstance of death! More than willingly, we got up at 3 a.m. to take a ferry across the Nile and climb by long-suffering donkey into the Valley of the Kings.

Nearly a million destitute Cairenes, it is estimated, live among the city's burial grounds and gravestones: the extremes of poverty encroaching upon a past of wealth. At the magnificent temple of Abydos, for instance, mud houses crowd up to the perimeter fence.

In ancient times, cats and dogs were favoured animals, deified in some cases. Today, brittle rib cages signalling their most obvious need, their descendants pick over the garbage that litters so many of the streets.

Going south by train, with mice and dirt around our feet, the deprivation was less obvious. Myriad souvenir shops and illuminations made Luxor a curious mixture of Blackpool (without the tower) and Venice (without the gondolas). But after three hours of desert, Lake Nasser and Abu Simbel provided a different kind of drama. Unprecedented engineering lifted the temple from the lake bottom to its present site. Inside an enormous concrete dome, we looked down from a cat-walk to massive foundations supporting thousands of tons of transplanted statuary. Bats in the temple swoop down disconcertingly. Outside, 66 feet of Rameses II towers.

The great dam nearby is not readily discussed with visitors. It has supplied millions, but also displaced 60,000 Nubians and radically changed the local ecology – and weather. The people whose ancestors worshipped the Nile are alarmed to see clouds in the sky for the first time. Some panicked at their first experience of rain. Silting on one side of the dam has forced farmers on the other to use chemical fertilisers.

Back in Cairo a last visit to the bazaar where eager children shouted, as they had throughout the country, 'Hallo, what is your name?' A few cacophonous, hooting streets away from the clutch of Hiltons, Sheratons and Shepheard's poverty surfaces again. In streets where every other building seems to be held up by faith, goats and sheep meander at will. Islam protects them all. Noisy food stalls alternate with tiny clattering one-man workshops. From one, a barber rushed towards us, waving his cut-throat razor. At the top of his voice, he shouted 'Welcome to Cairo' and smiled.

Bibliography

* Indicates a work has been consulted but not quoted from.

*Aboudi, Mohammd, *Aboudi's Guide Book*, Luxor, 1963.
Athanasi, Giovanni d', *A Brief Account of the Researches and Discoveries in Upper Egypt Made Under the Direction of Henry Salt, Esq.*, 1836.
Baedeker, Karl, *Lower Egypt with the Fam and the Peninsula of Sinai*, Leipzig, 1878.
— *Upper Egypt with Nubia as Far as the Second Cataract and the Western Oases*, Leipzig, 1892.
— *Egypt 1929*, reissued by David and Charles, 1985.
*Baker, Anne, *For Morning Star*, London, 1972.
Reynolds-Ball, Eustace A., *Cairo of Today*, Boston, 1897.
*Barnsley, Emmeline, *Diary of a Trip to Egypt and Palestine*, unpublished manuscript, 1888.
Bartlett, W. H., *The Nile Boat or Glimpses of the Land of Egypt*, London, 1850.
Beaton, Cecil, *Near East*, London, 1943.
Belzoni, Giovanni, *Narrative of the Operations and Recent Discoveries in Egypt and Nubia*, 1822.
*Bemrose, William, *Recollections of Egypt and Palestine*, unpublished manuscript, 1882.
Bevan, Dr Samuel, *Sand and Canvas: A Narrative of Adventures in Egypt*, London, 1849.
Bibescû, Princess Marta, *Egyptian Day*, New York, 1930.
*Breasted, James Henry, *Egypt: A Journey through the Land of the Pharaohs*, Camera Graphics Press, 1978 (originally published in *Egypt through the Stereoscope*, 1905).
*Briggs, Martin, *Through Egypt in Wartime*, London, 1918.
Browne, W. G., *Travels in Africa, Egypt and Syria*, London, 1800.
Bruce, James, *Travels to Discover the Source of the Nile 1768–1773*, London, 1804.
Budge, E. A. Wallis, *Cook's Handbook for Egypt and the Sudan*, Thos. Cook and Son, 1906.
Burkhardt, John Lewis, *Travels in Nubia*, London, 1819 (also Katharine Sim, *Jean Louis Burkhardt*, Quartet, 1969).
*Burns, Rev. Jabez, DD, and Thomas Cook, *Help-Book for the Traveller to the East*, 1870.
*Butcher, E. L., *Things Seen in Egypt*, London, 1914.

Carne, John, *Letters from the East*, 1826.
— *Recollections of the East*, 1830.
*Caillard, Mabel, *A Lifetime in Egypt 1876–1935*, London, 1935.
*Caernarvon, the Earl of, and Carter, Howard, *Five Years' Exploration at Thebes*, 1912.
*Cecil, Lord Edward, *The Leisure of an Egyptian Official*, London, 1921.
*Chaill-Long, Colonel, C., *My Life in Four Continents*, London, 1912.
*Charles-Roux, F., *Bonaparte, Governor of Egypt*, London, 1937.
*Chateaubriand, Vicomte de F. R. de, *Travels in Greece, Palestine, Egypt, and Barbary 1806–7* (translated by Frederic Shoberl), London, 1811.
*Chennells, Ellen, *Recollection of an Egyptian Princess by her English Governess*, Edinburgh, 1893.
Christie, Agatha, *Death on the Nile*, London, 1937.
— *An Autobiography*, London, 1977.
Churchill, Winston, *The River War*, London, 1899.
Clarke, E. D., *Travels in Various Countries of Europe, Asia and Africa*, London, 1810–23.
Cocteau, Jean, *Maalesh: A Theatrical Tour of the Middle East* (translated by Mary C. Hoeck), London, 1956.
Conan Doyle, Arthur, *The Tragedy on the Korosko*, London, 1897.
*Cooke, E. W., *Leaves from my Sketch Book*, 1877.
*Coward, Noël, *Middle East Diary*, London, 1944.
*Curtis, George William, *Nile Notes of a Howadji, or the American in Egypt*, 1852.
Curzon, George Nathaniel, *Tales of Travel*, London, 1923.
Curzon, Robert, *Visits to Monasteries in the Levant*, London, 1849 (reissued by Century, London, 1983).
*Dawson, W., and Uphill, E. P., *Who Was Who in Egyptology*, London, 1972.
Denon, Dominique Vivant, *Travels in Upper and Lower Egypt during the Campaign of General Bonaparte* (translated by E. A. Kendal) 1803 (reprinted, Darf Publishers, 1986).
Diodorus of Sicily, *The Antiquities of Egypt, Asia, Africa, Greece, the Islands and Europe*, Book 1, London, 1653.
*Dorr, Benjamin, *Notes of Travel in Egypt, the Holy Land, Turkey and Greece*, Philadelphia, 1856.
Duff Gordon, Lucie, *Letters from Egypt* (reprinted Virago, 1983).
— *Last Letters from Egypt* (reprinted Virago, 1983).
Durrell, Lawrence, *Spirit of Place: Letters and Essays of Travel*, Faber, 1969.
Eden, Frederic, *The Nile without a Dragoman*, London, 1871.
*Edmonstone, Sir Archibald, *A Journey to Two of the Oases of Upper Egypt*, London, 1822.
Edwards, Amelia B., *One Thousand Miles up the Nile*, Longmans, 1877 (reissued by Century, London, 1982).
*Elgood, P. G., *Bonaparte's Adventure in Egypt*, London, 1931.
Elwood, Mrs Colonel (Anne Katherine), *Narrative of a Journey Overland by the Continent of Europe, Egypt, and the Red Sea, Including a Residence There and a Voyage Home, 1825–8*, London, 1830.
*Encyclopaedia Britannica, Supplement to 4th and 5th edition, *Egypt*, Thomas Young.

*Erman, Adolf, *Life in Ancient Egypt* (translated by H. M. Tirard), London, 1894 (reissued Dover, 1971).

The Excursionist, Thomas Cook Ltd, 1851 onwards, monthly.

Fabri, Felix, *The Wanderings of Felix Fabri*, translated A. Stewart, Palestine Pilgrims Text Society, 1892-7.

*Fairholt, Frederick William, *Up the Nile and Home Again*, London, 1862.

*Finati, Giovanni (edited by Wm. John Bankes), *Narrative of the Life and Adventures of Giovanni Finati*, London, 1830.

Flaubert, Gustave, *Flaubert in Egypt* (translated by Francis Steegmuller), Michael Haag and Academy Chicago, 1983.

*Forbin, Comte de, *Travels in Egypt in 1817-18, Being a Continuation of Travels in the Holy Land*, 1820.

Forster, E. M., *Pharos and Pharillon*, Michael Haag, 1983.

— *Alexandria: A History and a Guide*, 1922 (reissued by Michael Haag, 1986).

*Fuller, John, *Narrative of a Tour Through Some Parts of the Turkish Empire*, London, 1829.

*Gleichen, Count, *With the Camel Corps up the Nile*, London, 1889.

*Goddard, John, *Kayaks down the Nile*, Brigham, 1979.

Golding, William, *An Egyptian Journal*, Faber, 1985.

*Grant, Joan, *Time Out of Mind*, London, 1956.

Grey, Catherine, *Journal in the Suite of the Prince and Princess of Wales*, London, 1869.

Haag, Michael, *Guide to Egypt*, Michael Haag, 1987 (new edition entitled *Discovery Guide to Egypt*, 1990).

Haggard, Sir Henry Rider, London, 1887.

*Hall, Richard, *Lovers on the Nile*, London, 1980.

*Halls, J. J., *Life and Correspondence of Henry Salt*, London, 1834.

Hamilton, William, *Remarks on Several Parts of Turkey. Part I: Aegyptiaca or Some Account of the Ancient and Modern State of Egypt Obtained in the Years 1801-2*, London, 1809.

*Harrison, Thomas Skelton, *The Homely Diary of a Diplomat in the East 1897-9*, Boston and New York, 1917.

*Hay, Robert, *Illustrations of Cairo*, 1840.

Henniker, Sir Frederick, *Notes During a Visit to Egypt, Nubia, the Oases, Mount Sinai and Jerusalem*, London, 1823.

Herodotus, *The Histories*, Penguin, 1972.

*Hibbert, Christopher, *Edward VII*, Harmondsworth, 1976.

Hopley, Howard, *Under Egyptian Palms or Three Bachelors on the Nile*, London, 1869.

Hoskins, George Alexander, *Travels in Ethiopia above the Second Cataract of the Nile*, London, 1835.

— *A Winter in Upper and Lower Egypt*, London, 1863.

Huxley, Sir Julian, *From an Antique Land*, London, 1954.

Ibn Battuta, *Travels* (translated by Sir H. Gibb), London, 1958.

Ibn Jubayr, *Travels* (translated by R. J. C. Broadhurst), London, 1952.

Irby, The Hon. Charles, and Mangles, James, *Travels in Egypt and Nubia, Syria and the Holy Land*, London, 1823.

Jarvie, William, *Letters Home from Egypt and Palestine, 1903-4*, privately printed, New York.

Jarvis, Major C. S., *Oriental Spotlight*, London, 1937.
*Junker, Wilhelm, *Travels in Africa*, London, 1890.
*Kennedy, Douglas, *Beyond the Pyramids*, London, 1988.
*Kelly, R. Talbot, *Egypt*, London, 1912.
*King, Annie, *Dr Liddon's Tour in Egypt and Palestine in 1886*, London, 1891.
Kinglake, Alexander, *Eothen*, London, 1844.
Kingsford, W. E., *Assouan as a Health Resort*, London, 1900.
Kipling, Rudyard, *Letters of Travel (1892–1913)*, London, 1913.
*Kusel, Baron Samuel Selig de, *An Englishman's Recollections of Egypt, 1863–87*, London, 1915.
*Köning, Hans, *A New Yorker in Egypt*, New York, 1976.
*Lane, Edward, *The Manners and Customs of the Modern Egyptians, 1860* (New edition Dover, 1963).
*Lane-Poole, S., *The Story of Cairo*, London, 1902.
— *History of Egypt in the Middle Ages*, London, 1914.
Lear, Edward, *Selected Letters* (edited by Vivian Noakes, Clarendon Press, 1988).
Legh, Thomas, *Narrative of a Journey in Egypt and the Country behind the Cataracts*, London, 1816.
Leland, Charles, *The Egyptian Sketch-book*, London, 1873.
*Lepsius, Richard, *Discoveries in Egypt*, London, 1852.
Light, Henry, *Travels in Egypt*, London, 1818.
*Lindsay, Lord, *Letters from Egypt and the Holy Land*, London, 1838.
*Loftie, William John, *A Ride in Egypt from Sioot to Luxor*, London, 1879.
Loti, Pierre, *Egypt*, New York, 1910.
Lynch, Jeremiah, *Egyptian Sketches*, London, 1890.
*Ludwig, Emil, *The Nile: The Life Story of a River* (trnaslated by Mary H. Lindsay), London, 1936.
*Lushington, Mrs Charles (Sarah), *Narrative of a Journey from Calcutta to Europe by Way of Egypt in the Years 1827–8*, London, 1829.
Macaulay, Rose, *Pleasures of Ruins*, London, 1953.
*Macgregor, John, *Rob Roy on the Nile and the Jordan*, London, 1870.
*MacLaren, Roy, *Canadians on the Nile*, Toronto, 1980.
Madden, R. R., *Travels in Turkey, Egypt Nubia and Palestine*, London, 1830.
Mangles, James (*see* Irby, Charles).
Manning, Samuel, *Land of the Pharaohs: Egypt and Sinai – Illustrated with Pen and Pencil*, London, 1875.
Martineau, Harriet, *Eastern Life, Present and Past*, London, 1848.
Maspero, Sir Gaston, *Egypt: Ancient Sites and Modern Scenes*, London, 1910.
Melly, George, *Khartoum and the Blue and White Niles*, London, 1851.
*Menu von Minutoli, Wolfradine, *Recollections of Egypt 1820–21*, London, 1827.
Merrick, E. M., *With a Palette in Eastern Palaces*, London, 1899.
*Milner, Sir Alfred, *England in Egypt*, London, 1893.
*Montefiore, Lady Judith, *Private Journal of a Visit to Egypt and Palestine by Way of Italy and the Mediterranean*, London, 1838.
Moorehead, Alan, *The White Nile*, London, 1960.
— *The Blue Nile*, London, 1962.
Morris, James, *Cities*, London, 1970.
— *Places*, London, 1972.
Morton, H. V., *Through Lands of the Bible*, London, 1938.

— *Middle East*, London, 1941.

Nightingale, Florence, *Letters from Egypt*, London, 1987.

Norden, Frederick, *Compendium of the Travels of Frederick Lewis Norden through Egypt and Nubia*, Dublin, 1757.

Olin, Reverend Stephen, *Travels in Egypt, Arabia Petraea and the Holy Land*, New York, 1843.

*Owen, Robert, and Blunsum, Terence, *Egypt: The Country and Its People*, London, 1966.

*Palgrave, W. G., *Narrative of a Year's Journey*, 1865.

*Palin, Michael, *Around the World in Eighty Days*, London, 1989.

*Petrie, Sir Flinders, *A Season in Egypt*, 1887.

— *Ten Years Digging in Egypt*, 1881–9, London, 1892.

*Pfeiffer, Ida, *Visit to the Holy Land*, London, 1852.

*Pinkerton, John, *A General Collection of the Best and Most Interesting Travels in All Parts of the World* (17 volumes), London, 1808–14.

Plummer, J E., *Up the Nile, 1862–3*, unpublished letters.

*Pococke, Richard, *Description of the East*, London, 1743–5.

Poole, Sophia, *The Englishwoman in Egypt*, London, 1844.

Prime, William C., *Boat Life in Egypt and Nubia*, New York, 1868.

Pryce-Jones, Alan, *The Spring Journey*, London, 1931.

*Pudney, John, *The Thomas Cook Story*, London, 1954.

Pye-Smith, Charlie, *The Other Nile: Journeys in Egypt, the Sudan and Ethiopia*, London, 1986.

Quibell, Annie, *A Wayfarer in Egypt*, London, 1925.

Rhind, Henry, *Egypt, Its Climate, Character and Resources as a Winter Resort*, 1856.

— *Thebes, Its Tombs and Their Tenants*, 1862.

Richardson, R. R., *Travels*, London, 1822.

Riggs, Miss, *Diary of the First Cook's Tour to Egypt and Palestine*, unpublished diary, 1869.

Ripley, John, article in *The Excursionist*, May 1871.

Roberts, David, *Egypt and Nubia*, 1846.

*Robinson, Jane, *Wayward Women*, Oxford, 1990.

*Romer, John, *Valley of the Kings*, London, 1981.

*Rose, George (writing as Arthur Sketchley), *Mrs Brown up the Nile*, 1869.

*Ross, Janet, *Three Generations of English Women*, 1888.

— *The Fourth Generation*, London, 1912.

*Romer, Isabella, *A Pilgrimage to the Temples and Tombs of Egypt, Nubia and Palestine*, 1862.

*Russell, Rev. Michael, *View of Egypt*, Edinburgh, 1831.

*Russell, William Howard, *A Diary in the East*, London, 1869.

Sandys, George, *A Relation of a Journey Begun in 1610: The Turkish Empire of Egypt, the Holy Land, etc.*, London, 1615.

*St John, Bayle, *Adventure in the Libyan Desert*, 1849.

* — *Village Life in Egypt*, 1852.

* — *Travels of an Arab Merchant*, 1854.

*St John, James Augustus, *Egypt and Nubia*, London, 1845.

*Salt, Henry, *Egypt, A Descriptive Poem*, Alexandria, 1824.

*Sattin, Anthony, *Lifting the Veil: British Society in Egypt*, London, 1988.

*Savary, C., *Letters from Egypt*, 1787.

*Shaw, Thomas, *Travels and Observations Relating to Several Parts of Barbary and the Levant*, 1721.

*Shere, Moyle, *Scenes and Impressions of Egypt*, 1824.

Sitwell, Constance, *Lotus and Pyramid*, London, 1927.

— *Bright Morning*, London, 1942.

Sladen, Douglas, *Egypt and the English*, 1908.

— *Queer Things about Egypt*, 1910.

Smith, Rev. A. C., *Attractions of the Nile and Its Banks: A Journal of Travels in Egypt and Nubia Showing Their Attractions to the Archaeologist, the Naturalist and the General Tourist*, 1868.

*Smith, Joseph Lindon, *Tombs, Temples and Ancient Art*, New York, 1956.

*Sonnini, C. S., *Travels in Upper and Lower Egypt* (translated by Henry Hunter), London, 1799.

*Sowden, Sir William, *Another Australian Abroad: Travel Notes in Egypt and Palestine*, 1924–5.

*Sopwith, Thomas, *Notes on a Visit to Egypt*, 1857.

Stanley, Arthur Penrhyn, *Sinai and Palestine*, London, 1856.

Steevens, G. W. *With Kitchener to Khartoum*, 1897.

— *Egyptian 1898*, 1898.

Strabo, *The Geography of Strabo*, Book 17.

Stuart, Villiers, *Nile Gleanings*, 1879.

*Sumner, Mrs George (Mary Elizabeth), *Our Holiday in the East*, 1881.

*Swinglehurst, Edmund, *Cook's Tours, the Story of Popular Travel*, Poole, 1982.

*Tafur, Pero, *Travels and Adventures 1435–39* (translated by M. Letts), London, 1938.

*Thackeray, William Makepeace (writing as Mr M. A. Titmarsh), *Notes of a Journey from Cornhill to Grand Cairo*, London, 1846.

Taylor, James Bayard, *Life and Landscapes from Egypt*, New York, 1878.

Thompson, Charles, *Travels through Turkey in Asia, the Holy Land, Arabia, Egypt and Other Parts of the World*, 1767.

*Traill, H. D., *From Cairo to the Soudan Frontier*, London, 1896.

Twain, Mark, *The Innocents Abroad*, London, 1870.

*Tyndale, Walter, *Below the Cataracts*, London, 1907.

— *An Artist in Egypt*, 1912.

*Volney, Comte de, Constantin François de Chasseboef, *Travels through Egypt and Syria*, 1783–5.

*Vyse, Howard, *Operations Carried Out at the Pyramids of Gizeh in 1837: With an Account of a Voyage into Upper Egypt*, 1840.

*Waddington, Very Rev. George, *Nubian Journey*, 1822.

Warburton, Eliot, *The Cross and the Crescent*, 1845.

Wilbour, Charles Edwin, *Travels in Egypt: December 1880 to May 1891* (edited by Jean Carpart, Brooklyn Museum, New York, 1936).

Wilkinson, Sir Gardner, *Manners and Customs of the Ancient Egyptians*, 1837.

— *Hand-Book for Travellers in Egypt*, London, 1847.

*Wyche, Sir Peter, translation of *A Short Relation of the River Nile, of Its Source and Current, of Its Overflowing the Campagnia of Egypt 'till It Runs into the Mediterranean and of Other Curiosities, Written by an Eye Witness*, printed by order of the Royal Society of London, 1569.

Index